CIVILIZATION
at the
CROSSROADS

By
**RADOVAN
RICHTA**
*and a
research
team*

CIVILIZATION at the CROSSROADS

Social and Human Implications of the Scientific and Technological Revolution

LONDON AND NEW YORK

This third, expanded edition of *Civilization at the Crossroads* is dedicated to the memory of *Dr. O t a K l e i n*, a member of the interdisciplinary team, who directed the preparatory work but did not live to see the results in print

The Authors

October 1968

First published 1969 by International Arts and Sciences Press, Inc.

Reissued 2018 by Routledge
2 Park Square, Milton Park, Abingdon, Oxon OX14 4RN
711 Third Avenue, New York, NY 10017, USA

Routledge is an imprint of the Taylor & Francis Group, an informa business

Copyright © Radovan Richta 1969

Translated by Marian Šlingová

No part of this book may be reprinted or reproduced or utilised in any form or by any electronic, mechanical, or other means, now known or hereafter invented, including photocopying and recording, or in any information storage or retrieval system, without permission in writing from the publishers.

Notices
No responsibility is assumed by the publisher for any injury and/or damage to persons or property as a matter of products liability, negligence or otherwise, or from any use of operation of any methods, products, instructions or ideas contained in the material herein.

Practitioners and researchers must always rely on their own experience and knowledge in evaluating and using any information, methods, compounds, or experiments described herein. In using such information or methods they should be mindful of their own safety and the safety of others, including parties for whom they have a professional responsibility.

Product or corporate names may be trademarks or registered trademarks, and are used only for identification and explanation without intent to infringe.

Publisher's Note
The publisher has gone to great lengths to ensure the quality of this reprint but points out that some imperfections in the original copies may be apparent.

Disclaimer
The publisher has made every effort to trace copyright holders and welcomes correspondence from those they have been unable to contact.

A Library of Congress record exists under LC control number: 68014154

ISBN 13: 978-1-138-03780-9 (hbk)
ISBN 13: 978-1-138-03782-3 (pbk)
ISBN 13: 978-1-315-17766-3 (ebk)

CONTENTS

Members of the Interdisciplinary Team 7
Foreword by Academician Šorm 11
Introduction: The Purpose of Change 13

CHAPTER 1
    The Nature of the Scientific and Technological Revolution 23
1.1. Changes in the Structure and Dynamics of the Productive Forces 24
    1.1.1. The Industrial Revolution as the Starting Point 24
    1.1.2. The Substance of the Scientific and Technological Revolution 25
    1.1.3. The Revolution in Technology, Raw Materials and Power Resources 28
    1.1.4 Changes in the "Subjective Factor" of Production and in Man's Place in Civilization 32
    1.1.5. Changes in Economic Growth Models 37
    1.1.6. New Dimensions in the Growth of Civilization 41
1.2. Technological and Social Innovations. The Scientific and Technological Revolution and Changes in the Relations of Production 45
    1.2.1. Social Implications of Technological Advance 46
    1.2.2. The Scientific and Technological Revolution and Social Progress 51
    1.2.3. The Imperative of Growth and World Systems 59
    1.2.4. The Scientific and Technological Revolution and the "Third World" 67
    1.2.5. Motive Impulse of the Scientific and Technological Revolution 70
    1.2.6. Time Economy 81
1.3. The Approach to the Scientific and Technological Revolution in Czechoslovakia 89
    1.3.1. The Divide in Growth 89
    1.3.2. Losses in "the Human Factor" Are the Most Serious 94
    1.3.3. New System of Management 100

CHAPTER 2
    Radical Changes in Work, Skills and Education 104
2.1. The Scientific and Technological Revolution and the Patterns of Human Activity 105
    2.1.1. Transformations of Work 105
    2.1.2. Structural Changes 119
    2.1.3. New Features in the Division of Labour. Need for Universality 125
    2.1.4. Changes in the Pattern of Skills 130

2.2. The Scientific and Technological Revolution and Education   135
    2.2.1. Educational Level: Onset of a Cultural Revolution   135
    2.2.2. Adapting the Educational System   141
    2.2.3. Technology and Education   148
    2.2.4. From Education to Self-Education   151

CHAPTER 3
    Modern Civilization and the Development of Man   155
3.1. The Scientific and Technological Revolution Changes the Way of Life   155
    3.1.1. Development of Man as an Independent Factor   156
    3.1.2. Changes in the Content of Life   161
    3.1.3. Man and His Changing Needs   164
    3.1.4. Technology and Human Contacts   170
    3.1.5. Disposable Time   172
3.2. Man in an Artificial Environment   178
    3.2.1. Problems of Civilization   179
    3.2.2. The Culture of Work   181
    3.2.3. Shaping the Environment   184
    3.2.4. Application of Nature and Seeking a Home   188
    3.2.5. The Necessity of Beauty   191
    3.2.6. Laying Hold of Space and Time   194
    3.2.7. Technology and Health   198
    3.2.8. Participation in Civilization and Man's Self-Realization   202

CHAPTER 4
    New Features of Social Development in the Era of the Scientific and Technological Revolution   210

4.1. Science and the Management of Affairs   211
    4.1.1. The New Status of Science   211
    4.1.2. Conditions of Integration   219
    4.1.3. Strategy of Science   222
    4.1.4. Atmosphere of Scientific and Technological Progress   227
    4.1.5. Technology and Management. Cybernetic Model   233
    4.1.6. Rationalizing the Flow of Information   240
4.2. Social Problems and the Ferment of Ideas in the Age of Science and Technology   244
    4.2.1. The Scientific and Technological Revolution and Social Stratification   245
    4.2.2. Forms of Social Organization and Leadership in the Age of the Scientific and Technological Revolution   252
    4.2.3. Dynamics of the Age and the Mode of Thinking   256
    4.2.4. New Light on the Individual   261
    4.2.5. Constructing Perspectives   267
    4.2.6. The Scientific and Technological Revolution in Modern History   273

Epilogue. Practical Aspects. Some Ideas for Consideration   279
Statistical Tables   291
Bibliography   355

Authors

RADOVAN RICHTA, M.A., D.Sc., Corresponding member, Czechoslovak Academy of Sciences (CAS), head of the interdisciplinary team for research on the social and human implications of the scientific and technological revolution, Institute of Philosophy (CAS), in cooperation with:

JAN AUERHAN, M.Sc., Ph.D., Institute of Economics, CAS

GUSTAV BAREŠ, Ph.D., Professor, Faculty of Journalism, Charles University, Prague

DRAHOMÍR BÁRTA, D.Litt., Institute for the History of Socialism

JAN BOLINA, D.Litt., Office of the Presidium, CAS

VLADIMÍR BRENNER, M.Sc., Associate Professor, Faculty of Technological and Nuclear Physics, Charles University, Prague

JIŘÍ CVEKL, Ph.D., D.Litt., Associate Professor, Institute of Philosophy, CAS

ZDENĚK DRÁB, M.Sc., Ph.D., Associate Professor, Centre for Automation and Computer Technology

IRENA DUBSKÁ, Ph.D., D.Litt., Associate Professor, Institute of Philosophy, CAS

EMIL DUDA, Ph.D., D.Litt., Faculty of Electrical Engineering, Slovak College of Technology

BLANKA FILIPCOVÁ, Ph.D., D.Litt., Associate Professor, Institute of Sociology, CAS

JINDŘICH FILIPEC, Ph.D., D.Litt., Associate Professor, Institute of Philosophy, CAS

RUDOLF FILKUS, M.Sc., Associate Professor, Institute of Economics, Slovak Academy of Sciences

MIROSLAV GOTTLIEB, D.Litt., Department for the Theory of Architecture and Environment Planning, CAS

MOJMÍR HÁJEK, M.Sc., Institute of Economics, CAS

JAROSLAV HAVELKA, Ph.D., LL.M., Ministry of Education

JIŘÍ HERMACH, M.Sc., Ph.D., Associate Professor, Institute of Philosophy, CAS

ANTONÍN HODEK, M.Sc., Professor, Institute of Philosophy, CAS

PETR HORÁK, Ph.D., D.Litt., Institute of Philosophy, CAS

ROBERT HORÁK, Research Institute for the Economics of Industry and Building

MILUŠE HORVÁTHOVÁ-HAVLÍNOVÁ, Ph.D., D.Litt., Institute of Philosophy, CAS

MICHAL HRONSKÝ, M.Sc., Labour Research Institute, Bratislava

MILAN HROUDA, Ph.D., D.Litt., Faculty of Nuclear Physics, Charles University, Prague

JAROMÍR JANOUŠEK, Ph.D., D.Litt., Associate Professor, Institute of Psychology, CAS

ZDENĚK JAVŮREK, Ph.D., D.Litt., Institute of Philosophy, CAS

BOHUMIL JUNGMANN, D.Litt., Institute of Social and Political Sciences, Charles University, Prague

JAROMÍR KLAUČO, M.Sc., Ph.D., Associate Professor, Faculty of Electrical Engineering, Slovak College of Technology

OTA KLEIN, M.Sc., Ph.D., Deputy head of the interdisciplinary team, Institute of Philosophy, CAS

JIŘÍ KOSTA, M.Sc., Ph.D., Institute of Economics, CAS

JIŘÍ KOTÁSEK, Ph.D., D.Litt., Associate Professor, Institute for Extramural Teacher Training, Charles University, Prague

MILOSLAV KRÁL, M.Sc., Ph.D., Associate Professor, College of Political Studies

FRANTIŠEK KUTTA, M.Sc., Ph.D., Institute of Economics, CAS

ZDENĚK LAKOMÝ, M.Sc. (arch.), Department for the Theory of Architecture and Environment Planning, CAS

BEDŘICH LEVČÍK, LL.M., Ph.D., Deputy head of the interdisciplinary team, Institute of Economics, CAS

BEDŘICH LOEWENSTEIN, Ph.D., D.Litt., Historical Institute, CAS

ERNEST MAGDOLEN, M.Sc., Institute for Research on Living Standards, Bratislava

KVĚTENA MARKOVÁ, M.Sc., Ministry of Technology

SÁVA MEDONOS, M.Sc., State Commission for Technology

VLADIMÍR NACHTIGAL, Ph.D., D.Litt., Historical Institute, CAS

JIŘÍ NEKOLA, M.Sc., Ph.D., Department for Study of the Social Function of Science, CAS

OTAKAR NOVÝ, M.Sc. (arch.), Department for the Theory of Architecture and Environment Planning, CAS

JAN ORLICKÝ, D.Litt., Institute of Philosophy, CAS

VLASTIMIL PAŘÍZEK, Ph.D., University of 17th November

MILAN PRŮCHA, Ph.D., D.Litt., Institute of Philosophy, CAS

VLADIMÍR PŘIKRYL, Ph.D., D. Litt., School of Economics, Prague

MIROSLAV RUMLER, M.Sc., Ph.D., Institute of Economics, CAS

LADISLAV ŘÍHA, M.Sc., Ph.D., Ministry of Technology

JIŘÍ SLÁMA, M.Sc., Ph.D., Associate Professor, Research Institute for the Economics of Industry and Building

JINDŘICH SROVNAL, Ph.D., D.Litt., Professor, Institute of Philosophy, CAS

MILOŠ SVOBODA, Ph.D., D.Litt., Institute of Philosophy, CAS

HANA SYCHROVÁ, Ph.D., D.Litt., Associate Professor, Univesity of 17th November

JAN ŠINDELÁŘ, Ph.D., D.Litt., Associate Professor, College of Political Studies

MIKULÁŠ TEICH, M.Sc., Ph.D., Historical Institute, CAS

MIROSLAV TOMS, M.Sc., Institute of Economics, CAS

LADISLAV TONDL, D.Litt., Professor, Department for Study of the Social Function of Science, CAS

LUDĚK URBAN, Ph.D, Associate Professor, Institute of Economics, CAS

FRANTIŠEK VALENTA, M.Sc., Ph.D., Associate Professor, School of Economics, Prague

JIŘÍ VRBA, M.B., Ph.D., Associate Professor, Institute of Hygiene, Faculty of General Medicine, Charles University, Prague

JINDŘICH ZELENÝ, D.Litt., Professor, School of Economics, Prague

JIŘÍ ZEMAN, Ph. D., D. Litt., Insitute of Philosophy, CAS

FOREWORD

The dynamic advance of scientific discovery in recent decades, together with the rapid development of the material base of human life, is assuming the magnitude of revolutionary changes that promise in the long run to transform the nature of civilization and open up boundless prospects for a new form of society. These considerations underscore the urgency of probing the substance of the scientific and technological revolution of our day — its social and human roots and implications.

In 1965, a systematic examination of these problems was undertaken in Czechoslovakia by a research team made up of workers in various branches of science. The group was attached to the Institute of Philosophy, Czechoslovak Academy of Sciences, and headed by Dr. R. Richta, who has been working in this field for some time. The original purpose was to make a brief report on urgent ideological and theoretical matters arising from the new advances in science and technology. However, a fuller analysis led to a more ambitious and long-term project. Its aim was to draw, insofar as this was possible, a synthetic picture of the scientific and technological revolution against the background of the two social systems — socialism and capitalism — while also attempting to suggest ways of handling the inevitable social and human issues involved. Although theirs was no easy task — owing in no small measure to past neglect of many aspects — the authors have tackled it successfully. The results of their work, which are now published in comprehensive form, offer both an inclusive outline of this intricate subject of modern times and an entirely new, optimistic view of the future. Understandably, some issues call for further investigation. A valuable feature is that the work is a collective effort, demonstrating that in the social sciences, too, team work can yield good results; undoubtedly, it will be useful to apply this method in studying other interrelated questions.

The project was discussed in the Academy of Sciences and at top political levels. It was ultimately decided to utilize it in developing the theoretical and practical aspects of social advance and in preparing long-term guidelines for a country which, having set out on the difficult and in many respects untrodden path of building socialism and communism, is searching for new, humanist variants of a technologically advanced civilization.

The novel concept of the project and the ideas embodied in it open the way to further investigation of the subject, which will undoubtedly make good progress in coming years.

> Academician
> F. Šorm
> President,
> Czechoslovak
> Academy
> of Sciences

INTRODUCTION

/The Purpose of Change/

We are offering our readers a rather unorthodox book: perhaps it may be best described as a scientific hypothesis or an attempt to analyse the social and human implications of the scientific and technological revolution. It has been compiled by a research group working in different fields (philosophy, economics, sociology, psychology, education, political science, history, medicine, the theory of architecture and environment, and branches of the technological and natural sciences).

The biggest obstacle facing our team has been the range and interlocking of the changes presently taking place in the foundations of civilization and in man's place in the world of his own fantastic creation. To the best of our knowledge there is today no generally accepted and satisfactory theoretical account of the revolutions under way in the sphere of the productive forces — not to mention their social and human implications.

The flood of literature on technology and on the "human factor" from the pens of social scientists in the USA and in Western Europe affords a wealth of material, but seldom penetrates beneath the surface of the current civilization processes. Moreover, some European authors consider that the theoretical concept should not go beyond the limits of a certain, though modified, "industrial society"[1]; others — insofar as they reflect some of Marx's ideas — conceive of the current expansion of the productive forces as a kind of second — or third — "industrial revolution"[2]. This promising approach does not, however, from the analytical standpoint, allow for an adequate distinction between two

---

[1] For example, H. Schelsky: *Die sozialen Folgen der Automatisierung*, Düsseldorf—Köln 1957; R. Aron: *Dixhuit leçons sur la société industrielle*, Paris 1962, etc.

[2] For example, F. Pollock: *Automation, Materialien zur Beuerteilung ihrer ökonomischen und sozialen Folgen*, Frankfurt a M. 1957 and 1964; similarly, G. Friedmann: *La crise du Progrès, esquisse d'histoire des idées* (1895—1935), Paris 1936; *Le travail en miettes*, Paris 1956; and R.F.W. Crossman: *Automation, Skill and Manpower Predictions*, address to a seminar at Brookings Institute, 1965.

epochs showing differing internal linkages and laws of motion: the era of the industrial revolution which heralded the rise of capitalism in the 18th and 19th centuries, and the present era of the scientific and technological revolution, linked, as we believe, by its intrinsic logic and in the broad historical perspective with profound social changes and the gestation of communism. Some authors at least show signs of recognising a turning point in the industrial structure of work when they use such terms as the "post-industrial" or "tertiary" civilization,[1] but here the true scale of the problems usually becomes obscured by unanswered questions concerning man's place and his future in the age that is rightly linked with science and technology. On the other hand, American authors, who are concerned with the relatively technically most advanced object of empirical enquiry, tend to lack the synthetic approach for interpreting the substance of the revolutions in the structure of the productive forces and in the social and anthropological dimensions; consequently, their treatment takes the form of interesting analyses of automation processes,[2] or broad enumeration of technological novelties,[3] or valuable studies of economic growth models,[4] social relationships[5] and, lastly, of the future in a cybernetic civilization[6]. But here, too, there are growing signs of awareness of a revolutionary change, already announced by N. Wiener,[7] and perhaps most clearly reflected in the well-known statement of *The Triple Revolution* manifesto[8] — that the current changes in the material base of human life ("the Cybernation Revolution") are assuming a new quality, outgrowing the confines

[1] J. Fourastié: *Le Grand Espoir du XXe siècle. Progrès technique, progrès économique, progrès social*, Paris 1958; C. Clark: *The Conditions of Economic Progress*, London 1941; J. Dumazedier: *Vers une civilisation du loisir?*, Paris 1962, etc.

[2] E. g. J. Diebold: *Automation. The Advent of the Automatic Factory*, Princeton, 1952, and other works by this initiator of research into automation.

[3] E. g. J. R. Bright: Opportunity and Threat in Technological Change, *Harvard Business Review*, 6/1963.

[4] R. M. Solow and other workers.

[5] Work by Mills, Riesman, Galbraith, Harrington and others.

[6] P. F. Drucker: *America's Next Twenty Years*, New York 1955. Much material on these lines has been gathered by staffs of experts in the US: Commission on the Year 2000, set up by the American Academy of Sciences and headed by D. Bell, the groups "Resources for the Future", "Tempo", "Rand-Corporation", etc.

[7] N. Wiener: *The Human Use of Human Beings. Cybernetics and Society*, Boston 1950.

[8] *The Triple Revolution. Complete Text of the Ad Hoc Committee's Controversial Manifesto*, New York 1964 — a manifesto signed by prominent personalities, including L. Pauling, H. S. Hughes, G. Myrdal, B. B. Seligman, R. Theobald, J. W. Ward, and others.

of the industrial revolution as we have known it and the capacity of the industrial system created by capitalism. However, the note of query at the conclusion that "the world is passing through a scientific and technological revolution" found in the official report of the National Commission on Technology, Automation and Economic Progress in 1966[1] in its polemic against the Triple Revolution manifesto suggests that a theory lacking the idea of productive forces encounters difficulties when faced with upheavals in their structure and dynamics.

At all events, much effort is being expended in the West to assimilate the theoretical substance of the technological revolution and its social and human implications. Many conferences have been held, more proceedings have been published on the subject than on many of the most voluminous branches of learning; the issues are debated by parliaments, governments, commissions, learned societies, universities and by thousands of experts. Indeed, some countries have launched long-term, 5 to 10-year research programmes with strong financial backing and employing the first-class intellectual resources of entire universities and research organizations.[2] Organizations engaged in planning or forecasting are advancing remarkable broadly-based concepts of the likely consequences of scientific and technological advance in the next 20 to 30 years.[3] Attempts are being made to give a broad scientific basis to reflections about the future in the era of technological revolution.[4] Yet the observer of this theoretic questing can hardly escape the feeling that the essence of the upheavals in our civilization today emerges only partially, in hazy and fantastic reflections, above the intellectual horizon of the times.

In the socialist countries, the social sciences lagged for a time in this sphere: primarily as regards empirical research and also in theoretic synthesis — which naturally has hampered the search for a practical, progressive view of modern civilization processes. Since the 1950's, when attempts were made by some Marxist thinkers[5] to register the stream of change in contemporary civilization under the concept

[1] *Technology and the American Economy*, Washington 1966.

[2] For example, the ten-year programme at Harvard, "Technology and Society", started in 1964 on the initiative of IBM; similarly Columbia University seminar, *Technology and Social Change* (ed. Ginzberg), New York—London 1964.

[3] The most significant and considered of which are undoubtedly the publications of *Groupe 1985* in France (*Réflexions pour 1985*, Paris 1964).

[4] The series New Scientist (ed. N. Calder), *The World in 1984*, London 1963 and *Wege ins Neue Jahrtausend* (R. Jungk and H. J. Mundt).

[5] E. g. J. D. Bernal, V. Perlo, S. G. Strumilin and others.

"scientific and technological revolution", Marxism has played a greater part in current research. The main thing is that we are able now to draw on the first steps in a Marxist approach to the scientific and technological revolution, contained in the Programme of the Communist Party of the Soviet Union; we have benefited, too, from some remarkable contributions by Soviet scholars,[1] for instance at conferences of the Soviet Academy of Sciences on social and economic problems of technological advance[2] held in 1961 and on aspects of the contemporary scientific and technological revolution in 1964,[3] and the writings of many Soviet authors.[4] Reference was also made to the contributions by German experts[5] and to the concept of the technological revolution submitted to a philosophical congress in Berlin (1965).[6] The work of Polish theorists of growth,[7] Yugoslav philosophers and sociologists,[8] and of Hungarian, Rumanian and other authors.[9]

A firm groundwork for exploring many aspects of the scientific and technological revolution has been laid by Marxists throughout the world, notably by J. D. Bernal, who coined the term "scientific and technological revolution"[10], and by Italian, French and British economists.[11] And it is certainly no accident that with its special concern for the interrelations between the contemporary scientific and technological revolution

---

[1] Especially, M. V. Keldysh: "Sovyetskaya nauka i stroitelstvo kommunizma" in *Pravda*, June 13, 1961; V. A. Trapeznikov: "Avtomatika i chelovechestvo" in *Ekonomicheskaya gazeta*, June 29, 1960; the reflections of Academicians Kapitza, Millionshchikov, Berg and others.

[2] *Sotsialno-ekonomicheskie problemy tekhnicheskogo progressa*, Moscow 1961.

[3] Problemy sovremennoy nauchno-tekhnicheskoy revolyutsii (conference reports) in *Voprosy istorii yestestvoznaniya i tekhniki*, 19/1965.

[4] E. G. Kedrov, Dobrov, Meleshchenko, Zvorykin, Osipov, Mayzel, Shukhardin and others.

[5] G. Kosel: *Produktivkraft Wissenschaft*, Berlin 1957; K. Tessmann: *Probleme der technisch-wissenschaftlichen Revolution*, Berlin 1962 etc.; E. Sachse: *Automatisierung und Arbeitskraft*, Berlin 1959; E. Herlitius: Historischer Materialismus und technische Revolution, in *Wissenschaftliche Zeitschrift* der TV Dresden 4/1966 etc.

[6] "Die marxistisch-leninische Philosophie und die technische Revolution" in *Deutsche Zeitschrift für Philosophie*, Sonderheft 1965.

[7] Especially the works of Kalecki, Flakierski, Chrupek (cf. *Teorie wzrostu ekonomicznego a wspolczesny kapitalizm*, Warsaw 1962).

[8] Supek, Marković, Vranicki, Petrović and others.

[9] Agoston, Jánossy, Suchodolski, Roman, etc.

[10] J. D. Bernal: *Science and History*, London 1955 and *World Without War*, London 1958; however, a forecast of the scientific and technological revolution was, in fact, contained in Bernal's book *Social Function of Science*, London 1939.

[11] E. g. Vincent, Grossin, Labini, Lilley, Dickinson and others.

and human problems the whole field of the Marxist philosophy of man has afforded a valuable source for our investigation[1], in common with the works of those who in one way or another take this position in their criticism of modern civilization.[2]

This, then, was a basis affording the opportunity and the obligation to try to work out a concept of the true substance of the scientific and technological revolution and of its social and human implications.[3] The interpretation here presented derives from Marx's criticism of capitalism and industrial civilization, which never restricted revolutionary tasks solely to changes in the relations of production. Marx envisaged the entire era of industrial civilization linked with capitalism as being transcended through revolution in the structure of production relations (elimination of class antagonism and introduction of a system of mutual cooperation followed by the common advancement of men) going hand in hand with structural changes in the productive forces (a revolution in man's place in the world of productive forces) — that is to say, Marx implied before the event that the changes we know today as the scientific and technological revolution would be an integral part of the communist transformation of society.

Experience of socialism has confirmed that the level of the productive forces in society has much wider implications than those foreseen by any theory based on the initial aims of revolution and the circumstances of socialist industrialization. The elementary function of the entire socialist stage of development would appear, from this standpoint, to be that of making way for and evolving economic, social, psychic and human

---

[1] R. Garaudy: *Perspectives de l'homme*, Paris 1959; A. Schaff: *Marksizm a jednotka ludska*, Warsaw 1965.

[2] E. g. E. Fromm, H. Marcuse.

[3] Our work was facilitated by the fact that in various areas aspects of the scientific and technological revolution have been studied in Czechoslovakia since the fifties. For instance, see J. Auerhan, *Automatizace a její ekonomický význam* (Automation and Its Economic Significance), Prague 1959; E. Vopicka, *Ekonomické a sociální podmínky a důsledky automatizace v kapitalismu a socialismu* (Economic and Social Conditions and Consequences of Automation under Capitalism and Socialism), Prague 1958; F. Kutta, *Úloha automatizace v technickém rozvoji a její ekonomické a sociální důsledky* (Role of Automation and Technological Development and Its Economic and Social Consequences), 1959, and many other books. With regard to the overall concept of the scientific and technological revolution, see R. Richta, *Člověk a technika v revoluci našich dnů* (Man and Technology in the Revolution of Our Times), Prague 1963 and a paper presented to a conference at Liblice in 1961 on the leading theoretical issues of socialism and communism.

conditions under which the most progressive productive forces can be created and the civilization base of human life revolutionized.

Of course, the productive forces cannot be visualized within the narrow and non-historical confines set by the vision of industrialization (which roughly corresponded to the conditions of the period) — that is, merely as a sum of the means of labour plus manpower — but in the broad sense conceived by Marx, as an abundant and mutable totality of all the productive forces of human life, that is, including social combinations and science, man's creative power and the mastery of natural forces. In modern civilization, every rational social integration, every application of science, every step forward along man's path brings into play new productive forces of human life. Socialism would be unthinkable if the advantages of a social structure freed of class antagonism were not manifested in such an open-minded and sensitive approach to these new dimensions in the growth of civilization — in the handling, motives and driving forces of the scientific and technological revolution.

On closer examination, the most surprising feature in this process is that the very logic of the materialized product of human labour does not exhibit a single and constant relationship to man. On the contrary, in man's remaking of the world and his self-creation, which are the matter of history, we meet with remarkable twists and turns. Consideration of the social and human implications of changes in the productive forces leads everywhere to the conclusion that in the course of its growth the groundwork of modern civilization reaches a divide beyond which the fundamental associations and proportions in the march of civilization are inverted — primarily as to the place of man. What seemed impossible below this divide appears above it as a necessity and vice versa: old, tried methods often turn beyond this point into backward, retarding factors. And this, naturally, has far-reaching social implications.

The concept here advanced traces this process in the endeavour to grasp its purely theoretical aspect, leaving aside some factors; it presents an analytical contrast between the industrial revolution and the scientific and technological revolution as the two fundamental civilization processes linked with divergent social and human conditions of life. In reality, of course, the transition proceeds as a continuous, gradual movement and a series of specific upheavals. In empirical reality we meet today at the surface of life with the resultant projection of both types of remaking the world and man's self-creation; the industrial revolution has shaped, and still to a large extent determines, the pattern in the economically advanced countries, but the scientific and technological revolution is beginning to reach out from this base to manifold facets of life, going beyond and transforming it.

Although the two civilization processes are interlinked, one passing into the other, they are intrinsically diverse and indeed, in many respects — mainly in their social and human implications — antithetic. Thus the progress of civilization today consists of various intersecting, merging or compensatory currents; what is more, it is subjected to disparities between the levels of science and technology and the nature of the social systems. From this, too, stems its obscurity. Under these circumstances it appears that the only way to gain any comprehension of the transformations in the basis of civilization is to work out theoretical models representing "pure" types of the structure and dynamics of the productive forces and to examine the specific social and human linkages in each separately. It is evidently just this inability to disentangle and grasp the two basic processes that has given rise to a measure of uncertainty and inexactitude with which the social sciences face contemporary civilization and its prospects.

Crossing the divide of modern civilization, which is coming to be our daily lot, makes exceptional demands on our ability to apply new methods and approaches, without which we would fail to understand the dimensions, laws and forms assumed by the movement of events accompanying the advance of the scientific and technological revolution.

Everything indicates that an understanding of these matters carries with it answers to many of the pressing problems of socialism, problems which have evoked surprise in some quarters. These considerations underscore the vital need for radical economic reforms now being introduced in the socialist countries. They also throw light on the need for a new, unorthodox course in developing the productive forces and show that profound, long-term changes in their structure and dynamics are essential to communist construction. The new status of science in society and the approaching shift of revolutionary strivings to new domains are coming to the fore: the economics of human resources assumes new significance, new conditions present themselves for shaping the socialist way of life and there is a growing need to solve the difficult problem of participation in civilization, to develop democratic forms of social life and so on.

The feeling we experienced throughout our work and that we would like to communicate to our readers was, in short, that our age can be comprehended only by those who are capable of grasping the import of big, unaccustomed changes.

Our team considered it its duty to throw these problems into sharp relief and show the need for new solutions in face of the scientific and technological revolution. In the short time available, it was not, however, possible to elaborate the concept in all its aspects; this is only the start of an undertaking that will require many years of joint research and our outline is intended as an introduction. On this plane it is, naturally, impossible to offer detailed and final conclusions on practical issues, particularly of a specialized nature; here the whole field of applied research and practical decision lies open. We therefore confine ourselves to appending in conclusion a summary of some suggestions that might come into consideration for practical application.

The work was projected at the request of political institutions and the presidium of the Academy of Sciences, and on the initiative of the President of the Academy, Academician Šorm. Many points were discussed with specialists in the fields of science, technology and practical affairs, especially members of the Academy, Charles University, the Czech Technical University and the Slovak Technical University, the School of Economics, the College of Political Science, the department of education and science, the ideological department and the economic department of the Communist Party Central Committee, the State Commission for Technology, the State Planning Commission, the State Commission for Management, the Ministry of Education, the Office for Patents and Inventions, the Institute for the History of Socialism in Czechoslovakia, the Scientific-Technological Society, the Centre for Scientific and Technological Information, the Czechoslovak Labour Research Institute, the Czechoslovak Institute for Research on the Living Standard, the Research Institute for Economic Planning and many other research institutes, institutions, enterprises, etc. Apart from members of the interdisciplinary team, Dr. M. Dýma, Dr. J. Kubálek, Prof. V. Tlustý, M. Zahrádka, M. Sc., and others have contributed written material on various subjects. Assistance in preparing statistical material was rendered by J. Coufalíková, M. Sc., A. Verner and others. Bibliographical information has been prepared by Dr. J. Orlický. We are indebted to all collaborators for suggestions, advice and assistance.

To the English-speaking reader not acquainted with the climate in which *Civilization at the Crossroads* came to be written, we would like to explain its special style. The work was conceived in an atmosphere of critical, radical searching and intensive discussion on the way forward for a society that has reached industrial maturity while passing through a phase of far-reaching socialist transformation. In the light of theoretical enquiries, we saw an image of all modern civilization. The choice advanced in our hypothesis emerged as a practical problem. We therefore tried to communicate it to as wide a public as possible. This led us to choose a readable, straightforward, economical style; every superfluous word was ruthlessly cut out. The Czech and Slovak editions of the book have run to over 50,000 copies and are again sold out.

In this English version we have included references and notes from the original studies from which the book has been compiled; in several places where brevity might have obscured the meaning, or where our team has gone ahead with its long-term research programme, we have added new matter and made some amendments in the interest of greater clarity.

The reader may find our style and terminology rather unusual, in which case we can only appeal to his patience and suggest that without worrying about matters of secondary importance he try to get at the heart of what we are trying to say. Understanding is, after all, a dimension of that human striving with which we are all concerned.

> THE AUTHORS
> Prague,
> Spring
> 1968

THE NATURE OF THE SCIENTIFIC AND TECHNOLOGICAL REVOLUTION

1

The speed and range of the revolution in the field of production, the technical innovations and scientific discoveries in the world today, signalize the inception of processes making for radical change in the structure of the productive forces and in the material base of human life; the prospect is that all previous achievements of civilization will be surpassed. With the rapidly accelerating stream of scientific advance, inventions can now be registered in minutes. Whereas at the start of the century technical innovations usually yielded slight rises in productivity, today, more often than not, entire operations are transformed. Man is penetrating the structure of matter and inaugurating the space age. Human activities are assuming new forms, life is changing under our eyes — distances grow shorter, time more intensive, man-made environments are replacing the natural — and at every turn we find science opening up new dimensions of mobility. People are gradually mastering the basis of their own being. Hitherto each generation has taken over from its predecessors a ready-made pattern of existence that had shaped the entire course of its life; now, however, it will evidently be necessary to reckon with the fact that each generation will experience more than one reconstruction of the nature of civilization and the entire pattern of human life.

Taking these processes to their conclusions from the initial stages or rudimentary forms we are witnessing today, we can see coming decades bringing a radical turn in the transmutation of the world and in man's shaping of his own self: in short, we are on the threshold of a *scientific and technological revolution*.

/Changes in the Structure and Dynamics of the Productive Forces/ 1.1

What is the substance of these innovations and how do they differ from the previous advances of civilization?

/The Industrial Revolution as the Starting Point/ 1.1.1

We stand today at the divide of a civilization evolved over the last 150—200 years, with its roots in the *industrial system* which dominated national economies and set the tenor of human life. Machines, systems of machines, conveyor belts — and alongside a vast army of workers, each performing a tiny part of the combined operation — that is the feature of production in an industrially advanced society. Harnessing the labour of generations, capitalism built up a production base that — in contrast to small-scale manufacture — no longer relied on the individual factor (tools and craft skills), but drew to the full on *social* production forces: the use of machines with a labour force to match.

The industrial revolution assumed various material aspects, but in substance it remained the same. Marx and Engels had already defined it[1] as a constant *revolution in the instruments of production* (the main component of the means of production). The continually developing *machine* — the main agent, the vital nerve of the industrial productive forces — pushed its accompanying object of production (which underwent no radical change) into the background and established a claim to its inseparable companion in the shape of the simple (essentially unchanging) labour power of an army of workers.

The working machine, which fragmented and took over the operations of the human hand, the power machine that excluded the human motive force, the transmission belt — these, in brief, were the stages leading up to the *mechanical principle* (involving the breakdown of complicated craft processes to abstract elements, with mechanization undertaking the main work, leaving to man the sole job of *machine-minding*).

The outcome was the *machine system*, installed in entire workshops and factories, engaging a mass of labour power, either in the form of

[1] K. Marx-F. Engels, *Manifesto of the Communist Party*, London 1935, p. 12.

series of universal or specialized machines with rows of worker-operators alongside them (traditional European industry) or in the form of the conveyor belt linking all operations in a more or less continuous mechanical flow which guided the movement of materials and of human labour (American type). The mass of workers were left to carry out simple manipulation or regulation at the fringes and in the pores of the mechanical system.

The starting point of the industrial revolution was the working machine[1] (first industrial revolution); its universal distribution was only possible in connection with the power machine, such as the steam engine (second industrial revolution)[2], while the spread of transmission devices, belts, transport facilities and especially electric equipment (all of which could be taken to signify a third industrial revolution) marked the virtual completion of the industrial base of civilization.

The industrial revolution disengaged the production process from the range and rhythm of individual labour. The original subjective unity of production, deriving from the producer (craft production) or a body of subdivided labour (manufacture) was fragmented to make its appearance anew in the form of the objective unity of the machine system which subjected the "aggregate worker".

Industrialization, in providing the production base of the capitalist epoch, made this structure of the productive forces general in the guise of the factory; varying in its material aspects, the structure was stable in the internal separation of machinery and labour power.

/ *The Substance of the Scientific and Technological Revolution* /

1.1.2

Recent decades have seen the onrush of science and technology breaki ing the bonds of the industrial revolution; the structure and dynamcs- of the productive forces are being transformed.

a) *The means of labour* are now passing beyond the confines of the machine, assuming functions that in effect elevate them to the position

[1] "...the industrial revolution does not spring from *motive forces* but from the part of mechanical equipment that the Englishman calls a working machine" (Marx in a letter to Engels, Jan. 28, 1963, Marx-Engels, *Ausgewählte Briefe*, Berlin 1953, p. 167).

[2] "...following this first great industrial revolution, the employment of the steam engine as a machine producing movement, was the second..." (Marx's Notebooks on Technology, quoted from the paper *Bolshevik*, Feb. 1, 1932).

of an autonomous productive complex; that is to say, modern technological advance is not merely a matter of innovations in plant and equipment.

b) Progress is spreading to the *objects of production* — the range of materials that have served for thousands of years, with the industrial revolution changing at most the proportions (iron, wood, agricultural raw materials, etc.).

c) The "subjective factor" in production is starting to move after centuries of immutability; step by step the jobs performed directly by simple labour power are being eliminated — technology is excluding man from his directly manual, machine-minding, operational and, ultimately, regulatory functions in production proper.

d) New productive forces, first and foremost *science* and its application in technology, are entering the production process on all fronts, and with them goes the base of all scientific activity — social integration and finally the growth of human capacities that underlies all creative activity.

What really distinguishes the coming advance, giving it the new dimensions of a scientific and technological revolution is, in short, primarily its development into a *universal transformation of all the productive forces* that is setting their whole elementary structure in motion and consequently radically altering the status of man. Everything points to the fact that we are no longer concerned merely with the constant advance of one objective factor in the productive forces (that is, the means of labour) — as was the case during the industrial revolution — or with the introduction from time to time of some new type of production that causes a stir, raises the level of civilization and then quietens down. On the contrary, we have an *unceasing, accelerating* stream of far-reaching changes in all productive forces, in the objective and the subjective factors in the production of human life — that is, in the structure and dynamics of the productive forces.

The upsurge of technology is excluding man with his limited physical and mental powers from production proper, introducing an intrinsic *technical unity* as the basis of automatic working. The technological revolution carries on from the point where the breakdown of labour into simple elements ended (in this sense it takes complex mechanization to its logical conclusion); but it employs, on the other hand, a *synthesis* which is a natural technical process that man has achieved and appropriated — and can therefore control; this synthesis signifies the victory of the *automatic principle* in the widest sense of the term (irrespective of the actual technical basis). We now have not merely tools or the means of labour interposed between man and nature, but an entire autonomous technical process embodying in one way or another a synthesized interaction of means and objects; and it is assuming an intrinsic pattern and dynamism.

The starting point of automatic production is no longer the individual machine, but a fully particularized, *continuous, mechanised production process*:[1] continuous production in the power industry, chemicals, metallurgy, cement production, mass-flow production in the manufacturing industries, and standardized work in offices — this is the most fertile soil for the automatic principle.

Man then stands *alongside* the production process proper (manufacture), whereas formerly he was its chief agent.[2] Simple human labour power is incapable of competing with the technical component of production; the average physical capacity of human labour power barely reaches 20 watts, the speed of sense reaction is of the order of 1/10 of a second and mechanical memory is limited and unreliable.[3] Only in the scope of his creative potentialities and his accessibility to cultivation does man tower above the most mighty of his creations. The traditional employment of man as simple, unskilled labour power therefore necessarily becomes in one sector after the other a brake on the productive forces, involving wastage of human abilities.

To the extent to which man allows the products of his past labours to operate as natural forces, with a consequent withdrawal of human labour power from participation in the immediate production process,[4] there enters into production a far more powerful force of human society

---

[1] Search for the starting point of the present technological revolution still leads some authors to the working machine (Zvorykin); others look to the motive force (Friedman, Osipov); some even to changes in raw materials (Forbes). Theoretic considerations and practical experience, however, increasingly point to its true source in the fragmented production process (conveyor belt) as the outcome of industrial progress, that is, in all components constituting the synthesis of the new quality of production as an application of *science*.

[2] K. Marx, *Grundrisse der Kritik der politischen Ökonomie*, Berlin 1953, p. 593.

[3] Cf. K. Steinbuch, *Automat und Mensch, kybernetische Tatsachen und Hypothesen*, Berlin—Heidelberg—New York 1965, p. 193 and other works; A. M. Turing, "Computing Machinery and Intelligence", *Mind* 236/1950.

[4] N. Wiener has compared this trend with man's control of a "most effective collection of mechanical slaves" which is equivalent to "the devaluation of the human arm" (i. e. simple operations) — cf. *Cybernetics*, Paris 1948, p. 37; he spoke of a new model of productive forces and was much closer to the truth than those who confronted him with the authority of empirical industrial statistics.

— *science as a productive force* in its own right, operating on a basis of all-inclusive social cooperation. The production process then ceases to be labour in the immediate sense; it finds its support in "man's understanding of nature", which implies equally mastery of his "own general productive powers" — i.e. in science, "the accumulated knowledge of society".[1] Science is now penetrating all phases of production and gradually assuming the role of the central productive force of human society and, indeed, the "decisive factor" in the growth of the productive forces.[2]

The more man gives up the jobs that he can leave to be done by his handiwork, the wider the prospects opening up before him — prospects that would have been inaccessible without the backing of his own achievement.

/*The Revolution in Technology, Raw Materials and Power Resources*/   1.1.3

By its very nature the scientific and technological revolution starts on a much wider front than was the case with the industrial revolution. Speaking in this wide sense of the automatic principle[3] (converting production to a technical process controlled by man), we have in mind a number of components:

a) *Cybernation* is the classical procedure. Automation equipment has been evolved as a means of internal autonomy in the working of the most advanced mechanical systems:

Its embryonic form is represented in technical *feelers* ("artificial senses") which eliminate the remnants of human operation and leave merely the need to *set* the various complexes.

When these devices take over the entire machine system, the control and *backset points* are converted into a system of technical reflexes ("nervous system") that ensure a feed-back and simply require to be guided by special apparatus (control desk), or perhaps feeding in of

---

[1] K. Marx, ibid. *Grundrisse*, pp. 586, 593, 600 et seq.

[2] Programme of the Communist Party of the Soviet Union, Moscow 1961, p. 114.

[3] We use the concise term "automatic principle" not in the restricted sense applicable to machinery, which is just one of the trends of contemporary advance, but in the wider sense to denote the sum total of revolutions in technology, raw materials and power, because this concept embodies the cardinal change in its entirety — the elimination of man from participation in immediate production.

programmes; the function of man is now on the fringe of operations.

The third and highest form of automation[1] comes with the *computer* (technical "brain centre") which operates as a new internal dominant throughout the continuous flow of production, making use of information linkages and coordinating the technical process in workshops, factories and complex units; human activity is then relegated to the pre-production stages, to technological preparation, research, science and the welfare of man.

The simpler types of automation equipment are flooding mechanized industrial undertakings, while advanced cybernetic equipment capable of automatically controlling entire units is still fairly rare and will evidently come to the fore in the next stage. Nevertheless, the number of "mathematical machines"[2] (computers) presently in use throughout the world amounts to some 50,000, of which 1,000 are performing process control in production; in the early seventies it will evidently exceed 100,000 and cybernation will find its way right into production, while by the year 2000 we can expect it to be a normal feature not only in factories, but also in transportation, commerce and services (cf. Table 1-1).

b) The application of *chemical processes* is another typical procedure. The industrial revolution afforded scope primarily for sectors relying on mechanical means. The scientific and technological revolution will for the first time open the way to all kinds of procedures in which the automatic principle can also find its application through the development and active role of the *object of labour* (raw materials). When their qualities are selected and controlled, the materials will make their own contribution to by-passing the related operations of external mechanical action on a massive object. On the one hand, chemical processes are, therefore, relatively economical in unit labour inputs, showing a higher proportion of skilled labour, offering unlimited scope for the application of science and being highly receptive to automation; on the other

---

[1] Most publications on the subject distinguish three levels of automation, e. g. *Automation, Great Britain*, Department of Scientific and Industrial Research, London 1956, refers to Detroit-automation, control-automation, computer-automation.

[2] Technical terminology still fails to make an adequate distinction between the levels of technical advance. A machine appears as a perfected tool, and an automatic device as a perfected machine. In reality, however, a machine is not a mere tool but a mechanism employing its own tools, implying a switch-over between subject and object. Similarly, an automatic system is not a machine, but an aggregate unit, or better, process, using machines, implying a new level of subjectivity, and consequently the automatic system carries quite different implications for man than the machine.

hand, they are in themselves a most effective element of automation in the national economy and the degree to which they are applied can, in a sense, be taken as a criterion of the progress of the scientific and technological revolution.

Today, chemicals usually show a growth rate double that of other branches. World output of new man-made materials is roughly doubled over 5—6 years (cf. Table 1-2) and at this rate synthetic substances would by the end of the century reach a level comparable to present-day steel output. In any event, the main point is that chemical processes break out of the narrow circle of natural raw materials with their established qualities and encourage their substitution by a range of man-made materials endowed with properties chosen at will. This opens the way to the mass application of more sophisticated methods than the mechanical.

A similar outlook (technologically uncharted as yet) is offered by the application of *biology* to automatic techniques, whereby still higher structures and a wider range of internal linkages in the objects can be exploited — and the prospects that may be opened up as science pursues its exploration of the substance of life, with the development and application of bionomics, are almost inconceivable. The use of antibiotics first confirmed the possibility of applying biology to industrial processes.

c) Application of automatic principles makes enormous demands on power resources; electric power output is trebled every ten years in the USSR, in the USA it is doubled; the trend here is exponential (cf. Table 1-3) and the classical sources are clearly inadequate. It seems that it is *nuclear energy* that is today capable of meeting the demands of universal growth in technical productive forces — here we have unlimited resources of energy, which is released, moreover, through application of the automatic principle as a technical necessity (cf. Table 1-4). Forecasts published by technically advanced countries anticipate that by the end of the century all increments in power inputs and a good part (50 per cent) of total consumption of electric energy will be met from nuclear sources.

In the decades before us the share of human labour put into producing human life will drop to a fraction of the technical means employed (cf. Table 1-5); probably around the turn of the century nuclear energy will take the lead in the power balance over all other sources (cf. Table 1-6).

Combining all these trends, we have a picture of constant radical change in the *industrial structure:* the progressive sectors will forge ahead (electronics, chemicals, etc.), while the traditional branches will decline (coal-mining, textiles etc.), and the entire profile of industrial production will change (cf. Table 1-7).

The automatic principle passes through several stages according to the degree of technical "automobility"; where the production process remains divided into cycles, with operations interrupted between them, we have only *partial* automation of systems, workshops, units and production lines. Where there is continuous mass production, we have *full* automation — the automatic factory. In many cases, and in entire sectors, application of the automatic principle first requires a change-over to continuous technology (e.g. chemical). Modern flexible types of automation (building-brick system, programming system, etc.) ultimately react back on short series or piece production.

The transition to the automatic principle is still in its *early stages* and even in the most advanced countries and types of production it does not account for more than a small proportion of capacity (e.g. the figure of 6—8 per cent is quoted for the US). Nevertheless, progress is rapid: in the USSR many hundreds of partially automated lines and units go into production each year — by 1975 there is to be a total of 35,000. The first fully automated works are appearing, in which, from feeding in of raw materials to the despatch of the final products, nothing is touched by human hand. Although they are few as yet, their existence marks a milestone in the march of civilization. It is generally assumed that by the end of the century the automatic principle will dominate mass industrial production, thereby revolutionizing the whole structure.[1]

Industrialization transformed the basic industrial sectors, and to some extent transportation and construction; agriculture was affected by the backwash; and although the "tertiary sector" (commerce, services, administration, etc.) expanded, it underwent no special change in quality — until recently. The scientific and technological revolution, on the other hand, has made its impact from the start on all *spheres of civilization*,[2] human activities and life in general — indeed, it often

---

[1] Eg. S. Lilley (*Automation and Social Progress*, London 1957, p. 215) expects that at the turn of the century we may find ourselves in an age of fully automated industrial production.

[2] Views defining the beginnings of the scientific and technological revolution as a "new", "second", or "third" industrial revolution (e. g. L. Brandt, C. Schmid, G. Friedmann, W. Buckingham, M. Pyke) increasingly come up against the fact that the present innovations are not confined to, and are not even rationally comprehensible in the context of, advances in industry.

induces sharper reactions here than in manufacturing or mining.[1]

Apart from a few operations in farming, forestry, fisheries, and services, the *prospective* outlook for complex automation of basic production and related processes has already been theoretically demonstrated by current scientific findings — and this goes for sectors for which a mere twenty years ago it was unthinkable (e.g. mining or administration). Much discussion is being devoted to projects for automating transportation, commerce and services. The most sophisticated computers are capable of adapting to circumstances and of self-organizing; the future seems to hold the prospect of the automatic production of automation equipment, marking the peak of the scientific and technological revolution.

Furthermore, the *perspectives of science* suggest some foreseen, but as yet unfathomable potentialities that may revolutionize production techniques and man's whole way of life during the next decades: application of magnetoplasmodynamic effects, quantum generators of electromagnetic radiation (lasers and masers), controlled mutagenesis, induced changes in the structure of the organism, etc. While their practical application will be a relatively long-term matter, their existence underlines the deep-lying intrinsic acceleration trends of the scientific and technological revolution.

/ *Changes in the "Subjective Factor" of Production and in Man's Place in Civilization* /

1.1.4

Essentially, automation and current technological advance as a whole are not mere sequels or appendages to mechanization; on the contrary, they imply a higher principle of production.[2] So far as the "human

---

[1] In the fifties, for example, output per man-hour in US agriculture rose almost twice as fast as in manufacturing and mining. But in its technical make-up, the civilization trend in agriculture was inferior, moving for the most part along the lines of elementary mechanization. Only with the application of chemical and biological principles can automation make its way into agriculture (cf. Table 1-8).

[2] J. Diebold, one of the first pioneers of the "automation" idea, views this process not from the standpoint of its content, the structure of the productive forces, but solely from the aspect of its technical form. Although he frequently stresses that it marks a "turning point", the introduction of a new type of production system "that regulates itself", he still tends to look on automation as merely "a distinct phase in industrial progress" and "part of the long continuum of man's mechanization of his

factor" is concerned, the industrial and technological revolutions have exactly the *opposite* effect.

Mechanization subdivides craft work, taking division of labour to an extreme, making *simple*, monotonous labour (with each job confined to a narrow sector) the foundation of modern industry.[1] And so the more industrialization and the factory technique progress, the greater the army of simple labour absorbed and the more glaring the disparity within this civilization.

In its results, automation halts and reverses this trend,[2] that is to say, when we take it as a model (leaving aside for the meantime the fact that with only partial automation the amount of simple auxiliary operating may increase). It eliminates the simple work of unskilled labourers, then of machine operators, and of office workers, etc.[3] — potentially, on various estimates, by up to 80—90 per cent. First, their place is taken by new job types on the fringes of direct production (job-setting, maintenance), in most cases of wider scope and with higher demands on scientific skills: the share of such professions rises to over 50 per cent in progressive lines of production and works in which automation has a foothold. Ultimately, the bulk of the work is taken over by highly skilled *technicians and engineers*, standing aside from the direct stream of operations — today they already number 20—50 per cent

work" (*Automation, The Advent of the Automatic Factory*, Princetown 1952, p. 6). As a result, he loses sight of the vital change in man's role in the world of productive forces, a change which is not evident in the purely technological context. A similar idea, that automation is simply an extension of mechanization, is to be found in the analyses made by T. R. Bright and in the report of the National Commission on Technology, Automation and Economic Progress (*Technology and the American Economy*, Washington 1966). Special stress on the similarity between mechanization and automation is placed by H. Schelsky (*Die sozialen Folgen der Automatisierung*, Düsseldorf—Köln 1957, p. 36) and by some participants in the second international meeting held by IG Metall (*Automation — Risiko oder Chance*, Oberhausen 1965).

[1] Rationalization of mass conveyor-belt production on the principles of F. W. Taylor (to split up every job into elementary operations) and Henry Ford ("the keyword of the mass production is simplicity") is just the last, extreme stage of the industrial development defined by Marx: "...simple labour has become the pivot of industry" (*The Poverty of Philosophy*, New York 1963, p. 53).

[2] "Automation is not simply an extension of mechanization... automation is a contemporary phenomenon of a revolutionary nature" (C. Vincent, W. Grossin, *L'enjeu de l'Automatisation*, Paris 1958, p. 26).

[3] Data for the USSR in *Spravochnie materialy po trudu i zarabotnoy plate*, Moscow 1960; for the USA, *Factory Management and Maintenance*, New York 1957. An analysis of the data is given by J. Auerhan in *Automatizace a její ekonomický význam*, ibid. and *Technika, kvalifikace, vzdělání* (Technology, Skill, Education), Prague 1965.

of the personnel in some modern establishments. In general, we can expect that within the next few decades, set-up men, repair and maintenance men and laboratory staff will form the core of production personnel (due to partial automation combined with not entirely reliable internal linkages of the automatic systems); later, as automation is completed and structural changes ensue, their place will largely be taken by technicians, engineers and other highly skilled personnel. There is a lasting and intensifying shift bringing the bulk of human labour into the preparatory phases of production, to technical management, design, research and development.[1] Estimates suggest that by the end of the century production in the most advanced countries will no longer be a *working process* (in the present sense of simple, fragmented labour); a considerable and growing part of the work concerned with acquiring the means of life may be at the level, though not identical with, the work of technicians and engineers.

We see that the scientific and technological revolution is bound up with a transformation in fundamental levels of human activity, whereby man assumes a new role in the world of productive forces — and, indeed, attains a new status in general[2]. This far-reaching social-human change constitutes one of the leading dimensions of the scientific and technological revolution; so long as we see that revolution purely in terms of technical happenings, we shall be incapable of grasping its true purport. In other words, all investigations that fail to assess current trends in the light of man's role in the world of productive forces and confine themselves to considerations of technical resources, power etc., will come up against the insoluble question — how to decide whether the present technical advances are truly revolutionary.[3] After all, is not every

---

[1] "Automation will tend... to enable man's energy and powers to be used to the full in the sphere of material production not for directing the production process, and still less as physical labour, but for projecting and carrying out new technological ideas" (V. A. Trapeznikov, "Avtomatizatsiya i chelovechestvo", *Ekonomicheskaya gazeta*, 29. 6. 1960. In *The Challenge of Automation* (Washington 1955, p. 32), W. S. Buckingham foresees that direct human labour would be largely eliminated from production and replaced in principle by analysis of the entire process, drawing up production programmes, maintenance and setting of machines, and by enterprise management.

[2] Marxist scholars are increasingly convinced that in examining purely technical changes, their impact on the productive forces and the role of man has to be borne in mind. See, for example, K. Tessmann, *Probleme der technischwissenschaftlichen Revolution*, Berlin 1962; G. Heyden, *Die marxistisch-leninistische Philosophie und die technische Revolution*, Deutsche Zeitschrift für Philosophie, Sonderheft 1965.

[3] "It is beyond our knowledge to know whether the computer, nuclear power,

technological innovation revolutionary in its way? And, indeed, with such an approach there is no hope of finding a measure for the revolutionary nature of current changes; nor can it elucidate the character of the present epoch in civilization. However, when we take into consideration the more profound criterion of changes in the structure and dynamics of the productive forces, especially in the relation of man to these forces, the revolutionary nature of the coming transformations emerges in sharply defined terms.[1]

Whereas in the age of industrialization growth in production was accompanied by rising employment in manufacturing and mining, the very beginnings of the scientific and technological revolution point to a reverse tendency: output rises without a growth in the amount of industrial labour. On the contrary, slowly but steadily the *traditional work in production is falling off*. The shift is relative at first (deployment to the "nonproductive" sphere) and then absolute: in the USA the average volume of labour employed directly in production has remained roughly the same for decades (about 75 billion hours a year) and signs of shrinkage are increasingly frequent. Between 1953 and 1963, employment in mining dropped by 15.6 per cent, in agriculture, 24.7 per cent, in communications, electricity and gas production and transportation by 7.2 per cent, in manufacturing by 1.4 per cent[2]; technology writes off 30,000—40,000 job openings a month; and of the "hard core" of unemployed, 59 per cent are unskilled, 19 per cent trained and 19 per cent clerical workers; building, services, new branches, however, still absorb the greater part of labour laid off by technology — nevertheless, the

---

and molecular biology are quantitatively or qualitatively more 'revolutionary' than the telephone, electric power and bacteriology... Our broad conclusion is that the pace of technological change has increased in recent decades, and may increase in the future..." (Report of the National Commission on Technology, Automation and Economic Progress, *Technology and the American Economy*, Washington 1966, p. 1).

[1] Automation "constitutes a new stage in this strange evolution through which man, little by little, retires from the operations of industry, ceasing, as the philosopher would put it, to be the *object* in order to remain solely the subject" (G. Friedmann, *Industrial Society*, Glencoe 1955, pp. 174—175). "Automation indeed appears to be... the technical instrument of the turn from quantity to quality. For the social process of automation expresses the transformation, or rather transubstantiation of labour power, in which the latter, separated from the individual, becomes an independent producing object... This would be the historical transcendence toward a new civilization". (H. Marcuse, *One-Dimensional Man*, Boston 1964, pp. 36—37).

[2] *Year Book of Labour Statistics*, Geneva 1955 and 1965, *Statistical Abstract of the US 1954—1964*.

trend towards eliminating traditional industrial work is clearer every day[1].

While the industrial system did undoubtedly open the door to science as a productive force, its operation remained largely dependent on the customary empirical procedures accumulated over the generations. But now we are witnessing a much wider application of science; it is everywhere shouldering out the routines unprocessed by accumulated human knowledge. The flow of production is transferred from start to finish to a basis of equations and algorithms, thus preparing it for the change-over to the automation principle. Science starts to function *universally* as a productive force, and industry, on the other hand, is turning all along the line into "the technological application of science". We are faced with a transformation of the production process "from a simple working process to a scientific process."[2]

In place of simple, fragmented work, which has so far been the basis of production, we now have the entry of *science* and its application in the guise of technology, organization, skills, etc. The sphere that used to be separated from industry and was merely brought in now and then from without in small doses is now penetrating the heart of production and the entire life of the community. This sphere, which not so long ago engaged a few hundreds of thousands of people, is growing into a vast *material force*, comprising, alongside its wide technical basis, an army of over three-and-a-half million specialists and 11 million associated workers throughout the world. Some experts estimate that in a historically short span of time (by next century) 20 per cent of the total labour force will be employed in science and research.[3]

In range and importance science and research will gradually catch up with industry to become the *decisive* area of human activity. These prognoses take into account the remarkable dynamism of scientific life, which no other field of endeavour possessed to such a degree — the fact that the more science is used, the greater the opportunities offered for its use. Consequently, new branches of science keep appearing as direct

---

[1] B. B. Seligman talks of a dramatic reduction and elimination of industrial personnel (*Automation und technischer Fortschritt in Deutschland und der USA*, Frankfurt-on-Main 1963); E.R.F.W. Crossman refers to "entirely eliminating human labour as a factor in producing goods and very largely in producing services" (*Automation, Skill and Manpower Predictions*, lecture at Brookings Institute, April 15, 1965, p. 12).

[2] K. Marx: *Grundrisse*, ibid., pp. 587, 588.

[3] J. D. Bernal, *World Without War*, London 1958, p. 88. Estimates of up to 50 per cent are given by N. N. Semyonov and P. Kapitsa.

productive forces, and the mechanical sciences are no longer alone in this, but are joined by all the natural sciences and gradually by social studies, too; the other side of the coin is the move by one branch of production after the other towards being "an experimental science".

Hand in hand with this change in function, and shaping it, goes a transformation of the actual nature of science.

All in all, the changes in the "subjective factor" of production signify more than a turning point in the structure of the productive forces, because they throw the field wide open to ever new and more potent factors — productive forces generated at first hand by society, and ultimately, by human beings, on their forward march. This is the point where the dynamics of productive movements, the civilization base of human life, assume their most radical, or we may say more and *more open*, quality.

/*Changes in Economic Growth Models*/   1.1.5

Every mode of production has its principles and parameters of growth. The leading factor in small-scale craft production was the number and quality of the people engaged in it; for industrial production the decisive and limiting condition was the *mass of capital, the means of labour* and the *labour power* employed. Now, with the changes in the productive forces, development is evidently starting to depend on the overall *state of science* (and its application, whether it be through technical advance or through management, organization and skills), rather than on the amount of simple living labour expended directly in production and even on the amount of production means and the volume of materialized labour — i.e., on the total amount of capital. These changes in the sources of growth carry untold consequences for all fields of community life and human activity.

As sources of growth, different productive forces possess entirely divergent *economic qualities*. The economy of craft production was typified by a permanent correlation between the amount of directly expended labour and the quantity of articles produced in the community. The two poles of the productive forces on which industrialization relied were, on balance, governed by a more complicated linkage — growth in the mass of the useful product, always readjusted in general to rises in the sum total of living and materialized labour engaged in production. To gain a larger quantity of use values, there always had to be more factories, machines and manpower, more capital or "capital and labour".[1] If we term the relationship between output and total inputs of living and materialized labour *"integral productivity"*[2], industrialization is, as a basic type of growth — however surprising it may seem — a period marked on the whole by stable, constant *"integral productivity"*.[3] It follows that during industrialization (insofar as technical means are substituted for human labour), the capital-output ratio steadily grows[4] (see Table 1-9), while continuous growth in output requires a rising rate of supplementary input (in relation to consumption), so that *accumulation of capital* then dominates economic growth.[5] Since the basic type of growth in the productive forces during industrialization continues to be *expansion* in the magnitude of industrial output with a relatively *stable* structure of the productive forces — that is, putting up more and more factories with better and better machines and more and more workers — we can say that industrialization represents an *extensive* element in economic growth.

A different picture is presented by a society in which the structure and dynamics of the productive forces overstep the upper limits of the

---

[1] In Marxist terminology this means simply the mass of capital, which includes wages (variable capital).

[2] In economic writings we usually meet with the marginal values of this ratio under the heading of "total factor productivity" — cf. E. D. Domar, "On the Total Productivity and All That" in *The Journal of Political Economy*, December 1962; J. W. Kendrick, *Productivity Trends in the US*, Princeton 1961, etc.

[3] Hence the deep-rooted idea of classical political economy about "the fixed degree of efficiency of capital" already pointed to by Marx (cf. *Capital*, Vol. 1, Dent, London 1933, p. 671) which has persisted as an axiom to this day (cf. J. Robinson, R. Harrod et al.). Marx, of course, takes capital to be the sum of constant capital ("capital" in the language of classical political economy) and variable capital (which often figures in economic writings as "labour").

[4] The main contribution to elucidating the secular trend of the capital-output ratio (for the era of industrialization) was made by calculations by S. Kuznets and R.W. Goldsmith.

[5] Economic growth theories have assumed that in an "industrial society" capital is the leading factor (cf. E. D. Domar, *Essays in the Theory of Economic Growth*, New York, p. 18). In contradistinction to these original assumptions it appears, however, that the advance of science, technology, organization and skills has — in one way or another — to be regarded as an independent parameter which, above a certain level of civilization, exerts a growing influence on the rate of economic growth (cf. R. M. Solow, "Technical Change and the Aggregate Production Function" in the *Review of Economics and Statistics*, August 1957, and other works. Indications of this concept were to be found in the Marxist theory of growth factors dating from the twenties). This circumstance lends the modern theory of growth a new and deeper content, because it inverts the original meaning.

industrial system. The peculiar status of science and its application as a growth factor is deeply rooted in its distinctive economic nature compared with abstract labour. Marx pointed out that "the product of mental labour — science — always stands far below its value, because the labour-time needed to reproduce it has no relation at all to the labour-time required for its original production".[1] The application of science is a sphere of human activity in which man learns at first hand to use the freely available natural resources and forces.[2]

As soon as science — whether through technics, organization or skills — enters production on the whole front and becomes the leading growth factor, the output curve inevitably breaks free of the curve of expenditure of human labour, both living and materialized. A rise in "integral productivity" is evident, opening the way to a decline in the capital-output ratio (see Table 1-9[3]), while the relentless need for a rising rate of accumulation drops out (at the expense of consumption). At this point, even from the purely economic standpoint, the process of extended reproduction and priority accumulation of capital ceases to be essential for all-round industrial advance.

In other words, science is emerging as the leading variable in the national economy and the *vital dimension* in the growth of civilization. There are signs of a *new* ("post-industrial") *type of growth*, with a new dynamic stemming from continual structural changes in the productive forces, with the amount of means of production and manpower becoming less important than their changing quality and degree of utilization. Herein lie the *intensive* elements of growth, the acceleration intimately linked with the onset of the scientific and technological revolution.

Economic growth today is, naturally, a sum of these two tendencies. As long as its predominant source lies in expansion of the labour supply and means of production (capital), as long as economic progress draws

[1] K. Marx, *Theories of Surplus Value*, Moscow, p. 343.

[2] "Insofar as natural science shows how without the help of the machine system, or just with the same machine as before (possibly even more cheaply...) to substitute natural agencies for human labour, it costs the capitalists (and society) nothing and cheapens the goods absolutely" (K. Marx, *Theorien über den Mehrwert* Berlin, 1959, 1921, p. 550).

[3] Cf. D. Creamer, S. P. Dobrovolsky, I. Borenstein: *Capital in Manufacturing and Mining, Its Formation and Financing*, Princeton 1961; B. N. Mikhalevsky: *Perspektivnyje raschoty na osnove prostykh dinamicheskikh modeley*, Moscow 1964. Evidently the tendencies towards a downturn in the capital-output ratio, which are a recurrent feature in the industrially most advanced countries, are reflexes of the scientific and technological revolution in its early stages.

predominantly on growth of capital ("capital and labour") — and these are the typical conditions of the industrial epoch — we can speak of an *extensive* type of growth. On the other hand, when the quality and degree of utilization of "capital and labour" become dominant — that is, factors stemming from scientific and technological advance in a broad sense, from structural changes in the productive forces — we have the onset of *intensive* growth, with new and distinctive features.[1] It is evident, however, that a radical change in growth types can come about only at a quite definite and relatively high level of development, in general when industrialization has been carried out.

Attempts to particularize the sources of economic growth lead us to the conclusion that at the start of the century some 70 per cent of growth (US data) still came from extensive factors; at the present day, on the other hand, some 70 per cent (in the US and the most rapidly growing West European economies) is, according to these estimates, attributable to intensive factors linked with applied science, new techniques, rationalization of organization and management, higher skills, etc. (see Table 1-9). Indeed, in the history of recent decades we can find confirmation of how intensive growth is gaining the upper hand — to the extent to which industrialization reaches its climax and the scientific and technological revolution makes itself felt.

---

[1] A mathematical distinction between the two types can be deduced from the interpretation given by R. M. Solow to the production function when he introduced technical advance as a dynamizing factor in place of the growth constant R. We get for a rate of national income (Y) in relation to "capital inputs" (K) and "labour" (L).

$$\frac{\Delta Y_t}{Y_t} \times = \alpha \frac{\Delta K_t}{K_t} + (1-\alpha) \frac{\Delta L_t}{L_t} + \frac{\Delta R_t}{R_t}$$

By the relative share of the growth rate of "integral productivity"

$$\left(\frac{\Delta R_t}{R_t} : \frac{\Delta Y_t}{Y_t} \right)$$

we can readily distinguish between two growth types according to which elements (the extensive or intensive) dominate (M. Hájek, M. Toms, "Determinanty ekonomického růstu a integrální produktivita" (Determinants of Economic Growth and Integral Productivity, *Politická ekonomie* No. 10, 1966). Taking other growth models, we arrive at a similar result, e. g. from Kalecki's model, V. Nachtigal, K. Kouba and J. Goldmann deduced a similar expression.

/ New Dimensions in the Growth of Civilization /

At a certain stage in the course of the technological revolution and of the changes in growth models evoked by it, all the laws and proportions of society's development appear in a new light. This is primarily true of the relationship between *science, technology and production proper;* one may say that a divide is reached beyond which these relationships assume as vital a role as that occupied by the relation between Departments I and II of production proper in the age of industrialization. In the circumstances of the scientific and technological revolution, growth of the productive forces follows a law of higher priority, that is, *the precedence of science over technology and of technology over industry.* As the President of the Academy of Sciences of the USSR, M. Keldysh,[1] has put it: "In the new historical situation... it is necessary that our technology should grow and develop faster than heavy industry and that the natural sciences, representing the main basis of technological advance and the main source of the most profound technological ideas, should exceed the rate of development of technology".

We find here a new circumstance, unknown in the days of the industrial revolution, which is an essential condition for intensive growth: there must be adequate research capacities and funds of scientific knowledge in readiness to allow for new and more effective technical, organizational and similar measures, always (and to a growing extent) to anticipate, and so forestall, rises in capital-output ratio and rates of accumulation. This is the only way to compensate for and offset the heavy costs involved in the initial phases of the current revolutions in the technological base of production.[2]

---

[1] M. V. Keldysh: "Sovetskaya nauka i stroyitelstvo kommunizma" in *Pravda*, June 13, 1961; we can find an indication of a similar idea in S. Kuznets, *Six Lectures on Economic Growth*, Glencoe 1959, p. 30. J. D. Bernal gives it mathematical expression: the advance of technology corresponds to the first derivation of the production curve, that of science to its second derivation.

[2] The more rapid the advance of science, the wider the range of new, revolutionary technical processes found to be highly effective. While the application of chemistry and other modern industrial processes are generally known to belong to the types of technology that "save capital", many economists (A. Vincent, W. Grossin, Z. Chroupek, H. Flakierski, G. H. and P. S. Amber and others) suggest that automation equipment and later even nuclear technics are also approaching this category, i. e., their introduction is starting to involve lower costs — in relation to output — than the construction of traditional industrial plant. However, there is no question that outside

From the standpoint of shaping and multiplying the productive forces in society, development of science and research can be, in this case (above a certain level and in certain proportions) much more important than expansion of industry pure and simple; structural changes in technology, modernization, management, rationalization, spread of education, care of man, etc., may carry much greater weight than building further factories at the existing level and recruiting the traditional type of manpower.

And it is in connection with the scientific and technological revolution that these factors emerge. Below a certain level of the productive forces (and, therefore, of capital accumulation) growth was always best served by concentrating all resources in industry. Beyond this divide, the situation is reversed. This strange dividing line now transects our age, everywhere upturning the fixed order of things. In the age of industrialization we get used to gauging economic growth by the expenditure on increasing the number of factories. Now, however, we find that above a certain limit and in certain proportions the vital factor is coming to be the amount of resources *released*[1] from production proper to the pre-production phase and to the cultural and social services. Hitherto the advance of civilization depended on growth of capital and absorbing greater and greater masses of manpower into industry. Now, on the contrary, progress in the productive forces is typified by the displacing of labour power by technical processes and "release of capital". Formerly, all-round growth demanded that consumption by the masses be restricted within limits required for reproducing their labour power. Now, on the contrary, this restriction is seen as an obstacle; a degree of expanding consumption (even by the masses) is coming to be the essential condition for growth today — and other examples could be cited. In these circumstances the urgency of a scientific, dynamic approach to alternatives of growth in the productive forces emerges with full force. This, too, is why "growth theories" have come so rapidly to the fore.

The new productive forces that are spreading through the sources of modern life also possess distinctive *human* qualities: science and its

---

the sphere of production proper, on the other hand, the means required for science (e. g. expenditures on laboratories) are now rising sharply.

[1] Marx pointed out the profound significance of the move towards "released capital" (*Capital*, Vol. III, Kerr ed., p. 131) which has assumed vast proportions since his day.

manifold applications are far more intimately connected with man's progress than was simple abstract human labour.[1]

In the industrial model, man's sole value for the growth of the productive forces was essentially that of a unit of simple labour power. With the scientific and technological revolution, however, the reverse tends to be true: now the leading factor is the extent to which the content of science — as a productive force — is harnessed by human activity.[2]

Since the progress of science and technology is to a large extent dependent on *the level of man's creative powers*, and so on the development of man himself, we are faced here with a new element in economic growth, and in the entire history of our times — an element revealing the secret of the present scientific and technological revolution:

At a certain stage in the advance of modern civilization the most effective means of multiplying the productive forces of society and of human life is inevitably found to be the *development of man* himself, growth of his abilities and creative powers — development of man as an end in itself.[3]

Compared with the industrial age, when overall growth stemmed primarily from the amount of capital ("capital and labour"), while the human element was of little concern in the economy, man's own powers are appearing today — through scientific and technological progress and the accompanying revolutions in organization and skills — as a

---

[1] "The development of science, that ideal and simultaneously practical wealth, is only one aspect, form, in which the development of human productive forces is manifested" (K. Marx, *Grundrisse*, ibid. p. 439).

[2] Taking as the unit of productive force the annual output of simple labour power engaged in immediate production, according to Academician Strumilin (the American economist Schultz gives a similar picture) a skilled worker attains a "useful effect" of about 1.5 units of labour power ("Effektivnost obrazovaniya v SSSR" in *Ekonomicheskaya gazeta* No. 14, 1962). Expressing the economies flowing from the work of innovators as savings of total social labour, we have a further equivalent (for the USSR in 1960) of 0.7 to 0.9 labour units (i. e., a total of 2.2 to 2.4 units); for the leading rationalizers and technologists the figure is 5—20 labour power units. On the estimate of the Soviet expert Kurakov, the average scientist saves about 36 labour units. Obviously, no other power in the world than that of human knowledge is capable of endowing human labour with such potency.

[3] Only when "the all-round development of each individual producer" coincides with "a great expansion of the productive powers of social labour" (Marx-Engels, *Ausgewählte Briefe*, Berlin 1953, pp. 370—371) can human development for its own sake become a law of historical progress. Without this concurrence, all humanist endeavours would be purely quixotic.

factor of growing importance in the march of civilization. In this practical context we see the emergence in the most advanced countries of theoretical disciplines concerned with the economic aspects of man's development ("the economics of human resources"), and so with human welfare. Even such expressions as "investment in man" and "human capital"[1] reflect new elements in the civilization released by the beginnings of the scientific and technological revolution.[2]

We are evidently reaching a point when productive forces are being generated in *other* spheres and in *different* proportions than was the case in the age of *industrialization*. The old division into "productive" and "nonproductive" spheres, "productive" and "nonproductive" work[3] and the like appears superficial and inadequate in this light — as do the priorities born of this division — insofar as they fail to take into account whence and in what measure the productive forces are flowing today and insofar as the traditional priorities are not subjected to their new dynamism.

* * *

The whole range of changes taking place on the *divide* that the advance of the scientific and technological revolution has introduced into the historical process of transforming the world and man's self-creation points to a deep-lying link between these movements of civilization and social revolution. Indeed, the scientific and technological revolution also appears as a cultural revolution in a new, and more profound and far-reaching sense; not stopping at internal changes, it proceeds to overturn the very position of culture in society, even making the provision of the material prerequisites of civilization directly dependent on the cultivation of human capacities.

---

[1] T. W. Schulz in an address to a congress of economists in the USA in 1960. Similarly, Tinbergen, Corea, Dennison and others. A conference on "investment in human beings" held in the USA in 1961 attempted to include investment in "human capital" among growth factors.

[2] C. C. Killingsworth, too, despite his one-sided concept, agrees that "the most fundamental conclusion is that automation and the changing patterns of consumer wants have greatly increased the importance of investment in human beings as a factor in economic growth" ("Automation, Jobs and Manpower" in *Manpower Revolution*, 1963—1964).

[3] An open question that has not yet been tackled is how this changed situation is manifested in the logic of the historical process.

/Technological and Social Innovations. 1.2
The Scientific and Technological
Revolution and Changes in the Relations
of Production/

Changes in the structure and dynamics of the productive forces may appear — especially at the start and when revolutionary social processes have not yet developed their full potentials and classical aspects — to be a purely technical concern of no interest to the social order and human relationships; indeed, from this angle technology may figure as a socially and humanly "neutral" factor. On closer investigation, however, we always find that the separation of technological from social changes is valid for a certain segment of history to a certain degree and for a limited time. Essentially the divorce of man from the means of production, of society from technology, is simply a special form of their inner unity — a stage typical of industrial civilization. Insofar as we associate the term "technology" with machinery (and with it alone) and insofar as we take "man" and "society" to imply simple labour power alone, or its sum — in other words, if we proceed from the specific reality of the industrial system and absolutize it in the past and the future[1], the technological base appears to lack any direct dependence on the social system and to be indifferent to it, and vice versa.

Right at the start, however, the scientific and technological revolution reveals the limits of this special type of disparate abstract relationship between technology and social conditions, and points to the profound *social* and *human* connotations of the shifts in the groundwork of civilization.[2]

---

[1] It is significant that all theories of social and human "neutrality" of technology have grown in the soil of industrialization. The reason is that "Never, in any earlier period, have the productive forces taken on a form so indifferent to the intercourse of individuals *as* individuals..." (K. Marx-F. Engels, *The German Ideology*, New York 1963, p. 65).

[2] "Under this aspect, 'neutral' scientific method and technology become the science and technology of a historical phase which is being surpassed by its own achievements — ..." (H. Marcuse, *One-Dimensional Man*, Boston 1964, p. 233).

/Social Implications of Technological Advance/

1.2.1

The structure of the productive forces — and consequently every specific type of production and technology — always possesses an implicit social attribute and, in its turn, demands an appropriate structure of social life. The relations of production are no more nor less than the mobile form of the productive forces, which are always the productive forces of a specific type of human life and a source of specific relationships among people.[1]

Every change in the productive forces is charged with social significance and no relation of production exists that does not in one way or another evoke changes in the world of productive forces.

The range of productive forces employed by society is in no way fixed or postulated once and for all; on the contrary, the extent and content are all open to change.[2] Different social systems are founded on different sets of productive forces, depending on the nature of the society. While the community itself (elementary division of labour and cooperation of labour) was the first great productive force of primitive society and on this foundation the antique world converted the mass of slaves into a mere means of production, later the key productive

---

[1] Today it is generally recognized that "Marxist-Leninist doctrine has long valued technology as a determinant of social change '...whose ideas have had more to do with shaping the lives of all of us than we might care to believe" (*Jobs, Men and Machines. Problems of Automation*, ed. C. Markham, New York—London, 1964, pp. 12—13). In an authentic interpretation of Marx we should, of course, substitute "productive forces" for the word "technology" — which includes man as labour power alongside the technical components; this view of changes in the structure of the productive forces presents their social implications in a comprehensible form.

[2] Marx and Engels spoke of naturally given productive forces serving society (the human body, the soil, natural materials and energy) and of general productive forces directly created by man; among the latter they mentioned cooperation and division of labour, machinery and technology, application of science, human skills, large-scale production, means of communication, the collective power of labour, the mass of the population and even at times the world market (Marx-Engels, *The Communist Manifesto*; Marx, *Grundrisse*, ibid.pp. 215, 651 etc.: *Arkhiv Marxa i Engelsa*, vol. II (VII), Moscow 1933, p. 98 et seq.). This broad historical concept was deformed in Stalin's definition, by which the productive forces were equated with instruments of production + people with a certain production experience and labour skill (*History of the Communist Party of the Soviet Union*, Moscow 1939, p. 120), a definition that gave absolute significance to the conditions of elementary industrialization, and it was certainly not by chance that it came close to the characterization of the structure of manufactories and early factories given by de Jaucourt in the French Encyclopaedia.

force came to be the land, with which, as a component part, the serf was associated. In manufacture and industry, the lead among productive forces was assumed by free human labour power, but its effectiveness was soon undermined by the force of machinery, so that the revolutions in modern production again tended to relegate simple labour power to the status of a "subalternate element" of the productive forces,[1] and this proceeds to the extent that the forces of science — the most potent productive force yet known in human society — are harnessed to production.

The fact that *capitalist* conditions of production opened the road to the *industrial* revolution stemmed from deep-rooted causes. The instruments of labour became independent of the worker, the intellectual powers of production were divorced from manual labour and concentrated to confront the worker in increasingly powerful machines; the directing and operative elements of human activity were separated. The material means of labour were developed at the expense of wasting potential advances in human labour power. Throughout this epoch of industrialization, civilization was passing through a period when progress sprang not from the worker but from the instruments of his labour existing in the form of capital, when growth of the productive forces was accomplished by harnessing simple labour power to the machine system. For this reason, too, the relations of production embodying this conflict were able to spur the productive forces — as long as their extended reproduction did not implicitly require, and did not even allow of, a general advance of human powers. Herein lies the indubitable civilizing role of capital as a relation of production that inevitably conceals within its conflicting social nature the fundamental logic of industrialization.

In mechanized flow production, where the system of machines in itself constitutes a oneness — an agency that subjugates the workers collectively and controls the simple labour of the whole group — the contradictory relation of production also finds its appropriate technical materialization. The self-expansion of capital through labour, the domination of labour itself by the conditions of labour, find their corresponding material and technical expression.

The mechanical techniques of industry differ radically from craft production in the structure of the productive forces and their social linkages. *Tools* were once genuinely the "extended hands" of the pro-

---

[1] K. Marx, *Grundrisse*, ibid. p. 587.

ducer, obedient to his aims and skills. On the contrary, the *machine* — in its social and anthropological quality, its subject-object structure, etc. — is essentially different; the machine system is not an organ of the individual worker[1]; on the contrary, it represents a *social* productive force that subjects the individual and employs entire groups of workers to serve it.

Thus the very technical make-up of machine industry embodies social connotations corresponding to the *inversion* of the subject and object characteristic for capital as a relation of production[2] — both in the actual process of production (it is not the individual worker who uses the means of production, but rather the social means of production now use the mass of the workers), and in the manner of industrial growth (from this standpoint the mass of capital materialized in machines is, indeed, an infallible sign of the extent to which the total material wealth confronting the worker has expanded and also of the degree to which social development has been monopolized).

We may also conclude from the above that so long as progress proceeds along the lines of mechanization and extensive industrialization, capital is the *appropriate* and effective medium. Herein, in the historical view, undoubtedly lies the justification for capital as a transitional outward manifestation of civilization's advance — while being simultaneously its true internal *limitation*.

The crux of industrialization was originally promotion of the extended reproduction of capital, the social substance of which lies in the separation and contradiction between the industrial means of production and the labour power of man. Capital cannot operate permanently and independently on a production base that lacks the two typical components of the industrial productive forces; it cannot exist without workers. Where human labour has been replaced by technical equipment,

---

[1] "The machine appears in no respect an instrument of labour for the individual worker. Its *differentia specifica* is in no way, as with an instrument of labour, to mediate between the worker's activity and the object; but this activity is far more that of a mere intermediary to the work of the machine, to its operation on the raw material ...the machine, which possesses skill and strength for the worker, is a virtuoso in its own right, having its own soul in the mechanical laws that operate within it... the activity of the worker, restricted to mere abstract activity, is determined and controlled on all sides by the movement of the machinery, and not the other way round... unity exists not in the living workers, but in the living (active) machine system" (Marx, *Grundrisse*, pp. 584—586.).

[2] "However, it is only in machine production that this inversion acquires a technical and palpable reality" — K. Marx, *Capital*, Vol. I, p. 451 (Dent).

capitalism has compensated and until recently over-compensated it by directing simple labour power to other sectors. Consequently, the classical industrial *structure of the productive forces*, with the cleavage of machinery and labour, has remained relatively *constant*, despite the rapid growth of machine technology. This was the starting point for the movement of civilization during the industrial revolution, and these were the confines to which it always returned.

In the immediate sense, capitalist production relations can be eliminated and industrial production can be taken over for the aims of *socialist* society — and this may be regarded as the true achievement of socialist revolution.[1] However, the *concurrence* reached between the *social* nature of the productive forces (the machine system as an essentially social production apparatus and the working collective) and the social nature of the newly-introduced relations of production at once engenders a *contradiction* at a different level: the state of overall social cooperation so established comes into conflict with the divided structure of the productive forces, fixed in machine industry with its limited growth potential. One aspect in this is the abstract nature of the basic mass of labour necessary to the inherited machine industry — the simple, operative work that in view of its duration saps a large share of the energies of people working directly in production. A further circumstance is the inadequacy of the resources provided by traditional industrial production to a community aspiring to expand the lives of all, but in which the realities of social development still require that the majority of working people be quite appreciably confined within the bounds of simple reproduction of labour power — the reason being that the greater part of surplus resources is absorbed in the course of industrialization by accumulation of means of production, and by spreading industry to new areas; in fact, production for production (for expanding production)[2].

[1] Large-scale machine industry in all fields was considered by Lenin (*The Immediate Tasks of Soviet Government*, Sochineniya, Vol. 27, pp. 238—239) to be an essential minimum for building socialism. Without this basis of industrialization it was impossible to speak of socialism in the truly scientific sense. However, it sets merely the lower limit for socialist change.

[2] The existence of this dilemma was already pointed out in documents on the first Five-Year Plan in the USSR. The Soviet economist G. A. Feldman revealed the economic nature of this conflict between the actual logic of industrialization and the long-term demands of socialist development (*K teorii tempov rosta narodnogo dokhoda* in *Planovoye khozyaistvo* 11—12, 1928). In current socialist writings — e. g. works by M. Kalecki — this problem presents itself in the much milder terms of the conflict between short-term and long-term growth of consumption (*O podstawowych zasadach planowania wieloletniego* in *Zagadnien gospodarszo-spolecznych Polski ludowej*, Warsaw 1964).

However, such progress cannot in the long run meet the needs of a new social order. It would inevitably — if it were artificially reproduced and maintained — lead to conflicts of principle, because the circumstances would be such that expanding production would be tied to stagnation in consumption and vice versa.

It goes without saying that in countries where capitalism did not play its historical role to the end and socialist society had to complete industrialization, or indeed to put the industrial base into operation from the beginning, the progress of industrialization was linked with that of socialism; in the minds of many people the laws, customs and proportions of the industrial era assumed a connotation as the lasting and sole form of socialist advance.[1] Experience showed that in its revolutionary onslaught socialism could accelerate industrialization and to some extent curb or even paralyze the traditional accompaniments of the industrial revolution: mass impoverishment, expulsion of people from the land, formation of a reserve army of industrial unemployed, etc. However, not even socialism could eliminate many profound and grave consequences of industrial advance; it could not stem the inherent tendency of industrialization towards fragmentation of work, separation of managing and operative activity, the need to maintain certain social distinctions, restriction of growth in mass consumption within the bounds of the simple reproduction of labour power, the propensity to devastate the natural environment, etc.

These tendencies are built into the very nature of industrial civilization, and herein lies the reason why a new life and new relationships among people cannot be permanently founded on this inherited base. In the final analysis, industrialization is one of the *preconditions* and *starting points*, rather than the goal of socialist progress. And, therefore, as in the past, all attempts to found the society on the industrial system alone must be doomed to failure.[2]

---

[1] The idea that the new socialist society could be built up entirely by carrying out the slogan "Everything for industry, everything through industry" belongs not to Marx, but Saint-Simon and his school. But thanks to historical circumstances, the idea that socialism and the industrial system were in full accord came to be generally accepted. For instance, Max Weber considered socialism to be simply a generalization of the principles of factory industry (*Gesammelte Aufsätze zur Soziologie und Sozialpolitik*, Tübingen 1924, p. 501).

[1] The authors of such schemes, from the days of Saint-Simon and his followers, have always ended in one way or another with "positivist catechisms" à la Comte, that is, recipes for a new life within the old industrial system that were forced to confine all man's activities and logically culminated in proposals for weeding out all

The limits of the industrial system assert themselves within the socialist community with a stubborn insistence; they are projected in ever more serious discrepancies, the longer socialism is involved in the elementary processes of industrialization. It would be utopian to imagine that the problem can be by-passed or swept aside by further shifts in ownership or by political power alone, or simply by enlightenment, or, indeed, that it can be dealt with in a matter of days or years. History has proved to the full that the traditional industrial structure of the productive forces and the groundwork of industrialization are too weak to support community life based on the full, free development of men as individuals and members of society; consequently, socialism has to evolve its *own civilization base*, overstepping the bounds of the industrial system, if the sources of communist life are to be tapped.

/The Scientific and Technological Revolution 1.2.2 and Social Progress/

While Marx's criticism of capitalism was directed first and foremost at the relations of production, it was never limited to this aspect; on the contrary, the entire system of industrial civilization as shaped by capitalism came in for critical analysis, penetrating to the roots of the civilization process, embracing the way in which nature and its social relationships have hitherto been appropriated and the mode of man's self-realization within the confines set by capitalist property. The supercession of this stage was conceived as a revolution in the relations and *forces of production*[1], anticipating the laying of a new foundation for civilization — and including what we term today the scientific and technological revolution — as an integral component of future communist reconstruction.

Socialist production relations born of revolutions in the realms of power and property cannot be expected alone to provide a solution for the problems inherent in industrial civilization or to eliminate the conflicts it engenders. The only new circumstance of significance that we may note in this respect is that the opportunity is provided for solving the major problems of the industrial groundwork of civilization,

"industrially useless" life on earth — proposals that, in his criticism of Comte, John Stuart Mill already referred to as civilization madness.

[1] "...transformation both of industry and of the social structure" (K. Marx, F. Engels, *The German Ideology*, New York 1966, p. 37).

but solely on the condition that there will be a *transformation of the entire structure of the productive forces* and the entire foundation of civilization.

The role of capital, as a relation of production, in the march of civilization was to exploit and extend the productive powers of divided labour, to expand the massive machine technology that confronted the army of labour. The industrial productive forces, which were divided and brought into operation against each other by the external agency of the circuit of capital, find in socialist production relations a common basis for a deeper and wider unity. This is from the start the distinctive feature of socialism — that it brings in a *new productive force*, the force of social integration (the unity of the workers' interests, limited and conflicting as it is) providing a potential basis for science as "universal" social labour, society's collective reason, as the social productive force par excellence[1], to penetrate far more deeply into the process of production. But only when all the procedures of actual production are reproduced in *scientific* form will technology be able to transform the direct role of man on an unprecedented society-wide scale; it will enable all elements to be brought by degrees into their intrinsic unity on a new, technical basis in the shape of the fully implemented automatic principle.[2]

On the other hand, when science is harnessed on a basis of social integration, the power of human development will be released and brought to bear on the side of civilization.

Understandably, the scope and significance accorded to these specific productive forces of the social revolution will vary with the conditions, and below a certain level of civilization they will find little outlet.

Nevertheless, from the standpoint of the general model, the transfor-

---

[1] Only when "all relationships are established by society and not determined by nature... is the application of science possible" to the full (K. Marx, *Grundrisse*, ibid. p. 188).

[2] Kapp, one of the founders of the "philosophy of technology" in the age of mechanization (*Grundlinien einer Philosophie der Technik*, Braunschweig 1877), could still manage with the view that the machine merely reproduces various operations previously performed by the worker. At the present level of technology, however, this anthropomorphic approach is inadequate; automatic techniques are making far more direct incursions into social procedures (management, information, etc.) and are increasingly performing functions that man himself never performed. Kapp's modern successor, J. Diebold (*Automation. The Advent of the Automatic Factory*, New York 1952), has already characterized the view that the purpose of the new technology is to substitute for operations performed by men, as a blind alley for automation.

mation of civilization consisting in replacing the simple labour of the mass of people directly engaged in production by the application of science — a productive force founded on a much deeper social quality than that of mere cooperation within the work force of simple labour — undoubtedly has its social roots and correlation in a far-reaching reconstruction of society.[1]

In this sense the changes introduced by socialism do open up wider, in principle *unlimited prospects*, for a much more radical civilization process than that of industrialization and an expansion of the productive forces within their given structure — that is to say, prospects of the universal development of all productive forces, of transformations in their entire structure and dynamics — in short, of the scientific and technological revolution. On the other hand, only social production relations that genuinely afford unlimited scope for science and its technological applications and thereby for development of man's creative powers are capable of putting the scientific and technological revolution into *full* operation. In this light, the advance of socialism appears as the constitution of an entirely new civilization, of a new mode of production that "is not founded on the growth of productive forces in order to reproduce a given state and at the most expand it," but where the free, unhampered, progressive and universal development of the productive forces themselves prepares the ground for a society in which "the full development of the productive forces is the condition of production," where "no definite condition of production is set as a boundary to the growth of the productive forces."[2]

In contrast to industrialization, which originally shaped the technological base of socialism — within boundaries that do not permit steady mass progress of human power — the scientific and technological revolution represents a process of civilization that not only allows of, but makes imperative, the steady and all-inclusive expansion of abilities and powers in every individual — in other words, it meets the requirements of the communist way of life. Logically, then — from the standpoint of the deeper linkages of the model — the chances of carrying out the scientific and technological revolution to the full lie with a society advancing towards communism. And, on the contrary, for a society pursuing this aim and "whose fundamental principle is the full and free

---

[1] These considerations of the model lead to recognition that, in the words of J. D. Bernal, "the scientific and computer age is necessarily a socialist one" (*Science of Science*, ed. Goldsmith-Mackey, London 1966, p. 306).

[2] K. Marx, *Grundrisee*, ibid. pp. 438, 440.

development of every individual"[1] it is essential to advance by degrees beyond the traditional industrial system and the industrialization model of growth to the scientific and technological revolution.

In its general implications and inner logic, the scientific and technological revolution is a *social process* — as was the industrial revolution.[2] Capital originally operated on an inherited base of handicraft industry and through the industrial revolution it acquired its own material base. Something similar, but in the opposite sense, applies in the case of the emerging social order — socialism and communism. In the course of the scientific and technological revolution this society, which at first relies on what is essentially an alien, inherited base, begins to shape its own productive resources.

Taken as a whole, however, the scientific and technological revolution is a social process in a different and more profound sense; in the age of industrialization the march of civilization relied primarily on progress in the means of labour — on the self-expansion and accumulation of capital, with reduction of the mass of immediate producers to abstract labour power. The essential limits of this civilization remained in the impossibility or inability to revolutionize *"the subjective side"* of production to the full — that is, human power[3] — which, of course, hampered technology, too. On the other hand, the scientific and technological revolution, judging by some indications and their summing up in the theoretical model, bases the course of civilization on advance on *both*

---

[1] K. Marx, *Capital*, Vol. I (Dent 1933), p. 651.

[2] The social nature of the scientific and technological revolution is coming to be acknowledged — although in a variety of interpretations — by authors in many countries: in Marxist writings reference is commonly made (by Tessmann, Herlitius, Shukhardin, Gauzner, Shibata and others) to this or that aspect of social correlation in the industrial and scientific and technological revolutions. F. Pollock also sees "the common feature in the processes that we associate under the concept of the first industrial revolution and what is happening today" in "far-reaching changes in the structure of the economy and society" (*Automation, Materialien zur Beurteilung ihrer ökonomischen und sozialen Folgen*, Frankfurt a. M., 1964, p. 171). C. Schmid links current technological innovations with fundamental changes in "the social order, in our modes of life and, indeed, in the forms of human existence" (*Mensch und Technik. Die sozialen und kulturellen Probleme im Zeitalter der 2. industriellen Revolution*, Bonn 1956, p. 5); however, the quality of these changes is not defined here.

[3] The gloomy view often taken of the present upsurge of technology usually stems from extrapolation of the factor that, throughout the industrial system shaped by capitalism, the creative activity of the majority and the attendant development of human powers were not to the fore; this whole area tended to be an "apathetic segment" of civilization (Berelsen, Lazarsfeld in *Social Sciences*, Vol. VIII, Chicago 1957, pp. 121—123, 135—136).

fronts — requiring radical interventions in the technological components; it requires equally or even more radical changes, equal or even more active progress, on the part of society and man,[1] and in all dimensions of life:

a) It is indubitably linked with the prospects of *transforming* the basic mass of *labour*, which has been the deepest stratum of life in civilization so far. This, in effect, signifies a radical change in the structure of the "aggregate worker" and in the position of the various sectors of human activity.

b) The same may be said of *division of labour*. The growing application of science and increasingly evident restriction of simple labour point to new technical prospects for overcoming the fixed division of work, especially the gulf between operative and managing, physical and mental activities — which would involve both eliminating the intelligentsia as an exclusive stratum and a radical change in the nature of the working class, and altogether radical intervention in the concept of occupations.

c) The industrial revolution converted the majority of European nations into workers, enveloped them all in the bonds of mutual dependence and spread its conflicting, class structure around the world. Now, the general course of the scientific and technological revolution, once the present social brakes have been released, is evidently moving towards a new, classless and entirely mobile *social structure*, rooted in the development of man by man.

d) As technological innovations progress, we see signs of an appreciable change in the position of science, education and culture. While in past centuries culture took its place somewhere on the fringes of human life, apart from the mainstream of civilization, it is now finding its way to the very centre of events. The scientific and technological revolution thereby signifies a *cultural revolution* of unprecedented proportions.

e) It seems that the scientific and technological revolution cannot take place unless the present bounds of human life are set into constant

[1] In the traditional view, Marx's design for revolutionary practice is simply a transformation of the objective conditions of human life; in reality, however, the element of self-transformation of the subject occupies an equal place; the crux of the matter is the "coincidence of the transformation of circumstances and of human activity or self-transformation" (Marx-Engels, *Gesamtausgabe*, I. 5, Moscow—Leningrad 1933, p. 534). This feature is to the fore in connection with the vital part played by the development of man and the mass transformation of people in the scientific and technological revolution. A rather divergent view from that outlined above is suggested by J. Filipec in an essay *Člověk a industriální společnost* (Man and Industrial Society), Prague 1966.

motion — affecting not only living standards, but the *level of life*, too. The cycle cannot be closed unless it leads at a certain stage to a comprehensive cultivation of creative human abilities in the fields of technology, science, economic affairs, the arts and human welfare.

These tendencies pose the crucial question: in what social order and under what conditions will these processes of civilization be capable of realization?

Clearly capitalism can take hold of and admit such changes, and even do quite a lot to speed them up in a given measure or zone — in workshops, factories and perhaps in sectors of the economy — insofar as the process does not go beyond a *critical point*, insofar as it is obscured or compensated for by other circumstances; insofar as new elements can be fitted into the old structure, or directed along the old channels, and their growth subjected to some measure of deformation. But will this contradictory system of social relationships be capable of coping with the problems of the scientific and technological revolution beyond this point? Not only critics,[1] but also adherents of the industrial system express their doubts.[2]

The more scientific and technological innovations and the corresponding social changes merge into the advancing stream of civilization, the more they assume the proportions of structural changes that impinge on the position of man[3] and the clearer the contrast between the traditional social form of industrial growth and the new scale of advance in the productive forces — in other words, the fact that "changes in technology have gone far beyond any to which the Western world has been accustomed".[4]

In all probability the groundwork of capitalism, on which the scientific and technological revolution is progressing fairly smoothly in its initial phases, will prove *inadequate* at crucial points and moments as soon as the process has assumed large proportions. In the historical view, various

---

[1] "But the industrial system does not possess any adequate mechanism to permit these potentials to become realities" (*The Triple Revolution*, ibid.).

[2] "There is no ground for complacency. Our society has not met the challenge of technical progress with complete success" (*Technology and the American Economy*, Washington, 1966, p. 6).

[3] The inability of capitalism to revolutionize the human factor in civilization today prompts the contention of C. and L. Longo that the framework of the capitalist mode of production is too narrow for the current scientific and technological revolution (*Il miracolo economico e l'analisi marxista*, Rome 1962).

[4] *Technology and Social Change* (ed. E. Ginzberg), New York—London 1964, p. 141.

upheavals and clashes[1], bordering on disaster, would seem to be very probable.

Theoretically, the social groundwork capable of carrying out the scientific and technological revolution thoroughly in all respects — while avoiding any disastrous alternatives — is to be found in the advance of socialism and communism in their model aspect.[2] The truth of this thesis — and simultaneously the maturity of the new society — must, of course, be demonstrated in practice; undoubtedly in these circumstances, too, it will be a most difficult task.

The limits within which the disparate nature of the production relations can find expression are firmly set by the level of the civilization base. The essential superiority of new social relations is fully revealed only where and insofar as they are backed by productive forces of sufficient level and mobility[3], i.e., where and insofar as the divide of industrialization has been crossed, where and insofar as the new production relations emerge as motivators impelling the productive forces into new dimensions. However, the potential human claims posed by, and the consequences flowing from, the incipient revolutions in the structure and dynamics of the productive forces reflect *correlation* within the scientific and technological revolution — all in all it is not merely a social process, but also a social revolution, that is, an organic imperative of the communist revolution, an essential stage and form of that revolution.

But, of course, the relations of production do not always keep in step with the level and movement of the productive forces. We may find that where the socialist revolution has been carried through, the productive forces — including specific factors brought in by the new social order —

---

[1] N. Wiener has long since pointed out that compared with such potential collisions all previous crises look like "a pleasant joke" (*The Human Use of Human Beings, Cybernetics and Society*, New York 1956, p. 162). Only in the course of the years, during which they assured each other that automation was simply a continuation of mechanization, did economists, industrialists and experts gradually begin to realize that "automation is not just a new kind of mechanization but a revolutionary force capable of overturning our social order" (A. J. Hayes in *Jobs, Men and Machines. Problems of Automation*, ed. C. Markham, New York 1964, p. 48).

[2] But the relations of production under capitalism are much too narrow for a scientific and technological revolution. Socialism alone is capable of effecting it and of applying its fruits in the interests of society" (*Programme of the Communist Party of the Soviet Union*, Twenty-Second Congress of the CPSU, Moscow 1961, pp. 27—28).

[3] "People have always liberated themselves to the extent that they were constrained or permitted not by their ideal of man, but by the existing forces of production" (*The German Ideology*, MEGA, Vol. I. 5, p. 409—410).

are for a time much weaker in comparison with industrially advanced countries; socialism may, in fact, be faced with a long list of elementary measures of industrialization. In such case, of course, severe tension is bound to be set up within the community, with a danger of the level of civilization being out of step with the social transformation. Should these conditions be prolonged, they may lead to some degree of immaturity or deformation of the corresponding production relations — in view of the possibility that features dictated by emergency may become fetishes and allowed to persist.

On the other hand, capitalism may be compelled by various causes to overstep the bounds of the industrial revolution and adapt itself to productive forces operating at a higher level, which inevitably generates various unaccustomed features in the economic and social life of the advanced countries.

The process of completing industrialization and of initiating the scientific and technological revolution will exhibit, when the two cases coexist — as we find them today — many divergences in principle, but also many analogous features which may be puzzling at first glance. The predominating structure and dynamics of the productive forces evoke at each stage some similar tendencies in the process of civilization, depending on the level of the productive forces and hence of consumer resources, on the material conditions of life and work — which exert strong pressure on the entire life of the community.

However, movements in the civilization base are modified by production relations and assume diverse forms; for instance, socialist industrialization does not involve primary impoverishment and pauperization, but it has meant long years that could be overcome only by the self-denial of millions. On the other hand, the early stages of the scientific and technological revolution under capitalism are probably strongly marked by inadequate economic utilization of the prospects potentially available for science[1], and the growth of human power — although the level of research and education has undoubtedly shot up in the foremost capitalist countries.

These conflicting currents produce appreciable deformation of the scientific and technological revolution as a world process in its early stages, altering and transposing its various features; the outcome is that the inner logic of the revolution, seen as a social process, and the deeper

[1] In this connection, American sources point out that total US expenditure on armaments and war in the fifties was four times the total expenditure on science.

implications of the technological and social upheavals are obscured; investigation is thereby confused.[1]

These existing superficial circumstances also offer theorists the choice of turning a blind eye to the new elements and dimensions of civilization processes[2] or of continuing to interpret them in the context of the traditional industrialization procedures,[3] treating them as another phase or a mere repetition of the industrial revolution, etc. In these circumstances, the essence of the scientific and technological revolution remains, even in the technologically advanced countries of the world, veiled in conflicting conjectures[4] and this tangled web obscures the true picture of the crossroads at which the civilization of our day has arrived.

/ *The Imperative of Growth and World Systems* /

1.2.3

Naturally, the course of the scientific and technological revolution is not a simple copy of a logical pattern; it is refracted by the prism of mediation that is typical of industrial civilization, whereby causes and effects are always made to appear inverted.

Hitherto many scientific discoveries and technological achievements have undoubtedly made their first appearance in capitalist countries.

---

[1] After a decade of intensive study, J. Diebold declared, for example, in a report delivered in 1960 on "The Basic Economic Consequences of Automation" that we know very little about the actual economic and social implications of automation. The incipient revolutions in production — writes G. Morgentau — "create economic and social problems unaccounted for by traditional theory and practice" (*The Crossroad Papers. A Look into the American Future*, New York 1965, p. 10).

[2] Such an attitude is adopted by S. Balke (*Vernunft in dieser Zeit*, Düsseldorf—Wien 1962, pp. 117 et seq.); he considers quite seriously that the revolutionary changes in the ground-work of civilization have been invented by the French and spread abroad by Toynbee.

[3] Dr. De Carlo noted at a seminar at Columbia University that such views originate among those captains of industry who "attempt to use the past to present the image of the future, conserving the values and attitudes which have made present institutions and organizations successful. They search for ways in which the present technological changes can be viewed as normal evolution" (*Technology and Social Change*, ed. Ginzberg, New York—London 1964, p. 21).

[4] "...neither Americans nor their leaders are aware of the magnitude and acceleration of the changes going on around them... mankind is at a historic conjuncture which demands a fundamental re-examination of existing values and institutions" (*The Triple Revolution*, ibid.).

Contrary to the model patterns, most socialist countries have so far been passing through the phase of industrialization, while advanced capitalist countries have been confronting the alternative of using the fruits of the scientific and technological revolution or succumbing to stagnation.

It is in the nature of capital that it is an essential relation for growth of the productive forces. Its historic role is in harnessing the mass of *social* productive forces — machinery and labour power. Nevertheless, capital is not an absolute form for the production of wealth because it operates solely at a certain level of association — that is to say, abstract association, fraught with contradiction, "...if we understand it correctly, it appears as a condition for growth of the productive forces, so long as they require an external spur, that simultaneously appears as their curb."[1] Beyond a point, however, growth of the productive forces sets bounds for capital, which is constrained by its own purpose — that is, to expand its own value with the aid of labour power. Theoretically, in direct proportion to its growth, capital puts a brake on the productive forces: "The very nature of the capitalist method of production prevents a reasonable improvement beyond a certain point"[2] — insofar, of course, as it operates from purely internal incentives with no modification or compensatory elements contributed by external or internal factors, control, etc.

This ambivalence of capital in relation to the productive forces is still stronger in the case of *monopoly*, which by its nature possesses far greater opportunities for using or misusing social resources, technology and rationalization; there is greater scope for specialization and combination, and for research, than in the case of classical capitalism — because the monopolist operates at a higher level of association than the classical capitalists.[3] On the other hand, monopoly has, or at least originally had, far greater cause and power to put a brake on productive forces in society that it cannot keep in its own hands — as happens when applications of modern science lead to radical technological inno-

[1] K. Marx, *Grundrisse*, ibid. p. 318.
[2] K. Marx, *Capital*, Vol. I (Dent), p. 520.
[3] "Competition becomes transformed into monopoly. The result is immense progress in the socialization of production. In particular, the process of technical invention and improvement becomes socialized" (V. I. Lenin, *Imperialism, the Highest Stage of Capitalism*, Selected Works, Vol. 1, Moscow 1963, p. 692). Socialist theory has long since taken into account the fact, pointed out by J. A. Schumpeter, that monopoly is in a position to devote greater resources to research and to bear heavier risks of innovation (*Capitalism, Socialism and Democracy*, New York, 1950).

vation, when full automation techniques are introduced, etc.; from this stems the tendency to rigidity so typical for monopoly.

This sharp contradiction has been felt in the most advanced industrial countries throughout the present century.[1] Which tendency has the upper hand at any given time depends on the intrinsic and extrinsic conditions af capital reproduction, to which monopoly is exceptionally sensitive.

From the end of the last century and in the first half of the twentieth century monopoly capitalism undoubtedly allowed a wealth of technological resources, and still more human potentialities, to remain untapped.[2] Speculations about a chronic "secular stagnation" and the approaching "maturity" of an economy with arrested growth[3] à la John Stuart Mill — combined with anti-technological attitudes and romantic damning of science à la Bergson — were typical for the atmosphere of those days.

The high growth rates of industrialization visibly faltered around 1903—1913 (see Table 1-11). The falling off in growth of per capita output in the first decades of this century is estimated[4] for the U.S. at at least thirty per cent, and for Western Europe at considerably more.

However, the thirties (the Depression), the forties (World War II)

[1] "...One often gets the impression that the scientific age is just beginning, and that once monetary problems are solved, technological advance will proceed at a tremendous rate. On the other hand, one also cannot escape the impression that certain institutional developments, particularly the growth of huge corporations and monopolies, are not conducive to rapid technological change, and that the mere assurance of an adequate effective demand will not solve the whole problem" (E. D. Domar, *Essays in the Theory of Economic Growth*, New York 1957, p. 60).

[2] The monopolies practised a complicated and two-edged manipulation with inventions ("patents protection"); investigatory commissions invariably noted a direct connection between technological stagnation and the degree of monopolization of a given sector. The U.S. Administration intervened to restrict output (agriculture); the idea of taking steps to curtail research was mooted (Great Britain); there was even legislation against technical labour-saving processes (Germany, 1933); and finally an outlet was found in turning a big share of the productive forces to destruction (rearmament).

[3] In 1929, in an article "Retardation of Industrial Growth" (reprinted in *Economic Change*, New York 1953), S. Kuznets generalized the facts about the slow-down in economic growth. Similarly Alvin Hansen and others.

[4] Kuznets puts this drop in per capita output at one-half and considers it to be a world-wide phenomenon (*Six Lectures on Economic Growth*, Glencoe 1959, pp. 39—40). A. Madison, using Kendrick's data, calculated that the increment rate of the per capita national product dropped from 2.2 per cent in 1870—1913 to 1.3 percent in 1913—1929; in Great Britain the figures were 1.2 per cent and 0.3 per cent for the same periods. (*Long Term Economic Growth 1860—1965*, U.S. Department of Commerce, Bureau of the Census, Washington 1966, p. 101).

and quite obviously the fifties (competition between two world systems) have brought an appreciable *change* in the metropolises of capital. The monopolies have been putting their accumulated inventions and patents into circulation, and increasing pressure towards innovations[1]. There is a sharp increase in funds for research and development. Technology is regaining its status. Growth rates are showing a new acceleration (Table 1-11); per-capita output, again on the upgrade, especially in the fifties and sixties, has reached a remarkable level in the U.S., and the heights reached in Europe are unprecedented and quite unexpected.[2] There has also been an unmistakable acceleration in output per man-hour.[3]

Structural changes in production follow one another hard and fast. Indeed, the apparatus of *state monopoly* is now giving all possible encouragement to progress by redistributing the surplus product and in general covering losses incurred by capitalist concerns in the course of rapid technological advance. There are here some unmistakable signs that the scientific and technological revolution is getting under way.

Whence the change?[4] Some people believe that capitalism has undergone a complete regeneration, others are loath to admit any substantial modification. The reality is, however, more complicated. In its social and class basis, capitalism has not changed, but there has been a substantial change in the conditions under which the self-expansion of capital can and is taking place; this imposes a new relationship to the productive forces, and important innovations throughout the reproduction process:

[1] "...Technological innovation is today being carried out to a growing extent by already existing big concerns" (P. Sylos Labini: *Oligopolio e progresso tecnico*, Torino 1961, p. 181).

[2] According to Madison's figures, per capita annual output increment rose in the U.S. from 1.3 percent in 1913—1929 and 1.6 per cent in 1929—1950 to 2.0 per cent in 1950—1965 (3.2 per cent in the sixties). In Great Britain, from 0.8 per cent in 1913—1950 to 2.4 per cent in 1950—1964; in France, over the same period, from 0.9 per cent to 3.8 per cent and in West Germany from 0.5 per cent to 5.9 per cent (*Long Term Economic Growth 1860—1965*, U.S. Department of Commerce Bureau of the Census, Washington 1966, p. 101).

[3] The report of the U.S. National Commission for Technology, Automation and Economic Progress recognizes that this advance is substantial: "In the 35 years before the end of the Second World War, output per man-hour in the private economy rose at a trend rate of 2 per cent a year. ...Between 1947 and 1965 productivity in the private economy rose at a trend rate of 3.2 per cent a year" (*Technology and the American Economy*, ibid., p. 2).

[4] Various answers to this question are contained in *Has Capitalism Changed? An International Symposium* (ed. S. Tsuru, Tokyo 1961).

a) From the days of the great crisis, it has been clear that traditional industrial growth had reached its limit[1]; without intervention by the monopoly state aimed at expanding purchasing power, the capitalist system is incapable of functioning normally; government measures can be directed to expanding parasitic consumption,[2] but to a limited extent; it soon becomes necessary to add public investments and military contracts, with artificially regulated growth (to prevent unemployment); and finally the problem shifts to the question of expanding mass consumption. And since the consumer system makes labour relatively dearer, and changes the structure of consumption so that the market is far more fluid for the producer[3], the incentive to make use of technological innovation is automatically strengthened — that is to say, technological progress becomes essential for the viability of capital.

b) These practices spread during World War II with the rise in military consumption and the breaking down of much of the monopolist resistance to technological innovation in face of external necessity.

c) Finally, the *pressure* of the growing *socialist world* is manifested in the economies of the capitalist countries as a long-term and most insistent (if indirect) factor.

In this connection there are two vital intermediary links: primarily, the *internal* class conflict has reached such proportions that it has posed expansion of mass consumption — although it conflicts with the reproduction needs of capital itself — as a vital imperative. Under these circumstances, when all opportunities for expanding absolute surplus value have been barred and, what is more, when its existing level is threatened, production of relative surplus value, relying on technological and organizational advance, comes to be the only solution. Capital is therefore resorting increasingly, with state assistance, to rapid growth

[1] Some Marxist economists have suggested that the depth and extent of the crisis in the thirties might have had something to do with the first indications of the scientific and technological revolution, for which the capitalist system was completely unprepared at the time.

[2] This was Keynes' original idea. But from the start his underlying concept went far deeper, as he said in his commentary on the Peace Treaty in 1920. He proceeded from the fact that the capitalist world was shaken by the pressure of socialist revolution. The state interventions he recommended to expand the consumer system and relieve the pressure of class conflict were framed to meet this threat. Yet at first he met with little understanding among capitalists — and it was not until the great crisis that he won recognition.

[3] A. Štraub, "Vývoj spotřeby a přechod do stadia intensivního růstu" (Trend of Consumption and Transition to the Stage of Intensive Growth). *Politická ekonomie* 5/1967.

and technological development as an alternative to impending social conflicts at home[1] and every step in this direction urges the operative interests towards further growth, for which new conditions are found in the structure and dynamics of the productive forces.

The *external* influence exerted by socialist forces follows a still more intricate path. Let us take good note of how Marx conceived the relation between capital and the productive forces: "And as soon as the formation of capital were to fall into the hands of a few established great capitals, which are compensated by the mass of profits for the loss through a fall in the rate of profit, the vital fire of production would be extinguished"[2]. The conditional tense is not used by chance; insofar as monopoly of production makes headway, capitalist society develops tendencies to halt the progress of technology and the productive forces. But the idea can be reversed: where capital fails to gain a monopoly of productive resources, it has no alternative but to drive the productive forces and technology forward, even at the risk of their running ahead of it. The existence of the socialist system, accounting for one-third of world industrial output, and possessing valuable research capacity, etc., signifies *de facto a breach in the monopoly system*, gradual loss of the monopoly of science, technology and production in the world.[3] The monopolies no longer possess (at least in many sectors) the supreme power to hold back revolutions in production; at the very least they are losing their freedom to manoeuvre, and they operate merely as big oligopolies; moreover, competition among the advanced capitalist countries is intensifying; the one-time "outsiders" are improving their positions — whether they be countries or concerns.[4]

An impulse is given to the reversible, paradoxical logic of monopoly, which leaves the top-rankers in peace and forces the rest to move; there

[1] Galbraith interprets Keynes' concept as follows: "In the advanced country... increased production is an alternative to redistribution. And, as indicated, it has been the great solvent of the tensions associated with inequality" (*The Affluent Society*, 1958, p. 95).

[2] K. Marx, *Capital*, Vol. III, p. 304. Similarly Lenin: "Since monopoly prices are established, even temporarily, the motive cause of technical and, consequently, of all other progress disappears to a certain extent and, further, the economic possibility arises of deliberately retarding technical progress" (ibid. *Imperialism*, p. 754).

[3] "...A rival economic system has appeared on the scene. ...our system must prove its worth by its performance" (G. Colm: Economics in the Atomic Age, in: *Zur Ökonomik und Technik der Atomzeit*", Tübingen 1957, p. 89).

[4] This circumstance has a strong impact, for example, on the economic growth of Western European countries; in the competition between two worlds their prospects are much brighter.

follows an effort to save, through a certain monopoly progression, the lead that could not be gained on the basis of a given state of monopoly holding. The self-expansion of capital is thereby presented with unaccustomed dynamic conditions and growth in the context of the scientific and technological revolution evokes a variety of new features in the monopoly economy and in the social life of capitalist countries.[1] State monopolism has to some extent adapted the capitalist economy to the conditions set by an exceptionally high degree of technological progress. However, the resultant movement of the productive forces ultimately tends to restrict the operative base of capital in one way or another, and enforces a progressive curtailment of this base as a condition for its maintenance.[2]

Evidently the interplay of social and technological revolutions does not take a direct course, but operates through innumerable *media*. In the totality of changes, the impetuous growth of the productive forces, with the ever more rapid advance of science and its applications, appears in the hitherto unknown guise of an independent social factor, as an autonomous elemental power soaring above people, countries and systems — a power that no monopoly in the world is now capable of restraining or resisting forever, however hard it might try — it can be harnessed solely by those who submit to it completely. So the scientific and technological revolution is entering the world scene as a concealed ferment, and anonymous "imperative of growth",[3] bearing no mark of its origin, but signifying everywhere a vital condition[4] that cannot be ignored. The spread of modern "growth theories"[5] is typical of this new atmosphere.

[1] "As to the West: the former conflicts within society are modified and arbitrated under the double (and interrelated) impact of technical progress and international communism" (H. Marcuse: *One-Dimensional Man*, Boston 1964, p. 21).

[2] So "capitalism is being killed by its achievements" (J. A. Schumpeter, *Capitalism, Socialism and Democracy*, New York 1950, p. 119.)

[3] V. Largentière, "Le Capitalisme contemporain et la croissance", (*Economie et politique*, 107—108, 109/1963).

[4] Compare the dilemma "automate or perish" that was a commonplace in economic treatises — from General Electric's practical circulars to the theoretical analyses by Newberg or Buckingham.

"Our existence depends on the fact that we have a technological lead" (K. Steinbuch, *Automat und Mensch. Kybernetische Tatsachen und Hypothesen*", Berlin—Heidelberg—New York 1965, p. 347).

[5] "Current growth theories" stem from the new dynamics of the productive forces as their theoretic expression. Leading exponents such as E. D. Domar recognize that the present concern with growth is no accident; it is evoked by the fact that the socialist

The complexity of these factors may, however, obscure the fact that in the underlying impulses, out of which the manifold dialectic of history has composed this imperative of growth, lies the challenge of the nascent social structure that sets no limits to the growth of the productive forces — the *technological challenge* of the communist revolution. The very birth of the scientific and technological revolution is intrinsically linked with the penetration of socialist trends into the body of the contemporary world; to say the least, the existence of socialism in the world bears the credit for the fact that the divide in the path of the industrial productive forces — the divide beyond which the traditional impulses of capital have been threatened with stagnation — has not become the boundary of civilization's progress and has been overstepped.

But there is no need for socialism to disguise the fact that its lead in branches of science, technology or education[1] is just a beginning and far from universal; for the present, these successes in some critical areas emerge at the surface of the world today as direct impulses towards a new acceleration of the productive forces and social change.[2]

Labour productivity in the most advanced socialist countries is still 2—3 times lower than that in the U.S., and if the present growth relations are maintained[3] it may take some decades to close the gap on the whole front.

With the present *competition between two systems*, the scientific and technological revolution operates as a process exposing all shortcomings and penalizing those who cannot keep in step or adjust their pace in time. The decisive struggle for socialism (on a world scale) is now being fought out in the field of capacities for productive, scientific and techno-

part of the world is "strongly and quite successfully committed to rapid growth" — that is, by the existing international conflict that makes growth a vital matter (*Essays in the Theory of Economic Growth*, New York 1957, pp. 15, 18).

[1] In 1959, following the successes of the Soviet space programme, a Congressional committee discovered for the first time that in some vital areas of science and technology the Soviet Union was starting to outstrip the USA (*Comparisons of the United States and Soviet Economies. Hearings before the Joint Economic Committee of the United States*, Washington 1960, pp. 245 et seq.).

[2] In reflections on these critical areas it is usually found that they have originated in the course of "our breathtaking movement into a new technological era" and that "the USSR has served as a rude stimulus to awaken us to reality" (*Prospect for America. The Rockefeller Panel Reports*, New York 1961, p. 368).

[3] If the causes of growth acceleration that we have stated are correct, we have to envisage not a decline, but maintenance and more probably some rise in the growth rate in the West, too — an assumption that has appeared in forecasts for some time now (e. g., *Long-Range Projections for Economic Growth*, Washington 1959, etc.).

logical progress, bringing into play many unaccustomed elements and requirements.

Capitalism can be surpassed only by being compelled to give the maximum weight to what has been the strongest element in industrial civilization and on which — and that is the main point — it still bases its position[1] — progress in production, and to the extent to which it shows itself incapable of realizing this progressive human undertaking.[2]

/ *The Scientific and Technological Revolution and the "Third World"* / 1.2.4

While in the initial phases the impact of the scientific and technological revolution is confined to the most advanced industrial countries, it is bound, in view of the level of the productive forces (science as a world-wide force), to be essentially a *world process* from the very beginning and can ultimately proceed solely on a world scale. Through various intermediary paths, it quickly penetrates all continents. We may assume with good reason that it will exert a strong influence on the position and development of the *"third world"*; conversely, the problems of the underdeveloped countries may also prove to be fateful factors for the course of this revolution.

Modern industrial civilization as formed by capitalism has culminated in a terrible and growing gulf between economic movements in the metropolitan countries and the "eternal" elemental privation endured by the majority of mankind. The average gap between the level of civilization in the industrially advanced countries and the third world is shown by economic data[3] to be of the order of 1 : 10, and in some cases (the USA

---

[1] "The problem posed by contemporary Russia", writes W. W. Rostow, "lies not in the uniqueness of its story of modernization, but in whether the United States and the West can mobilize their ample resources... of spirit, intellect, will and insight quite as much as steel and electronic gadgets..." (*The Stages of Economic Growth. A Non-Communist Manifesto*, Cambridge 1960, p. 104). This broad interpretation reflects certain changes at the surface of the historical mechanism, but stops short of the question of the specific nature of these contemporary sources.

[2] "This necessary drive for technological leadership — on which increasingly rests our economically privileged position — will sharpen and intensify the as yet largely unperceived social problems of automation," writes J. Diebold in *Jobs, Men and Machines*, ibid., p. 12. Of course, the stumbling-block for this society is not automation as such, but man under the conditions of automation.

[3] According to calculations by S. Kuznets, published in *Economic Development and Cultural Change*, the average per-capita national income for seven industrial countries

compared with Indonesia) it reaches 1 : 50 — allowing of no comparison in modes of life. Today, at the start of the scientific and technological revolution, the gap is widening. But there is now no place in the world that can permanently coexist with the mass poverty of the part inhabited by the majority of mankind. The mighty forces of technology and communications have made this world too accessible from all sides, and too small; under these circumstances, the catastrophic backwardness of one part of the world signifies a threat to all.

Modern advances in science and technology have so far touched only the fringes of the third world, but they have already managed to do much to upset the natural equilibrium maintained for thousands of years by hunger, epidemics and natural disasters. The scientific and technological revolution invades this dissimilar world from without, lacking any connection with its inherent organic development. It aggravates the contradictions of human existence to extremes, accumulating highly inflammable material and creating many bizarre combinations of natural principles of life and the dynamics of modern civilization.[1]

The backlash is felt, for example, in the *"population explosion"* in these countries at the rate of a quarter increase every ten years[2], always outweighing their economic advances, so that in many developing countries the per capita national income is not growing, but even decreasing. Education has never shown such progress in the world as today, but in face of the population explosion in the developing countries the world level of illiteracy is not only not falling, but tending to rise.

These startling paradoxes in the condition of the third world are a clear indication that in their one-sided, spontaneous aspects the effects of the modern revolutions in civilization can overshadow the initial impulses of the scientific and technological revolution and even — at least at the start — halt and reverse it. If these effects were not consciously developed and rationally mastered, they would be bound in time to bar the way to intensive economic development and therefore to the mass cultivation of human powers.

---

amounts to 1,000 dollars, and for 24 developing countries, 100 dollars (cf. the summary in *Industrialization and Society*, ed. B. F. Hoselitz, W. E. Moore, UNESCO 1963).

[1] Many critics of contemporary civilization envisage a salutary compensation for Western life through assimilation of some elements in the Oriental concept. In reality, however, they stand little chance of reaching a synthesis by employing such divergent elements — they tend rather to demonstrate the depth of the contradictions contained in modern civilization itself.

[2] Which means that in 120 years the population of these countries will be tenfold.

The third world will inevitably have to pass through a long process of industrialization, requiring the full mobilization of internal resources in the countries concerned[1] — but with things as they are industrialization alone will be unable to solve their problems, just because it will be taking place at a time when the scientific and technological revolution will be in full swing in the advanced countries and will be overstepping the bounds of the industrial system. This disparity cannot be by-passed. It would be possible to take the edge off it and reduce it to a minimum if the advanced countries managed to reach much higher levels of the scientific and technological revolution, enabling them to channel resources to release the civilization dynamic of the developing countries.[2]

Economic balances elaborated on these lines indicate, however, that the resources needed for such an alternative would be much greater than has been assumed. They would evidently amount to many times the present world total under the heading of minimum aid to the third world.[3]

As the scientific and technological revolution starts to operate under socialism, it could gradually provide new openings for bridging this widening fissure in the foundations of civilization today[4], with its threat to the whole world — while also acting as a limiting factor in view of its own inadequate development. Should this process in future assume considerable proportions, should it enforce the release of world resources

---

[1] With a limited, essentially pre-industrial structure of the productive forces, introduction of elements of the scientific and technological revolution is often found to be uneconomic. On the one hand, because the low cost of labour makes manual work cheaper than modern technology (cf. A. I. Brown, *Introduction to World Economy*, London 1959, p. 56), on the other, because under these circumstances the intensive development of production generates an insoluble manpower surplus.

[2] "It depends on the spread of the scientific revolution all over the world. There is no other way. For most human beings, this is the point of hope... It may take longer than the poor will peacefully accept..." (C. P. Snow, *The Two Cultures and a Second Look*, New York—Toronto, 1964).

[3] J. Tinbergen mentioned a minimum annual sum of some 20 billion dollars; F. Benham estimates (in *Economic Aid to Underdeveloped Countries*, London 1961, p. 37 et seq.) that if the backwardness of the third world were to be speedily overcome, it would require 85 billion dollars a year. At present, according to UNO figures, the capitalist countries provide about 3.5 billion dollars annually in aid; some 4 billion dollars represents the annual export to the third world, of which, however, 2.5 billions is simply reinvestment of the surplus product of the developing countries, while over 2 billions a year are siphoned off to the metropolitan countries in the shape of profits, and a much larger sum in the shape of losses from non-equivalent exchange.

[4] Economic aid by the socialist countries to the third world is estimated at 2 billion dollars annually.

for a peaceful solution of civilization problems, should it make contact with the realistic autoreflexes of the entire industrialized world, it might be able to cut to a minimum the present trials and tribulations of primary industrialization for the developing countries and offer a way out of the otherwise almost inescapable dilemma hitherto presented by civilization. In this event, industrialization itself might in these countries be freed of many otherwise unavoidable conflicts and might proceed in a very modified form.

Indeed, this alternative appears to be almost a condition of existence. That is to say, if there were to be a continuation and domination of the trend that converts the technologico-economic lead of the industrial countries into neocolonial practice, creating tension in the world, with the armaments race swallowing up enormous resources released by the nascent scientific and technological revolution, the position of the developing countries — especially those with million-strong populations — would in time become insoluble for entire generations. There is, for instance, no doubt that the sharp rise in the productivity of agriculture on a world scale — based on technological innovations and the application of science (especially biology) — offers real prospects for tackling the terrible problem presently facing the world — that of mass hunger.[1]

The scientific and technological revolution is beginning to throw a new light on the conditions for the operation of many civilization factors and entire social movements, on the outlook for solving, and on the methods hitherto used in solving, many of the most vital questions of world politics. Its reflection in the military field has long since brought to the point of absurdity the traditional methods of resolving international conflicts, the ultimate means of politics. There is every reason to believe that many other fields will undergo similar development.

/*Motive Impulses of the Scientific and Technological Revolution*/ 1.2.5

In the economic sense, the industrial revolution — industrialization — was evinced as a process of *expanded reproduction* of capital. It was set in motion by a set of interests engendered by the self-expansion of capi-

---

[1] F. Baade assumes (*Der Weltlauf zum Jahre 2000 — Unsere Zukunft: Ein Paradie oder die Selbstvernichtung der Menschheit*, Oldenburg—Hamburg 1960) that by the yea 2000 world food output will have to be trebled if famine on a vast scale is to be avoided This would, however, call for a radical change in existing trends.

tal. Through the intricate economic mechanism, the fundamental tendency of capital — "with a given mass of wealth to make the surplus product or surplus value as large as possible"[1] — to all intents and purposes dominated the scene.

With the universal validity of commodity forms and the underlying competition of capital, this economic base appeared in a dual, divided guise: as the immediate motive impulse of enterprise, driving industrial progress forward without respite and without scruple, there emerges *profit* on capital, whose incentive is felt, however, solely by the minority. The more superficial view usually overlooks the fact that another motive impulse is at work as the antithesis and indispensable accompaniment of capital profit, that is, the *concern for existence* evoked in the majority by the need to win day by day the means for reproduction of the worker's own labour power.[2] These two contrasting bodies of interests are linked by the general legal forms governing private property and by the ethics of *laissez faire*.

Indeed, Hegel was already aware that all such separate interests were in reality "merely something subjective"[3], mediated in fact by the operation of the entire system whose interests they served as motive forces by means of which Adam Smith's invisible hand weaves from the activity of their bearers the spontaneous march of industrial civilization.[4]

The requirements of the expanded reproduction of capital and the profit interests induced by it did not tie the process of industrialization to the productivity of aggregate social labour directly, but only conditionally, partially, in a certain *relation* — allowing, that is, on the one hand, for economic movement even in circumstances when there was no growth in the productivity of aggregate social labour whatever (and when social wealth was accumulated merely by restricting the majority of the community within the limits of simple reproduction of labour power), and on the other hand, essentially not permitting increase in the

---

[1] K. Marx, *Theorien über den Mehrwert*, part 2, Berlin 1959, p. 563.

[2] Max Weber pointed to this negative type of interest as a constituent element of industrial civilization, equally vital as its positive parallel, profit: "The decisive impulse to all undertaking in a society of free exchange is *normally* for the propertyless... the threat of complete destitution..." (*Wirtschaft und Gesellschaft*, Tübingen 1922, p. 48).

[3] G. W. F. Hegel, *Phänomenologie des Geistes*, Stuttgart 1951, p. 382.

[4] In fact the whole classical teaching on interests is connected with Locke's and Condillac's theories of man as a product of external circumstances. Balzac showed a brilliant appreciation of the nature of economic interest in the cry of his romantic critics of industrial civilization: "Instead of having faith, we have interests."

productivity of aggregate social labour to be valued to the full, because only a part of such a general advance of the productive forces could be realized in the form of profit[1]; moreover, this part was the smaller, the greater the dimensions assumed by accumulated capital, the more industrially advanced was the country.[2] On the contrary, the other part of absolute growth in the productivity of aggregate social labour may appear in the shape of a depreciation of the operating capital.[3] The more intensive the progress of technology, the greater the anxiety about depreciation of capital,[4] the wider the gap between "vested intersts"[5] and the growth of the productive forces, which is revealed in the monopolies.

The duality by which profit and the worker's concern for existence serve as impulses to the growth of the productive forces is inherent in industrial enterprise to this day[6]; in the broader context the inadequacy of these factors in face of modern developments in science and technology in the West is an open secret.[7] Nevertheless, it is impossible to

---

[1] "The law of increased productive power, then, does not apply absolutely to capital. So far as capital is concerned, the productive power is not increased by the enhancement of productive labour in general, but only by saving more in the unpaid portion of living labour than is expended in past labour..." (K. Marx, *Capital*, Vol. III, Kerr ed., p. 308).

[2] An expression of these limitations of capital in relation to the productive forces is the general tendency to a decline in the rate of profit. Its extent is indicated in the forecast given by J. Fourastié in *Le Grand Espoir du XXe siècle*, Paris 1950: "Technological progress tends wherever it operates, i. e., mainly in the primary and secondary sectors, to elimination of absolute rent" (i. e., profit).

[3] "This is another one of the causes which... tend to check the fall of the rate of profit, although it may under certain circumstances reduce the mass of profit by reducing the mass of capital yielding a profit" (K. Marx, *Capital*, Vol. III — Kerr ed., p. 277).

[4] The endeavours described by some writers, to reject modernization (S. Lilley, *Men, Machines and History*, London 1948, pp. 198—205), or to restrict technological advance merely to saving labour (P. M. Sweezy, *The Theory of Capitalist Development*, New York 1956) usually stem from the fear of capital depreciation.

[5] T. Veblen, *Vested Interests and the State of the Industrial Arts*, New York 1919. L. von Mises perceived that the antagonism between businessmen and scientists and technologists is in this sense deep-rooted (*The Anti-Capitalist Mentality*, Princeton 1956, p. 20).

[6] The peculiarities of the ambivalent relationship of capital to technological advance today have been well expressed by J. R. Bright: "We must learn how to assess technological progress, to employ it, to delay it, and to defend our companies against technological change, if necessary..." ("Oportunity and Threat in Technological Change", *Harvard Business Review*, November—December 1963, p. 86).

[7] "The present system encourages activities which can lead to private profit and neglects those activities which can enhance the wealth and the quality of life in our

overlook the fact that many circumstances today are adapting the profit motive to the level of technological progress (without *prima facie* changing the social basis). Through state monopoly, a new factor is entering the economic life of the advanced Western countries — an agency that does not itself work for profit, its enterprises being in fact usually accepted as unprofitable, but that operates as an instrument to preserve profit as such. Apparently Adam Smith's invisible hand, which keeps the interest mechanism in capital in operation over the heads of people, needs itself to be guided.[1] For some decades now all capitalist countries have been injecting increasingly vast sums at the points where the profit motive is misfiring — and this function of government has gradually developed into a permanent, organic part of the system; profit becomes an instrument of politics, and the allocation and redistribution of the surplus product assumes decisive importance in stimulating the productive forces.[2] This creates artificial conditions under which the direction in which the structure of interests operates is modified. Significantly, state intervention has gone furthest in the areas where science — as a productive force that is inherently averse to private enterprise and continually breaks through it — is most active. The US Administration finances 65 per cent of expenditure on research and development (though only 18 per cent is actually government work), for France the figure is 64 per cent, for Britain 54 per cent, etc.[3] J. F. Kennedy justified[4] the system of subsidizing technological innovations by the fact

society" *(The Triple Revolution. Complete Text of the Ad Hoc Committee's Controversial Manifesto,* New York 1964).

[1] "Laissez-faire capitalism cannot work perfectly or even satisfactorily. The invisible hand needs some assistance and guidance." — In commenting on this statement by T. Yntema of the Ford Foundation in an address at the Carnegie Institute of Technology on November 11, 1964, G. S. Wheeler rightly remarks that "the technological revolution is an impelling factor for the expansion of state functions" (Technological Revolution, *Political Affairs*, May 1965, p. 14). Similarly, L. Brandt: "The headlong progress of technology and the need to keep in step with it have led to new forms of cooperation between industry and the state" (*Die zweite industrielle Revolution,* Bonn 1956, p. 11).

[2] "Thus it comes about that the redistribution of the total surplus value in favour of monopoly capital acquires greater significance, as regards expansion of production, than surplus value itself" (G. and L. Longo, *Il miracolo economico e l'analisi marxista,* Rome 1962).

[3] *International Statistical Yearbook for Research and Development. A Study of Resources Devoted to R and D in Member Countries,* 1963—1964, Vol. I. *The Overall Level and Structure of R and D Efforts in OECD Member Countries.* Other sources cite even higher shares (around 70 per cent).

[4] *Economic Report of the President,* Washington 1963.

that profit is not capable of stimulating scientific and technological progress to the requisite degree. Similar aims are followed by the automation, taxation and credit policies of the modern state — to the point of boosting purchasing power and contriving armaments booms. Such measures go a long way to accommodating profit incentives to the imperatives set by the new developments in the productive forces. On the one hand, capital meets with the ready-made conditions for rapid scientific advance offered by the good offices of the state; on the other, government funds cover the overall losses incurred by the onrush of technology. In these circumstances, the drive for super profits from innovations takes precedence over the vested interests. The secular tendency to a falling rate of profit is even reversed.[1] All these interventions naturally underscore the *optimalizing* aspect of the profit motive, turning enterprise towards *intensifying* growth, driving the advance of the productive forces far beyond the boundaries of the industrial system.

The wage labourer's *indifference* is also increasingly felt as a drag on technological progress.[2] Modern capitalism endeavours to compensate these limitations by offering bonuses, by profit-sharing, "people's shares"[3], and first and foremost by intervention to expand consumption within the consumer system — the system that reproduces external work incentives on a broader basis. At bottom, however, lies the selfsame money form of wages, allowing for the endless driving of the employee, turning the worker into an industrial being[4]; linked with expanding consumption — however illusory as a form of man's self-realization — this stimulation does exert a much wider influence than mere concern for a livelihood — indeed, to such a degree that some critics consider it possible and desirable to eliminate uncertainty about a livelihood completely from economic motivation.[5] Under the new conditions of ex-

---

[1] J. M. Gillmann argues that in recent decades, with the revolution in technology, the compensatory elements already mentioned by Marx have grown so strong that they have, in fact, led to a rising rate of profit in private enterprise. (*The Falling Rate of Profit: Marx's Law and Its Significance to 20th Century Capitalism*, London 1957, p. 67).

[2] M. Pike considers that the existence of sports fans "is simply a reflection of the lack of interest that ordinary people are able to feel about their everyday industrial lives". (*Automation, its Purpose and Future*, London 1956, p. 183.)

[3] "People's shares" are today held by some 10 per cent of the US population, including a section of the better-paid workers.

[4] K. Marx, ibid. *Grundrisse*, p. 200.

[5] R. Theobald, M. Lovenstein and other American authors pose the interesting questions of whether with cybernation the traditional wage stimulation of work is not losing its meaning, whether the worker's economic uncertainly is not tending to turn

panding productive forces, state interventions to raise consumption need not weaken the profit motive — as was the case at earlier stages — on the contrary, they tend to provide a groundwork for this motivation, saving it from extinction and stimulating its effect.[1] In this sense a new element has actually been added to economic motivation[2], although not really new enough.

The force capable of setting the scientific and technological revolution in motion, and of carrying it through to the full, can be, by the logic of things, none other than the effort of masses (or at least the majority) of people, of *each* personally, to achieve a steady maximum growth in productivity. In a highly developed economy that has overstepped the bounds of industrial maturity and has been freed of internal class antagonism, this universal need merges with concern for *expanding consumption and the whole process of life*.

Economic interest itself[3] rests upon a certain position occupied by people in the expansion of the productive forces. Insofar as the nature of work and the level of the consumer resources do not in general offer sufficient *inner* incentives — i.e., incentives operating widely and intensely, linking man directly with his own activities and his human motives — the socialist structure of interests is also bound to be split up into various components made up of this or that combination of *external* stimuli; on the one hand it produces "material interest", consisting of concern with wages and a share in profits (whereas negative incentives, stemming from preoccupation with earning a livelihood, lose much of their force when work is guaranteed by law); on the other hand, it emerges in the shape of the ideal social expression of these material stimuli, reflected in "moral interest", which in the final analysis — being still an external incentive to work, a mere duty — is not really an advance of "material interest", but rather the reverse of the medal. In this sense "material interest" and "moral interest" share the common boundaries

---

against technology as a destroyer of job opportunities, whether technological civilization does not demand some form of "guaranteed income" (*The Guaranteed Income. Next Step in Economic Evolution?* New York 1966).

[1] E. D. Domar explains that at the roots of his growth theory lies the endeavour "to show that there exists a rate of growth of income... which if achieved will not lead to diminishing profit rates" (*Essays in the Theory of Economic Growth*, New York 1957, p. 8).

[2] J. K. Galbraith, The Affluent Society, London (Penguin) 1962, p. 95.

[3] In the shape of wages, profit and the like, the impulses to action do not appear as definitive wants connected with man's personal active self-assertion, but as abstract economic interests, external stimuli, mediating a variable content.

of the industrial system, transferred to their mutually distinct existence; what one expresses in the narrow guise of claims, the other reflects in a general demand; the personal and the collective, interest and duty, operate here as *divorced* and opposing, although essentially associated stimuli — so long as their deeper inner union on the basis of the common advance of all is not possible — an advance in which the social and human impulses are incorporated in man's active self-assertion, and no longer face people as the interest of one redeemed by the duty of another, and vice versa. A contradictory unity arises: the "material interest" of the socialist man or group, insofar as it is based on *their own* work, their own effort expended as part of aggregate social labour — and insofar as it does not overstep a given limit — represents interest in extending the life processes of individuals or groups, which in its outcome is to the benefit of other people, too. Consequently, insofar as *personal* interest coincides with *social* interest, it is derived from the social; this is not a matter of "a relic of the old days", but a logical motive force of socialist society, a necessary transitional form, necessary for the emergence of new inner motivations in the conditions of industrial civilization.

The domination of material interest undoubtedly presents some pitfalls, but it cannot be rejected by comparing it with private acquisitiveness, to which it can, however, easily revert; the danger is that these interests may become ends in themselves, submerging the newly-won opportunities in an artificial expansion of mere "reproduction life", instead of gradually striking out beyond these limits. However, to the extent that external stimuli lead in one way or another to growth of the capacities and creative powers of man, to enriching human life, there is a strong moral element, too, and on the contrary, every substantial rise in living standards simultaneously implies a moral obligation for everyone under socialism to perfect all the socially useful abilities he possesses. Therefore, when private ownership has been abolished, there is no question of eliminating material interest and replacing it by moral stimuli, but of freeing economic interest from the abstract limits drawn by the social conditions under which it operated, in other words to *develop* abstract interest into a social and human value.

At a certain stage of development, the more the resources acquired are turned to the cultivation of human abilities, as intrinsic social forces, the more the once purely "material" stimuli will become equated with "moral" interest, also freed from its narrow limits of mere obligation. In other words, as the motive of man's identification with his activity and life emerges from the existing world of human interests, man's *"interest" in his own development*, in creative self-assertion and hence the development of all, will begin to dominate the scene. Indeed, should this motive of man's development as an end in itself fail to take the lead among the forces behind civilization's progress, there seems little prospect that a full-scale advance of the scientific and technological revolution will avoid the pitfalls of production for production's sake or consumption for the sake of consumption.

The essence of socialist change is not to abolish economic interest in profit, insofar as growth in the productivity of social labour is among the aims to which it is directed, but simply to:

a) abolish the situation where profit is *exclusive* to capital — where the decision on how to dispose of it does not lie with society — and to create a general interest in the level of social profit accruing to all working people, in which they all share;

b) hence, simultaneously, to link interest in profit with interest in wages, that is, to constitute an overall interest in the gross income, or the national income, produced by aggregate social labour;[1]

c) and finally, to raise the general interest in gross income to the level of interest in *raising the productivity of aggregate social labour*,[2] in expending each part of this labour usefully, in obtaining maximum performance in terms of gross income with a minimum expenditure of social labour. Gross income (generally equivalent to net value added) which plays the role of the economic *instrument* of socialism, and the source for the direct economic motivation of all, represents in this respect the true counterpart to profit on capital. True, still being an external impulse, it is also (similar to profit) merely the expression of a deeper

[1] We meet here with the first entirely new phenomenal form of the economy of social labour, since "...gross income is for capital a matter of complete indifference. The only thing that interests it is net income" (K. Marx, *Theorien über den Mehrwert*, part II, Berlin 1959, p. 566). Gross income is equivalent to value added.

[2] L. von Mises's classical argument about the impossibility of socialism rests on the assumption that interest in gross income is not for socialism just an economic instrument, but the sole and unfettered substance of the economy that consequently prevents the economical use of social labour — in fact, his criticism applies not to Marx's concept of socialism, but to Proudhon's syndicalist ideas. Von Mises's observation that "a socialist society, too, has to take the net not gross earnings as the yardstick of the economy" (*Die Gemeinwirtschaft*, Jena 1932, p. 125) did, nevertheless, have some rational meaning in contrast to the then prevalent underestimation of the category of social profit in the structure of socialist stimuli and overestimation of the purely wage motivation, which by itself, without being linked to a share in profit, undoubtedly evokes some resistance to technological change, evinced in efforts to "nurse the job" and the like.

economic substance — that is, the value-producing process of *aggregate social labour* (living and materialized, fixed and circulating, paid and unpaid) which under socialism possesses a similar, and similarly decisive, subjective role as capital in the bourgeois formation, but without contradiction.[1] In this sense, interest in gross income can operate purely as an intermediary — as the numerator of a fraction, the denominator of which is interest in savings on aggregate social labour — in other words, as a stimulus to growth in the productivity of aggregate social labour which alone can ultimately provide the groundwork for the general structure of incentives under socialism.

The worker, actuated by the material incentive, assumes under socialism (as worker and consumer) the role of a particle of aggregate social labour — just as formerly the capitalist functioned as the personified agent of capital. To this extent, the economic mechanism of socialism still retains to some extent the nature of an external power above people, whose "will" is obeyed by individuals — as an external spur carrying external sanctions.[2] The new element in this economic network of interests is, however, that this "will" does not spring — as was the case under capitalism — from outside people's own interests, but within its rational boundaries also represents the worker's personal interest; all working people are participants in the general social labour, while from capital they were *a priori* excluded.

We see then that socialism does not imply doing away with the spirit of *enterprise*, but its *generalization* on a social basis, so that it no longer has to embody a contradiction[3]. The special nature of socialist stimuli in relation to growth of the productive forces lies in their overstepping the bounds of profit, not in exerting an influence below this level (or

[1] Capital itself is, indeed, a kind of limited mode of existence of social labour in its totality, which is involved in contradictions; it is "the existence of social labour — its combination as subject equally as object but this existence as itself existing independently in face of its real element" (K. Marx, *Grundrisse*, ibid. p. 374).

[2] If under capitalism most of what people do is clearly manifested as an inescapable imperative, carrying "superhuman sanctions" (J. Schumpeter, *The Theory of Economic Development*, Cambridge 1949, p. 91), socialism surmounts this fatal barrier, but only indirectly, by employing "objective factors operating apart from our will" (G. S. Lisichkin, *Plan i rynok*, Moscow 1966, p. 8) for the gradual shaping of a higher human subjectivity.

[3] According to E. Denison (*The Sources of Economic Growth in the US and the Alternatives Before Us*, New York 1962, p. 164), some 400,000 people launch out into some form of enterprise in the US each year. But this figure represents only a small fraction of the active population, and only a tiny percentage actually make good. The potential reserves for socialist forms of enterprise are evidently boundless.

being indifferent in this respect). A socialist economy, therefore, can and must *employ* — as forms of detailed expression and subordinate parts — interest in profit and wages, gross income and labour-saving of all kinds. The only way to make the superiority of socialist incentives effective, and overcome the influence of the capitalist profit motive coupled with worker's concern about winning a livelihood, is to evolve an interwoven, yet differentiated structure of economic stimuli. It should operate in *every constituent part* of social labour (at top-management as at works level, and among individuals) and find ways and means of arousing an equal interest in stepping up the productivity of all social labour. Such a system — especially in the context of the socialist enterprise — has not yet been fully established, and this undoubtedly hampers socialism in the pursuit of scientific and technological advance.[1]

Moreover, the structure of interests retains its dynamism only when stimuli are steadily renewed and extended, that is, when they rely on objective economic feed-backs, which for the present exist solely through the medium of commodity-money and market relations.[2] These economic forms also provide an objective yardstick enabling the productive forces to be built up by planned intervention.

Of course, it can equally well be said that the economic stimuli of socialism, if they are not to be purely nominal, can really only be formed and operated when the dynamics of the productive forces have reached such a level that the share in profit, spread in one or another proportion among the masses of the working people, represents an item substantial enough to act as an effective incentive. Experience shows that so long as these sources of new motivation are not released by intensive growth, and the workers tend to be subjected to the negative economic

---

[1] "...In the practice of our economic construction there is still little use made of the principle of providing material incentives for workers, engineers and technicians in enterprises and building projects, specialists in scientific research, design and construction organizations to create new technology and speed up its application in production" — Resolution of a plenary meeting of the Central Committee of the Communist Party of the Soviet Union held in June 1959 (*Materialy yunskogo plenuma TsK KPSS*, Moscow 1959, p. 11).

[2] The idea of making planned use of material incentives and economic forms was already contained in Lenin's NEP. According to a resolution of the Twelfth Congress of the CRP(b), a socialist state should "...leave individual enterprises freedom of economic activity on the market and should not try to replace it by administrative decision" (*KPSS v rezolutsiakh...* Vol. I, Moscow 1953, p. 691). A theoretic model subordinating the market to the plan was elaborated by O. Lange in his work "On the Economic Theory of Socialism" in *The Review of Economic Studies* 1936—1937, and by other socialist authors.

risk alone, it is easy for the inclination to sacrifice economic forms in favour of "social certainty" for the majority in society to prevail, without regard for the effects this may have on technological advance.

When, today, the socialist countries are starting to use the market, value forms and the like, the casual observer may take this to be a step back towards capitalism.[1] The reverse is, however, true. Whatever the detours or pitfalls, the socialist countries are approaching a remarkable improvement of their own socialist economic structure, corresponding to the new movements in the sphere of the productive forces. On close examination of the concepts of "new systems of planned management" or "economic reforms", we cannot but see that the categories with which they work (production, price, profit, interest, etc.) go far beyond the bounds of simple commodity production and primary forms of value. We have here commodity forms in which the specifically socialist economy moves as the economy of social labour and which are entirely derived from the contradictions of aggregate social labour.[2]

A universal, multidimensional and steady growth of the productive forces, corresponding to the scientific and technological revolution, can therefore only be expected when:

a) interests are shaped under conditions of mutual cooperation to correspond with the *general* interest of every enterprise (working group), every worker and the whole community in unconditional growth in the productivity of aggregate social labour, i. e., in growth in the national income, while economizing in all the social labour engaged in production, which is equivalent to the most intensive harnessing of the new general productive forces of society;

b) the socialist structure of interests is made fully *dynamic*, capable at every stage of development of generating new and higher demands to match the changing course of the productive forces, i. e., it should be able at every step to create a new progressive economic subjectivity in society.

These are also the conditions for a higher form of planned growth

---

[1] Such arguments usually have a clearly ideological purpose — to persuade simple-minded people that by such economic experiments socialism is well on the way back to capitalism, while incidentally trying to discredit the bold innovations evident within the socialist countries.

[2] It is, in fact, the nature, limits and contradictions of social labour under socialism — that is, the general level attained in man's active self-assertion in industrial civilization — that engenders the need for mediating commodity-money forms (cf. O. Šik, *K problematice socialistických zbožních vztahů* (Socialist Commodity Relations), Prague 1964, pp. 26—27).

throughout society. There can be no shadow of a doubt that without a fully elaborated economic structure, without the free operation of a *developed system of interests*, it will be impossible to throw open the doors to the scientific and technological revolution, to give it its own economic soil and enable it ultimately to prevail.

/*Time Economy*/ 1.2.6

The indications are that the economic changes induced by the onset of the scientific and technological revolution will lead in the long run to a breakdown in the criteria of wealth and progress of civilization that emerged from the industrial processes and the traditional capitalist forms.

Whatever the reactions among people might be, the fact remains that the wealth attained hitherto has been manifested in the accumulation of capital[1], and the measure of progress in civilization has been the degree of capital valorization through human labour. In this type of *economic rationality*, which separated means (of economic undertaking) from ends, and which Max Weber once and for all identified with" capital accounting"[2], wealth was assumed to be founded on poverty, and enrichment to be its reproduction at the opposite pole. In the interests of modern civilization, the soil for this contradictory type of wealth remains, but there comes a point when it develops grave shortcomings as a direct measure. This happens when the amount of capital shows a falling growth rate[3] and a surplus appears, when growth is halted ane

[1] The extent of capital indicates "the degree of development of wealth" or "to what degree the social productive forces are produced... as direct organs of social praxis; of the real process of living" (K. Marx, ibid. *Grundrisse*, p. 594).

[2] For Max Weber, as for Mises, Schumpeter, Sombart, Gottl and others, capital calculation is actually the basis of European civilization i. e. "capital accounting *(Kapitalrechnung)*":" when the economy of today rationalizes, it views reasonable ordering of the economy from the standpoint of the interests of capital" (*Fragen der Rationalisierung*, Zürich, p. 9). From this angle the well-known argument about the impossibility of rational economic operation under socialism is in fact a tautology. Insofar as Weber admits some workers' demands, he places them outside economic rationality and allots them an eternal sphere of irrationality.

[3] The median growth rate of the mass of all fixed capital in the US was in 1889—1929 about 3.3 per cent, in 1929—1957 under 1.5 per cent (J. Kendrick, *Productivity Trends in the US*, Princeton 1961, pp. 320—322): at constant prices the difference is even less.

capital-output ratios start to shrink,[1] when the economy passes to a stage of intensive growth accompanied by release of capital,[2] when elements of science and technology, organization and skills endow operating capital with an unprecedented power of expansion, independent of its amount and of the amount of labour it directly uses.

In the light of these realities, capital itself appears as a persisting contradiction — on the one hand, it extends work on all sides; on the other, it endeavours to reduce necessary work to a minimum. It mobilizes the forces of science, social combinations, etc., in order to "make the creation of wealth independent of the labour time", while "it wants to measure the enormous social forces so created in terms of labour time".[3] The faster the progress of structural changes in the productive forces, the more the further formation of wealth appears to depend not directly on the amount of labour used, but on the power of factors that are being set in motion in this process and "whose powerful effectiveness itself bears no relationship to the actual labour time required for their production, but depends much more on the general state of science and the progress of technology."[4] True, these new sources of wealth continue to be expressed in terms of an economic yardstick evolved in fact by the reverse conditions[5] — at least so long as elimination of industrial labour

---

[1] According to S. Kuznets' figures (*Capital in the American Economy*, Princeton 1961, pp. 205, 209, 217), the capital-output ratio in US manufacturing rose in the period 1870—1929 by 59 per cent, while in 1929—1957 it dropped by 33 per cent; mining showed a still sharper reverse. B. N. Mikhalevsky demonstrates that such turning points are not evident in Soviet data because the USSR is still engaged in extensive industrialization and intensive growth simultaneously (*Perspektivnye raschoty na osnove prostykh dinamicheskikh modeley*, Moscow 1964, p. 28).

[2] Marx already characterized various types of extended reproduction: "...extensive expansion, if the field of production is extended; it is intensive expansion, if the efficiency of the instruments of production is increased" (*Capital*, Vol. II — Kerr ed. — p. 195) and demonstrated that the second type is connected with the new role of the amortization fund as a source of growth. Rapid expansion of *"self-financing"* in present investment practice is a sign of these changes. While up to World War I the sources of accumulation in the US were dominated by profit, the majority of investment resources have since appeared under the heading of amortization funds (cf. S. Kuznets, "Proportions of Capital Formation to National Product", *The American Economic Review*, May 1952, p. 516).

[3] K. Marx, *Grundrisse*, ibid. p. 593.

[4] K. Marx, *Grundrisse*, ibid. p. 592.

[5] The value and the productive power of labour are entities standing in inverse ratio to one another. Surplus value, on the contrary, is directly related to productivity, but not in proportion to increase of productivity. "Every increase in the mass of capital utilized can increase the productive power not only in arithmetical, but also

and the release of capital have not become absolutely dominant. Nonetheless, the beginnings of the scientific and technological revolution are already making appreciable inroads on the economic mechanism and disturbing the traditional criteria of performance.[1]

In terms of value and profit an economic rationality of a new type is emerging in the background of society's wealth — rationality embodied in the *absolute growth in productivity of total social labour* — i.e., all items of labour embodied in a given quantity of useful products (materialized and living labour, fixed and circulating, paid and unpaid) are curtailed, in contrast to the relative growth of output per man-hour, linked with the substitution of materialized for living labour, typical of the industrialization era.[2] The priority of this higher rationality of the scientific and technological revolution is felt through various channels even where economic operation itself is still immersed in the rationality of "capital accounting".[3]

---

in geometrical progression — while profit can increase it only to a much lesser degree." (K. Marx, *Grundrisse*, p. 252.)

[1] "With automation, you can't measure output of a single man; you have now to measure simply equipment utilization..." (*Automation and Major Technological Change: Impact on Union Size, Structure and Function*, Washington 1958, p. 8). E.R.F.W. Crossman points out that with automation, the connection between labour-input and product-output is broken and this is accompanied by the disappearance of the spontaneous feed-back of the economic cycle linking production, distribution and consumption. (*Automation, Skill and Manpower Prediction*, lecture at a seminar at Brookings Institute on April 15, 1965.)

[2] Productivity of growth is always reflected in falling labour costs embodied in a product. This, however, allows for a relative variant involving higher inputs of past labour if this is compensated by corresponding savings on living labour. On the contrary, absolute growth in productivity presupposes cuts in all types of labour engaged in production. The customary methods of examining productivity abstract from the inputs of materialized labour and simply state output per capita or hour, which can easily be outweighed by a decline in the effectiveness of assets; from this angle such methods have often met with criticism among socialists (cf. for example, S. G. Strumilin, *Problemy ekonomiki truda*, Moscow 1957, p. 663). The actual trend of productivity of total social labour (all-factor productivity) can be traced only by combining data on productivity of living labour and the effectiveness of materialized labour.

[3] When he was developing the implications of Max Weber's "occidental rationality", F. Gottl-Ottlilienfeld constantly came back to the idea that "technological rationalization can only be allowed to take place according to the rules of commercial rationality", and that "the dictates of Technological Reason must always bow to the dictate of Economic Reason" — i.e., of "capital accounting" (*Vom Sinn der Rationalisierung*, Jena 1929, pp. 9, 13). In the ideas of Max Weber's successors today there is, however, a growing consciousness — though expressed in one-sided form — that this rationality is not supreme. It is voiced in the idea that capital and technology are changing places,

Scope for the growth of all-factor productivity can, however, only be won by the practical realization and theoretical mastery of the *economics of total social labour*. As distinct from the economics of capital, the economics of social labour is completely dominated by the drive for maximum saving of all labour engaged in production.[1] The degree of wealth is here given by the growth rate of the mass of national (or gross) income formed by aggregate social labour (living and materialized) in unit time, in other words, by the degree of "valorization" of total social labour.[2] All criteria of rational operation, of the actual effectiveness of growth, etc., must necessarily derive from this law.

True, the economics of social labour embodies a contradiction when as its measure of wealth it employs labour, which is ceasing to be an immediate agent in the formation of wealth;[3] nevertheless, it also conceals within itself — although still in an inverted form — the ready-made, new yardstick of *time economy*[4], which can come into full operation only

that "economic reason" now has to adapt itself to the hard realities of technology, that technological rationality is becoming "the primary dimension" that "dominates the main field of tension in society", etc. (J. Ch. Papalekas, "Wandlungen im Baugesetz der industriellen Gesellschaft", *Zeitschrift für die gesamte Staatswissenschaft*, 1959, p. 22).

[1] E. D. Domar gives a good explanation of the difference between the economics of capital and of social labour in relation to present technological advance. Innovations and new technology, he says, are wanted in both the USA and the USSR. In the USSR, however, mainly because they "save labour", i. e. for their σ-effects. In the US, on the other hand, "technological progress is wanted as the creator of investment opportunities, and investment is wanted because it generates income and creates employment. It is wanted for its multiplier effect" (*Essays in the Theory of Economic Growth*, New York, 1957, p. 107).

[2] Both the productive power of labour and the effectiveness of materialized labour belong here. The decisive factor is the total input of social labour, not merely the costs borne by capital. In the background of this rational economy lie changes in the structure of the productive forces (applications of science, technological innovation, growing skills, division or combination of functions and professions, and finally the creation of human powers).

[3] Labour is the sole source of value, but is far from being the sole source of wealth, use-values, in the formation of which, on the contrary, all the productive forces participate and the share of direct productive labour itself is constantly shrinking: "It is wrong to say of labour, insofar as it yields use value, that it is the *sole* source of the wealth it creates, namely material wealth" (Marx-Engels, *Zur Kritik der politischen Ökonomie, Werke*, Band 13, Dietz Verlag, Berlin 1964).

[4] "Time economy, into this all economy is ultimately resolved" (K. Marx, *Grundrisse* p. 84). In class societies, time economy has found only partial application, within the limits of the contradiction that time has always had to be won for the ruling class by depriving the majority of it. Basic here was the fact that the law of time economy had no absolute force.

when labour in its present form has been transcended through changes in the entire civilization base of human life.[1]

The economics of labour today does not exclude the *time dimension* introduced into production by capitalism[2], but rids it of its contradictions and limitations, giving it a new meaning as the measure of the valorization of total social labour, i.e., also the measure of man's appropriation of the social productive forces, and giving every saving of time relevance to the expansion of the life process of all. The ground is thereby being prepared for an economic form that, combined with revolutions in the structure of the productive forces, will extricate the time dimension from its immediate linkage with expenditure of labour and make time — the measure of movement — an autonomous value for man.

Without the time dimension[3] the economic structure is incapable of inducing progress in the productive forces and is therefore of no use in the scientific and technological revolution. Technologically advanced socialist society is indubitably faced with the task of working out, on the basis of a developed structure of interests, by means of value forms and with the assistance of an integrated computer network and mathematical modelling, a *scientific system* of time economy. This is the only way to provide the exact picture of the effectiveness of different productive forces that will be indispensable in the future; then it will be possible to guide the mechanism of economic levers and instruments of management, to manipulate them in a rational way through rapid movements and universal transformations, while harnessing productive forces that — as in the case of science — possess entirely divergent economic characteristics. Failing this, disproportions will ensue and the opportunity to bring the future nearer to the present will be missed.

Time economy, consisting in saving the total social labour embodied in production in unit time, records the immediate level at which new productive powers are being created[4] and also the level of opportunities

---

[1] "When labour has ceased in the immediate form to be the great source of wealth, the labour time ceases, and has to cease, being its measure and consequently the exchange value (the measure) of use value" (K. Marx, *Grundrisse*, p. 593).

[2] "Time is money" in fact has two quite distinct meanings: time as the measure of labour performed by man (the more elementary meaning) and time as the measure of self-expansion of capital (specific meaning tied to labour only insofar as it is a means to capital expansion, where man is subjected to time).

[3] We refer to a time dimension stemming from the valorization of total social labour; it assumes, for example, that every part of it will be "interest-bearing".

[4] "True economy — saving — consists in saving of labour time (minimum — and reduction to minimum — of production costs); but this saving is identical with the

being offered for the creation of man's productive forces. The wealth engendered and measured by time economy is the time freed for man, *his disposable time* — space for the development of human powers, for the development of man as an end in itself. In these circumstances the law of time economy emerges as the first economic law — at a much higher level than hitherto — by which the claims of maximization and optimalization merge[1], because growth of the productive forces, accumulation of wealth, winning a "time reserve", the development of man and his relationships come to be identical.[2]

Seen from this angle, beyond a certain point in production proper, progress in education, improvement of services or any other release of means serving to develop man's creative powers become *equivalent* to each other. In these circumstances, the division of work and economic sectors into "productive" and "non-productive"[3] loses its former meaning, because the productive forces that determine human progress are then engendered in the whole field of human life. On the contrary,

---

development of the productive forces" (K. Marx, *Grundrisse*, p. 559). The correspondence between the language of the economy and the productive forces that occurs at a certain level of development in a society freed of class conflicts has not infrequently been interpreted in terms of a transition from economic to technological criteria (energy supply, etc.) — as once proposed by the technocrats. But in this concept we again come up against a reduction of the productive powers to technology. In reality, they represent a *social* category in the sense that the position of man is included; their yardstick is time, but it is the disposable time for man.

[1] "...when the narrow bourgeois form has been peeled away, what is wealth if not the universality of needs, capacities, enjoyments, productive powers, etc., of individuals... the absolute elaboration of his creative dispositions, without any preconditions other than antecedent historical evolution which makes the totality of this evolution — i. e., the evolution of all human powers as such, unmeasured by any *previously established* yardstick — an end in itself?" (K. Marx, *Grundrisse*, p. 387, quoted from K. Marx, *Pre-Capitalist Economic Formations*, London 1964, trans. J. Cohen).

[2] It can be demonstrated that as the productive forces gather momentum and break out of the industrial limits, maximization of growth in all-factor productivity increasingly approaches optimalization of economic growth in respect of consumption and human development. M. Kalecki (*Zarys teorii wzrostu gospodarki socjalistycznej*, Warsaw 1963), O. Lange (*Teoria reprodukcji i akumulacji*, Panstwowe Wydawnictwo Naukowe, 1965) and others are already coming up against this fact quite often.

[3] We know that Marx understood the term "productive labour" primarily in a historical sense and not with Saint-Simon in its material form. In bourgeois society, productive = producing surplus value. The fact that it concerns the production of material products is secondary (cf. *Theories of Surplus Value*, Part I, Moscow, p. 384). Consequently Marx believed that under socialism the sphere of "productive labour" would tend to expand.

a failure to draw on this area in the creation of human capacities inevitably leads to waste of growing productive forces.[1] We may therefore foresee the standards and criteria of the time economy gradually penetrating all social and human life. Time economy will in all probability afford the *appropriate economic form for advancing the scientific and technological revolution.*

True, time economy is a quite special type of economic rationality, distinguished from all previous types by its scope (embracing all spheres of civilization and culture) and extent (defining in effect the economic preconditions for the common advance of all people, that is, communist human relationships). It annuls the constitution of economic rationality (and all rationality) as a matter of mere means divorced from aims, breeding irrationality by its own movement. It points to a shift in the subjectivity of this rationality; the "ratio" that in industrial civilization quite evidently lies apart from man and essentially represents the reason of circumstances or the reason of man simply as an executive of these circumstances, the "ratio" that has been imposed on man from without[2], reverts to man as the *rationality of human development*[3] at the moment when man's development for its own sake merges with the highest

---

[1] If this imperative is fully operative in the economics of social labour, it is also felt in the economics of capital today. C. Freedman, R. Poignant, I. Swennilson (*Ministers Talk about Science*, OECD, Paris 1965, p. 95) point out that the economic programmes of the fifties placed too much emphasis on accumulation of capital and underestimated investment in education and research. D. Bell sees in the limits to "human capital" "...the fundamental element limiting the growth of the society" ("The Post-Industrial Society", in *Technology and Social Change*, New York—London 1964, p. 49). Denison, who evidently gives the effects of education, science, etc., the lowest rating, admits that from the standpoint of society (far more than of concerns) expenditure on science and education may yield much higher returns than expansion of production (*The Sources of Economic Growth in the U. S. and the Alternative Before Us*, New York 1962, p. 245).

[2] Rationalization *à la* Taylor is a typical example of this external application (cf. *Modern Technology and Civilization*, Ch. R. Walker, New York—Toronto—London 1962). When rationalizers like Henry Ford invoked the Cartesian reason and economists like Max Weber the Kantian rationality, they demonstrated the inherent limits of the rationality of the entire industrial epoch. The very concept of rationality demands — as we see — critical analysis.

[3] Answers to the question of whether the rationality of the production system can change into a truly human rationality (M. Harrington, *The Accidental Century*, New York 1965), whether technological reason can prove to be the technological liberation of man (H. Marcuse, "Industrialisierung und Kapitalismus" in *Max Weber und die Soziologie heute*, Tübingen 1965) lie beyond the borders of rationality based on the antinomies of reason and the economic system from which it sprang.

development of society's productive forces — at the critical moment linking the scientific and technological with the social revolution of our age.

Contrary to the concept of the Marxist classics, when scientific socialism came to be put into practice the conviction prevailed for some time that communism could be achieved by way of changes in the field of power, forms of ownership and ideology, possibly accompanied by a general growth of production. The course of political revolutions, expropriation and industrialization in the socialist countries provided a factual basis for this view. This, however, implied attributing absolute and lasting significance to the forms of social development taken over from the culminating phases of the industrial revolution and the class struggles bred of it. The whole question of changes in the productive forces, in work, in the mode of man's self-realization, was regarded as a purely external circumstance of communist construction and was even excluded from the field of Marxist scholarship. But the model of communism and concept of Marxism that failed to recognize the scientific and technological revolution as an *inherent part* — which, indeed, at a certain level decides the fate of the revolution — ran into the blind alley of the personality cult and will always run into a blind alley wherever it is applied. The trend of developments today is throwing into ever sharper relief the ideas put forward at the Twentieth Congress of the Communist Party of the Soviet Union, which directed socialist theory and practice to far wider goals, to "a shift in the focal point" of revolution to new positions, to the need for qualitative changes in the productive forces and to consideration of their social and human essence. Everything indicates that the first outline of a theory of the scientific and technological revolution, and of communist construction carried out in its course, which is to be found in the Programme of the Communist Party of the Soviet Union, heralds the most *fundamental* discovery and *positive development* of Marxist theory since the days of Lenin. Evidently the practical accomplishment of the scientific and technological revolution will be a no less vital element in the communist revolution than the winning of power by the working class or socialization of the means of production — indeed, in many respects it will *surpass* them.

/The Approach to the Scientific
and Technological Revolution
in Czechoslovakia/

1.3

The scientific and technological revolution is a world process. The special question for each country lies only in the mode, degree, specific features and intensity of its participation. For socialist countries there is also, as a matter of their international duty, the question of how they will contribute to the dynamics of socialism in the world, and to success in the competition between social orders.[1]

/The Divide in Growth/

1.3.1

During the first years of post-war economic construction, Czechoslovakia passed through a phase of socialist *industrialization*, when what had been left unfinished by the industrial revolution of capitalism was completed in the main under socialism.[2] Moreover, Czechoslovakia played a big part in helping to industrialize the East European countries. Without question, this process of industrialization, which drew on a growth in quantity of the productive forces, progressed rapidly and prepared the ground for a change in orientation.[3] But it also piled up internal problems, shaped a set structure (organization, management,

[1] This chapter is not concerned with evaluating the achievements of socialist construction in Czechoslovakia, but with directing attention to the lines of approach to the scientific and technological revolution and elucidating the obstacles standing in the way of the transition. The figures cited — when not otherwise stated — are taken from Czechoslovak statistical abstracts and the volume *Ukazatelé hospodářského vývoje v zahraničí 1965* (Indicators of Economic Development Abroad 1965) published by the Centre for Scientific, Technological and Economic Information, Prague 1966.

[2] Czechoslovakia experienced the main phase of industrialization at the end of the last and the beginning of the present centuries. Before World War II, she was a fairly advanced industrial country. Nevertheless, her production potential in those days lagged by about 30—50 percent behind the most advanced European countries and she bears some unmistakable marks of her involved historical background.

[3] To this extent the Communist Party's Twelfth Congress could point to the success of this stage. In volume and intensity of industrial production, the country had taken its place among the ten most industrialized countries in the world; in the share of industry in the nation's work and the share of engineering in output, Czechoslovakia is today roughly comparable with West Germany or Belgium, slightly behind Great Britain and ahead of Sweden and France. In industrial production per head she is on a level with Great Britain and Switzerland, a little behind West Germany and ahead of France and Belgium (cf. *Industrie-Kurier* 113/1966).

output pattern, etc.) and outlived its usefulness under the given conditions, notably holding back technological progress and the application of science in the economy; the results were not adequate to the means expended. Growth of the productive forces was weighted in favour of multiplying industrial plants with the traditional type of equipment,[1] which swallowed up comparatively large amounts of investment, manpower, raw material, etc. No substantial structural changes were made within the existing production and technological base, and therefore there was no increase in dynamism, while growth of the productive forces demanded increasing inputs of all factors embodied in output (living and materialized labour) — considerably more than in many countries that are otherwise at the same level of development.[2]

Czechoslovakia's industrialization during the fifties was strictly *extensive*. Breaking down the growth in the mass of net output (in 1950—1964, 6 per cent per year on average), we find among the sources (see Table 1-13) 80 per cent extensive factors — primarily capital expansion (in industry also about 30 per cent growth in employment), while the share of intensive factors remained below 20 per cent; of the latter, only about 6 per cent was attributable to new technology; an appreciable contribution from advance in skills was for the most part paralyzed by the dead weight of organizational factors and the system of management.[3] Under these conditions, the opportunities for acceleration deriving from the new production potentials of the social revolution, i.e., nationalization, broad application of science, development of human powers, remained largely untapped (except for the first, easily mobilized reserves).

Similarly the movement of all-factor productivity bore the unmistakable marks of extensive industrialization and was unsatisfactory (see

[1] At first the equipment of new plant usually showed no advance over the prewar technological level, and even later much of it fell short of world standards. Assuming the viability of the new capacities, this will complicate the transition to progressive technology, automation, chemical processes, etc. for some time yet.

[2] Compared with the leading European countries, Czechoslovak industry absorbs twice the input of primary energy resources and steel per unit of output (cf. Z. Vergner, M. Souček, *Teoretické otázky ekonomického růstu ČSSR* (Theoretical Questions of Czechoslovakia's Economic Growth), Prague 1967, p. 89).

[3] Cf. M. Toms, M. Hájek, "Determinanty ekonomického růstu a integrální produktivita" (Determinants of Economic Growth and Integral Productivity) in *Politická ekonomie* 10/1966; the extensive character of economic growth in Czechoslovakia was stated by F. Valenta, *Efektivnost socialistického průmyslu* (Effectiveness of Socialist Industry), Prague 1964.

Table 1-14). Of two components making up all-factor productivity,[1] productivity per man-hour (living labour) in immediate production showed an annual growth of 4.2 per cent through 1955—1965 (two-thirds of the output increment): the figure for industry alone was 3.9 per cent, representing not quite one-third of net increment in output. The efficiency of capital assets (materialized labour), on the contrary, dropped in the same period by 1.0 percent a year (in industry 0.2 percent) — with an especially noticeable drop in the efficiency of machinery and equipment as a result of inadequate modernization and technological development. By and large, the global effectiveness of all factors remained unchanged.[2] The capital-output ratio, which for some years had shown a downward trend, finally recorded a noticeable rise at this stage (cf. Table 1-9) and investment efficiency took a definite downward turn.[3]

The curves that together show the movement of all-factor productivity indicate, in fact, that at the latest since 1958—1959 the sources of extensive growth have been exhausted and industrialization has reached a ceiling. This is the signal for cutting expenditures on the traditional lines to absolutely essential development capacities and for comparing the effectiveness of the old method of augmenting the productive forces with the new prospects offered by *qualitative changes* that give priority to science as a productive force, drawing on new technology, modernization of production, and all-round release of man's creative powers.

Statistics also bear witness to a typical industrial pattern and dynamics of investment (see Table 1-15) which is the exact opposite of the advance of science over technology, and of technology over industrial production, that we have pointed to as the underlying requirement for the scientific and technological revolution (Keldysh's proportion). For instance, from 1955 to 1962, with industry expanding, the growth of investment in building work was ahead of that in machinery and technology, and both outran science and research. Only in 1964 did the proportions become more progressive, but at that stage the volume of investment was restricted.[4]

---

[1] The statisticians have not yet enabled us to follow the level of all-factor productivity directly; they refer us to its components.

[2] Cf. V. Nachtigal, "Extenzita a efektivita hospodářského vývoje ČSSR" (Extensiveness and Effectiveness of Czechoslovak Economic Growth), *Politická ekonomie* 4/1966.

[3] Cf. O. Šik, "Příspěvek k analýze našeho hospodářského vývoje" (Contribution to Analysis of Our Economic Development) in *Politická ekonomie* 1/1966.

[4] At the start of the sixties, nearly one-half of total investment in Czechoslovakia went into industry, and even in 1964 — after cutting expenditures on industrializa-

The economic difficulties of recent years, with the imbalance induced by the drain on resources, are probably a symptom of a much more deep-seated cause, and that is the impossibility of clinging to the procedures and proportions of industrialization. In other words, we are feeling the actual presence of the kind of divide beyond which growth of the productive forces can no longer be handled by existing methods, but solely by a transition to the *scientific and technological revolution*. In some sectors (agriculture, building, etc.) and in some regions (Slovakia), industrialization will have to go on, but in general the overriding consideration will be to steer the country into the stream of the scientific and technological revolution. The groundwork for this process would be:

a) technological modernization of the entire economy, especially integrated mechanization and automation, use of chemical processes and structural shifts in favour of progressive types of production;

b) eliminating simple unskilled labour wherever the technological, economic and social conditions allow, and much more effective valorization of human labour;

c) opening up spheres that release man's creative powers, advance the application of science in all fields of life and so build up reserves for a new departure in the trend of growth.

Experience has shown that the system of management employed hitherto, and the theoretic concepts associated with it, which sprang from different conditions, are not capable of registering and handling the turning point between industrialization and the scientific and technological revolution. At this point it proves more advantageous from the standpoint of creating productive forces and of the time economy to devote resources to changing the quality of the productive forces, to factors of intensive growth, modernization, new technology, advance of science, education and skills, to human welfare, the working and living environments, shortening working hours, etc., than to building more of the traditional industrial plants. The inability of the old system to handle this leads to an increasingly obvious lag in the approach to the scientific and technological revolution, the main currents of which are only just beginning to make themselves felt in the country's life — at the lower preliminary levels and in some respects at an experimental

tion — the figure was 44.7 percent compared with 30—37 percent in Western Europe and the USSR. While in Czechoslovakia overall building investment (excluding housing) still overtopped investment in machinery and equipment, in many other advanced countries the reverse was the case (cf. *National Accounts Statistics*, OECD 1955—1964; *Narodnoye khozyaystvo SSSR v 1965 godu*).

stage. They have not yet made any appreciable impact on the leading trends and proportions of social development. Although Czechoslovakia can compare with the most advanced countries in the volume of her output of traditional industrial products,[1] she is well behind in the growth of the structure (and hence dynamics) of her productive forces, in the transformations that are the key to progress today.

While the country's industrial capacities, individual workshops, departments or plants are at a fairly high level of technical equipment, the degree of automation is relatively low. To this one must add the circumstance that the hub of industry (engineering) relies to 70 per cent on piece or short-series production, so that in many cases automation would involve complicated intermediate links — either a transitional phase of completing mechanization, with aggregation and stepping up serial operations, or a switch to new technology based on sophisticated, flexible forms of automation, programming, the building blocks system, etc. The magnitude of these problems is indicated by the fact that the amount of automation elements in Czechoslovakia's mechanical and technical equipment is one-third to one-sixth that in the USA.[2] Especially serious is the lag in the highest forms of automation — those based on *cybernation* — and in the utilization of computer technology in general. In the number of computers installed per million of the population, Czechoslovakia remains far behind the technologically advanced countries.[3]

Despite a good standard in research chemistry and fairly rapid progress of the chemical industry over the past decade, the share of this progressive sector in Czechoslovak industrial production is still around 8.5 per cent (and increments show a decelerating trend), while in many

[1] In steel output per head, Czechoslovakia was on a par with the USA and West Germany, and ahead of Great Britain and France in 1965; in cement output on a level with France and Sweden, ahead of the USA and Great Britain; in overall output of primary energy, behind the USA and ahead of Great Britain, West Germany, Sweden and France (cf. *Statistische Grundzahlen der EWG 1966; Monthly Bulletin of Statistics*, UNO 3/1967, etc.).

[2] The share of automation equipment, electrical equipment and electronic elements in total industrial and in engineering output is still one-half to one-third that of the most advanced countries (cf. L. Říha, *Ekonomická efektivnost vědeckotechnického pokroku* (Economic Effectiveness of Scientific and Technological Progress), Prague 1965, p. 17 et seq.).

[3] In 1965, Czechoslovakia had not quite four computers per million inhabitants, i.e., one-fortieth the figure for the USA, one-seventh to one-twelfth that for Sweden, West Germany, France and Britain. Despite a sharp rise in 1966 and further installations planned, some years will be needed before this gap can be closed.

advanced countries the figure is nearly double. Output of plastics per head in Czechoslovakia is about one-third of that in the top countries (USA or West Germany).[1]

Czechoslovakia's fuel and power balance relies 83 per cent on solid fuel (compared with 40—70 per cent in the most advanced countries); the share of liquid and gaseous fuels shows only a slow rise, and adequate industrial utilization of nuclear energy is also lacking (no marked advance is envisaged until the seventies). This detracts considerably from the high level of primary energy sources and ties a disproportionately high share of labour to mining.[2]

Other sectors of key importance for the approach to the scientific and technological revolution are facing similar problems. Sectors that were overlooked by the industrialization pattern (services, transportation, communications, etc.) suffer an often alarming technological lag. In view of the high demands on Czechoslovak technology, its *quality* is also unsatisfactory.[3] Unwieldiness and a high breakdown rate, alongside the material losses incurred — such shortcomings undermine the country's reputation for technical ability and run counter to the traditions of sophisticated work that have earned Czechoslovakia her place in the international division of labour.

/*Losses in "the Human Factor" Are the Most Serious*/ 1.3.2

In the long run, however, the gravest losses arise on the side of *man* and concern the development of his *creative powers*, which lies in the target area of economic construction in the socialist countries, while emerging equally as a direct and increasingly weighty factor in the course of this construction. We have seen that the industrial revolution and the phase of industrialization are intrinsically linked with restriction of "the human factor"; the repercussions of the stage when overall

---

[1] The share of man-made materials in the Czechoslovak textile industry is a quarter of that used in France or Japan. The input of fertilisers per hectare of arable land is half that of West Germany or Belgium.

[2] The share of mining in the structure of production and labour is one of the highest in the world.

[3] According to a check-up in 1964, about 36 per cent of products attained world technological level or surpassed it, 37 per cent were below the mark and 27 per cent were completely obsolete.

progress proceeded independently of man and at the expense of the mass of people are still felt. Not even a socialist order, with its social measures, could entirely escape its influence.

The prime outcome of unilateral industrialization is *irrational* use of human powers and, above a certain level, widespread (under the previous system of management, uncontrollable) *wastage of human labour* below the level of socially necessary costs.[1] The effects can be seen, on the one hand, in exhaustion of manpower reserves, on the other in inflation of the unskilled and manual functions, and finally in the propensity to maintain employment in works operating at a loss (not infrequently for social reasons). A serious aspect of this is the growing number of workers who have been operating with outdated tools and equipment.[2]

The overall picture of workers' job classification in Czechoslovakia is 57 per cent in predominantly manual jobs, 42 per cent in mechanized work and around one per cent operating under conditions of partial automation. Materials handling, works and inter-operations transportation alone tie down some one-and-a-half million people — largely engaged in low-skilled and purely operative activities with a minimum of creative elements. This accounts for a large part (about one-third) of all workers (in mining and manufacturing up to 40 per cent). About 20—22 per cent of handling operations in Czechoslovakia are performed by technical means, while in the technologically advanced countries the proportion is much higher, and in the USA the figure stated is over 80 per cent. In materials handling Czechoslovakia has up to four workers where under modern conditions one can do the job.[3] Using contemporary means of modern organization, mathematical records, intra-works transport, palletization and containerization, standardization of packaging and storage, etc., it would be possible to rephase the flow of materials and divert hundreds of thousands of people to better utilization of capital

---

[1] Average labour inputs in Czechoslovak industry in 1964 were about 25 per cent higher than in West Germany, 10 per cent higher than in France and at about the same level as in Britain.

[2] Through 1955—1964, the proportion of machinery and equipment scrapped in Czechoslovak industry was only slightly over 2 per cent (*20 let rozvoje ČSSR* (Twenty Years Development in Czechoslovakia), Prague 1965, p. 32). The outcome was that the proportion of machines older than 5 years rose in the same period from 53.8 to 56.1 per cent, while buildings older than 5 years dropped from 82.8 to 71.8 per cent.

[3] Although Czechoslovakia possesses a well-developed engineering industry, equipment for materials handling accounts for only 2.5 per cent of output, while in the USSR and France the figure is 8 per cent and in the USA 14 per cent.

assets, to saturating the service industries and reinforcing the pre-production stages — with repercussions on an overall reshaping of the job structure, improving its quality, or helping to release disposable time — in short, raising the creative potential of society.

The situation is similar in other sectors with a large proportion of simple, unskilled labour, such as building (finishing work), agriculture, clerical work (especially in accounting and records.)[1]

It has to be borne in mind that extensive industrialization, which discourages modernization and qualitative changes, always fragments and simplifies work. Without any doubt, the processes of industrialization have done much to alter the traditional *profile* of the industrial work force in Czechoslovakia. Craft work, with its comparatively higher content of manual skill and some measure of intellectual creativeness, has been debased, but a higher form of human accomplishment has not replaced it to any adequate degree. The mature core of the workers has thereby been degraded and diluted.[2] Hundreds of thousands of housewives have been brought into industry with the minimum of training.[3] If we add the all-too-frequent lack of cultured working conditions, environments unsuitable to physical and mental health, we see an ominous gap between man and his work. The situation is aggravated by a similar trend induced during the process of laying the approaches to the scientific and technological revolution by the shift of manpower to the elementary commercial services, where the level, culture and skill of work is often equally low.

These processes in the structure of work, tending to endow it with an increasingly abstract nature, are in fact objective and unavoidable. But whenever, in this situation, simple labour is not used with the

[1] A contributory factor in the unsatisfactory utilization of manpower is the relative cheapness of labour due to the fact that the socialist state employs its "social consumption fund" to meet the costs of social, medical and cultural welfare, that is, the indirect costs of reproducing labour power (at the level of nearly half of wages) that in other parts of the world are usually paid by the employers.

[2] Today over 50 per cent of workers in Czechoslovakia are semiskilled, while the proportion of the fully trained is shrinking. In 1962, about 43 per cent of workers in industry had served an apprenticeship; although the share of the highly skilled is fairly big, the fact remains that Czechoslovakia is lagging behind some of the technologically advanced countries in the level of skills: in West Germany about 45 per cent of workers are fully skilled, in Britain over 55 per cent (cf. *Economic Growth and Manpower*, London 1963).

[3] In 1963, for every 100 men in all forms of employment there were 79 women at work (as in the other socialist countries), while the figure for West Germany was 58, for the US and France 52, Britain and Sweden 44.

maximum of economy, the resultant loss is twofold, because on the one hand the benefit it gives to society is too meagre, and on the other hand it devours too many opportunities for developing individual abilities, activity and creativeness. This dilemma of industrialization underscores the urgent need for technology that would compensate and outweigh the above trend, first maintaining and then gradually improving the national work structure. Obviously, if technology and the accompanying organization fail to outpace the growth of production proper and the industrial shifts to simple labour — i. e., do not enable the transitional phase of deterioration in quality and dehumanization of work to be curtailed to the utmost, and fail to impel a large part of the work force to skilled occupations, to the pre-production stages and to the sphere of human welfare — people's creative powers will be irreparably impaired; the potential of skills and drive will drop to an untenable level, ultimately leading to new difficulties, because the advance of socialism is incompatible with human labour of such a type and with such a structure of the productive forces.

At the present level of industrialization, a faulty take-off to the scientific and technological revolution involves other troubles of a *sociological, psychological and anthropological nature*, which hold back the creation and social application of human potentials in our modern civilization.

The high demands on labour exert a pressure on working hours.[1] The result is a *shortage of free time* which is a real obstacle to more rapid and massive shifts in the content and pattern of people's lives. Only individuals of exceptional physical and mental vigour are able, after an average 46 hour week (including overtime), to embark to any extent on educational activities, pursue technical or cultural interests, and use their talents for the public benefit.

Another trouble is a chronic lag in the *infrastructure*, making itself felt in serious shortcomings in the elementary services (with the exception, for example, of the cultural and health services provided from public funds), inadequate transport to and from work, an underdeveloped network of retail outlets, which are in need of modernization[2], and so

---

[1] The working week in Czechoslovakia is 44 hours.

[2] In Czechoslovakia, 10 per cent of the work force is engaged in commerce, in France, Belgium, Britain and West Germany 14—18 per cent, and in the USA 23 per cent; only a minor part of the difference can be accounted for by actual savings due to rational use of the opportunities for organizing buying and selling on a large scale under socialism.

on — in short, breakdowns in the sphere that was sidetracked by industrialization and starved of resources. Statistical surveys[1] show that acquiring the everyday necessities of life absorbs about 30 hours a week for the average adult of active age (twice as long for women as for men). To this we must add time spent on visits to public offices[2], a propensity to overorganize the business of life and some fluidity in its new patterns.

All in all, these factors constrain the lives of many working people, despite the changed social structure, rising consumption and quite extensive provision for social welfare, keeping them within the bounds of *simple reproduction of labour power;* a wealth of socially beneficial qualities and creative powers of individuals is squandered.

Quite evidently, the old course of industrialization has outlived its day. The administrative, directive system of management that set things going and was intimately linked with this course is now an *obstacle*, and thorough implementation of the new economic system of planning and management is a condition for Czechoslovakia's entry into the stream of the scientific and technological revolution.[3]

The administrative, directive system creates a state of affairs in which it is economically advantageous to expend immense amounts of superfluous labour[4]; it allows unqualified personnel to be retained at various levels of enterprise management, curbs socialist initiative and independent efforts at innovation. The general run of employees — from manual workers to technicians — are actuated by incentives that have nothing in common with scientific and technological progress, they feel no link with productivity and the social usefulness of their own activities. Moreover, years of neglect and subjective deformation of economic categories has deprived instruments and yardsticks of their true basis, making people oblivious to waste and giving the community no chance to see its way clearly in the world of rationally utilized technology and labour power — and still less to find its way along the optimal paths of time economy. Man's creative powers are *de facto* excluded from the

[1] Computed on a per-capita basis from data published by J. Bezouška and J. Vytlačil, "Šetření o využití času v Československu" (Investigation of the Utilization of Time in Czechoslovakia), *Demografie* 3/1962 and 4/1963.

[2] In their composition and practical activities some offices remain completely out of step with the fact that the citizen's free time is an increasingly valuable commodity and that to waste it is an offence against the public interest.

[3] Cf. Report of the Thirteenth Congress of the Communist Party of Czechoslovakia, Prague 1966, p. 396.

[4] Enterprises have hitherto kept reserves of inoperative labour and, in view of the payroll total fixed by directive, they preferred cheap, unskilled labour.

economy, they are not taken into account and are considered irrelevant in the type of construction that accompanied the industrial revolution, but is inadequate for the new conditions of growth.

What is more, this *system of management* has led to wastage of human potentialities and hampered the active creation of human abilities, thereby squandering the powers of acceleration they could engender. The reflection of the system in the lives of men and society has operated in the same sense. An overgrowth of directives vainly trying to replace economic stimulation and inner human motivation expels the actual subjectivity of socialist man — already gravely burdened by the nature of work and the amount of "reproduction cares" — from the social sphere. People see this either as a lack of confidence in them, or the course of civilization loses altogether in their eyes the character of an accessible process in which their choice plays any part. This deals a severe blow to the "human factor" in technological and scientific progress, blunts initiative, destroys the sense of responsibility, breeds mediocrity, teaches people to swim with the stream, not to stand up for their own opinions, not discover and propagate new things, but rather to find loopholes in the directives and turn them to their own account, to be wrapped up in their private lives — an unhealthy atmosphere for the approach to the scientific and technological revolution, which demands for its success completely free scope for the full *self-assertion* of every individual, with all his dispositions.

The impact of all these circumstances is felt in the level of creative *human powers* in society. It is seen in a decreasing interest in education[1], especially higher education; in some branches the demand for university graduates is falling off, while less and less people are showing interest in part-time study, or in any kind of further education. Comparing the stagnation in social activity with the boom in private occupations[2], one can glimpse the wealth of capacities untapped by society. Recent years have shown no growth in technical *initiative* among workers and technicians; the upward trend in numbers of inventions and improvement suggestions so typical of the fifties has halted since 1960, or has even taken a downward turn. In comparative figures for domestic notices of inventions and patents granted (see Table 1—15), Czecho-

---
[1] The demand from industry for educated personnel now usually falls short of the numbers of university and college graduates. In some subjects (technological) applications for university entrance fail to come up to expectations.

[2] There is a sharp rise in the numbers of collectors and people immersed in various hobbies — which is otherwise a thoroughly healthy phenomenon.

slovakia is lagging behind some of the top countries with which she had formerly kept in step;[1] indeed, the lead in improvement suggestions by factory workers has in some cases been lost.[2] Moreover, the *prestige* of science and technology as professions, which was much higher in Czechoslovakia than in capitalist countries (see Table 1-17), has been showing a tendency to drop in recent years.[3]

A *vicious circle* has been formed — technological shortcomings curtail opportunities for cultivating man's creative powers, and this in its turn aggravates the tardiness with which science and technology are permeating community and individual life. Extensive industrialization, overexpansion of unskilled work, free time swallowed up by the obstacles of civilization, initiative ousted by administrative direction — all this smoothes the way to equalitarian trends, perpetuates the set pattern of reproduction life, strengthens the element of technological and social conservatism, weakens people's creative qualities, nourishes prejudices against skills and education, damps the efforts of foremost workers, technicians and scientists, and finally stands in the way of resolute management and gearing socialism to the scientific and technological revolution.

To break out of this circle will only be possible by bringing *both sides* into action — modern technology and cultivation of human powers. It looks as if at the present stage in Czechoslovakia there are good chances on the side of the human factors, mainly as a product of trends in the management of society.

/ *New System of Management* /   1.3.3

For some time now the key issue for Czechoslovak policy has been to draw on all the potentialities offered by productive forces operating

[1] The number of domestic patents applied for and filed per million inhabitants in 1964 was less in Czechoslovakia than in Sweden and Switzerland, about the same as West Germany and Britain, more than the USA and many other countries (data from the journal *Propriété industrielle*, 1965 and 1966).

[2] Some capitalist firms in Britain and Austria and elsewhere, which — impressed by socialist experience — are intensively introducing analogous forms of improvement suggestions on a commercial basis, are now achieving similar (or even better) results than Czechoslovak enterprises.

[3] A sociological survey among young people in the Ostrava region showed, for example, that only 1.3 per cent chose scholars and scientists as their examples in life (Edison, Křižík, Marx, Lomonosov, Comenius, among girls — Mme. Curie, Pavlov); only 6—7 per cent aspired to be experts with university training.

within socialist production relations, to reap all the advantages that lay dormant during the phase of industrialization. To bring them to life is, however, no easy matter, not to be solved simply by adopting certain measures and establishing forms of ownership (this is just the beginning). The operative forces lie in forging really active relationships among people in the production of their own lives, in providing day-by-day motives and impulses for thoroughgoing changes in the structure of the productive forces.

All the indications are that the first internal brake on the scientific and technological revolution, which according to their own reports is felt by many socialist countries, is the insufficient development of the *economic structure*, and of the system of impulses and instruments of management that stem from the essence of socialism. What is still lacking is a fully dynamic system that would link all working people with advances in science and technology, thereby giving socialism an undisputed advantage in the growth of its productive forces — an advantage lying not solely in ending the exploitation of man by man, but also in releasing the positive impulses concealed in a world of all-round cooperation and coming to the surface in the course of the scientific and technological revolution. It remains to work out economic instruments of socialism that will be capable of stimulating a socialist spirit of enterprise and economic initiative at all levels, that will give due recognition to the risk of innovation, while penalizing passivity and backwardness.

As Czechoslovak experience has shown, administrative, directive management is intrinsically linked with the phase of industrialization when broad application of science and technology and overall development of human capacities played no vital role. That being so, it ties the impulses of society to the single dimension of growth in quantity of output, by engaging the aggregate force of social labour; it has no means of enforcing a universally economical expenditure of social labour and, therefore, cannot achieve economic optimization or effective growth.[1] It subordinates the stimuli inherent in socialism to the one goal of maximum output demanded from the centre; and in practice it conjures up a multitude of subsidiary, non-social interests and petty concerns, in enterprises and among individuals, in maintaining the *status quo* —

[1] A widespread feature in the socialist countries under directive management was immobilizing of social labour: in 1960, 4.5 per cent of the national income in Czechoslovakia was tied up in growth of inventories, in the GDR 5.8 per cent, Poland 6.9 per cent, while in the advanced West European countries the figure (in comparable terms)

interests that deliver society into the power of *spontaneous*, extensive movement, running counter to the course indicated for the scientific and technological revolution. And since it simply expands existing procedures, this extensive industrial growth has no particular need for science and research, or new types of organization and skills. Quite clearly there is no prospect of entirely new processes making headway in the industrially developed socialist countries until radical steps have been taken to put through economic reforms and introduce management systems relying on the market mechanism.

The prime claim of the scientific and technological revolution on the economic structure is that it be made *dynamic*. In this respect the former management system in Czechoslovakia was static, because it lacked an economic feed-back.[1] Every new trend or proportion was given absolute significance and turning points could never meet with a prompt response. True, with industrialization, the changes occurring from time to time — confined on the whole to the instruments of labour, i.e., tools, machinery and the like — could be carried through by a simple directive transfer of resources to new types of production and by stabilizing some newly-acquired proportions. A hang-over from these days is the conviction that the scientific and technological revolution can be called into being by the selfsame directive methods — by something in the nature of a technocratic procedure. But this stems from a misconception about the substance of the revolution, which is not just a structural shift that can be carried out by one simple operation, but involves a continuous, universal stream of structural changes, with a multidimensional dynamic as the very essence of its progress. Consequently, only a flexible, steadily developing and improving system of planned management, commanding a fully elaborated economic feed-back, can clear the forward road. In order to accomplish "the full

was 2-3 per cent; a similar picture is seen in the growing volume of capital-under-construction, and the inadequate use of rapidly mounting capital assets (cf. J. Goldmann, K. Kouba, Economic Growth in Czechoslovakia, English edition, Prague 1969, p. 71). In the USSR, too, according to I. Kurakov, before the economic reform "there was in fact no material incentive in state-owned works to improve the utilization effectiveness of fixed and circulating assets" (*Nauka i tekhnika v period razvernutogo stroyitelstva kommunizma*, Moscow 1963, p. 41).

[1] The economic categories (prices, profit, costs, etc.) "were degraded to mere instruments of recording and control" by the directive management system, and they lost the property of being economic expressions of real interests (cf. O. Šik, *K problematice socialistických zbožních vztahů* (Socialist Commodity Relations), Prague 1964, p. 341) and thereby the capacity to serve as effective economic instruments.

development of the productive forces" — as Marx pointed out — it is not enough for "certain *conditions of production*... to be established"[1] and then reproduced; it is necessary that the dynamics of the productive forces be built into the social relations of production, the structure of interests in human life, and the source of all strivings that determine human action. Such mobile, regenerating production relations alone can allow for a proper appreciation of science and technology — and the underlying human abilities — enabling them to be used in a planned way as social productive forces.

The very job of industrialization in which Czechoslovakia was engaged offered, under the given circumstances, soil conducive to the use of directive management (immobilizing operation of the market, socialist forms of enterprise, etc.) in place of economic methods, accompanied by a deformation of the social structure (wage levelling, conservative interests emerging, with consequent conflicts among social groups) and finally by freezing the system of political administration (democratic centralism replaced by bureaucratic, the rights of the working people and their participation in decision-making constrained). There came a stage when opportunities for breaking out of this circle arose on several occasions, when fresh alternatives could have been found — but progress was barred by the whole system of managing public affairs, especially by the socio-political system, where it was becoming increasingly obvious that eliminating the shortcomings was the key to an approach to a new stage of development.

We may conclude that Czechoslovakia's decision — as that of other socialist countries — to carry out radical economic reforms and operate a new system of planned management, to extend socialist democracy and throw open the doors to initiative in society, signifies a far deeper purpose than simply to correct shortcomings that at a certain stage of industrial maturity are evinced in ineffective performance. It implies working out, developing and introducing dynamism into the economic structure of socialism in tune with the new mobile conditions of civilization in the coming epoch; hand in hand with this goes the handling of the key issues in the approach to the scientific and technological revolution, which simultaneously opens up the far-reaching prospect of bringing to fruition the fundamental motives embodied in the socialist revolution.

---

[1] K. Marx, *Grundrisse*, ibid, p. 440.

RADICAL CHANGES IN WORK, SKILLS AND EDUCATION

2

Gradually, with cross currents, with all kinds of modifications or deformations, with many regressions, but nevertheless ever more clearly and vigorously, the revolutions in the structure of society's productive forces — most evident in the accelerating transformation of technology — are impinging on the *nature of human labour*, its division, its material and human qualities.[1] What is more, they are upturning the whole area of preparation for work, disturbing the accepted structure of industrial skills and professions, shaking up the traditional system of education and social institutions that surround man in his work. In the long view they are demonstrating the profound intrinsic connection between the universal changes in the productive powers and the revolutionary social processes, which according to Marx and Engels necessarily assume an active role at a certain stage, clearing the way to the most radical transformation experienced by mankind since the transition from barbarism to civilization — the transformation of the entire preceding mode of activity, the very substance of human labour.[2]

---

[1] Socialist writing sometimes employs two terms — "the character of labour", meaning the social conditions of work under given production conditions, and "the content of labour", denoting its material features (cf. *Tekhnichesky progress i voprosy truda pri perekhodye k kommunizmu*, Moscow 1962); but this division in itself assumes the existence of a quite definite, i.e., industrial, type of labour. When we speak here of a change in "the nature of labour", we have in mind a deeper historical process concerning at bottom the material and the social and anthropological dimensions of human activity.

[2] "In all revolutions up till now... the mode of activity always remained unscathed and it was only a question of a different distribution of this activity, a new distribution of labour to other persons, whilst the communistic revolution is directed against the preceding *mode* of activity, does away with labour" (K. Marx, F. Engels, *The German Ideology*, New York 1966, p. 69).

/The Scientific and Technological Revolution and the Patterns of Human Activity/

2.1

In civilization as we have known it up till now, work has dominated the lives of the vast majority of people. In the first place, work is man's fundamental means of life and to this point it lies in the sphere of necessity; but it is also a specific historical form of man's innate self-realization, of his active self-creation, and in this respect it oversteps the bounds of necessity and marks a measure of freedom. So it holds the secret of the mode, but also of the bounds within which human existence has developed. By work man is "acting on the external world and changing it," but "he at the same time changes his own nature."[1] From this source, then, we may expect the most vital impulse or the heaviest curb to social and human development. We start, therefore, from the assumption that changes in the field of work, of human activity, are the key to an understanding of the movements in civilization today and to prognosis in all other spheres of human life.

/Transformations of Work/

2.1.1

When tracing the processes going on beneath the surface of work at the present time, we always arrive in the end at a few fundamental phenomena. They are related to the very substance of work, because — at least for the future — they go beyond the interrelationships of necessity and freedom embodied in it hitherto, or shift them to new positions.

The growth of the productive forces that we are witnessing today is generating in this respect two conflicting series of processes whose effects on the internal and external linkages of the basic mass of work in society are opposed. Industrial mechanization is still breaking up complicated human labour into the simple elements of machine-minding. The spread of the automatic principle, on the contrary, is beginning to eliminate the simple operation of labour power at one point after another; it is pushing man beyond the limits of production as such — on the one hand to exacting jobs in the application of science and development of culture, on the other to new, formerly underdeveloped spheres (services, etc.), where he is again caught up to some extent in industrialization processes.

[1] K. Marx, *Capital*, vol. I, p. 196 (Dent ed.).

On the surface this inner contradictory movement appears as a persistent revival of traditional industrial work in new sectors.[1] But with the advance of the scientific and technological revolution, the closed circle of these processes opens out into a spiral of universal transformations in human labour.

Today the ordinary *simple* labour of the manual worker (and similar jobs in offices, etc.), which was the basis of industrial civilization and the industrial way of life, carries with it in its material pattern and its content the social conditions of its origin — it emerged as the material implementation of wage labour. This social relationship, embodied in the specific utilization of human labour by the machine, in the fragmentation of man's activity into the simple elements of industrial operations, moulds the pattern of work, too, to its own likeness, that is, separated from man, appearing as external necessity, a mere means of an existence whose purpose lies outside work.[2] On the other hand, it consumes his best capacities, it is not his self-determination or his self-affirmation, and is not therefore his true life[3]; man does not live in this activity but merely earns a living that begins after work has ended. This separation of means and ends is at the heart of the alienation inherent in industrial labour, which finds its appropriate embodiment in the simple tending of the industrial mechanism.[4] In the cogs of the classical machine factory, man's activity as a manifestation of his self-assertion is converted in

---

[1] Empirical sociological investigation of work trends, insofar as it deals with a summation of divergent movements, is bound in these circumstances to lead to the conclusion that it is quite impossible to establish the overall trend of changes in human labour (cf. G. Friedmann, *Le Travail en Miettes, spécialisation et loisirs*, Paris 1956).

[2] The labourer "does not count the work itself as part of his life", his true life starts after work (K. Marx, F. Engels, *Wage-Labour and Capital*, London 1935, p. 19). This fact has become so fixed in people's minds that it is taken as an argument for the impossibility of transforming work into a vital need: "*Ex definitione* labour cannot be an immediate source of enjoyment, because after all the term labour has in general been applied to the very thing that evokes no sense of enjoyment..." (L. von Mises, *Die Gemeinwirtschaft*, Jena 1932, p. 147).

[3] As A. R. Heron writes in *Why Men Work* (Stanford 1948, p. 121), to fill a space in a factory or office, to perform motions that have been calculated by others, to expend their physical strength, cannot suffice to provide human beings with an outlet for their inherent abilities.

[4] The point is not merely that the conditions of work are alien to the worker under the system of wage labour. Labour power too, in relation to living labour, "behaves as something alien and if the capitalist wanted to pay it *without* allowing it to work, it would accept the deal with pleasure. So its own labour is just as alien to it" (K. Marx, *Grundrisse*, p. 366).

effect into action subjected to an alien will and alien mind, embodying an alien subjectivity based on alien objectivity.

The chief expression of life remaining for the mass is the simple employment of muscles, senses and nerves in production, the mere expenditure of labour power. And man himself is reduced to the status of labour power, his life revolving in the circle of its simple reproduction. Satisfaction can be obtained solely on the condition that man regards himself in his working activity purely as labour power.[1] The growth of big industry deprives labour of anthropological values. Work loses all correlation with the individual and his special abilities, needs and intentions. Whenever it has been emptied of any lingering craft skills, it is a purely operative, monotonous mechanical performance, simply *abstract activity* divorced from any special form it may assume.[2] In classical industrial operation, at the conveyor belt, it becomes in practice "the abstraction of the category 'labour', 'labour in general', 'labour sans phrase', that starting point of the modern economy"[3]; "abstract labour" is then no longer just one aspect of activity nor a concept derived by comparing different kinds of work, but something that emerges at the surface as "real abstraction" carried out daily in the social process of production and comprising the ever growing mass of al-labour in the industrial system.

The contradictions of industrial labour are the leading factor in determining man's status in modern civilization. They carry to extremes the alienation of the entire man-made conditions for humanity's active self-assertion by turning man himself into an "alienated being"[4] — a being who is not only immersed in the production and consumption of

---

[1] Identification of human nature with simple labour power is at the root of Ford's theory that large numbers of people engage in simple activities because work not requiring creative thought is just what suits them (*My Life and Work*, 1928, Vol. II, p. 7). This confusion of cause and effect ignores the fact that the main reason why people are not inclined to do creative work is that their dispositions have been shaped by factory work which robs them of the opportunity to cultivate their creative powers.

[2] According to G. Friedmann, in advanced industrial civilization ninety percent of people perform simple work that holds no interest whatsoever for them (*Où va le Travail humain?*, Paris 1950).

[3] K. Marx, Anleitung (zur Kritik der politischen Ökonomie) in *Grundrisse*, ibid., p. 25).

[4] K. Marx, *Aus den Exzerptheften*, MEGA, vol. I. 3, p. 536. With this concept Marx stands from the outset head and shoulders above Moses Hess and the romantic critics of civilization, who connect all alienation and inversion purely with the objective conditions of human life.

things, but who also figures in this prime function of his life as a thing,[1] which though living, is a mere appendage of its conditions, of the industrial system, and consequently replaceable by mechanical elements.[2]

This quality of labour, the social and material limitations of man's active self-assertion, are the factors that envelop the pattern of human life in an industrial civilization with their web of internal and external relationships.

On the one hand, the industrial separation of labour from man sets off the process of emancipation whereby man grows to be something for himself even apart from work[3] and independent of his natural surroundings[4], or the instruments with which he works.[5] On the other hand, since industrial work gives man no chance to realize himself as a developing being, he is endowed with interests and motives that lie apart from his productive activity — that is, they are primarily concerned with consumption. The confines into which industrial work, by its quality and quantity, compresses human life make "reproduction claims" insatiable and truly disposable time more or less an illusion.[6] Naturally, as long

[1] As a "bouche-trou de la mécanisation", filling in the interstices of the machine system (G. Friedmann, *Problèmes humains du machinisme industriel*, Paris 1946, p. 179).

[2] Hegel was the first to grasp the connection between the real abstraction of labour on the one hand and the mechanization that follows from it on the other (*Grundlinien der Philosophie des Rechts*, Berlin 1956, p. 174). But in Hegel's day Babbage already went much further in elaborating the prospects of technological application implicit in this development (*On the Economy of Machinery and Manufactures*, London 1832).

[3] "The animal is one with its life activity. It does not distinguish the activity from itself. It is *its activity*. But man makes his life activity itself an object of his will and consciousness. He has a conscious life activity. It is not a determination with which he is completely identified" (K. Marx, *Economic and Philosophical Manuscripts*, quoted from E. Fromm, *Marx's Concept of Man*, New York 1966, trans. T. B. Bottomore, p. 101). The great advantage of simple industrial labour lies in its most critical feature — the absolute separation of labour from man. Because only with this separation can the basic work functions be taken over by technical means and human activity be purposefully remoulded.

[4] Industrial work broke up the primitive natural unity of man and his natural surroundings, the harmony that once existed in "the ploughman, ox, ploughshare and soil" (K. Marx, *Theorien über den Mehrwert*, vol. III, Stuttgart 1921, p. 576). But thereby all aspects of human activity were again exposed to the intervention of man.

[5] "Every medieval craftsman was completely absorbed in his work... to which he was subjected to a far greater extent than the modern worker, whose work is a matter of indifference to him" (K. Marx, F. Engels, *The German Ideology*, New York 1966, p. 47).

[6] "Most often impoverished work is matched by free time of the same kind" (J. Dumazedier, *Vers une civilisation du loisir?*, Paris 1962, p. 82).

"The reason so many actually prefer horror movies, quiz programs, and panel

as man does not find work itself to be his wealth, the form assumed by wealth is, on the contrary, his inducement to work. The fact that socially beneficial activity in the guise of such work is not felt as an inner need, but merely as an external necessity of existence (or perhaps a social duty) relegates man's wants to the private sphere alone.

Thus all the leading elements in the mode of life followed by working people in an industrial civilization — leisure, consumption, living standards, cultivation of abilities, etc. — are determined by the nature of industrial labour. All forecasts for civilization advanced in the West bear unmistakable marks of this boundary. The only lasting solution is to be seen in negating the entire complex of conditions governing work.[1] A considerable curtailment and transformation of industrial work is, indeed, coming to be the key question for social and technological advances — without this the circle of modern civilization is closed — quite apart from the radical tone that may be assumed by its critics.

True, socialism — in its material aspects — is based by and large on the selfsame type of labour that evolved under the industrial system it has inherited. Although people living in the changed conditions of a socialist society are placed in a different relationship to their work (being now genuinely particles of the total social labour)[2], and even if no socially useful and necessary activity, whatever its material guise, can be ignored in a community of labour, it is nonetheless obvious that, being stamped by its typical industrial limitations, much of this work reproduces[3] its inner cleavage at a new level — man cannot realize himself

---

games on TV is that their daily lives, especially their jobs, are so dull and meaningless" (W. Buckingham, *Automation, Its Impact on Business and People*, p. 155, New York 1961).

[1] Indeed, the workers who show interest in work are those who at the same time express their dissatisfaction with the work they are performing (cf. A. Andrieux, J. Lignon, *L'ouvrier d'aujourd'hui. Sur les changements dans la condition et la conscience ouvrières*, Paris 1960, p. 51).

[2] "Under socialism, then, the jobs of individuals are essentially shaped beforehand by work for society... but they are not yet universally self-satisfying jobs" (O. Šik, *K problematice socialistických zbožních vztahů* (Socialist Commodity Relations), Prague 1964, p. 224). This is, in fact, the reason why socialism still has to employ wages and hence the whole complex of commodity forms.

[3] Influenced by the Soviet psychotechnical school of the twenties and thirties (e.g. *Die Arbeiter und die Fliessbandarbeiter*, Moscow 1929), G. Friedmann admitted in his *La crise du progrès* considerable differences between materially similar work at the conveyor belt in Soviet and American factories. Later, evidently actuated by the undiscriminating attitude to the features of industrial work common to different social systems adopted by some socialist writers, he fell into the opposite extreme of maintain-

in it directly as a creative, developing being, he finds in it no immediate source of satisfaction and enrichment, he does not live in it, but wins through it the means for a life that begins when the working day has ended, when the space for life has been more or less consumed by work and the reproduction of the capacity to work.[1] Consequently, socialism cannot be content with these abstract boundaries inherited from industry.

In this context profound significance is assumed by the impact of the scientific and technological revolution, seen from the angle of the logic and the empiricism of the changes in the nature of work. If we break down the *work cycles* in types of production (craft, mechanized, automatic) with different structures of the productive forces, taking as our criterion the functions performed by man or technology in the various phases (preparatory, managing, operative and control) and compare the diagrams obtained (see Table 2-1), we find[2] that in the course of mecha-

ing that work at the belt was identical in Detroit and Gorky (*Sept Etudes sur l'homme et la Technique*, Paris 1967). However, undoubtedly only long-term development will be able to demonstrate the true significance of differences implicit in the social characteristics of work, whereas at present their explicit material features are seen merely in slight and, on the whole, external disparities.

[1] Hence the dissatisfaction with the legacy of simple industrial jobs to be found among workers in socialist countries: "We often hear and repeat ourselves," writes V. Gaganova, worker-innovator at a spinning mill, "that work should be a pleasure in our society. But what pleasure can one get from mechanical repetition of operations that have been learnt once and for all and have long lost any interest, if one doesn't progress in one's work and think how to improve it? Can one feel satisfied if one's work simply helps towards someone else's innovation? Real pleasure in work that is worthy of people in a communist society comes only from creativeness and one's own insatiable desire to keep on improving things" (*Nesobecké rozhodnutí* (Unselfish Decision), Prague 1960, p. 25). A similar view was expressed by a woman worker from the press shop of the Tesla works at Hloubětín, Prague: "we don't want just to carry out the set operations mechanically and unthinkingly" (*Tvorba*, no. 41, 1960). And this dissatisfaction with industrial work and the endeavour to break out of its bounds carries vital implications for the whole progress of modern civilization.

[2] The model of the work cycle based on microanalysis that is employed here was constructed by F. Kutta "Podstata a postavení automatizace v technickém rozvoji" (The Substance and Place of Automation in Technological Development), *Politická ekonomie* 10/1960). J. Auerhan has confronted it with models of technological development and worked out on this basis a *classification of technological development* with eleven grades of production development, two grades using tools, three based on mechanization and six on progressive automation. He has also proposed a dynamic model for the growth in skills of the aggregate worker at various technological levels (cf. *Automatizace a její ekonomický význam* (Automation and Its Economic Significance), Prague 1959, *Technika, kvalifikace, vzdělání* (Technology, Skills, Education), Prague 1965). In its method and results, Auerhan's classification comes, in a sense, close to the

nization, individual operations become independent, and some belonging to the immediate sphere of production (primarily the operative phase) are taken over by machines. In contrast, in the process of automation the technological components take over all functions in production proper (and the entire managing phase), and a large part of the control, with even some elements of the preparatory phase (see Table 2-2).

The chief prop of mechanized industrial production is the *worker-operative*, minding the machine or tied to the movement of the conveyor belt, with perhaps the semi-skilled labourer filling in the spaces of the imperfect machine system. In the short term, during the advance of industrialization into new sectors, with further mechanization of processes, etc., growth in the numbers of worker-operatives has to be envisaged (perhaps of the semi-skilled, too), that is, of the classical industrial workers. This implies that there is no getting round some awkward civilization problems stemming from the ill effects of the manually-operated machine system on human beings, especially where arduous and stereotype operations are involved.

However, even the first steps in automation, cybernation, chemical processes, etc., eliminate this type of work. They incorporate the basic operations in immediate production into a technical system and put man out on the fringe. The proportion of operatives drops sharply (from 60—70 per cent to under 10 per cent of the work force).[1] In place of armies of machine workers, we find much smaller groups of *job-setters*[2] (in shops undergoing progressive automation they account for up to half the labour force, while in mechanized around 6—7 percent[3]), and of *main-*

concept of J. B. Kvasha (*Klasifikatsiya mashin uchota oborudovaniya*, Moscow 1934). Auherhan has also examined some later proposals: that of V. I. Lossiyevsky, using an 18-grade classification (see *Avtomatizatsiya proizvodstvennykh protsessov*, II., Moscow 1958), J. R. Bright's with 7 grades (see *Harvard Business Review* 7—8/1958), H. Schenkel's with 6 (see *Technischer Fortschritt — wie messen und beobachten?*, Berlin 1960), A. Touraine's 3-grade model (see *L'évolution du travail ouvrier aux usines Renault*, Paris 1955), and S. Leonardi's work (*Studi Gramsciani, Atti di Convego tenuto a Roma*, 1958).

[1] Soviet research estimates a drop from 63 percent in mechanized works to 9 percent in automated (see *Spravochnye materialy po trudu i zarabotnoy platye*, Moscow 1960, p. 40).

[2] Originally job-setters belonged to the semi-skilled category; they were so few that British factory statistics did not even include them. With automation they appear as the most numerous group; thus the traditional profile of the worker is completely changing.

[3] J. Auerhan, *Technika, kvalifikace, vzdělání*, ibid. pp. 226—227. This is the case, for example, in the First State Bearings Works in the USSR (cf. A. Osipov, I. Kovalenko, E. Petrov, *Sovietsky rabochy i avtomatizatsiya*, Moscow 1960). In some partially

111

tenance and repair men (in partially automated works about 20—30 percent or more; in modern chemical plants they comprise up to 50 percent of the labour force[1], compared with 3—5 percent in mechanized works) or of personnel performing optimalization jobs. These changes are beginning to impinge on the general pattern of manpower, too[2] — job-setters, maintenance and repair men have been (alongside managers) the most rapidly growing category both in the USSR and the USA[3]; while the number of skilled machine operatives is rising at half the previous rate in the USSR, and in the US it is stagnant or falling (see Table 2-3).

As far as one can judge from the rather scanty evidence available at present, complex automation always goes further in that it proceeds to abolish human operation in the control phase, too; it cuts the job-setting, maintenance and repair personnel, freeing man altogether from direct participation in the production process. It relieves him of his role as a mere cog in the machine system and offers him the position of inspirer, creator, master of the technological system, able to stand apart from the immediate manufacturing process. The hub of human activity is shifted to the *preparatory phases* of production. This is the soil for a sharp rise in *technological-engineering* and *technical-managerial personnel* with the emphasis on creative technologists, technicians, design-

automated shops this proportion rises even higher (P. P. Petrochenko, *Organizatsiya i normirovaniye truda na promyshlennykh predpriyatiyakh*, Moscow 1962). On the Ford production lines the proportion of job-setters reaches 70 percent (cf. J. R. Bright, *Automation and Management*, Boston 1958).

[1] For example, in Shell refineries (Vincent-Grossin, *L'Enjeu de l'Automatisation*, Paris 1958, pp. 67—71) or in Soviet oil works (*Sotsialistichesky trud* 8/1959). In top plants, however, the proportion of maintenance and repair men drops again thanks to the reliability of the automation equipment. According to a model of changes in personnel structure with a view to ensuring optimal effectiveness after automating the Automobile Works at Mladá Boleslav (Czechoslovakia), the percentage shares of *operatives: job-setters : maintenance men* should change *from 89.2 : 3.3 : 7.5* in mechanized production to *30 : 50 : 20* with automation (cf. F. Kutta, S. Rufert et al., *Metodika mikrorozborů a projekce nové techniky na pracovní síly*, EÚ-ČSAV, Prague 1965, p. 79).

[2] But the overall picture obscures many reverse processes and bypaths that complicate matters; e.g. assembly shops show much slower change in work or none at all, while the direct processing phase is strongly affected. There is, therefore, a shift in the relations between these areas. While in the USA in 1950 there were 43 operators in assembly shops per 100 in processing, in 1960 the figure was 61 (cf. E. A. Connant, *Papers*, University of Chicago, March 1960).

[3] See the report of the Central Statistical Administrations attached to the Council of Ministers of the USSR (*Voprosy ekonomiky* 1/1961) and data given by M. Rutzick and S. Swerdloff of the US Bureau of Labor Statistics (*Monthly Labor Review* 11/1962).

ers, automation experts, systems analysts and scientists, and of management personnel, industrial psychologists, sociologists, people concerned with industrial aesthetics, hygiene, etc. In the last few decades the number of graduate engineers has risen in the USSR by 6 per cent, in the USA by 5 per cent a year (see Table 2-3), which is over twice in the USSR, and in the USA three times, the growth rate of the total labour force. In long-term projection, the growth of the specialist technological intelligentsia appears as the steadiest and most pronounced shift in the job pattern of the advanced industrial countries.[1] While in industry to date the proportion of engineers and technicians has not as a rule amounted to more than 10 per cent — and traditionally has been much less[2] — the signs are that during coming decades their share will rise severalfold and in the most sophisticated works will reach 50 per cent of all personnel.[3] In automated production the technical staff will probably be in the majority. Among the technologists, the proportion of scientific and research work is growing; in some chemical and radio-engineering works it comprises about half of such personnel.[4]

We may assume that the advance of the scientific and technological revolution will first engulf the operative type of work involving manual machine-minding, and later the less sophisticated regulatory and control activities — in a word, the traditional simple industrial work, insofar as man does not need it and it is enforced by external necessity, or will cut

[1] In the USA, the work force per engineer and scientist dropped between 1930 and 1963 from 189 to 59; in Czechoslovakia between 1953 and 1963 from 174 to 85 (cf. F. Kutta, B. Levčík, "Vliv vědeckotechnické revoluce na změny v obsahu práce a struktury pracovní síly" — Influence of the Scientific and Technological Revolution on Changes in the Content of Work and the Structure of the Work Force), *Sociologický časopis* 2/1966).

[2] Marx was still able to refer to this group as being "few in number" (*Capital*, Vol. I, p. 448 (Dent ed.)).

[3] Technological-engineering personnel in US manufacturing numbers about ten per cent, but in the aircraft industry it has already passed the fifty per cent mark. Figures for the share of engineers and scientists in the work force are: food industry 0.7 per cent, metallurgy 2.9 per cent, engineering 4.2 per cent, electrical engineering 7.5 per cent, chemistry 9.8 per cent, aircraft 13.0 per cent, oil 20.5 per cent, atomic industry 34.1 per cent (cf. P. N. Ivanov, *Tekhnichesky perevorot i rabochy klass v glavnykh kapitalisticheskikh stranakh*, Moscow 1965, pp. 136—138).

[4] In 1962, of the total of engineers and natural scientists in the USA, 30.1 per cent were engaged in research and development, taking the economy as a whole. For the manufacturing industries the figure was 36.6 per cent, for chemicals 44.9 per cent, in the aircraft industry 52.5 per cent, in communications engineering 52.7 per cent, in office machine and computer production 54.2 per cent (cf. *Scientific and Technical Manpower Resources*, Washington 1964, p. 57).

it down to a degree not exceeding people's need for movement. Then, when man stops doing the things that things can do for him, he is offered the prospect of creative activity as the normal occupation through which he can exercise all his powers — activity imbued with scientific elements, discovery, invention, pioneering and cultivating human powers. Should such a type of human activity become universal it would, of course, signify the *transcendence of work* in the accepted sense, a process that Marx and Engels saw as the cardinal issue of the social revolution.[1] For as soon as human activity in its material shape coincides with the nature of man's creative self-assertion, external necessity, imposed either by the struggle for a livelihood or by social obligation[2], gives way to man's inner need, a need for man himself that enriches him; at this point the abstract cleavage between work and pleasure, labour and leisure, vanishes, and human activity merges with life itself.

Nevertheless, the transformation of human labour into *creative activity* cannot take place unless both the social conditions and material contours of man's doings undergo a change, unless his active self-assertion assumes a scientific character[3] and aesthetic qualities, in other words, unless the conflict of means and ends that has bedevilled industrial labour is overcome. Human activity has to, in fact, gain qualities whereby it will be as a means equally man's goal and as a goal equally a means. Creative scientific, technical, inventive (like artistic) activity is a type fundamentally different from simple industrial work, because (at least potentially) the cleavage between means and ends is eliminated from it; universal labour, transformation of the world, then merge with man's self-creation; consciously-directed activity combines with the free play of human powers that is an end in itself. Through creative

---

[1] We may note that Marx did not consider the "transcendence of labour" or "annulment of labour" to be the "sweet idleness" of hackneyed bourgeois dreams, but "the full development of activity itself, in which natural necessity in its immediate form has disappeared", and which is therefore no longer labour in the true sense (*Grundrisse*, p. 231).

[2] Such active self-assertion "is not, like labour, decreed by the pressure of an external purpose that has to be fulfilled, whose fulfilment is a natural necessity, or social duty, as you will..." (K. Marx, *Theorien über den Mehrwert*, III, Stuttgart 1921, p. 305). The currently employed economic stimuli, and also the consciousness of social obligation, may be regarded as temporary substitutive external impulses with the help of which a new internal bond between man and his activity is only just starting to be forged.

[3] Human activity in production "can acquire this character solely through: 1. being given a social character, 2. having a scientific character and simultaneously being universal labour, not human exertion as a specially drilled natural force" (K. Marx, *Grundrisse*, p. 505).

activity man will no longer be a mere means in expressing his life, but will come forward as an active intermediary[1] — the agent of his own development and thereby of that of others, too. This radical change is, of course, bound to carry incalculable consequences for the world of human values and the contours of human life. This change alone will be capable of demonstrating the genuinely profound humanist implications of technological progress, without which every social revolution would be doomed to frustration.

True, the capitalist world accepts the transformation of labour as long as it takes place in workshops, plants or sectors — insofar as it does not assume universal proportions and is overlaid by the spread of industrial work in other sectors. From this stems the "compensation theory" that presently interprets the changes in the nature of labour as a matter of simply transferring industrial work to other fields.[2]

In reality, however, "compensation" is merely a superficial phenomenon of temporary equilibrium among conflicting processes, at the limits of which stepping up the value of human activity paradoxically emerges in the guise of "redundancy" for the mass of workers once engaged in simple operative work.[3] With a social background where the worker himself is not an end, he ultimately loses his significance as a means, too. The magnitude of this threat can be judged from the discrepancy between various calculations in the USA. On the one hand they show how many jobs will be scrapped by automation and declare that if science and technology were to be given free rein the greater part of the present labour force in works and offices would be made redundant,[4]

---

[1] K. Marx, *Aus den Exzerptheften*, MEGA, I. 3, p. 546.

[2] Empirical investigation has revealed the difference between "machines that provide job openings" (mechanization), and "technology that eliminates job openings" (automation); to imagine that these processes will maintain a lasting balance is tantamount to assuming that the scientific and technological revolution will not go forward. But the Triple Revolution memorandum has already shown that no substantial job creation is now to be expected in the USA. B. B. Seligman has computed that the net decline in simple work, after deducting all types of "compensation", amounts to 156,000 jobs a year, and the trend is accelerating: "The idea that everyone who has been pushed out by the machine can quickly find new employment is ridiculous. It reminds one of the man who whistles gaily as he walks through a graveyard" (*Automation und technischer Fortschritt in Deutschland und den USA*, Frankfurt a. M. 1963, p. 73).

[3] The very formation of a reserve army of unemployed is simply a paradoxical "expression of the greater real value of the producer" (J. Davydov, *Trud i svoboda*, Moscow 1962, p. 105).

[4] On W. Reuther's estimate, technology may displace in the near future 60 percent (in the opinion of the Subcommission for Economic Stabilization as much as 65 per-

on the other hand, long-term forecasts for the US economy do not envisage in the meantime any substantial curtailment and general transformation of work. Least of all is this technological society prepared for any upheavals in the quality of elementary human activity. The chief hope (and central argument) of official reports remains the bold assumption[1] that changes in work will not be so far-reaching and rapid as the scientific and technological revolution might allow, and that they will, therefore, present no threat to the operation of the "industrial system". Should we need proof that the revolution is proceeding purely spontaneously within this system, here is the place to find it. Paradoxically enough, the latest know-how is directed just to this end — to create fresh openings for the old type of work, to preserve the very industrial utilization of man that it is capable of abolishing. The old simple labour that dominated man and called the institutions of the industrial system into being is to be maintained "in the public interest" by the "active policy" of modern administration aimed at compensating the impact of technological upheavals by artificially contrived extensive industrialization processes. The alienation embodied in work then reaches the point of absurdity — people uphold a level of the old, abstract work that their own creative powers are making more and more superfluous, in the belief that they would otherwise become "superfluous" themselves.[2]

cent); taking the MacGraw-Hill calculations of the net job loss induced by computer instalment, this alone would be capable of displacing about 15 million people from simple production work by the year 2000.

[1] The report *Technology and the American Economy* (Washington 1966, p. 9) makes the contention that "the basic fact is that technology eliminates jobs, not work", that is to say, the intensive growth induced by the scientific and technological revolution can in future, too, be counterbalanced by an appropriate dose of artificially evoked extensive industrialization. The rapid advance of labour productivity engendered by science and technology is here taken as a given quantity and the search is for a growth rate of the gross national product (higher than the sum of the expected productivity and population growth) that would avert the danger of "technological unemployment" and lay the basis for "compensation". This gives a clear indication of how far this society is adapted to the conditions of industrialization, to which it repeatedly looks for a way out of the contradictions evoked by the advance of the scientific and technological revolution. Should such a "balance" be artificially maintained, the present development may really assume a form suggestive of an extension of the industrial revolution.

[2] The idea of people being "useless" has for some decades been regarded as the central problem of technological civilization (cf. *The Margate Conference: The Automatic Factory — What Does it Mean?* London 1955, p. 28). Karel Čapek's Dr. Gall *(RUR)* already posed the question whether in "the realm of robots" man is not an anachronism, indicating thereby that he looked on man purely as a living robot.

The industrial system ties them so firmly to the role of mere labour power that they identify themselves with it; so the work that constrains and robs them of life seems to them to be the sole guarantee of free existence, and, indeed, of life itself. By this, however, they in fact bear witness to the utter futility and tragedy of the conditions that make their lives into the simple reproduction of labour power.

Once upon a time Rousseau expressed through the mouths of Caribbean savages his astonishment at the nascent industrial civilization which relegated work to the sphere of necessity and made it into a mere means of preserving existence — and this feeling runs to this day through much humanist criticism. But now, in the twilight of the industrial epoch, we are presented with a still more bizarre picture of a civilization that, through the vast wealth it has accumulated, has converted human existence into a mere means for maintaining industrial labour — divorced from any necessity.

The crucial issue posed by the revolutions of our day is how to open the road to a universal transformation of human labour, and herein lies the mission that socialism has to accomplish for civilization. With their concept of "transcending labour", Marx and Engels expressed a humanism distinguishing them sharply from their predecessors who built up the European and American system of ideas on the positive soil of industrial labour.[1] In this sense it contains at least a theoretical indication of the conditions and contours of a new civilization emerging beyond the frontiers of the industrial world created by capitalism.

---

[1] The most extensive analyses of labour at our disposal usually take up the theme of Marx's appreciation of Hegel, who "conceives *labour* as the *essence*, the self-confirming essence of man". (*Economic and Philosophical Manuscripts*, ibid. p. 177.) They assume that Marx took over from Hegel either the whole key concept of labour (G. Friedmann, *Le Travail en Miettes. Spécialisation et Loisirs*, Paris 1958) or at least all essential characteristics (H. Marcuse, "Über die philosophischen Grundlagen des wirtschaftswissenschaftlichen Arbeitsbegriffs", *Archiv für Sozialwissenschaft und Sozial politik* 3/1933; similarly, *Reason and Revolution*, New York 1941). But Marx goes on at once to criticise Hegel, who "observes only the positive side of labour, not its negative side" (ibid., p. 177) and this standpoint became the limiting factor for Hegel's philosophy, the source of his uncritical positivism. At bottom he identifies active self-assertion with labour existing in the form of alienation; Marx and Engels, on the contrary, see the transcendence of alienated labour and the complete transformation of human activity into free creation of human powers as the condition for man's genuine self-assertion. Marx and Engels are not philosophers of labour but its critics: "The point is not that labour should be emancipated, but that it should be abolished, transcended" (*The German Ideology*, MEGA, Abt. 1, Band 5, Moscow—Leningrad 1933).

Attempts to make radical changes in the course of civilization by less arduous means, for instance merely by activating leisure or expanding consumption, or even by appealing for an improvement in human relationships without any change in the nature of human activity (however needful progress in these fields, too, is becoming) are still no more than half-hearted rebellions.[1] Labour, consumption, leisure and human relationships are so intertwined in the industrial system that critical projects directed at partial solutions are bound in any case to abandon any prospects of radical civilization changes, relegating them to some unknown future[2], or to the realm of illusion, or losing sight of the positive anthropological connotations of changing human activity[3], and so of the prospects of social transformation, too.

We find, then, that an indispensable condition for transcending industrial civilization — and a constituent part of any genuine criticism we may make of it — is that man's basic activity be completely changed through radical measures affecting its social background and the civilization on which it rests, measures involving both the nature and content of labour.

---

[1] Some authors (Popper, Friedmann, Popitz and others) believe that in later years Marx revised his theory of "transcending labour" (primarily in Vol. III of *Capital*). But it is enough to look into the preparatory work for *Capital*, or the much later *Critique of the Gotha Program*, to find the same idea of transforming labour into man's creative self-assertion, which will also be his vital need. In his later works Marx simply specifies the difference between socialism, as a stage drawing primarily on the traditional material nature of labour, and communism that is based on a new, creative type of human activity.

[2] One of the leading industrial sociologists, G. Friedmann, has sought all his life for ways of *revalorizing* industrial work in the intellectual, human and social fields (*Problèmes humains du machinisme industriel*, Paris 1946). He welcomes every humanizing element in existing labour; yet, in view of the above standpoint, he has no faith in a general radical change; he even relegates Norbert Wiener's enunciation of the potentialities offered by cybernation of production processes to the realm of a technological utopia.

[3] H. Marcuse sees that present-day technology offers possibilities for transcending existing labour. He admits that it would imply a radical change in the status of technology altogether. But in view of his standpoint, he interprets Marx's idea about *"transcending labour"* purely in terms of *"pacifying existence"* (*One-Dimensional Man*, Boston 1964, p. 16), and not as a positive mode of man's development. Marcuse does not then view the future of civilization from the angle of creatively-active people who are transforming the world and themselves, but from that of people displaced from activity and opposing the onrush of the technological world.

/ *Structural Changes* / 2.1.2

Industrialization transferred the focal point of human labour from the fields into the factories, assembling a growing proportion of the population in industry. In the classical industrial countries this influx halted when 35—50 per cent of the economically active population was concentrated in mining, manufacturing and building (see Table 2-4), with a large share absorbed by big industry.[1] In a parallel — and even more rapid — movement, industrialization reduced the share of farm labour from an original level of 70 per cent to under 30 per cent, so that, all in all, the work force in these two sectors[2] gradually shrank.

We can observe in the industrially developed countries today a tendency towards *redistribution* of manpower:

a) Eliminating the bulk of manpower from agriculture through technology, concentration and rationalization is assuming massive proportions. Taking into account only countries that are self-sufficient or at least strong in agriculture, we find a drop in the US farming population from 27.6 per cent (1920) to 6.3 per cent (1965); forecasts show a further decline to 5.4 per cent (1972) and 2.5 per cent (2000).[3] Similarly, in France the trend was from 41.5 per cent (1921) to 20.7 per cent (1963) and the forecast anticipates 11.0 per cent by 1985.[4] An analogous trend in Czechoslovakia can be estimated as proceeding from the present 22 per cent

---

[1] The frequently employed term "industrial society" derives from this typical manpower structure. R. Aron defines it as "a society where industry, and large scale at that, becomes that most typical form of production" (*Dixhuit leçons sur la Société industrielle*, Paris 1962, p. 97); and again in *Le développement de la société industrielle et la stratification sociale* I, Paris 1957, pp. 25—27). This theory on the one hand fixes the definition of contemporary society solely in a single projection at the surface of the complicated transformations of civilization, on the other hand it remains, in consequence of this, impotent in face of the deeper-lying departures of the modern world.

[2] We employ the historically established division into three economic sectors: I. agriculture, II. mining, manufacturing and building, III. services. It can be demonstrated that the interpretation of these sectors according to C. Clark (*The Conditions of Economic Progress*, London 1941), i.e. on the basis of the material effect of activity, and J. Fourastié's mobile definition (*Le Grand Espoir du XXe Siècle*, Paris 1958) delimited by the degree of growth in productivity (average in Sector I, above-average in Sector II and below-average in Sector III) agree in essentials for the conditions of industrialization and within the sphere of industrial civilization; indeed, they derive from common roots reaching back to the ideas of the physiocrats and classical political economy.

[3] Cf. *Statistical Abstract of the US; Resources in America's Future*, Baltimore 1963.

[4] J. Fourastié et al., *Migrations professionnelles*, Paris 1957; *Réflexions pour 1985* (ed. P. Massé), Levallois-Perret 1964.

to 10 per cent within two to three decades and later to a still lower level. The model[1] indicates that in the initial phase of the scientific and technological revolution (see Table 2—5), the share of agriculture ranges around 20 to 3 per cent, becoming a relatively small fraction of the nation's labour.

b) An entirely new phenomenon, demonstrating the disparity between the scientific and technological revolution and industrialization, is the turn to a relative *decline* in the amount of labour absorbed by *industry* and associated activities — accompanied by a strong shift[2] from the traditional branches to the progressive within industry (see Table 2-6). This tendency clearly refutes the standpoint giving absolute validity to the industrialization process and the structure of "the industrial society". The proportion of US manpower engaged in mining, manufacturing and building[3] dropped from a peak of 36.8 per cent in 1950 to 33.6 per cent in 1962; forecasts suggest a further decline to 31.6 per cent in 1972 and to below 30 per cent later. The decline in the mining and manufacturing industries is much sharper in view of an opposite movement in building. From the 1950 maximum of 30.4 per cent, these industries sank to 27.2 per cent in 1962, while the outlook for 1972 is 25.2[4], with a prospective limit of 20 per cent. There are signs of a similar phenomenon in Great Britain;[5] having maintained a level of 50 per cent for some time (1950), the share of mining, manufacturing and building is now 48.1 per cent, and a further shrinkage seems likely, with a still stronger trend in the non-building industries. Several European countries (France, GFR, GDR) now envisage a stabilization of the share of the secondary sector. This also applies to Czechoslovakia, where growth in the share of industry[6] is halting; assuming a transition to the scientific and technological revolution, a gradual decline may be anticipated. In the overall

[1] This model was constructed on the basis of extensive empirical material by T. Frejka (*Rozbor odvětvové struktury pracovní síly*, Economic Institute CAS, Prague 1965; *Politická ekonomie* 8/1966).

[2] Cf. *The Growth of World Industry 1938—1961. International Analyses and Tables*, New York 1965.

[3] Cf. Nation's Manpower Revolution, *Senate Hearings*. P. 5, 1963.

[4] Cf. *Hearings before the Subcommittee on Employment and Manpower of the Committee on Labor and Public Welfare*, US Senate — 88th Congress, Washington 1963, p. 1399.

[5] *Manpower Statistics 1950—1962*, Paris 1963; *Yearbook of Labour Statistics 1965*, Geneva 1966.

[6] Between 1948 and 1962, the share of mining, manufacturing and building in Czechoslovak manpower rose from 34 per cent to 47 per cent (cf. Czechoslovak Statistical Abstracts for 1957 and 1963).

model of shifts in manpower structure (see Table 2—5), the initial phases of the scientific and technological revolution show a drop in the industrial labour force to 34—25 per cent, with building stable or rising to 8—10 per cent.

c) Insofar as we adhere to the traditional division of economic sectors, the advance of the scientific and technological revolution is manifested in the resultant of the two foregoing trends, as an accelerated shift of human labour in the industrial countries from the "production sectors" (the sectors of "immediate production", primary and secondary) to the "nonproduction sectors" ("services"). The outlook of the revolution is evidently linked with a *strong advance of the "tertiary sector"*, i.e., "services" in the widest sense (including commerce and transportation). This shift has assumed varying intensities in different countries (see Table 2-7); in the USA the ratio of "immediate production" to "services" has been completely inverted from 59 : 41 (1940) to 47 : 53 (1946); in the USSR it has dropped from 82 : 12 (1940) to 76 : 24 (1964); in Canada from 61 : 39 (1940) to 54 : 46 (1960)[1]. The rule during industrialization was that the degree of the process was directly proportional to the share of the secondary sector and indirectly to the primary sector. Now a converse and considerably extended relation applies: beyond a given limit, the share of "immediate production" stands in inverse ratio to the degree of the scientific and technological revolution, and the fall of the former is indirectly proportionate to the rate of the revolution's progress.

In general, we can assume that in the course of the scientific and technological revolution the volume of "services" will grow to the point of occupying 40—60 per cent of national labour in coming decades (see Table 2-5), with a still bigger share in the long term[2]. The civilization to which we are advancing might accordingly quite well be called "postindustrial civilization", "tertiary civilization", "services civilization", etc.[3] But this definition is obscured by the superficial phenomenal ele-

---

[1] Cf. F. Kutta, B. Levčík, "Vliv vědeckotechnické revoluce na změny v obsahu práce a ve struktuře pracovní síly" (Influence of the Scientific and Technological Revolution on Changes in the Content of Labour and the Manpower Structure), *Sociologický časopis* 2/1966.

[2] The US forecast for 1975 mentions over 60 per cent (The Outlook for Technological Change and Unemployment, *Technology and the American Economy*, Appendix I, Washington 1966). Fourastié usually speaks of 80 per cent of the work force in services in the USA by the year 2000.

[3] Cf. J. Fourastié, *Le Grand Espoir du XXe Siècle*, Paris 1958; D. Bell, "The Post-industrial Society" in *Technology and Social Change*, New York—London 1964.

ment of the transition stage and the initial phases of the scientific and technological revolution; the "services" sector is not in fact homogeneous, either in structure or outlook; it comprises several components that are divergent as regards the structure and dynamics of the productive forces.[1]

Today, in the first phases of the scientific and technological revolution, the classical *services* are recording an explosive rise, with impressive increments in *commerce, financial services, administrative departments, etc.* But this applies preeminently to some European countries; in the USA, where commerce and financial services already account for 24 per cent of national labour, and the services proper for 14 per cent, where nearly 15 per cent of actively employed people are office workers, one can observe a reverse trend[2] — through 1950—1964 employment in commerce increased no more than 17 per cent (in West Germany over the same period by over 70 per cent), i.e., at a much lower rate than previously, so that it accounted for a smaller share of the total work force as a result of progressive methods in wholesale trade and retail outlets, and of computer techniques in financial and insurance offices. While the number of white-collar workers has risen quite considerably in the USA (by 40 per cent), the curve is flattening out under the impact of cybernation, which in the central, best-equipped units will ultimately

---

[1] Clarke's concept of economic sectors, derived from the external material form of industrial production, is not sufficiently sensitive to changes in the structure of the productive forces, especially to the specific status of science; in fact it assumes their immutability. J. Fourastié's classification, on the contrary, absolutizes the traditional industrial dynamic, placing sectors with an average growth of productivity in the primary sector, with above-average in the secondary, and below-average in the tertiary, and is built on the assumption (also valid in the era of industrialization) that the tertiary sphere is in principle inaccessible to technological progress. But the beginnings of the scientific and technological revolution have refuted these assumptions. Productivity per hour in US agriculture is known to be rising at nearly twice the rate attained in industry.

M. Lengellé (*La Révolution Tertiaire*, Paris 1966) demonstrates on the basis of V. R. Fuchs's figures for the USA and his own French data that the growth in productivity of living labour in several service sectors matches that in industry. D. N. Michael (*Cybernation: The Silent Conqueror*, Santa Barbara 1962) signalizes a sharp advance of the scientific and technological revolution, which is making the service sector especially a domain of scientific and technological progress.

[2] Cf. J. Kosta, "Strukturální změny společenské pracovní síly ve světle mezinárodního srovnání" (Structural Changes in Manpower in the Light of International Comparison), *Politická ekonomie* 1/1967; based on US statistical abstracts and Yearbook of Labour Statistics 1965, Geneva 1966.

lead to stagnation and a decline.[1] Moreover, it has to be remembered that by its very nature the economic and social order in the United States absorbs an inflated amount of labour in some service branches, especially in commerce, financial and administrative posts (irrational dispersion of retail outlets, overgrowth of financial operations, alarming expansion of the military machine, insatiability of advertising, etc.), which retards the outflow of manpower from the classical service sphere that modern information, communications and transportation techniques and organization have made possible. Comparative studies illustrate this fact in terms of differences in the structure of the "tertiary sectors" of the most developed countries.[2] In Sweden, for example, commerce, finance and clerical occupations account for a much smaller proportion than in the USA, while a relatively more important place is assumed by social, health and cultural services (with the exception of education, which is highly developed in America); moreover, in Sweden the share of commerce, finance and clerical occupations is starting to shrink more rapidly than in the USA. With the tertiary sector at an equal level, socialism would have even better opportunities in this direction.[3] All in all, we may envisage certain growth thresholds in the tertiary sphere in the course of the scientific and technological revolution. After an initial sharp rise, there apparently comes a point when growth of the labour force in commerce, finance and transportation is halted; improvement of management systems and rational use of cybernetic techniques on a society-wide scale may also reverse the trend in white-collar occupations; at a later stage, technological development will make a strong impact on the services proper. During this process, some areas of activity are detached from the tertiary sphere, and on

[1] In 1952, US central federal offices had 2,420,000 employees, in 1964 the figure was 2,348,000 (cf. *Manpower Report of the President*, March 1965, Washington, p. 233).

[2] M. Lengellé (*La Révolution Tertiaire*, Paris 1966) polarizes Sweden and the USA in this respect as two divergent "tertiary types" and poses the question in which direction France (and other West European countries) will move.

[3] Dividing the tertiary sphere into groups A (science, education, health services, social welfare, housing) and B (commerce, finance, administrative work, the armed forces), we find a comparatively much higher proportion of group A in the socialist countries. By converting data from Soviet and American publications (*Vestnik Moskovskogo Universiteta* 6/1964 and *Manpower Report of the President*, March 1965) to a comparable base, we find that group A predominates in the USSR and group B in the United States. In view of the lag in commerce and the usual services in the USSR, and the expansion of science and education induced in the USA by the start of the scientific and technological revolution, there are signs of an approximation between the two, but the disparity is still great.

closer examination they exhibit a lasting divergence in their nature and growth acceleration.

The trends indicate an undoubted tendency towards a jump in the proportion of the labour force engaged in *science, research and development;* until recently measured in fractions of one per cent, this figure now amounts to about two per cent in the technologically advanced countries and by the end of the century may rise to 10 per cent, and in the first half of the next century to 20 and more. This is certainly a significant proportion of all gainfully employed people, and remains so despite the retarding effect of automation applied to routine jobs in research operations. In any case, science, research and development constitute a specific sector in the formation of productive forces apart from immediate production; in its structure and dynamics it is clearly distinguished from the classical services.

A similar trend within the tertiary sector delimits the sphere of *human welfare*, in the sense of unfolding man's abilities and powers. It comprises first and foremost education and culture, to a large extent the health services, social welfare, etc. — an area that together with the cultural and technical growth of the working people generates productive forces, while over and above this role it possesses a social and human content that bridges the gulf between means and ends, work and leisure, which is typical of industrial activity, and is renewed in the commercial services, white-collar work and the like. From data available today we may justifiably assume that after some saturation of elementary services, the current of change in the national work structure will turn more decisively to the area of science, technology, production preparation, education, the arts, cultivation of human powers and care of man in the wider sense — that is, to areas that are distinguished by their special social and anthropological features both from the traditional "production sphere" and from the classical activities in "services"[1] and

---

[1] Attempts are being made today from various angles to convey the substance of these new trends in categories going beyond the traditional division into "production" and "nonproduction" spheres, which are clearly inadequate to the reality of the day. F. Machlup has set out to define the new division of sectors on the basis of "production of knowledge" (*The Production and Distribution of Knowledge in the United States*, Princeton 1962). H. Schelsky (*Die Sozialen Folgen der Automatisierung*, Düsseldorf — Köln 1957) suggests a quaternary sector comprising culture and recreation, that is, areas connected with non-working activity. What is lacking, however, is a theoretical basis for such changes in the classification of labour, and this can be provided only by a rational comprehension of the role played by these activities in the structure and dynamics of the productive forces.

might be termed *quaternary*. The scientific and technological revolution will probably shift a large part of human labour to this sphere, in the course of time raising its share in the work force up to the level of industry, and later to a higher level.

/New Features in the Division of Labour — Need for Universality/ 2.1.3

Taking civilization to be typified by the fact that the labour of all members of society constitutes a unity, in which each separate piece of work in some way represents an element in the total labour, we find that the industrial system extends this *division of labour* to its limits. The unity of labour in society is no longer just a primary matter of external exchange, the market, etc., but is moulded into the material form of production and the entire industrial machine system, which, independently of the individual workers or even of their aggregate, directs and combines all elements within the entire complex of labour as its appendages.

The industrial revolution reproduced the division of labour in society on a new basis. It dissected the originally intricate production operations that constituted life-long professions into the most abstract elements. Since the days of the French Encyclopaedists, production has been turning more and more into a process whereby many people do the same type of work[1] — namely, minding machines. For the vast majority, industrialization imposed a lifelong specialization in a new guise — in place of the former inclusive specializations, it made into a general rule "non-inclusive specialization", "specialization in abrogated speciality"[2], that is, levelling down the basic mass of labour in industry to the simplest, almost identical elementary operations. Finally, division of labour deprived the fundamental human activity of all the attributes belonging to specific human self-assertion; it transferred the creative elements to the machine; it divorced operative functions from management;[3] the separation of physical operations from the intellectual elements was

---

[1] *Encyclopédie* of Diderot and d'Alembert (1751—1772), under "Manufacture".
[2] K. Marx, Notebooks on Technology, quoted from an excerpt in *Bolshevik* 1-2/1932, p. 19.
[3] Max Weber already took labour to be "activity, subject to disposal" not a "disposing activity" (*Wirtschaft und Gesellschaft*, Tübingen 1921, p. 62).

converted into a principle of production;[1] the workers were estranged from the intellectual potentialities of the working process in the same measure that science entered production as an independent power; by depriving entire groups of people of the need and opportunity to think about their work, the power of thought was reserved for exclusive individuals. Artistic talent was cultivated at the price of suppressing aesthetic sense and understanding among all except the elect; professions turned into exclusive institutions and anyone outside the circle ranked as unprofessional. Alongside specialization and experts, industrialization engendered "craft-idiocy".[2] At the fringe of this industrial development it became clear that division of labour no longer implied simply an expedient distribution of activities, and had evolved into an overt power over people[3], embodied in the whole object-directed apparatus of civilization.

What is more, industrialization undermined the previous course followed by the division of labour in society. It wiped out the differences among the activities of a vast mass of people; for a worker performing simple operations in large-scale industry it is more or less immaterial what mechanism he tends and what kind of product he turns out.[4] He no longer has a trade, but simply a job.[5] We have here a renewal of

---

[1] F. W. Taylor was convinced that the price of a product would be the lower, the more the intellectual function could be divorced from the manual labour (*Shop Management*, New York—London 1921, p. 121.)

[2] K. Marx, *The Poverty of Philosophy*, New York 1963, p. 144.

[3] Observers of contemporary civilization have come to the conclusion that "division of labour has gone wild" far in excess of what might be rationally necessary (J. C. Worthy, "Organizational Structure and Employee Morale", *American Sociological Review*, April 1950).

[4] "Qualitative differentiation among workers, insofar as it is not natural... but expresses division of labour and its differentiation, is itself a product of history and for the great mass of labour is again cancelled, in that such labour is simple" (K. Marx, *Grundrisse*, p. 506). Durkheim's attempt to transfer division of labour to a natural, biological base (*De la Division du Travail Sociale*, Paris 1893) is simply an indication of the craft traditions prevailing in French thinking at the time (and later).

[5] While the development of tools extended the range of trades, with the application of the machine system they were fragmented into tens of thousands of specializations, among which, however, all substantial differences were erased. Consequently, catalogues of occupations that once ran to a few hundred titles spread in the days of mechanization to tens of thousands of entries (e.g. the *German Systematik der Berufe 1924*, the Soviet catalogue of work and the *Dictionary of Occupational Titles*, Washington 1939). In recent times, however, job surveys are increasingly pointing to the conclusion that a whole array of specializations are in fact identical. The latest Soviet census was able to summarize an enormous number of specializations in effect into

workers' mobility, the readiness to change jobs, the capacity to perform various functions; but in the immediate sense only in a negative guise — alienation of the worker from the content of his activity[1] in his indifference to his work. Nonetheless, herein lies the ground on which it is possible to organize and change the modes of cooperation among people in accordance with their own inner needs.

By its inner logic the scientific and technological revolution points to the possibility of superseding the old industrial division of labour and replacing it by a conscious organization of human cooperation,[2] where the conflict between operating and managing activity is done away with, the general and prime function of all is the application of science, the split between the intellectual forces of production and labour, between physical and mental work, disappears — where, in short, one and all can affirm themselves through creative activity, whatever form it may assume.

Analysis of changes in the structure and dynamics of the productive forces in some sectors enables us to demonstrate these trends today. The process of *specialization* in production, accompanied by displacing people from the immediate cycle of making things, diverges from specialization among the producers — at least as it has been understood hitherto. The progress of specialization in production is compatible with a growing *universality* among the producers and, indeed, demands it.[3]

---

300 general occupations (*Tekhnichesky progress i novye professii*, V. S. Belkin, Moscow 1962).

[1] In this respect the industrial division of labour, although it dissects man to the state of performing simple, detail operations, is nevertheless a step forward compared with the original poetic oneness of the craftsman, which made a single limited trade the condition and boundary of life.

[2] Both Marx (*Grundrisse*, p. 89) and Engels (*Anti-Dühring*, p. 289) already expressed this idea. Of course, it has nothing in common with the vulgar concept of liquidating the division of labour in the sense of abolishing professionalism and returning to do-all dillettantism.

[3] An interesting point here is the critical revision of Taylorism in the USA, which has revealed the ineffectiveness of extreme division of labour. The Edincott surveys conducted in the United States by IBM, and the findings of the British "National Institute of Industrial Psychology", have initiated a movement for job enlargement and functional integration of occupations. In a commentary on this movement, C. R. Walker writes: "Significantly that swing began not because of the preaching of humanitarians... but because practical production men found it often paid to enlarge the job and so release more responsibility, skill and judgement to the mass production worker" (*Modern Technology and Civilization*, New York 1962, pp. 76—77). Nevertheless, there is obviously a strong element of ideology involved.

"Inter-industrial occupations" such as maintenance and repair are coming to the fore. At a higher level of automation, conditions are ripe for aggregation of functions and for "job-enlargement"[1]. The capacity of specialization is not abrogated, but is given a universal base and dynamized.[2]

Even in the occupations remaining at the fringes of production (job-setting, maintenance) intellectual elements are coming to the fore; the work calls increasingly for engineering and technological skills. The number of brain workers is definitely surpassing that of manual workers.[3] The signs are that a point will come when the disparities between mental and manual work, on which the old division of labour was based, will be wiped out; in some cases, the distinction is already of very limited significance.

In the sphere of intellectual work (especially among engineers) a similar tendency can be observed, at least in some branches. The speed of technological advance and the growing opportunities for applying the most advanced principles of "self-movement" make it imperative to acquire a wide theoretical and methodological foundation (cybernetics, mathematics, physics, chemistry) extending to the social sciences (economics, sociology, psychology) as well. Even specialized scientists are evidently being impelled today — when routine work is taken over by technical procedures — towards greater universality, especially in areas

---

[1] Industrial psychologist W. Lejeune of Essen refers to these developments as implying degradation of the classical worker, the robot-type operative, the man of muscle unthinkingly following a one-track routine, in favour of a new-type "poacher", who combines several specializations, has no particular need to be industrious, but needs to "know the ropes", be able to make up his mind promptly and independently, and to cope with things without sticking to regulations (*Spiegel* 14/1964, pp. 39—42).

[2] "...the perfect adaptability of the individual human being to the changing demands of different kinds of labour," was seen by Marx as the condition for the emergence of "an individual with all-round development, one for whom various social functions are alternative modes of activity" (*Capital*, Vol. I, p. 527 — Dent ed.). But Marx did not suggest, as Fourier had, that people should change their work about every two hours (*Théorie de l'Unité Universelle, Oeuvres Complètes*, vol. II, pp. 15—16). He believed that so long as it would be impossible to eliminate much of the old type of work, alternation would pave the way to the complete transformation of human activity. Today, the scientific and technological revolution allows us to consider the prospect of a far more radical transformation of labour.

[3] According to M. Rutzick and S. Swerdloff *(The Occupational Structure of US Employment, 1940—1960)*, the number of intellectual workers already outnumbers that of manual workers; although the classification they use is debatable, the trend is hardly open to doubt.

of contact between branches.[1] Of course, "specialization" here has another social and anthropological meaning — it does not confine man within the bounds of his profession, as was the case with specialized machine work, but cultivates his special talents, enabling him to concentrate his creative abilities, and in this sense it is undoubtedly of lasting value.

While of the two components in which man's development is accomplished — namely, specialization and universality — the first was given priority during industrialization, everything now indicates that the second is coming to the fore in the course of the scientific and technological revolution, and is paving the way to a higher synthesis.[2]

To this we should add that, with the progress of civilization, some activities that are particularly open to the human factor (e.g. jobs involving inventiveness, teaching, public information, social participation, human welfare, cultural creativeness) are entering more and more into people's work; indeed, they are to some extent coming to be a condition for the real mastery of specialized problems. The combination of changes in work and expenditure of the growing amount of leisure undoubtedly offers big opportunities for manifold cultivation of talents. The mounting power of human achievement is rolling back the frontiers of a rigid division of labour and of occupations to which man has hitherto been bound for life. But these restrictions can be abolished only when all distribution of labour in society is directed to the purpose of *man's development*.[3] Indeed, it seems that complete mobility of human activity in society will be essential in the civilization of the future in view of the need of seeking all possible ways of harnessing and developing the creative abilities of every individual. The alternative of retaining the old division of labour with its contrast between the simple operative work performed by the mass of the population and the outstanding performance of a few scientists is, indeed, assuming quite a tragic

---

[1] So alongside the growth of specialization the idea is emerging that — at least in a sense — the era of narrow specialists is ending (cf. R. Goetz, V. Girey, *Aspects économique et sociaux du progress technique et de la recherche scientifique*, Paris 1964, VIII).

[2] As K. Varshavsky puts it in *Sotsialistichesky Trud* 8/1962, "With two opposed tendencies existing in work — specialization and integration — the second holds the lead."

[3] These were the lines along which Marx and Engels envisaged the existing division of labour being overcome, because the universal human "profession" is all-round development, realizing one's creative gifts (*The German Ideology*, MEGA Abt. 1, Band 5, Moscow—Leningrad 1933, p. 270).

quality in the circumstances of our day. Evidently a generation of people with all-round training and a capacity for consistent development will be needed to cope with the problems posed by the scientific and technological revolution.

/ *Changes in the Pattern of Skills* /   2.1.4

The industrial revolution *debased* the traditional craft work, making simple labour the pivot of industry,[1] it founded its own division of labour on unskilled operations,[2] replacing dexterity by the capacity to perform the monotonous, simple routine of operative work,[3] requiring a minimum of training. While industrial mechanization did at least gradually enhance the role of experts outside immediate production, the same logic of events reduced the share of the skilled worker at the factory bench (impact of Taylorism) — in the USA, from 32.3 per cent in 1920 to 30.1 per cent in 1940 (see Table 2-8). In the most advanced industrial country, the core of the work force was increasingly composed of semi-skilled operatives[4] — to a much greater degree than in the European countries. This phenomenon matched the spreading mechanization,[5] and it has to be remembered that industrial mechanization will always make for such consequences.[6]

By degrees, however, in the most advanced works, sectors and finally countries, this trend from skills has been halted. In 1940—1964 the curve for skilled workers and foremen in the United States took an

[1] K. Marx, *The Poverty of Philosophy*, New York 1963, p. 53.
[2] K. Marx, Capital, Vol. I, p. 523 (Dent ed.).
[3] "Thus the workman and the artist tend to view technology as the destruction of an artistic and humanly wholesome way of life" (W. Ogburn in *Technology and Social Change*, New York 1957, p. 4).
[4] For instance, in the twenties, 85 per cent of Ford workers were not skilled but had simply undergone training, not longer than one month, and half of them just for one day. (Cf. J. Hirsch, *Das Amerikanische Wirtschaftswunder*, Berlin 1926.)
[5] In Great Britain, for instance, where the decade 1951—1961 was still dominated by the advance of mechanization, the proportion of skilled workers dropped from 54.6 to 50.1 per cent (see Table 2—8).
[6] In the USSR mechanization did not engender such an open trend away from skills, because industrialization was compressed into a minimal space of time and extensive extra-economic measures were introduced by the socialist state to encourage the spread of skills. Nevertheless, in the thirties — and up to 1950 — the semi-skilled category showed the largest growth (cf. A. M. Omarov, *Tekhnika i chelovek, sotsialno-ekonomicheskye problemy tekhnicheskogo progressa*, Moscow 1965).

upward turn — from 30.1 to 36 per cent,[1] and by all appearances the new trend is gaining the upper hand as the scientific and technological revolution gets under way.[2]

The most striking effect is, however, induced by the growing numbers of *technical and professional personnel* in all sectors of the economy outside immediate production. In the fifties and sixties this group outpaced all others in the United States in its rate of growth, which was twice that for clerical workers (the category that held the lead in the forties) and seven times more than the overall rate for workers.[3] Moreover, the most skilled sections showed the biggest advance.

There are big changes in the quality of skills. Craft and manual skill born of habit, tradition and experience is certainly still on the wane, but as the trained operatives who held the field at the classical conveyor belt disappear from automated works and from modern plants altogether, skill founded on *science and technology* is acquiring growing weight. True, a section of the job-setters still need no more than ordinary training, but this is by no means general; at a progressive automatic line, for instance, a setter has to command the knowledge of a former lathe worker and electrician, master the principles of heating and ventilation and be capable of dealing with common faults. Maintenance and repair men in the most modern plants are increasingly required to possess elements of knowledge previously exclusive to technically trained personnel. With the progress in technology and transition to the more sophisticated types of automation, technicians need the theoretical training of engineers — especially in branches such as mathematics, electronics, etc.[4] Engineers, in their turn, are often faced with research jobs for which they have to study all the time. Leaving aside various reverse processes and intermediary stages, we can see here an overall growth in *educational requirements* as one of the foremost features of the scientific and technological revolution.

Using analyses of the changing pattern of skills according to the

---

[1] *Economic Report of the President*, 1965; in Britain, the 1961—1971 decade is expected to show a jump in skilled manpower from 50.1 to 60.4 per cent.

[2] It is found that "more or less complete automation appears to increase the skill level..." (E.R.F.W. Crossman, *European Experience with the Changing Nature of Jobs Due to Automation*, ed. Univ. of California 1964). But, as Lilley has pointed out, this only comes with the highest stage of automation and it is the feature that clearly distinguishes the actual process of the scientific and technological revolution (*Automation and Social Progress*, London 1957).

[3] *Manpower Report of the President*, March 1965.

[4] Cf. E. Sachse, *Technische Revolution + Qualifikation*, Berlin 1965.

structure of the productive forces, we can work out *"personnel models"*[1] of skills for the key production principles (see Table 2-9); they throw a revealing light on the specific implications of the scientific and technological revolution. The following table shows the pattern of skills required in different types of production, in percentages.

Types of production	Un-skilled	Semi-skilled	Skilled	Medium-grade professional education	University or college education
a) Traditional industrial principle					
series of universal machines	15	20	60	4	1
mechanical line	—	57	33	8	2
b) Automatic principle					
partial automation	—	38—3	45—55	13—30	4—12
full automation	—	—	40—0	40—60	20—40

This suggests that demands on educational attainment may be expected to soar above the present level, which is still largely conditioned by the industrial system. The magnitude of the change is indicated by the finding that the demands on skills in fully automated works are at least the same or even higher than the level of education found hitherto in the entire stratum of intelligentsia (and also of the average technological-engineering personnel today). Overall introduction of automation would, in that case, lead to closing the gap in educational attainment between workers and intellectuals. And since the level of skill has a substantial influence on the creative content of activity, on man's self-realization and self-creation[2], we are faced with an entirely new situation from the cultural and human standpoint.

Projecting the above theoretic models on to the Czechoslovak economy,

[1] The model we have employed was elaborated by J. Auerhan on the basis of his own research and of critical examination of American, Soviet, French, German and Czechoslovak work (cf. *Technika, kvalifikace, vzdělání* (Technology, Skill, Education), Prague 1965.

[2] According to C. W. Mills (*White Collar, The American Middle Classes*, New York 1951), only 41 per cent of industrial workers and 42 per cent of office workers consider their jobs as sources of self-realization, while the corresponding figure for highly skilled personnel is 85 per cent.

structured in the proportions envisaged in the forecasts, we are presented with a remarkable picture of skill requirements induced by the initial phase of the scientific and technological revolution. Within two decades it will be necessary to achieve a substantial rise in the skills of the basic work force,[1] to supply adequate numbers of medium-grade specialized and technical personnel (with the requisite secondary education)[2] and strongly reinforce the proportion of trained engineers within the total industrial labour force.[3]

Naturally, the advance in skills has not, even in the most advanced countries, followed a linear course and will not do so for a long time yet; in the first stages of the scientific and technological revolution, so long as the emphasis is still on completing mechanization accompanied by more or less partial automation, the skill level may even sink. A similar effect is sometimes evoked when full automation in industrial sectors shifts manpower to the service sphere — at least as long as the technical equipment of services, and therefore the skills required, are lower than in industry. But since within the tertiary sector we find the most rapid growth in the specific areas linked with science, education, human welfare, where exceptional demands are made on education,[4] these regressions are only temporary.

True, to the empirical observer who fails to link the trends of skills with the corresponding changes in the structure and dynamics of the productive forces and regards them purely as coherent entities, their overall aspect must appear confused and their movements unpredictable.[5] For a rational view of the present situation it is necessary to understand that in the end two opposing trends, matching two

[1] In contrast to today's minority, 60—70 per cent of workers should be equipped with modern skills by 1980.

[2] The proportion of technicians should rise from the present 13 per cent to 25 per cent, while instead of 30 percent as now, almost all should have the requisite secondary and medium-grade professional training.

[3] Hitherto the proportion of engineers in the Czechoslovak industrial labour force has been 1.2 per cent — that is, much less than in the United States and the Soviet Union; by 1980, it should rise to 6—6.5 per cent.

[4] In "Automation, Jobs and Manpower", *Nation's Manpower Revolution 1963— 1964*, C. C. Killingsworth points out that the most rapidly growing parts of the service sector are the health services and education, both claiming a large majority of highly skilled people (p. 1475).

[5] Such extensive investigations as that, for example, by P. Naville (*Essai sur la Qualification du travail*, Paris 1956 and *L'automation et le travail humain. Rapport d'enquête* (France 1957—1959), Paris 1961), have failed to demonstrate any substantial change in work. However, the valuable data collected by Naville reveal a great deal

distinct civilization processes, are merging, clashing and possibly coming to terms — and this view is gained by using the theoretic models of skills. They also throw light on the outlook shaped by the growing ascendency of elements provided by the scientific and technological revolution, which will push the curve of skills more and more in an upward direction.

*

In the realm of the key issues posed by human activity, various theoretical concepts of modern civilization take the field and the alternative paths of development diverge. The ideas advanced by Marx and Engels on this subject could long be regarded as merely extreme formulations of much less dramatic tendencies.[1] Nevertheless, observing the changes presently taking place in the nature, structure, division and skill of human activity, leaving aside transitory, superficial influences and concentrating on the outlook for some decades, we are justified in assuming that — given a favourable social background — there will be an upturn in the nature of work, its distribution and implications, its technological and cultural level, in short its totality, and that this will involve almost the entire basic mass of the population. The consequences of a victory for creative work on the whole front are still incalculable.[2]

as soon as they are linked with theory capable of discerning the outcome of deeper processes within this empirical picture. The fact that in the fifties the total of skilled workers in French manufacturing industries showed no change or rather tended to drop, points to the dominance of mechanization processes in this area; on the other hand, it is significant that in the progressive branches (e.g. chemicals) there was a strong advance in the proportion of skilled personnel. According to similar data given by S. Buckingham in *New Views on Automation*, New York 1960, reports from firms showed that installing new equipment reduced the need for skills in 43 percent and increased it in 27 percent of cases; this gives us a pointer on the nature of the technical innovations (for the most part they probably involved mechanization); however, the result presumably also implies the simple fact that modern technology gradually displaces all labour from the immediate sphere of production — including the skilled workers.

[1] H. Klages and other opponents of Marxism describe Marx's humanism, founded on the concept of transforming human labour, as "a code of technico-scientist eschatology" (*Technischer Humanismus*, Stuttgart 1964, p. 108). But they cannot deny that today they are quite definitely confronted, entirely in Marx's terms, with the fact of a "permanent technico-scientific revolution advancing on all sides" (ibid. p. 131) which is impinging from all quarters on the existing modes of human activity.

[2] J. Diebold puts at the fringe of these changes a question that is significant from his standpoint: "Are we capable of developing culture that does not depend upon work to give meaning to our lives?" (*Automation. The Advent of the Automatic Factory*, Princeton 1952, p. 165).

Probably it will be only at that point that man will be truly aware of his own activity as an immanent value in his life, irrespective of external purposes. Yet even at an earlier stage he will experience the value of the human powers and abilities achieved. The abbreviated and condensed cycle of civilization will evidently react with the question: How is man prepared to meet these opportunities?

/The Scientific and Technological Revolution and Education/ 2.2

The paradox we are facing is this — the traditional system of education takes 12—20 years to prepare people for life, that being the usual time span accepted today, and this preparation has actually to equip people for life fifty or more years ahead, because their active lives will last that long; but the methods we use correspond to today's and not to the future stage of development. We have no choice — either we have to comprehend the perspectives to that extent and direct training for life accordingly,[1] or we assume implicitly that life in the future will be much the same as it is today, or perhaps that changes in human abilities will play no substantial part in future civilization processes — in other words, we project the present aspect of the world and its industrialization processes into future decades, abstracting from the nascent scientific and technological revolution and the social transformations of our day. And to the extent that this picture is divorced from reality, we shall be confining society within its present dimensions and making education a drag on the future progress of civilization.

/Educational Level: Onset of a Cultural Revolution/ 2.2.1

The type of work and the way of life prevailing in a society make their imprint through various media on the level of education, and vice versa. The *educational groundwork* enforced by the industrial revolution as appropriate to its needs — and to which it confined the bulk of the

---

[1] "The estimation of long-range human resource requirements is a difficult but absolutely indispensable step in planning for social and economic development" (T. Harbison, C. A. Mayers, *Education, Manpower and Economic Growth. Strategies of Human Resources Development*, New York—Toronto—London 1964, p. 208).

population[1] — was general versing in the three R's (basic-type school) and elementary knowledge for manual skills (middle-type school), in short, mainly attainments making simple labour power suitable for manipulation in the factory.[2]

For almost half a century — from the time when compulsory school attendance had become general in the industrial countries — the level of education[3] and its predominant type showed little substantial change. From the thirties, and still more the fifties, however, the educational systems of all industrially mature countries have been on the move. The spread of high schools, vocational schools, universities and colleges, and of out-of-school education, heralds a break that may be denoted as the onset of a new *cultural revolution*. Linked with technological advance and the onset of changes in the general conditions of human life, this revolution can be compared in scope to the introduction of universal elementary education, but its implications go much further, because the course of events today is giving education a new status in the life of man and society. The transformations are assuming the nature of a cultural revolution in its own right, with no direct dependence on advances in technology.

The past twenty to thirty years have seen an upswing in secondary education with a vocational bent, or with an emphasis on general education. The high school, or secondary school that not so long ago was still for the élite, is now generally accessible. In some countries (USA, Japan, Holland, Sweden, Finland), the bulk of young people now attend high school — 60—90 per cent of the age-group (see Table 2-10).[4] In the USSR and Great Britain, secondary education for all is planned for the

---

[1] Up to the nineteen-thirties, a majority in the USA, and in the industrial countries of Europe 80—90 per cent of the active population, had no more than basic education usually lasting 8—9 years. P. F. Drucker (*The Landmarks of Tomorrow*, London 1959, pp. 146—147) therefore distinguishes between "a literate society" and an "educated society".

[2] "...the most essential parts of education... to read, write, and account, can be acquired at so early a period of life that the greater part even of those who are to be bred to the lowest occupations have time to acquire them before they can be employed in those occupations" (Adam Smith, *An Inquiry into the Nature and Causes of the Wealth of Nations*, Chicago—London—Toronto—Geneva 1952, p. 342).

[3] From the eighties of last century (when compulsory school attendance had been enacted in most countries) to the thirties of the present century, the proportion of students in the population was more or less stable; recent decades have seen an upswing. In the USA, of course, the explosion started earlier (cf. J. Auerhan, *Technika, kvalifikace, vzdělání*, pp. 265—266).

[4] *L'éducation dans le monde, III. L'enseignment du second degré*, Paris 1963.

seventies, in France for the eighties. The probability is that many industrially advanced countries will reach this stage in the course of ten to twenty years. On this assumption, the close of the century will see an advance in the share of people with full secondary education from 15—20 per cent in developed European countries, and from 40 per cent in the USA in the early sixties (see Table 2-11)[1] to a decided majority of the economically active population.[2]

The past ten to twenty years have witnessed a notable expansion of the *university* population. Around 1963, university and college intake for full-time study (see Table 2-10) was 34 per cent of each annual age group in the USA, 15—20 per cent in the USSR, Canada and Australia, 12—14 per cent in France and in leading European countries some 10 per cent.[3] Compared to the average for Europe in the thirties, four to five times more young people graduate from universities and colleges today and the trend is continuing with unexpected rapidity. The Soviet Union plans to increase university admissions to 35 per cent of the age group by 1980.[4] In the USA, the 1960—1970 decade will double the numbers of university and college students, causing a further shift beyond 40 per cent of the age group.[5] In Britain, student numbers will be multiplied 3.5 times over 15 years.[6] At this rate we may expect that at the turn of the century the most advanced countries will reach a new frontier and cross it — half their young generation will have higher education — so long as these trends are not blocked by barriers set by society.

So far as we can judge from the inner logic of the scientific and

---

[1] *Deployment and Utilization of Highly Qualified Personnel*, Paris 1966.

[2] According to C. C. Killingsworth's data (see *Nation's Manpower Revolution, 1963—1964*), between 1950—1963 increased demand for manpower in the US was confined to people with over twelve years' education.

[3] World Survey of Education, IV Higher Education, 1966; West Germany shows a marked lag in this respect.

[4] *Programme of the Communist Party of the Soviet Union*, 1961. The sharp advance of Soviet higher education has aroused lively interest and had a considerable effect on educational programmes in other countries. As C. P. Snow put it, "...the Russians have judged the situation sensibly. They have a deeper insight into the scientific revolution than we have..." (*The Two Cultures and a Second Look*, New York—Toronto 1963, p. 39).

[5] See *Ressources en personnel scientifique et technique dans les pays de l'OCDE*, Paris 1961; *Digest of Educational Statistics*, Washington 1965. American data include about ten percent of junior college students, which we have deducted in our figures — but this does not change the picture substantially.

[6] *Higher Education Report* (Lord Robbins), London 1963.

technological revolution, as revealed by analyses of the empirical tendencies and synthesis of the model elements detected (changes in the relative position of physical and mental work, spread of creative activity, etc.), the future need will be for an educational base involving:

a) *full secondary education* for all — "polytechnical", combined with a balanced education in the humanities, and founded on a scientific approach;[1]

b) wide-scale advance in elementary *scientific, university-level* training — of such scope that no opportunity for cultivating the questing spirit will be lost and such potentialities will be constrained by nothing else than human abilities themselves.

Her economic structure has traditionally ranked Czechoslovakia among the countries requiring large numbers of educated personnel. It was no coincidence that in the twenties and thirties she recorded a higher ratio of university students to the population than all other European countries (except Austria, and Switzerland)[2], including France, Sweden, Germany (cf. Table 2-10). During the sixties, Czechoslovakia can record a gradual compensation for the postwar shortage of educated personnel.[3] As things stand today, 36 per cent of general-school-leavers pass on to secondary education,[4] a figure still below the level of many

---

[1] The idea of "polytechnical education" derives from Marx's broad concept of technology, which "reveals man's dealings with nature, discloses the direct productive activities of his life, thus throwing light upon social relations and the resultant mental conceptions." (*Capital*, I. p. 393 n.). Projects of polytechnical education in the Soviet Union and the socialist countries put the school on a scientific basis of production linked with a planned approach to activity, practical training and a broadly-conceived liberal education. Lenin was among the first to point out that there should be no question of "craftmongering" (*On Polytechnical Education*, 1920). Under the pressure of industrialization, the idea of polytechnical education was unfortunately quite often narrowed down to manual training in production.

[2] According to figures collected by C. Clark (*The Conditions of Economic Progress*, London 1951, pp. 480—481), in 1925 university students per thousand of the population numbered 2.04 in Czechoslovakia, 1.45 in Sweden, 1.44 in France, 1.42 in Germany; the figures for 1930 were Czechoslovakia 2.33, Germany 1.98, France 1.88, Sweden 1.84.

[3] The shortage was caused by the war-time gap, when the Germans closed down the Czech universities, and by the slow progress made in education during the fifties, when everything was concentrated on industrialization.

[4] Cf. J. Havelka, "Vědeckotechnická revoluce a změny ve struktuře práce, v kvalifikaci pracujících a v úrovni vzdělání" (The Scientific and Technological Revolution and Changes in the Structure of Work, in Skills and the Level of Education), *Sociologický časopis* 2/1966.

advanced countries. The labour force now includes 13 per cent of people with secondary-school training and by 1970 the figure should be 16 per cent; this in general meets the needs of the economy at the present stage. Some ten per cent of the relevant age group enter the universities, which is the average figure for advanced countries. University-trained personnel number three per cent of the labour force and by 1970 will reach 4.4 per cent; here Czechoslovakia is behind the USSR and Britain (where 4.5 per cent have university training), and, of course, far behind the US figure of 9 per cent of the active population; she is at about the same level as France and West Germany. Demand for university graduates is now met to about 90 per cent (see Table 1-11).

Naturally, we cannot confine ourselves to the situation as it has evolved so far. If we really envisage radical changes in the structure of work being induced by the scientific and technological revolution, we are faced with a serious choice of alternatives in the field of educational advance:

a) The next five to ten years may be expected to reveal an urgent need for improvements in general education. Today, we are already aware of serious gaps in the teaching of economics; neither the methodological grounding nor liberal education provided can satisfy modern requirements. Unquestionably, secondary education for all will become indispensable within the next fifteen to twenty years.

b) The outlook for university education presents a wide range of possibilities. Should present trends continue, university graduates will number 6.4 per cent of the active population by 1980. But we have to bear in mind the prospect that the structure of the economy may have undergone profound change by that time. Czechoslovakia, as a country with fairly modest resources of raw materials and manpower, may be inclining more decidedly to the sophisticated work that conforms to her traditions and this would mean that she had found her appropriate approach to the scientific and technological revolution. In this event, the country would need between 1980—1985 to be able to rely on nine or more per cent of her active population being university trained — this would involve an intake of at least 20 per cent of the relevant age group, and the existing capacity of the universities would prove inadequate.

Every country reaching industrial maturity has to expect that the standing of its educational system in the national economy will acquire new and unaccustomed implications, which inevitably involves reconsidering some of the accepted proportions of resource allocation. Compared with the start of the century, the advanced countries now devote about threefold shares of their national incomes to education;[1] in absolute terms, expenditure grew, between 1950 and 1960, 5.8 times in France, 3.4 times in West Germany and Sweden, 2.8 times in the USA.[2] While in the days of industrial development it seemed irrelevant as far as the economy was concerned to extend general education beyond the level of literacy, this distinction is seen to be out of place today:[3] there is talk of "industrial education" as a powerful "growth sector" at an exceptional level of effectiveness and steadily growing,[4] with an impact on economic growth surpassing that of the classical factors,[5] and therefore calling for priority attention.[6] But the matter goes deeper; in face of the new constellations of modern society — many only belatedly discovered — and of the enormous material power now within man's grasp, the level of education presently obtaining in many of the

[1] In terms of comparable national income, education received at the start of the sixties 9 per cent in the US, 7—8 per cent in the USSR and GDR, 6 per cent in Britain, around 5 per cent in Czechoslovakia, Poland and West Germany. The share of total investment expenditure going to education was 7 per cent in the USSR, 6 per cent in the USA, 5 per cent in Poland, 4 per cent in Sweden and Czechoslovakia (cf. H. Maier, H. Schilar, *Bildung als Ziel und Faktor des ökonomischen Wachstums in der sozialistischen Produktionsweise*, Berlin 1967; J. Havelka, *Vývoj a ekonomické postavení nevýrobní sféry* (Development and Economic Status of the Nonproductive Sphere, Prague 1966). These figures show quite clearly that — in relation to their economic level — the socialist countries devote much greater resources to education, in fact about as much as non-socialist countries with per capita national incomes 50—100 per cent larger. Nevertheless, at this level even the substantial outlay on education in Czechoslovakia appears rather restricted, especially in respect of investment, the prime cause being deficiencies to be made up in the equipment of the universities.

[2] According to data from F. Ebbing, quoted by O. Pavlík in "Škola ve svetle súčasnej vedeckej a technickej revolúcie" (School in the Light of the Current Scientific and Technological Revolution), *Pedagogika* 2/1967.

[3] H. Philp, *Education in the Metropolis*, 1967, p. 10.

[4] E. Renshaw puts the standard for educational effectiveness at 8 per cent ("Estimating the Return of Education", *Review of Economics and Statistics* 3/1960; G. Becker suggests 8—9 per cent "Underinvestment in College Education?", *American Economic Review* 2/1960, and T. Schultz 10 per cent ("Capital Formation by Education", *Journal of Political Economy* 4/1960). All three authors agree that education is becoming increasingly effective.

[5] Soviet and American economists have arrived at very similar results on this point — cf. S. Strumilin, "Effektivnost obrazovaniya v SSSR", *Ekonomicheskaya gazeta* 14/1962; M. J. Bowman, "Schultz, Denison and the Contribution of 'Eds' to National Income Growth", *Journal of Political Economy* 5/1964.

[6] Cf. *Conditions Favourable to Faster Growth*, London 1963; *Policy Conference on Economic Growth and Investment in Education*, 1—5, Paris 1962.

most advanced industrial countries of the West is seen to be inadequate;[1] potential human resources are not being used. To accomplish the approaching cultural revolution and to release all its latent forces — therein lies the great opportunity for socialism, and this opportunity has to be seized if the initiative is to be taken in advancing the scientific and technological revolution.

/ Adapting the Educational System /　　2.2.2

Although the implications of changes in the level of schooling are undoubtedly far-reaching, the scientific and technological revolution makes perhaps still greater claims on the entire concept and system of education — claims posed by the new function of education in the life of the individual and society.

Under the industrial system shaped by the capitalist era, mass schooling was chiefly concerned with producing ready-made labour powre. The educational system was therefore constructed as a closed system of limited content (the three R's), extended only for a restricted social stratum through the different types and grades of exclusive schools. But in this sphere, too, the impact of science and technology is evident. Pressure towards *expanding* and *democratizing* secondary education is growing. In recent years there has been undisguised talent hunting in some sectors, employing modern methods of pedagogy and psychology. The restricted selection imposed by class barriers is more and more felt as a drag and the response is seen in a measure of "democratized selection" to expand the "pool of capacity" required for competitive purposes.[2] Here socialism has a big advantage with its genuinely democratic selection, providing an almost inexhaustible source of abilities.[3] Nevertheless, the socialist countries face a problem of talent selection, though of a different kind. Their educational systems sometimes tend to train average ability, to lead a hundred per cent of their pupils to a successful

---

[1] J. Vaizey notes in *The Residual Factor and Economic Growth* (Paris 1964) that there is a disbalance between "physical" and "human" capital in the West.

[2] Cf. P. W. Musgrave, *The Sociology of Education*, London 1965.

[3] In West Germany, France and Czechoslovakia, manual workers constitute the majority of the gainfully employed. But while in West Germany only 7—8 percent of university and college students come from worker families and in France a bare 13 percent (cf. J.-J. Servan-Schreiber, *Le défi Américain*, Paris 1967, p. 87), the figure for Czechoslovakia is 40 percent.

conclusion. And this course, too, seriously conflicts with a true economy of human powers at a stage when the prime need is for quality, building up a potential — in fact, for quite informal searching for, refining and *unfolding of talents and abilities* at all levels.[1] In this respect a universal and modern educational system acquires an independent role of its own, with no direct subordination to any claims of production. The issue is no longer what training for life can be instilled into people's heads or hands, but on the contrary what can be made of each individual, what unfettered creative forces of civilization can be cultivated in him during his lifetime. One can hardly imagine such an undertaking being possible without a complete change in the concept of the *pedagogical* process[2] and without equipping education with a solid sociological, anthropological, and especially psychological apparatus — either through separate advisory services, or through direct participation by the specialists in educational institutions.

As the scientific and technological revolution progresses, education takes on a *dynamic* quality, through its purpose, content, methods and finally its institutions. In the world of today the conditions are disappearing under which education could confine its aims to once-for-all preparation of labour power. The pupil of our times will have to spend his life adapting to changes in human knowledge, in work, the environment and the entire content of living.[3] The wall separating education from life is crumbling[4], "learning for life" is giving way to *lifelong education.*[5] In contrast to the traditional operative, the modern techni-

---

[1] When talent-seeking is the aim, student "drop-outs" are to be expected; the problem is rather one of using and regularizing incomplete education.

[2] O. Pavlík, *Automatizácia a škola* (Automation and the School), Bratislava 1959, p. 59.

[3] "When once we have admitted that change has become a lasting phenomenon and that it is continually accelerating... it is no longer possible that even the most complete education provided in childhood, in adolescence, or in the first years of adult life can prepare young people to solve all the problems which probably await them when they grow up..." (A. S. M. Hely, "*Nouvelles tendences dans l'education des adultes,*" UNESCO 1963, p. 10).

[4] Both Robert Owen and Marx stressed the idea of combining work and education — "not only as a means for increasing social production, but as the only way of producing fully developed human beings" (*Capital* I, p. 522), which itself engenders a new productive force in society.

[5] P. Lengrad, "Adult Education", *Fundamental and Adult Education* 3/1958, pp. 91—92. This idea has appeared in one form or another in earlier pedagogical theories, and in its developed form in the British "Final Report of the Adult Education Committee of the Ministry of Reconstruction" of 1919, in Soviet pedagogical projects of the

cian needs to keep up with new developments all the time; in this age of explosive advance and rapid obsolescence in knowledge, he is compelled to *learn throughout his life*. By present estimates, without supplementary training, a technician loses touch with modern developments in his subject within ten years. After twenty-five years, half of what a scientist has learned as a student is outdated. The traditional education fails even more disastrously when it comes up against deeper areas of emergent scientific synthesis, or entirely new concepts that for many people meeting with them in adult life remain completely incomprehensible. And since such developments are increasingly focussed on the very fundamentals of human life, and of social evolution, the onset of the scientific and technological revolution is manifested as a profound *crisis in concepts and systems of education* throughout the industrially developed world.[1]

The prospect offered by the inner logic of the scientific and technological revolution tends towards abolishing the present division of life into a phase of acquiring knowledge and a subsequent lifelong stage of giving it out. Furthermore, education is ceasing to be a mere preparation, but is becoming an integral and substantial part of life. In many branches today it is already a permanent component of "working time"; for the future it may be expected to occupy a growing share alongside the actual "productive time".

However, so long as lasting education is not an integral part of human work, the system of school education will have to be supplemented by a stage of further or post-graduate education, enterprise schools, "people's universities" and "academies", and use of the mass media — so that the vast diversity of educational media will gradually constitute a system of *adult education*.[2]

Assuming the above development, the very purpose of schooling will

---

early twenties (J. N. Medynsky, *Entsyklopediya vneshkolnogo obrazovaniya*, Moscow 1923) and in Thorndike's *Adult Learning*, New York 1928. It was implicit in Comenius's idea of "all life as a school" (*Všévýchova* (Universal Education) Prague 1948, p. 214). But for centuries the idea was obscured by the empirical finding of the industrial age that under the given circumstances the only group generally susceptible to education were the young. Only when the dynamism of change had deprived once-for-all schooling of its basis could lifelong education become a practical proposition, and this is brought about by the onset of the scientific and technological revolution.

[1] Th. Litt describes the situation as a "victorious advance of things" and "impotence of education" (*Technisches Denken und menschliche Bildung*, Heidelberg 1957, p. 12).

[2] *L'éducation des adultes, tendences et réalisations actuelles*, Paris 1950; again in *Conference mondiale sur l'éducation des adultes*, Paris 1960.

change, because it will ultimately have to conform to the concept of lifelong expansion of human powers. Here we are faced with a new and as yet unresolved question as to the *optimal* regime for this type of education; the components will have to be distributed through the levels and types of school and out-of-school education in a manner best suited to the nature of contemporary knowledge of the world and how it can be transformed, while giving due weight to man's natural abilities at various stages of his life, in other words, starting from the requirements of man's self-realization, with their specific rhythm and claims on education.[1]

None of the traditional *concepts of education* has been capable of fulfilling these conditions. Anyone who pauses to consider the complex and mutable position of modern man in the world of his creations, with its shifting social relationships, will realise that it is no longer possible to make do with mere literacy supplemented by manual, craft training (the old type apprenticeship) providing no broad insight into the consistency of our civilization. Even supposing that such training could suffice for a lifetime of working activity — that is, as labour power — which in itself is rather improbable today, it would certainly not be enough for man as a participant in humanly ever more demanding transformations of society and civilization. A society that stayed at this level in the future would inevitably pay the price in stagnation and internal conflicts[2] evoked by its inability to achieve mutual understanding and cooperation among its people.

Nor, in shaping a system of lifelong learning, shall we get far with the classical concept of secondary education[3] which has its roots in the

---

[1] Man's perceptivity is related to the nature of his life. B. Suchodolski, for example, points out that understanding of the social sciences is on the one hand a necessary foundation for general education, on the other, however, it requires the experience of an adult ("Problemi upowszechnienia nauki w epoce wspołczesnej," *Pedagogika dorostlych*, ed. K. Wojciechowki, Warsaw 1962, pp. 276—282).

[2] Adam Smith was not alone in regarding universal elementary education (intended to prevent people from "judging rashly or capriciously" without elementary knowledge) as a condition for achieving a lasting constitution, civil rights, democracy of the bourgeois type (*The Wealth of Nations*, p. 343). By analogy we may say that a permanent system of lifelong education with appropriate universal schooling (probably at high-school level) is a condition and guarantee of lasting development for a socialist society.

[3] A critique of past concepts of education has been made by H. Sychrová in *Dlouhodobé změny vzdělávacích systémů a problémy naší vzdělávací soustavy* (Long-term Changes in Educational Systems and Problems of Our Educational System), Study materials no. 2/1967.

ancient world, draws on the Renaissance concept of "the humanities" and found its shape in the grammar-school type of school. The weaknesses of the concept were already revealed by the industrial age. It was incapable of embracing the modern natural sciences, its profound sense of order was predominantly contemplative and therefore readily deteriorated into formalism, and its laudable endeavour to cultivate the subject culminated in the shallow demand for circumscribed encyclopaedic knowledge.

We can still observe today how as a reaction to the limitations of this classical concept emphasis is placed on "modern", practical, specialized teaching[1], primarily based on the concept of "objective natural science" that in the spirit of Descartes and positivism eliminated man's subjectivity, or with Bacon, and more precisely pragmatism, reduced it to the external relation of expediency. But the specialist with a narrow skill now finds great difficulty in adapting to the rapid succession of technological change if he lacks a background of systematic broad training, new methods and overall concepts are hard for him to grasp and altogether he is handicapped for life in modern civilization.[2] The "utility education" proposition actually repeats the illusions of the industrial system whose unfettered and spontaneous course is in fact a sum of well-considered and elaborated special acts; the educational concept therefore oscillates fruitlessly between the modern and grammar-school types, between external utility and inner order, spreading wider and wider the power of things and the impotence of education.

The world confronting us today is largely one of man's own creation[3] that has assumed fateful dimensions for man himself. Purposeful mastery of his external creations is interwoven and conditioned by the unfolding of his inner potentialities. An education capable in these circum-

---

[1] In Czechoslovakia — as in some other European countries — this even results in an understimation of general education as being "without practical value" (cf. J. Kotásek, V. Pařízek, "Vědeckotechnická revoluce a vzdělávací systém" (The Scientific and Technological Revolution and the Educational System), *Sociologický časopis* 2/1966). Compared with the secondary vocational schools, schools giving general education are rather limited and their shortcomings are an obstacle to discovering talented students for higher education.

[2] In this connection J. B. Conant's critique of pragmatic concepts of education is instructive (*The American High School Today*, 1960).

[3] Indeed, Comenius (*De rerum humanarum emendatione consultatio catholica*, Prague 1966) already advanced as an argument in favour of universal education the fact that man had filled the world with his artificial inventions, thereby becoming a "competitor of the Creator" — of course, at that time only "in small measure".

stances of fortifying creative activity would have to provide a far more effective methodological equipment than that of narrow specialization, and a far deeper synthesis than that allowed by an encyclopaedic compilation of knowledge — it would have to give a broad scientific insight into the method of changing the world today and of man's self-creation, and come to terms with the present relationship between man and the technological world.[1]

Education cannot keep pace with all new discoveries and theories in detail, but it can fulfil its mission in depth, by enabling people to penetrate the fundamental dialectics of man and his handiwork in the civilization of the times. The best system for this purpose would seem to be one providing a *broad, general* education — probably in the form of universal high school attendance — which would draw people by degrees into the most various areas of human activity. With potential talent being awakened and stimulated on all sides, there would be no danger of erecting a barrier of narrow specialization that would condemn gifts discovered in later life to frustration, and conditions would exist for unfolding all abilities.[2] Such a higher stage of integrated general education corresponds to the perspectives of modern science — to its new methods, its urge to coordinate different branches and its typical developments at the fringes of disciplines. And it is equally relevant to changing human activities at a time when tens and hundreds of professions and models of life are being swallowed up or recast by advancing technology and organization. A well-founded general education gives a man greater mobility, flexibility, capacity to change, acquire new skills and embark on fresh training. A move in the same direction follows from the convergence of cultures in the world, the need to master the swelling stream of information, people's growing participation in social decision-making and — the strongest in the end — the claims of man's development for its own sake.

Yet hand in hand with the above it would be necessary to proceed from a solid basis of general education to a gradual and sensitive *differentiation* (choice of course, subjects, etc.) — and in this sense to *individualize* education — thereby cultivating all genuine bents in the

[1] In his *Social Function of Science* (London 1939, p. 246) J. D. Bernal already called attention to the need for "humanizing" science teaching.

[2] In the British discussions on the future of automation the view has been voiced that only a fifth of the population is fitted for university education. But it would be advisable to examine this proportion — insofar as it accords with the facts — to see if it is not a product of the present system of general education.

young, before their gifts have time to grow superficial and be dissipated. Lacking a broad base, specialized education today fails to cultivate the whole man; on the other hand, without the required specialization, man cannot make contact with the progress of civilization.

Such a system of schooling can provide the best groundwork for adult education. But with its present forms[1] adult education is in part just a substitute. Part-time study for employed people in the socialist countries is largely a way of making up for the injustices of economic discrimination and restricted access to higher education of capitalist days. Its value is declining, because the work load makes it difficult to guarantee the desired quality on a mass scale. But should leisure overstep a certain threshold, education while you work may evolve into a lasting symbiosis of working and learning. For the time being, factory schools and post-graduate university courses mainly serve a *supplementary* purpose, but with the growing interchange of scientific and technological knowledge, they will soon expand into an integrated system of permanent education involving a wide range of professional people as a matter of course.

Moreover, the mobile base of civilization and human life endows adult education with a *specific*, unique mission. Not being tied to formal marks of attainment, its motives spring from deeper sources of modern life, revealing the need for human powers to unfold, the urge to engage in blazing new trails for civilization, the longing to know oneself, the need to counter the uncertainty and instability born of overspecialization and to satisfy the curiosity evoked by the onrush of time and passing of values, to establish a creative relationship to one's own self. However diffused and unstable these motives may be today, they represent the immanent product of technological civilization, holding out the greatest promise for man's future. In time they will undoubtedly evolve their own institutional pattern.

As yet there is no knowing what agencies will take over such educational responsibilities or to what extent. Nor do we know how the flood of demands for teachers will be met.[2] Generalization of study will evidently lead in some degree to generalization of teaching, which will also come to be a more or less universal human function alongside the

---

[1] See J. Kotásek, K. Škoda, *Teorie vzdělání dospělých* (Theory of Adult Education), Prague 1966.

[2] The possibilities of special sources in this connection have been explored by R. Maheu (cf. "Weltweite Bildungsprobleme im Zeitalter der Technologie", *Unsere Welt 1985*, ed. R. Jungk, H. Mundt, München 1967, p. 204).

functions of work and membership in the community that are commonly accepted today. One thing is certain — we shall reach a point when all the conventional means of education will be found wanting.

/ *Technology and Education* / 2.2.3

Modern science and transformations in civilization are perceptibly revising views on the content of the educational process. The consequences are felt in the teacher-pupil relationship, in teaching methods and techniques. Hand in hand with the emergence of the new content of education, the methods and techniques take shape, and only in this context can they really prove their worth.

Although the teacher will undoubtedly continue to be the *leading* figure, the next few decades will see a third factor, *didactic technology*, entering the educational process on a wide front.

Until recently the school remained almost untouched by technological progress. In the age of atomic and rocket technology, it plodded on with *mass verbal* instruction dating at least from the days of manufactories. While ten to twenty years ago attempts to *individualize* teaching on a mass scale met with insuperable obstacles because teachers were unable to cope with the varied rates of progress in big classes, we can now look forward to an effective individual approach through wide-scale use of the techniques that have been finding their way into education since the fifties.[1]

The discovery that learning is a process that can be *controlled* — like other types of behaviour — by technically operated feed-back of information provided the basis for *programmed learning*[2], either in Skinner's original external (linear) programmes, or the subsequent tendency among Soviet authors to use a more all-round algorithmic approach on a deterministic basis (Landa) or in the strategic learning on a stochastic basis used by Pask's[3] analytic school. Modern cybernetics could then be applied to pedagogy, and so the door was thrown wide open to

---

[1] One of the founders of programmed learning, B. T. Skinner, believes that it was the endeavour to individualize, together with the growing structural shortage of teachers, that aroused interest in didactic technology (*The World in 1984*, ed. N. Calder, Baltimore 1965, p. 71).

[2] D. Tollingerová, V. Knězů, V. Kulič, *Programové učení*, Prague 1966.

[2] Cf. B. Skinner and G. Pask, in *Teaching Machines and Programmed Learning (a source book)*, Washington 1961; L. N. Landa, *Algoritmy i programmirovannoye obucheniye*, Moscow 1965.

management techniques, which in this case became techniques of learning.

A whole range of teaching techniques then emerges, with the most varied "teaching machines" capable of feeding back information, electronic language laboratories (audio-oral system), trainers and automatic testers, specialized class-rooms with technical equipment for handling and storing information, etc. Hand in hand with computer techniques, modern communications media come to the fore — closed-circuit radio and television, instructional films and transparencies, tape-recordings and especially video-tapes, earphone and optophonic apparatus, xerography, etc. The school of the future can be envisaged as using a multiple internal information system linked up with any external source (radio, television), which may play an important part especially at the higher levels. All in all, these techniques may be able step by step to relieve the teacher of monotonous routine, allowing him to choose from a range of teaching programmes and to employ the most suitable information medium. He will be in a position to combine the frontal, differentiated and individual approaches to the best advantage. And he will be able to "call all the human senses into play" during the process of learning.[1]

The teaching media grouped around cybernetic nuclei will rapidly expand into an intricate technical complex, which in the end will probably find its universal inner linkages. But the teacher, who will continue to play the guiding role, cannot be expected to master the entire system of modern teaching technology; there will have to be a *technical staff* responsible for designing, setting up and maintaining the complicated mechanisms and apparatus. An idea of the magnitude of this change can be gained from the forecast that teaching technology will prove to be one of the biggest investment projects in the last third of the century.[2] Despite its expensiveness, technologically-based teaching is remarkably effective, not only because without it schooling would have to be extended to 15 or 20 years, but also because it can be turned into an instrument for cutting the costs of instruction.[3]

[1] *Education for the Age of Science*, Washington 1959, p. 17.
[2] "...Industry must see education as a major market of the future" and the leading field for application of computer techniques (D. D. Bushnell, R. de Mille, J. Purl, "The Application of Technology to the Improvement of Instruction and Learning", in "Educational Implications of Technological Change", Appendix Vol. IV of *Technology and the American Economy*, Washington 1966, p. 7).
[3] According to the calculations by the above-quoted California experts, published in the appendix to the *Technology and the American Economy* report, one hour of pro-

The old familiar school with no other equipment than black-board and chalk is out of tune with the times in another respect, too — it is unfitted to the mentality of young people aware of the prospects offered by modern science; and it undermines the authority of education altogether. For people surrounded from childhood by the products of modern technology, blazing new trails for civilization will be an immanent need, and lasting education intrinsic to their way of life.

The revolution brought by *communications and teaching techniques* into the school will, however, probably be overshadowed by the impact on adult education. The forms tried hitherto — works and local clubs, cultural centres, educational centres and the like, with the emphasis on lectures[1] — are out of date and lack the appeal capable of inspiring people to cultivate their abilities. They can seldom compete with such "time-killers" as, for instance, the public house or bar. Modern communications and teaching techniques, linked with the schools, could turn adult education into a far more successful pioneer in the field of science, technology and the arts.[2]

Radio, the press, and most important, *television* and the *video-tape-recorder* seem to be the media capable of freeing adult education from the four walls of the classroom and transposing much of the activity to the home or workplace. Some countries (the USA, Japan) already have permanent educational channels,[3] with complete university courses by television in some subjects; others (USSR) are rapidly adopting such methods. Television is obviously destined to hold the field in

grammed instruction using the latest computers costs not quite 10 dollars, in three to five years the cost will drop to under one dollar, while ordinary verbal instruction by a teacher costs about two dollars an hour. The authors consider that to instal equipment linking up all classrooms in the USA (some 1,000,000) to a computer network will in the foreseeable future be an economic proposition without any danger of absorbing too large a share of the national income.

[1] Few institutions for out-of school education are equipped for more than verbal instruction. In Czechoslovakia, where they are numerous, one-third lack a gramophone, two-fifths a tape recorder and one-fifth an epidiascope. Film projectors are more common, but usually they are old types.

[2] A survey made by Illinois University of the extent to which the mass media are used in education throughout the world has shown a great potential of unused opportunities (*Mass Communications and Popular Conceptions of Education:* A Cross-Cultural Study, G. Gerbner, Urbana 1964).

[3] According to UNESCO reports, in the mid sixties there were about a hundred TV educational programmes in the USA, and around a thousand closed-circuit stations in schools. The Standford University research anticipates that by 1971 all larger schools will be equipped to impart a third of all teaching matter to pupils in this manner.

adult education, with a system of popular academies as its auxiliary. It would acquire even greater significance if its range were to be extended by video-tape recorders in the home — which could have a revolutionary effect in this connection — and by organizing the direct supply of reference material through modern media to individuals. Cybernetic techniques hold out even better prospects for the future; they could make learning equipment a feature of adult education on a mass scale. The key would be the operation of large computers, each accessible to some thousands of users simultaneously by means of instruments in the home — telephones or video-telephones, automatic recording and small domestic "printing presses". The linked-up network of computer centres would act as an "information bank"[1] ready to supply sources of instruction on request.

All this implies the approach of a profound revolution in all fields of education[2] capable of restructuring the entire foundation. A completely novel situation arises — modern technology is acquiring the ability to allow anyone at any time to comprehend whatever he may need about the current structure of the world and the basis of human existence.

/ *From Education to Self-Education* / 2.2.4

The point where the role of the scientific and technological revolution as an impulse to the development of human abilities will merge with its capacity to provide an opportunity for man's self-realization will be when each individual emerges in the interweaving objective processes of civilization as an *active subject.*

The rising generation, entering the educational process as the creator of potential reality, reaches out into the future; the world of today cannot satisfy it unless it finds satisfaction in what is actually already the

---

[1] Cf. A. Oettinger, *A Vision of Technology and Education* (Harvard program paper, Reprint no. 1). A project exists for a similar tie-up of 10,000 households to a computer centre in Columbia.

[2] Although the report of the National Commission for Technology, Automation and Economic Progress (*"Technology and the American Economy"*) is not favourably inclined to any views underlining the revolutionary nature of current changes in civilization, wherever in its appendices it lets the educationalists be heard, we find the consensus of opinion to be that coming developments in education "spell a revolution" (D. D. Bushnell and co-authors, p. 27), the entire institution of education is "moving into the general scientific-technological revolution" (J. D. Finn, p. 33).

past.[1] The endeavour to identify the individual completely with social reality and his awareness of it can bear no fruit in the civilization of our day. Unity has to be sought not so much in external affinity as in the *integrated oneness* of the individual. It is not the job of modern education to equip the pupil with a ready-made system of knowledge, but to give him the grounding and the method needed for his lifelong self-creation — above all, for the time when his teacher will not be there to guide him. The school of the future will have to turn the *object* of education into the *subject* of his own education, the being undergoing education into the being educating himself — education into self-education.[2] This radical change in man's attitude to his own self, which holds out the prospect of lifelong self-creation, presents the educational system with its most intricate problem for the coming decades of scientific and technological revolution;[3] its handling will provide the crucial test for the socialist course.

If man, having attained all-round development of his powers, is to be the creator of the material conditions of his life, self-education is his true path to realization and one of the fundamental modes of human existence in this day and age. The broader his approach to his world, the greater will be his ability to realize himself as a human being, that is, to develop himself. And all-round development can no longer — or at least to an ever smaller degree — be achieved by imparting a body of knowledge about everything existing in the world; it can, however, be promoted by making knowledge accessible to a man who is capable of mastering it through his own activity, who adopts a creative relationship both to the object and activity, and to his own self. With the progress of technological civilization it will no longer be possible to regard education as the attainment of a certain type of specialized qualification; the purpose will be to give people the groundwork for choosing their own spe-

[1] "In the past people could be educated by dealing with situations that their teachers knew, but now it has been recognized that the world that students enter will be widely, sometimes unpredictably, different from that in which they acquire their knowledge" (J. D. Bernal, "The Future, the Fundamental Factor of Scientific Education", article in Czech in *Věda a život*, 4/1963).

[2] M. Havlínová, "Nová povaha vzdělání v technicky vyspělé civilizaci" (New Character of Education in a Technologically Advanced Civilization), *Sociologický časopis* 2/1966.

[3] From this standpoint criticism is growing of concepts — including Skinner's — that reduce learning to outer-controlled reinforcement and demand its transference to an inner level (e. g. J. S. Brunner, *On Knowing. Essays for the Left Hand*, Cambridge 1962).

cializations. The aim of education will be to cultivate not a given type of person, but one able to shape himself to one type or another and to change from one to another.

Indubitably, this makes substantially greater claims on education.[1] Research on the frontiers of the human intellect usually indicates that *abilities* can be expanded indefinitely, but not factual *knowledge*. We have already reached a point when the sum of knowledge about the world cannot be encompassed even in its fundamentals; education based on acquiring pieces of knowledge will be an absurdity in the future. Moreover, the price of seeking encyclopaedic knowledge is paid in diminished capacity for logical thought. Nevertheless, a middle course exists whereby imparting knowledge goes hand in hand with cultivation of the ability to retain and use information, so that fresh information can be acquired and deeper comprehension gained throughout a lifetime. This course directs teaching to imparting the *structure of a subject*[2], involving the transfer of skills to ever new spheres, and generalizing the creative abilities.

The theory and practice of education have not yet come to terms with the sharp turns imposed by modern civilization on the process of scientific cognition. For the most part they fail to advance beyond the dividing line between the picturable concepts of classical theories and the purely rational concepts and systems of modern science. They move in a world where the all-inclusive creation of a new nature by man that leads directly to man's own self-creation is not a factor of any substantial weight. As presented hitherto, objects and institutions either remain within the bounds of qualities perceived by the senses, or are explicable by direct reproduction of the mechanical design embodied within them — in any case, demonstration by means of analysis and synthesis. But such a world is no longer a faithful picture of our times. A method of education based upon it can no longer afford an insight into the inner dialectic of current processes of civilization. In penetrating the reality of our day we discover on all sides areas of scientific finding that have to be grasped directly in their rationality and cannot be exactly matched by any graphic, purely objective models. Cultivation of abstract thinking attuned to this level of reality, comprehension of logical systems, systems approaches and methods that take the dialectics of the object

[1] "Our changing civilization will demand in the future an even greater devotion to learning and a greater pride in intellectual achievement" (*Education for the Age of Science*, Washington 1959, p. 30).

[2] J. S. Brunner, *The Process of Education*, New York 1963.

and the subject into account, these are emerging as the issue for truly modern education throughout the world.

In communicating the successes of modern science, which as fruits of human genius cannot be directly imitated, education can but proceed from a consolidated foundation of knowledge about the world, for perceiving which we are biophysically adapted, and from this range of knowledge ascend to the power of abstraction — in other words, retrace the adventurous path of getting to know (and transforming) the road trodden by mankind. Where this concentrated recapitulation up to the point of current human praxis is lacking, any preoccupation with learning some specific scientific finding, however up to date, merely serves the speedy obsolescence of this arsenal of facts which, together with the head in which they repose, are soon good for nothing.

If science is destined to be the leading force in the process of civilization, *education* assumes the key position for the present. The scientific and technological revolution will be accomplished by people who are now leaving school, or will leave in the next few years, and they bear with them the potentialities and the limitations given by the educational system of today. On their preparedness, their creative abilities, the mental dynamism manifested throughout their lives, will hang the fate of this civilization to a degree unknown in any previous epoch. We may safely say that the society with the best scientific, educational and cultural system will in future occupy the position in the world once held by the country with the greatest natural wealth, and later with the mightiest industrial potential.

MODERN CIVILIZATION AND THE DEVELOPMENT OF MAN

3

In the course of the universal and permanent transformation to which it subjects the structure and dynamics of the productive forces of human life, the scientific and technological revolution unfolds two new dimensions of social progress:

a) scientific discoveries and their applications, innovations in technology, organization and skills are imparting a dynamism to the whole life of man;

b) simultaneously the entire sphere of human life is gradually entering the movement of civilization as a new dynamic factor.

Not so long ago it was possible to assume that the life of man and advances in science and technology were separated by a layer of space and time so thick that its magnitude surpassed human capacities and the dimensions of human existence, making any real relevance between the worlds of man and of science an exception, or more precisely, relegating it to the realm of centuries-long history. Now, however, an intricate, two-way dialectical exchange is taking place between man and his handiwork; its windings extend the traditional boundaries of life *ad absurdum*, while starting to break free of them.

/The Scientific and Technological Revolution Changes the Way of Life/ 3.1

The advances in science and technology are beginning to impinge on the fundamental dimensions of human existence as fixed by industrial development — that is to say, the modes of work and living, interactions between man and nature, structure of personality and relationships among people.

Different productive forces exhibit different anthropological qualities. Consequently, fundamental changes in the structure and dynamics of these forces are bound to evoke radical turns and conflicting trends in human life and social development.

/Development of Man as an Independent Factor/ 3.1.1

The industrial production system relied on the mass employment of *ready-made* labour power. The advances of industrial civilization were accomplished, in one way or another, directly or indirectly, by the expenditure of the simple labour power of the overwhelming majority of the population. This structure of the productive forces has lent industrial civilization its anthropological qualities and limitations; simple expenditure of labour power has no need for an advance of human capacities; it requires a mere reproduction of labour power — coming to the factory gate each day in the same shape as the day before[1] — and the outcome is that masses of human potentialities and abilities over and above this reproduction are swallowed up.

The role of science as a productive force, which is emerging as a feature of modern civilization, carries quite different human connotations than the simple application of labour power. Creative activity inspired by science relies in all its forms and applications on progressive human abilities, bringing them into being and pressing for new advances in an ever-growing field. In this sense the scientific and technological revolution is for the first time an immediate reality, promoting the all-round social development of man, the cultivation of all his powers as a condition of progress in production.

Factory civilization brought a decline in the value of the "human factor" in inverse ratio to the magnitude of mechanical equipment; with the present revolution in the productive forces, on the contrary, the weight of the human factor is growing in line with the advance of the technical element. The surprising conclusion emerges that the highest level of technology (as a human achievement) witnessed in automation "enables man for the first time to turn his attention to his own self".[2] American speed-up methods of the twenties still saw man as a robot; but since the days when Mayo studied the role of human relations in production and, in the postwar period, the young Ford urged that attention be turned from the machine to man as a factor, these connotations of technical civilization are evidently imposing themselves in the capitalist environment, although there is reason to doubt how far the totality of such innovations can make headway.

[1] K. Marx, ibid., *Grundrisse*, pp. 202, 229.
[2] V. A. Trapeznikov, "Avtomatika i chelovechestvo", *Ekonomicheskaya Gazeta*, June 29, 1960.

The complexity and the limits of the scientific and technological revolution in its initial phases stem at each stage from the fact that, while relying on the advance of human creative power, it first induces this advance by the opportunities it provides. To the extent to which science permeates the world of production, the advance of people in the mass, and of the creative power of every individual, becomes the *decisive factor* in the development of civilization, in place of capital and labour. Sectors that were once of little interest for the generation of productive forces, such as mass culture and education, consumption and services, health care, travel and human contacts, organization of cooperation, leisure and recreation — in fact, the whole structure of human life — are emerging today in previously unknown contexts, because they now have in one way or another, and to a greater or lesser extent, direct relevance to the generation of the force that is coming to be the key factor for economic growth, i.e., science and its applications. In this sense the structure of human life is acquiring quite a different significance from that possible in the age of industrialization.

Up to a point in the advance of civilization, any shifting of reserves of material and time towards "investments in man" usually meant a loss, because the means expended either failed to raise people's creative powers to any noticeable degree (they were swallowed up by unsatisfied "reproduction needs" and worries), or the impact of new creative powers of man on the productive forces stayed within the bounds of simple extended production. But there comes a point when the tables are turned: the opportunity is offered for human abilities to be effective and for their advance to be harnessed by society to an extent far exceeding the mere multiplication of plants and labour inputs. The advantage of "investment in man" is steadily growing[1] and ultimately any

[1] "The economics of human resources" continually come up against this fact, whatever the method of analysis used: H. Correa demonstrates that at a certain level of accumulation of capital and technical progress investment in capital and in man are complementary, which was, of course, unthinkable in the industrial revolution (*The Economics of Human Resources*, The Hague 1962, p. 183). Similarly, P. R. Hanna writes: "Human resources have been traditionally thought of as one of the more or less inert input factors necessary in the life of the community. In contrast, we now consider that human resources creatively determine the subsequent nature and behaviour of society... Then that society will fall behind other societies which invest more intelligently in human development" (*Education, An Instrument of National Goals*, New York 1962, pp. 2—3). D. Bell, in considering the "postindustrial society", declares that "It is the limits to 'human capital' rather than to financial capital which have become the fundamental element limiting the growth of the society" (*Technology and Social Change*, New York—London 1964, p. 49).

failure to make use of human potentialities will amount to economic wastage.

Through science and its applications, and hand in hand with the progress of the technological revolution, the development of man emerges as an intrinsic part and *independent factor* in the growth of the material productive forces. This factor owes its peculiar vitality as compared with former agencies to the fact that it shares the specific accelerating property of science; the grander the dimensions assumed by human powers as an induced effect, the more forcefully they act as a generating cause. Through the medium of his own handiwork, man in advanced technical civilization provides the conditions enabling and indeed compelling him to be ahead of the whole sphere of his creations. As soon as the simple productive functions can be taken over by the fruits of human labour and people can be freed from mere concern for existence, full weight is given to the fact that there is no more vital agent of progress than the continuous cultivation of human abilities on a mass scale. Cultivation of human powers, *man's development as an end in itself*,[1] then assumes prime importance.

Throughout the history of civilization, changes in the level of human life and powers — except within a narrow circle, divorced from production proper — have never appeared as independent causes, but rather as secondary, induced, or even side effects, a kind of by-product of the general progress of civilization, whatever the ideas by which individuals motivated their practical activities. Extrapolation of the extended reproduction of capital (and its industrial reality) has hitherto provided the only real basis for forecasting the future.[2]

Modern technological advances induce sharp, irregular shifts; in contrast to the industrial revolution, they afford an explicit opportunity

---

[1] That is to say, "the absolute elaboration of his creative dispositions, without any preconditions other than antecedent historical evolution which makes the totality of this evolution — i. e., the evolution of all human powers as such, unmeasured by any *previously established* yardstick — an end in' itself" (K. Marx, in *Pre-Capitalist Economic Formations*, ed. E. Hobsbawn, London 1964, trans. J. Cohen, pp. 84—85).

[2] Most prognoses of social development still rely in one way or another on this approach (cf. *Resources for the Future*, the Ford Foundation, the Unilever forecast *Britain 1984*, etc.). In more long-term prognoses (assembled, for example, by N. Calder in a *New Scientist* poll, by the American organization Tempo, and in Jungk's "futurological" writings), the tone is set by aspects of scientific and technological development. An exception is "*Groupe 1985*" in France, which starts with some human elements of future development, but this welcome inversion of the order remains essentially declarative, because in fact the assumption is man "exposed to the pressures and implica-

for everyone to share (to greater or lesser extent) in the advance of civilization, while carrying, however, the spontaneous growth on the technological side to the borders of absurdity; if this process is not controlled (or at least guided) by collective reason, it will inevitably lead to disproportion, waste of productive powers, deterioration in people's physical and mental fitness, threatening catastrophe for civilization and, indeed, for mankind's very being.[1]

Use of nuclear energy and chemical processes, intervention in the structure of living matter and the genetic code — each of these present and future wonders of civilization carries untold prospects for people either to develop or to destroy themselves. This power of human handiwork gives a new dimension to the life of man,[2] it appears as an active agent in human destiny.

Because in the progress of the industrial revolution the emphasis was largely on the side of instruments of labour (machinery and equipment), requiring only that man as labour power should adapt himself to serving them, in the long run a hitherto unknown gulf was established between the worlds of civilization and culture.[3] And so, from the outset, the very concept of civilization, which had arisen in defiance of primitive barbarism, bore the taint of being the antithesis of culture. But today this rift in the foundations of human life, lying between the indirect and the direct levels of the selfsame process of man's appropriation of the world, the same self-realization of man, is assuming the proportions of a tragic abberation.

For a technically advanced society, on the contrary, human inertia — on which the industrial system was based — signifies destruction; an *advance of overall human development* ahead of the rushing stream of

---

tions" of spontaneous unfettered economic trends (*Réflexions pour 1985*), determined far more than determining. On the other hand, the prospect outlined in the Programme of the CPSU is concerned with primary social transformations; for the short term, however, economic considerations are followed here, too.

[1] "The development of technology has posed before man a problem engendered by his own power. Man's existence depends on his own decision" (R. Garaudy, *Perspectives de l'homme*, Paris 1959).

[2] "Man faces a terrible new abyss. Human history is acquiring a new dimension that formerly it did not possess. And consequently the whole question of relationships among people assumes a new dimension" (P. Togliatti, "Il destino dell' umo", *Rinascita*, March 30, 1963).

[3] This divergence was already sensed by Kant, Pestalozzi and others. A. Coleridge, J. Burckhardt and A. Weber identified it in the theory about the eternal hostility of civilization and culture.

material technology emerges as an imperative condition of life and finally the specific principle of freedom.[1]

This confrontation defines the justification for the existence of socialism. Taking socialism in its broadest historical connotations derived from the elimination of conflict between classes, we are witnesses of the process that allows man's scientific undertaking to operate in the social and human dimension, that starts to break away from the one-track course followed by civilization hitherto, and overcomes the rigidity of its subjective factors. The foundation is then laid for uniting the worlds of civilization and culture — whereas the shadow of their disparity never forsook the industrial system.[2]

If we take culture, as defined long ago by Kant,[3] to be cultivation of human abilities and powers, the scientific and technological revolution merges with the greatest *cultural revolution* known to history, because it transposes culture, which has hitherto tended to lie on the fringe, right into the centre of life.

Indeed, in this dimension of the scientific revolution — that is, cultivating the creative powers and talents of the working people at a higher level than hitherto, when only a tiny part has been able to find an outlet — lies the only realistic prospect for *overtaking* capitalism; on the condition that socialism will consciously steer its structure of interests, technological course, a rational system of production and consumption, incentives to constructive public activity and the like to this end. The true mission of socialism is to open the gates to development on the side of man by seeking human variants of technical civilization; such humanism is its inherent quality — if human development were not found at a certain level to be the most potent source of progress for civilization,

---

[1] From the first signs of the scientific and technological revolution L. Mumford perceived that the end of the "age of the machine" was at hand; the new epoch would either bring the "age of man" or the end of modern technology would also follow (*The Conditions of Man*, New York 1944). Both humanist critics and defenders of contemporary civilization like J. Fourastié (*La Grand Espoir du XXe siècle*, Paris 1950) are increasingly concerned with "the contrast between technical advance and the inadequacy of human progress" evident hitherto.

[2] When C. P. Snow returned with the "two cultures" to the divergence and even impossibility of understanding between the technological and humanist worlds that dogged the industrial system, he perceived a possible new way out in "the human aspects of the scientific revolution" (*The Two Cultures and a Second Look: An Expanded Version of the Two Cultures and the Scientific Revolution*, New York 1964).

[3] "Creation of the capacities of a reasonable being for any purposes whatsoever (that is in his freedom) is *culture*" (I. Kant: *Kritik der Urtheilskraft*, Berlin 1799, p. 391).

communism would recede into the world of far-off dreams. Freeing human creative powers to a *fuller extent*[1] than is usual under the industrial system based on capitalism can be taken to mark a vital step and will be a clear sign that the initiative in competition has been assumed; in its potentialities, this is a specific quality for the future course of the scientific and technological revolution under socialism.

/ *Changes in the Content of Life* / 3.1.2

Man, as distinct from animals, is not absorbed by his immediate activity; he employs it, embodying it in the motivations cultivated by his own living — in other words, he rises above it, having experienced changes in the nature of human life. The world around him and he himself are for him both a means and an end. The divergence and ultimate severance of these two poles lying at the roots of all manifestations of man's life reach an extreme, mass form in industrial civilization. The abstract antithesis of means and ends runs through all the life of this epoch like an impassable chasm: the elementary generic activity that saps the power of man without being an end in itself and, for man, finds its counterpart — beyond the bounds of work — in the sphere of ends, where man is deprived of his fundamental powers and means, and therefore cut off from active self-assertion. The more intensively man lives at either of these poles, the more hopelessly he is confined within the boundaries they erect between themselves and the more his life is reduced to a mere means to ends outside himself.[2]

The cycle of life in which the industrial system of capitalism enclosed the mass of people was indissolubly tied to the nature of human participation in the production process. The worker imagined that he worked to live; in reality, he lived for his daily repetition of given operations in the extended reproduction of capital.[3]

[1] But economists who are steeped in the traditions of the industrial civilization shaped by capitalism see these developments as "overinvestment of human resources" (Harbison, Myers, *Education, Manpower and Economic Growth*, New York, Toronto—London, 1964).

[2] This is "the stream of life" for which "it is immaterial what kind of mill it drives" (G. W. Hegel, *Phänomenologie des Geistes*, Glockner, dritte Auflage, Stuttgart 1951, p. 222).

[3] K. Marx, *Grundrisse*, ibid., p. 229.

Under these conditions, David Ricardo with some justification declared that the life of the entire population (including population trends, consumption, etc.) was a

Life for the majority was reduced to the level of the renewal, *reproduction of labour power*. The structure of consumption, leisure, interests, and claims of "private life" were swallowed up in the processes of renewing the capacity to work and in compensating the effects of one-sided, limited activities. For the mass of workers any rise above these limits was prevented by low levels of consumption and leisure time, or was absorbed by the set ideas and demands of the daily round, or it was ultimately deflected to the narrow aims of private aspirations that could not find a social outlet nor become a mode of full human self-realization.

In contrast to the earlier forms of society, industrial civilization carried the life of man beyond the bounds of mere subsistence at the level of his elementary natural needs; production of labour power was part of the general social reproduction process. A historically mobile element was introduced into the conditions of life, offering a prospect of change in the level of consumption. Nevertheless, in its essential structure, the life of the common man moved in an endless circle, a daily repetition of the selfsame functions. Existence was confined within the limits of "simple circulation" which, while allowing all manner of deviation and movements, in effect always signifies for the general run of mankind the simple reproduction of their labour power — at whatever level — as a condition for the extended reproduction of capital.[1]

Indeed, even beyond the bounds of capitalism, the material mould of industrial civilization, primarily the nature of work and the level of resources, absorbs man's physical and mental capacities, his outlook, mode of life and aspirations; it perpetuates the pattern of a system that had no place for man's development, or at least marked all his potentialities with a question mark. Man of the industrial age carries within him the limitations of his handiwork — in his needs and ideas, his abilities

---

derived quantity that "regulates itself by the funds which are to employ it" (*The Works and Correspondence of David Ricardo*, Cambridge, Vol. I, p. 78).

[1] "...such an operation cannot, of course, ever enrich, but must bring its performer at the end of the process to the very point at which he was at the start. This does not exclude..., but on the contrary embraces the fact that the circle of his immediate needs can to a certain extent be narrowed or expanded." (K. Marx, ibid. *Grundrisse*, p. 202.) Marx's concept of the life of a worker under capitalism as "the reproduction of labour power" has no relevance to whether the worker receives better or worse pay (*Arkhiv Marksa i Engelsa*, Vol. II (VII), p. 236) and therefore has nothing in common with the view identifying the value of labour power with a subsistence minimum commonly held by Grotius, Petty, Turgot, Ricardo and others.

and the motivations of his life, in which tendencies for self-development are still weaker than the opposing tendencies.[1]

Everywhere the first steps in the scientific and technological revolution are indubitably raising *living standards*, but within the limits of capitalism they are powerless to break through to make a radical change that would revolutionize the *level of living*. For socialism, too, this is fraught with difficulties, involving some dramatic happenings. Modern technology enables concern with the reproduction of life to be reduced to a minimum, clearing a space beyond the boundaries of the former circle of living; but the rhythm and forms of existence outlive their social and technological roots, frittering away resources and time, letting talents lie fallow and human potentialities run to waste in petty preoccupations.

In the initial stages it is evidently impossible to do more than set the bounds of "reproduction life" in motion, substituting extension of the life processes of all;[2] only when the transformation of activities, the level of consumption and the amount of free time is raised by technological advances to such a point that work and life will not devour each other and paralyse the potential cultivation of human abilities, but on the contrary will serve to stimulate them, when in fact "the opposition of labour to pleasure loses its basis"[3], will it be possible to foresee the conversion of all human life into a constant process of *man's development*, which is as much a consequence as a condition for an all-out advance in the scientific and technological revolution.

Where life for the general run of people is hemmed in by the need to reproduce their labour power, human relationships cannot escape from the confines of mere *mutual dependence* — that solitude amidst the universal links binding all men. Human relationships reflect the conflict

[1] J. Cvekl, "Vědeckotechnická revoluce a kultivace lidských sil" (The Scientific and Technological Revolution and Cultivation of Human Powers), *Sociologický časopis* 2/1966. How deeply these limitations are rooted in man himself is demonstrated by observations of the materially most wealthy communities, e. g., in *One-Dimensional Man* by H. Marcuse, Boston 1964. Moreover experiences of socialist revolution serve to confirm in another way Marx's and Engels's assumption that the "alienation" involved in industrial civilization is not confined to the objective conditions of life, but affects man himself in his own subjectivity (cf. Marx-Engels, *The Holy Family*, Marx-Engels, Gesamtausgabe, Vol. 3/1, Berlin 1932, p. 298).

[2] Marx describes socialism, as opposed to capitalism, as a society directed towards "an ever expanding system of the life process for the benefit of the society of producers", *Capital*, Vol. III (Kerr ed.) p. 293).

[3] Marx, Engels, *The German Ideology*, Marx-Engels Gesamtausgabe, Vol. 5/1, Moscow—Leningrad 1933, p. 197.

that bedevils life in industrial civilization — within this treadmill of work and living, man can serve the development of others only at the price of sacrificing his own development, and vice versa.[1]

Industrial civilization was founded on this contradiction of development in the material sphere and from it has stemmed all class privilege known to history.[2] And this drama of human relationships would continue unceasingly, shattering the best intentions and dreams, defeating the most ardent and determined movements — if it were not for the emergence of productive powers whose operation and expansion allow for and require the constant advance of all, or at least the great majority of people. In the circumstances of the scientific and technological revolution, any monopoly of human development is not merely superfluous, but indeed an obstacle to social advance. When the lives of each and every man reach such a level that the creative self-realization of each, man's delopment for its own sake, will be a means for the development of others, only then will society overcome the contradiction of means and ends, escape from mere mutual dependence and ultimately be able to convert the universal interconnection and cooperation among human beings into relationships in which the free development of each is the condition for the free development of all[3] — relationships which alone can provide the true communist dimension.

/ *Man and His Changing Needs* /   3.1.3

In pre-industrial communities, human needs — at least within the life span of a single generation — showed no appreciable change.[4]

During industrialization, expansion of the productive forces depended on accumulation of the bulk of the surplus resources produced; overall

---

[1] Over this practical dilemma of egocentric satisfaction and altruistic sacrifice in an industrial civilization — and as its theoretical expression — Kant's edifice of the moral imperative was erected.

[2] Liberals such as J. S. Mill still openly condoned the state where the mass of people are deprived of the right to their own development by pointing to the need to promote the advance of an "upper class" that would further the progress of civilization (*Elements of Political Economy*, London 1821, Vol. II, 2.)

[3] Marx-Engels, *Manifesto of the Communist Party*, London 1935, p. 28.

[4] "From the earliest times of which we have record...down to the beginning of the eighteenth century, there was no very great change in the standard of living of the average man living in the civilized centres of the earth" (J. M. Keynes, *Essays in Persuasion*... London 1931, p. 360).

growth took place at the price of stultifying the development of the majority, who had to restrict their needs to the level necessary for the simple reproduction of labour power. Although the age of industrialization gave an impetus to consumption by the mass of the people and, after the usual initial drop in real consumption, there was as a rule an upward turn, the degree of average satisfaction of needs shows in long-term projection a quite surprising stability or very gradual change.[1]

Despite the great efforts in the socialist countries to raise living standards, they, too, have found the simultaneous expansion of production and consumption in the phase of industrialization to be "an insoluble task",[2] at least so long as the watershed of industrial maturity has not been reached.

When modern civilization progresses to its peak, however, the productive forces can be seen to overstep the limits of the contradictory development; at a certain stage (transition to the scientific and technological revolution), indeed, the general *expansion of consumption* becomes just as essential a condition of economic growth (and of the viability of capital at the stage of its "saturation"[3]) as formerly restriction of consumption by the masses.[4] Compared with the phase of industrialization, when advance in real incomes was sharply divided from growth in labour productivity and (thanks to the dilemma of consumption and accumulation) tended rather to move in inverse ratio to productivity, there is now a growing tendency for the two values to show a direct pro-

---

[1] J. Kuczynski's long-term index of real earnings for all industrially advanced countries shows for the period up to the nineteen-thirties at the most a 10 per cent increment rate per decade (*"Die Theorie der Lage der Arbeiter"*, Berlin 1955, the series *Die Geschichte der Lage der Arbeiter*, Vol. I—IV for the USA, Germany, Great Britain and France).

[2] See the resolution of the Fifteenth Congress of the Communist Party of the Soviet Union, dating from the start of the First Five-Year Plan (*KPSS v rezolutsiakh i resheniakh syezdov, konferentsiy i plenumov TsK*, Moscow 1954, Vol. II).

[3] "Overproduction of capital never signifies anything else but overproduction of means of production — means of production and necessities of life — which may serve as capital" (K. Marx, *Capital*, Vol. III, (Kerr ed.), p. 300).

[4] Keynes' discovery that beyond a certain point "capital is not a self-subsistent entity existing apart from consumption" and that consequently encouragement of purchasing power is required in order to postpone "the day when the abundance of capital will interfere with the abundance of output" (*General Theory of Employment, Interest and Money*, London 1936) is given a dynamic interpretation by economic theorists today: a measure of growth in consumption is now a condition for the normal functioning of capital (cf. E. D. Domar, *Essays in the Theory of Economic Growth*, New York 1957, p. 8).

portionality.[1] This fact underlies all modern Keynesian doctrines of artificial stimulation of buying power by means of state monopolistic measures.[2] Intensively growing production capacities are scrapped, turned to destructive consumption (armaments), or caught up in the system of mass consumption that is turning modern technological civilization into a "consumer society".[3]

The significance of the mass consumption that has been spreading in the advanced capitalist countries in recent decades should certainly not be underestimated — although, of course, the system of exploiting human wants is dominated by the conditions under which the self-expansion of capital takes place. The level of real consumption (see Table 3-1) has risen in the U.S. over the past 20 years more than in the previous 50 years and the present outlook is that the pace will be maintained.[4] Britain's prospects up to 1984 suggest a doubling of per capita consumption,[5] an advance not previously achieved even over 70 years, while French prognoses[6] also speak of consumption in 1985 being 2.5 times that of today (a threefold acceleration). A *threshold* is reached where elementary needs are satisfied and the range of wants extends. Witness the shift in the pattern of consumption and family budgets — since the thirties the share of expenditure on food has been on the downgrade in the U.S., Sweden and Britain, and this trend is now common to all industrially advanced countries.[7] The curve for clothing began to take the same course after the war and alongside France, Austria and Italy (where the drop has started) a number of other countries see this outlook for coming decades. Since the fifties even the share of expenditure on automobiles in the U.S. has shown a similar trend and other countries are expected to follow in 10 to 20 years.[8]

[1] In 1906—1939 real incomes in the U.S. national economy (excluding agriculture) showed annual increments of less than one per cent, compared with advances in productivity per man-hour of about two per cent. On the other hand, between 1939—1959, real wages advanced by over 2.9 per cent and productivity per man-hour by 3.1 per cent (for instance, S. Lebergott, *Manpower in Economic Growth*, New York—San Francisco—Toronto—London 1964, pp. 524, 528 and other sources).

[2] At the present time this Keynesian attitude has become "the new conventional wisdom" (J. K. Galbraith, *The Affluent Society*, Cambridge 1958, p. 192).

[3] D. Riesman, N. Glazer, R. Denney, *The Lonely Crowd*, New York 1950.

[4] *Resources in America's Future*, Baltimore 1963.

[5] *Britain 1984*, London 1963.

[6] *Réflexions pour 1985*, ibid.

[7] *The New Europe and Its Economic Future* (20th Century Fund) 1964; *Europe's Future Consumption*, Amsterdam 1964; *Yearbook of National Accounts Statistics*, Geneva 1964.

[8] S. Kuznets, *Six Lectures in Economic Growth*, Geneva 1959.

But these developments, considerable as they are, offer little prospect, within the given order of society, of altering the social and anthropological substance of life. The theory of the "affluent society"[1] or of "high mass consumption"[2] indirectly — and critics of the consumer society[3] directly — come up against a dilemma posed by the inner limits of this consumption; evidently the system is incapable of breaking these bounds to give priority to the requirements of human development, while to continue as before implies converting rationalized "production for the sake of production" into irrational "consumption".[4]

With rapid technical advance, the system of external manipulation of consumption incessantly inflates mass demands for private enjoyment of amenities,[5] it imposes an array of senseless, fictitious wants, sponsored by advertisement, prestige appeal and undercutting. Man is made a slave of his consumption, human activity is turned into a mere means to this end; instead of taking possession of the world, we have the appropriation and consumption of things.

Should the scientific and technological revolution go ahead in the socialist countries during the coming decades, it will *advance* and probably break through the bounds of mass consumption. Statistics of consumption in Czechoslovakia at present (by its share in net family incomes and compared with the dynamics of the most advanced countries) indicate that reproduction needs[6] still occupy a foremost place

---

[1] J. K. Galbraith, *The Affluent Society*, Cambridge 1958.

[2] W. W. Rostow, *The Stages of Economic Growth, A Non-Communist Manifesto*, Cambridge 1960.

[3] "Man is transformed into the 'consumer', the eternal suckling, whose one wish is to consume more and 'better' things" (Erich Fromm, *Let Man Prevail*, The Call Association, New York 1960, p. 10).

[4] "Many of our wants are shaped by the very system of production which exists to supply them" (A. Cairncross, *Introduction to Economics*, London 1944, p. 213). Similarly J. K. Galbraith (*The Affluent Society*, ibid, p. 136 — Penguin ed.).

[5] In the foremost industrial countries today we can clearly see the extent to which wants are self-justifying in a system of mass consumption; they take on a life of their own (Dusenbury), they are determined by powers over which the individual has no control (Marcuse). Nevertheless, at a certain level just such a drastic forcing of growth of wants, this "self-deafening", this "civilization within the gross barbarity of wants", was denoted by Marx as "a civilizing element... on which rests the historical vindication, but also the present power of capital" (*Grundrisse*, ibid., p. 198).

[6] At present 41 per cent of expenditure in working class families in Czechoslovakia is on foodstuffs (i.e., 40 per cent more than in the U.S., 20 per cent more than in Sweden), 14 per cent on clothing and footwear, 10 per cent on essential services, etc. (see Table 3—2). The higher share of material goods (icluding food) is due to a considerable

(about 80 per cent); we can expect these *essential needs* to be fully catered for only when real per capita consumption has been considerably increased (about threefold), with a big shift to durables, housing facilities and services. A similar rise in real income (3.5 times) during the next twenty years is anticipated by Soviet prognoses[1] and by the forecasts for most of the socialist countries. Only when this *threshold* of reproduction needs has been crossed can the resources produced and consumed turn into a potential supplier of new human wants, while below this threshold they are always swept into the channels of existing reproduction needs. Satisfaction of needs cannot be by-passed; every delay can merely serve to prolong their domination. Heightened consumption, flowing from growth of the productive forces, is for socialism, too, a necessary stage of development. Wants tend to be refined by their satisfaction; things — if there are enough of them — call for cultivation of the ability to choose, they encourage the power of perception; beyond a certain point, *mass* consumption promotes development of the individuality; while introducing a democratic element into the groundwork of human progress, it cannot yet be identified with that progress — undoubtedly the socialist countries, too, will be faced with the problem of the "mass consumer", the *consumer attitude* to life with its accent on consumption in preference to human development (especially in the transition phase when work brings little satisfaction, education is underestimated, commitment to the group is weak and the participation in guiding the steerable processes of civilization is altogether slight).

Socialism is not, however, obliged to follow all the twists and turns made by consumer society in Western technical civilization; it can benefit by experience and shorten the path of mass consumption with the help of science, technology and a combination of factors throughout the community; wherever abundance is achieved, socialism can evolve its own style of life. Modern technology has demonstrated that elementary needs can be rationally provided for by a system of large-scale services. Socialist countries, to their own detriment, are failing to take advantage

degree to the fact that many services are provided free or at state-subsidized prices. B. Stíbalová and Z. Urbánek have calculated that these shifts compensate the divergence in consumption structure between Czechoslovakia and Austria, for example (cf. *Plánované hospodářství* 1/1966). In light of this, we can see that despite the divergent structures, the various curves of consumption in Czechoslovakia are following very closely the similar trends in other industrial countries. Outlays on foodstuffs are falling, relative expenditure on clothing has past its peak, and so on.

[1] Cf. *Programme of the CPSU*, section II. A.

of these methods. Moreover, there are now known to be good prospects for combining mass services (delivery of foodstuffs and ready cooked meals to the home, modern laundry and dry cleaning services, etc.) with an individual approach to home mechanization, and at low cost. A rational system of analysing consumer demand and setting scientifically based standards[1] (nutrition standards, "the rational wardrobe", models of transport, housing, etc.) backed by a considered policy of built-in economic and social stimulation, can serve to divert a maximum amount of resources to the development of human creative powers.

Every such step, however, demands the working out of both the necessary technical project, accompanied by publicity to explain things and persuade the consumers, and of a concept covering all the social measures impinging on the nature of work and the human motivations, the evironment, etc. — measures that will embrace all the interconnections of these intricate changes and give preference to alternatives promoting the advancement of human power and so paving the way to further acceleration. Only on such dynamic soil can a policy for modelling the style of life be a practical proposition.[2]

On this assumption, satisfaction of wants engenders *new wants* — and this is the very process in which people can take an active part (at a far higher level than when merely existing wants are to be satisfied), a part adequate to the demands of the scientific and technological revolution and simultaneously infusing it with a greater dynamism.

Revealing and creating new wants, cultivating in man a rich variety of wants, this was in Marx's view, contrasting with all previous views of civilization, the production of wealth peculiarly suited to mankind, for here is displayed the nature of man as a being distinguished by "the infinity of his wants and their capacity for expansion".[3] The cultivation of new wants always changes the nature of those already existing, so

---

[1] Among first attempts see, for example, collected papers published in Moscow in 1962, *Metodologicheskie voprosy izucheniya urovnya zhizni trudyashchikhsya*. A number of similar rational norms have been worked out in Czechoslovakia.

[2] Cf. O. Klein, "Vědeckotechnická revoluce a životní sloh" (The Scientific and Technological Revolution and Style of Life), *Sociologický časopis* 2/1966. The ideas that modelling the style of life can be accomplished by the romantic step of halting the growth of needs and diminishing the dominance of demands over capacities (Rousseau), or by creating a general static ideal of the desirable style of life (Saint-Simon, Fourier), or even by prescribing an order of life in the form of a "positive catechism" (Comte) — ideas that recur among critics of modern civilization in all countries — are being confuted at every turn in the socialist countries.

[3] *Arkhiv Marxa i Engelsa*, Vol. II (VII), Moscow 1933, p. 235.

that the whole traditional world of wants can gradually come to be dominated by *man's need to develop*, which is generated by human civilization itself. The age of science and technology knows many components of this need. We can mention only the foremost:[1] the need for creative work, the need for life-long education, the need for all-round abilities and self-assertion, the need for unsullied relationships and human sympathy, the need for complete mobility and information, the need for free physical activity, the need to enjoy beauty and nature, the need to see a way forward — all these are intrinsic, indissolubly linked human claims on the progress of modern civilization.

/ Technology and Human Contacts /   3.1.4

Industrial civilization dissolved the original bonds of cooperation and fellowship among people; it atomized society, substituting for direct personal contact its anonymously imparted *information.*

Thanks to technical advance, relationships among people are more extensive and frequent (people see, hear and meet each other more), but their contacts increasingly rely on intermediary agencies, they are more superficial and less authentic (we meet in cars, hear each other on the telephone and radio, or see people on the television screen). With growth of the productive forces, man acquires greater power to influence others, but still not enough to give this influence a purposeful, truly human and profound quality; on a mass scale its real intentions tend to be lost in the maze of interacting processes that make up our civilization. On the one hand, the bulk of the working people continue to be crowded under the roofs of vast works, offices and shops, while formal relationships grow more and more tedious — hence the escape to private life, the family circle, which is the patent outcome of industrial civilization. Tension between formality at work, in external contacts and concerns, and the intimacy pervading the sphere of friendship and family life is too great at present for there to be any hope of "balancing" one against the other, and retreat to the intimacy of emotional life is usually — with its limitations — of no avail.

True, the opposing tendency is man's growing loneliness in fully mech-

---

[1] J. Hermach, "Nástin řešení problému rozvoje socialistického člověka a jeho potřeb" (Some Notes on Handling the Problem of Developing Socialist Man and his Wants), *Sociologický časopis* 2/1966.

anized workshops, at control desks and the like, which weighs so heavily on the personality that it calls for a special system of remuneration ("loneliness pay") and is evoking with some urgency an unwonted demand for what promises to be an imperative need for human proximity. From this stems the interest in travel, getting to know people, holding discussions, and the propensity to associate in groups of close friends. An urgent lack of unfettered human contacts is a feature of this transitional stage of civilization.

As for the future, we shall have to be prepared for the atomization of society to last some time yet; a change may finally come from the already-known circumstance that *creative work* in groups provides some new opportunities for the "natural" linking of solitude and contacts, evidently related to the higher level of human cooperation, to the type of mutual development in which the enrichment of each is a condition for the enrichment of all. The more difficult, however, will it be to meet the needs of these relationships (even in a classless social order), which with the advance of the scientific and technological revolution are evidently going to spread throughout the system of human cooperation.

Technical advance will in the future provide new conditions for human contacts; through application of the new principles of transmitting and storing information evolved by radiotechnology and electronics (miniaturization, wave-guides, lasers and so on), by setting up systems of communications satellites and the international link-up of computer services. Almost all projects elaborated throughout the world envisage the coming two decades as bringing the telephone to every home in the industrially advanced countries.

In the foreseeable future — according to the experts[1] — we shall have the "videotelephone" or "telex"; when these audiovisual means of telecommunication become general it will be possible to operate multiple television communication, enabling conferences and talks to be held without travel or the direct physical presence of the participants. In connection with the now frequently mooted prospect of a "computer in every home" linked up with monster information and teaching centres,[2]

---

[1] J. R. Pierce, J. D. Clare, G. Barry, G. C. Cross et al. in a *New Scientist* poll (*The World 1984*, Vol. 1, London 1964).
Clare expresses the hope that one day other sense perceptions will be transmitted simultaneously with vision and sound (p. 155).

[2] Cf. D. D. Bushnell, R. de Mille, J. Purl, J. D. Finn, G. D. Ofiesh and others in an appendix to *Technology and the American Economy*, Washington 1966.

the new technology will enable us to inform ourselves about everything all the time.[1]

The scientific and technological revolution will evidently enormously expand and complicate the world of human contacts. The media of communications channels will open the gates to universal information and to misinformation, while new attitudes to information will present as crucial a problem as the attitude to things (and the corresponding forms of ownership) in the industrial epoch.

Even today communications engineering can at least potentially break down the barriers of privacy, exposing our entire lives to the eyes and ears of the world. When in the future there is no problem about transmitting and acquiring information at will, we shall face the formidable question of cancelling, toning down, regulating, selecting and controlling information. The technical facilities themselves compel everyone to master new skills, that is, to be a specialist in *human relations*.

/ *Disposable Time* / 3.1.5

Leisure is born as a mass phenomenon within industrial civilization with the progressive shortening of working hours; it appears when working time plus the time necessary for reproducing labour power ceases to occupy the worker's whole life, confining him in a circle of necessity (see Table 3-3). A product of technological advance, it is also an autonomous agent in releasing and shaping human powers — to such an extent that technologically advanced societies are sometimes treated as "leisure societies".[2] Compared with the limitations set to work in the industrial system, the growing sphere of leisure seems to offer good hopes for mankind — indeed, it is sometimes seen as the sole source of human development.[3]

From the social standpoint, however, the time a worker in industrial

---

[1] In discussing the advances of communications techniques French prognoses draw a parallel with the "ubiquitousness" of man (*Réflexions pour 1985*, ibid., p. 138).

[2] J. Dumazedier, *Vers une civilization du loisir?*, Paris 1962.

[3] For example, G. Friedmann takes the approach that industrial work is still "so limited and monotonous" that "it cannot offer a stimulus to forming the spiritual and moral capacities of man..."; he deduces from this for the future, too, that "...under the technical and social conditions of large scale industry, many workers can only live their real lives in their free time" (*Où va la travail humain?*, Paris 1950). He therefore turns to the cultivation of free time — on the lines of Proudhon's ideal of "free work".

civilization is at rest is equivalent to the time in which he reproduces his labour power.[1]

Leisure is, in this sense, an illusory reflection of predetermined behaviour patterns built into the process of work and embodied in the general living conditions. Moreover, even when extension of leisure time actually exceeds these bounds and there is no doubt about its availability, social conditions perpetuate its set limits and compress its content into the traditional mould, so that its specifically human dimension is again destroyed. From this stems the opposing, sceptical view that no manner of expansion will ever make leisure into a domain for man's development and self-creation.[2]

Although under socialism leisure is no longer charged with inevitable conflict, it still bears the marks of its origin in the cleavage fixed in the material forms of the industrial system. The concern with earning and getting that is the prime component in reproducing labour power still reigns supreme in human life, sapping energies, absorbing the attention and receptiveness of all who work (80 per cent of waking time). Figures for Czechoslovakia[3] show that simple work (men and women workers) accounts for an average of 30 per cent of the weekly time-table, while sleep takes 31 per cent, essential activities 21 per cent, etc., and about 15 per cent remains for leisure — which is, however, mainly taken up by the rest and distraction that are either a compensation for the nature of work and the one-sided conditions of civilization, or simply their prolongation through force of habit. A bare half of the leisure time (i.e., about 7 per cent of the weekly schedule) can be regarded as truly *time available to man* (disposable time), dedicated according to Marx's concept in one way or another to the development of man[4] — about 2.3 per cent falls to private study, while other activities include culture,

---

[1] K. Marx, ibid., *Grundrisse*, p. 440.

[2] H. Schelsky sees "no prospect that modern man will employ this newly-won free time for the cultivation of his individuality" (*Die sozialen Folgen der Automatisierung*, Düsseldorf—Köln 1957, p. 34). Similarly H. Arendt: "...the surplus time of the *animal laborans* will never be used for anything else than consuming" (*Vita activa oder vom tätigen Leben*, Stuttgart 1960, pp. 120—121).

[3] Based on statistical investigation by J. Bezouška and J. Vyskočil (Šetření o využití času v Československu, *Demografie* 3/1962 and 4/1963) and the elaboration of their results in a book by A. Červinka et al.: *Práce a volný čas*, Prague 1966.

[4] Disposable time is, in Marx's delightful phrase, time that "gives room for man's development" and that "changes him who has it into an entirely different being" (cf. K. Marx, *Theorien über den Mehrwert*, Stuttgart 1921, Vol. III, p. 302; *Grundrisse*, pp. 593—599).

technical hobbies, meditations and discussion, travel, social activities, active entertainment and sports, etc.

Judging by the findings of modern anthropology and psychology, mass participation in the scientific and technological revolution (linking work and education, etc.) could be practicable when the disposable time reaches a level of about 30 hours a week, i.e., three times more than today (and later it would have to be even more).[1] This would mean introducing the 30-hour working week, with about 40 weeks of work a year;[2] and an even more drastic reduction of time expended on reproducing labour power (to about 15 hours a week) — a situation that, according to various prognoses, can be expected towards the end of the century.[3] Disposable time would then be the leading component in human life; new powers of man and the community would spring from leisure time, signifying a radical shift in the boundaries of human potentialities and the imperatives of life.

In considering the freeing of time for man's own disposal, we cannot today be guided any more by the traditional standpoint of social policy. The role of the human factors in transmuting the structure and dynamics of the productive forces makes decisions about leisure with all its implications a complicated problem for society. From the standpoint of growth, the long-term course to be followed in reducing working time is not irrelevant (whether to shorten the working day, week, year or working life, etc.), so long as every lightening of the load in one place involves an added burden elsewhere and vice versa. Modelling of optimal variants will probably be the more effective the more it is linked with the transformation of work, and later, the more room it leaves for individual approaches; in any event, the point at issue in the economic, sociological and anthropological considerations underlying the time economy is to keep in mind the ratio of the amount of time released to the actual growth of human powers.[4]

---

[1] In the opinion of educationalists today this is also the time necessary to enable consistent study-while-you-work projects to be carried out.

[2] J. Fourastié, *Les 40,000 heures*, Paris 1965; most Soviet forecasts advance similar data.

[3] With the exception of some American prognoses, which do not envisage any substantial reduction of working time even by the year 2000 (*Resources in America's Future*, Baltimore 1963).

[4] For example, shortening the working day or week within certain limits raises productivity of simple work; indeed, for creative workers the sabbatical year is now considered to be a highly productive amenity. On the other hand, premature retirement when the span of human life is growing longer results in unnecessary delegation of

In distinguishing between kinds of leisure we reveal its ambiguity. Not only the measure but primarily the *content* of leisure is significant. Empirical research shows that below a certain level of living standards, there is a strong tendency to use the time to supplement incomes ("moonlighting" etc.). A similar correlation is found between simple, monotonous work and the inclination to spend leisure in activities that severely restrict its humanizing role.[1] Evidently, increasing the amount of leisure cannot in itself provide a source of creative powers. Here is the place for social modelling and the search for effective means of, on the one hand, not curtailing, but rather increasing the freedom of *choice*,[2] while on the other hand stimulating the emergence of subjective wants that are in harmony with the development of the individual and therefore of society, too. Naturally, vulgar utilitarianism has no place here, for the range of stimuli and experiences that develop the personality in leisure time is immensely varied.

a) In industrially advanced countries the scale of leisure activities is headed by television viewing,[3] cinema-going, listening to the radio, reading newspapers and magazines — that is, "mass culture", which plays a special and at present irreplaceable role. The mass media have made information, entertainment, culture generally available, but the cleavage inherent in the industrial system reappears as the dilemma of the creator and the consumer: so long as man lacks the connection between his own activity and his creative powers, he loses touch with art and science, which are founded on such activity. In the West, commercialism skilfully adapts and petrifies the desire for distraction, offering pastimes that foster trivial wants. Critics of mass culture have long since pointed out that modern entertainment, being tied to existing modes of production, is a projection of the rationalized and mechanical operations to which man is subjected.[4] Here socialism possesses unmatched

work to younger people and tends to disrupt the overall generation of creative powers in society.

[1] B. Filipcová, *Člověk, práce, volný čas* (Man, Labour, Leisure), Prague 1967.

[2] Polish research demonstrates an interesting correlation: the higher the skills and education, the greater preference people give to individual, unorganised holidays.

[3] Surveys show that in all industrial countries viewing time in families with televisions sets (in Czechoslovakia 50 per cent of families) represents a considerable item — in Czechoslovakia, as in the U.S., about 18 hours a week.

[4] "Distraction is bound in the present mode of production, to the rationalized and mechanized process of labour to which, directly or indirectly, masses are subject" (T. Adorno, On Popular Music, in: *Studies in Philosophy and Social Science*, 1941, p. 37; also discussed in M. Horkheimer, T. Adorno, *Dialektik der Aufklärung*, Amsterdam 1947).

advantages still waiting to be used. Of course, there is a general tendency towards "mass culture" (rise of a "culture industry", popularity of second rate entertainment, etc.) in the socialist countries, but the independent value of culture has greater opportunities to assert itself; entertainment is to this degree more open to the cultivation of human powers. Current advances in science and technology are steadily penetrating the structure of mass culture, and as the mass media become differentiated, they will be capable of offering a richer source for individual choice and shift the balance in favour of active entertainment. In all probability the unilateral flow of information will ultimately become multilateral, and this would impinge strongly on the nature of mass culture, intensifying demands for active participation and bringing it to the top.

b) In *sports*, too, we still find a clear reflection of the underlying cleavage in industrial civilization (the managers and the performers). In fact, the mass dissemination of sports in the industrial countries originated in the separation of the work of masses of people from their original anthropological dimension, which is then concentrated after work in play.[1] But this dichotomy of work and play again mirrors the abstract dialectics of means and ends, in the conflicting approach to play itself, in the guise of the sports-ace-onlooker nexus. In sports events, the onlooker looks for interruption of his daily life with its uninspiring work and emptiness, he wants escape from the tangled web of relationships with other people to the simple, transparent rules of justice and fellowship, to the sense of unbounded self-determination and the right to choose that is denied him by the industrial mechanism. No doubt the compensation for the restrictions of real life in industrial civilization is illusory, yet it betrays some signs of new wants, which find their genuine expression in active mass sports. We may assume that a more developed technological civilization will do much to encourage sports activities (not, of course, top rankers), in contrast to the previous stage when the emphasis was on the mass entertainment aspect, and that when a strong move towards the intellectual elements of work ensues, sport will be indispensable — i.e., the need will be both objective and subjective.

c) Hobbies, which have recently come to be one of the biggest time-spenders,[2] also involve some contradictory features. Their popularity is not just in their usefulness — on the contrary, in many cases it would

[1] J. Huizinga, *Homo ludens. A Study of the Play Element in Culture*, Boston 1950.
[2] According to an internationally organized survey in European cities, where gardening is included, these hobbies occupy 40 per cent of leisure (most among elderly people).

be easier to resort to the shops or services[1]. But the direct contact with things, physical work (compensating for an intellectual bias in working life), simplicity in execution (against the sophisticated power of technical apparatus), the free play of human skills for their own sake (against the direction of work from without) — these are values to be prized in an industrial civilization so long as the nature of work remains unchanged.[2] The success of the "do-it-yourself" industry speaks for itself. It reveals the widespread desire for creative effort, but also shows a tendency to deprive it of social utility. However, when leisure is extended, some progressive hobbies will undoubtedly provide the starting point for more fruitful pursuits among many present-day do-it-yourself fans.

If the age of science and technology sees the true potential of leisure to lie in the diversified cultivation of human abilities, the abstract antithesis of leisure and work will be overcome as soon as work is transformed into creative activity.[3] At this divide the time available to man which has been released for human development will take the place of "working time" as the measure of *social wealth*.

* * *

The boundaries set to the activities, wants and inclinations of "reproduction life" in industrial civilization possess a dead weight of inertia even when revolution has torn down social barriers and technological advances have deprived them of their justification. Man is not unchanging, as some anthropologists interpret the fate of the masses in history.[4] Under certain conditions his pattern of motivation becomes susceptible to the influence of his own handiwork.

[1] According to W. Buckingham, "it is a fair bet that amateur electricians, plumbers, and carpenters create as much repair work for the professionals as they perform themselves". (*Automation. Its Impact on Business and People*, New York 1961, p. 197).

[2] Cf. J. Ellul, *La Technique et l'enjeu du Siècle*, Paris 1954.

[3] Marx himself pointed out that when work merges with the creative self-assertion that is equivalent to man's development, the abstract antithesis of work and leisure will disappear and "disposable time" will be the total measure of the wealth of human life (*Grundrisse*, p. 599).

[4] The conflict between Marx's concept of man as a malleable being, capable of self-development, "of the true solution of the conflict between existence and essence" in: *Marx's Concept of Man*, ed. E. Fromm, New York 1967, p. 127, and that of traditional anthropology based on the immutability of man (Gehlen and others) lies deep at the roots of the diverse views of contemporary civilization; it provides constant food for attacks on Marx's "futurism", "anthropological eschatology" and the like (cf. H. Klages, *Technischer Humanismus*, Stuttgart 1964, p. 30 et seq.).

In this case, what keys can open the door to man's victory over his own apathy and rigidity — a task that Lenin saw as more difficult and essential than victory in the struggle for power?[1] What forces will crystallize in his inner being the free decision to follow his own development?

In some circumstances an *opportunity system* may provide the answer. From work, through education, consumption and leisure there is a wide range of big and small opportunities to promote technical, scientific, social or simply human creativeness. The time will certainly come when the traditional dominants of life prove inadequate. Here and now we should be thinking about new functions of factories, schools, mass communication and entertainment facilities, centres of technology, science and culture. We should consider establishing a network of institutions open to everyone who feels the need for active contact with the world of technology and innovation, with an atmosphere of developing human powers.[2]

We cannot pretend to know these paths; on the contrary, we still know too little of the distance lying between the scientific and technological revolution and the motivations underlying human development in the lives of millions who are emerging from the zone of industrial civilization.

/Man in an Artificial Environment/ 3.2

The world in which man finds himself today has long since ceased to be a world of untouched nature; invaded and adapted on all sides by human agency, it is being transformed into a second, man-made type of nature.

People cannot master the conditions of their own lives until they have created them themselves. But as they pile up their edifice of conditions, its backlash shapes and confines the makers. Man himself ceases to be a mere child of nature, and grows in all aspects into a social individuality moulded by civilization. The quality of his handiwork, which is carved into the environment in which he lives, comes to determine his development.

[1] V. I. Lenin, *A Great Beginning*, Sochinenya, Vol. 29, 1950, p. 379.
[2] In Soviet writings, experiences with "bureaux" of technological creativeness are usually discussed; in France, they propagate private and public laboratories of similar type; in the USA, they rely mainly on modern telecommunication.

/ *Problems of Civilization* /

In an industrial civilization shaped by capitalism, man has freed himself from dependence on nature at the price of becoming dependent on his own creations — on substances he has shaped and forces he has set in motion.

From factory work and life based on the social reproduction of labour power, there gradually emerged an *artificial environment*, and this environment is out of tune with the biological and psychic qualities common to human life through the ages — *it no longer corresponds* to man's natural disposition.[1] However, these conditions of life were not as a rule the fruits of human concepts, but rather the outcome of the utilization of man and of efforts to facilitate this process. They acquired an arbitrary and cold logic: the vast material impetus of industrial civilization overpowers masses of people day and night, forcing their activities along strictly defined channels, bringing them into ready-made situations, setting firm boundaries to their lives. Feeding the conveyor belts, caught up in the mechanism of urban agglomerations, in the thrall of the industrial hierarchy (with its fatal division of work and intellectual capacity), man beholds his own handiwork as an autonomous material power. Amidst the products of joint labours in the human community, he feels an increasing loneliness and least of all that he is a man.

This *inversion* and *alienation* are inherent features of industrial civilization. The conditions man has evolved for his own activities appear as an alien power, which is not only independent of the desires and actions of individuals and the community, but even controls human desires and actions.[2] Its social source lies, of course, in the alienation of the conditions of human life and in the domination of a social element — capital — over the diversified flow of things and endeavours. We should not forget, however, that this contradictory nature of social conditions was also materialized and confined for centuries in the one-track

[1] "The quantity of new elements and effects of technological advance is coming to be so vast that it is evoking a new quality in civilization in which new methods of psycho-sociological moulding of man by his environment are emerging" (G. Friedmann, *Sept Etudes sur l'Homme et la Technique*, Paris 1967, pp. 150 et seq.).

[2] It is by this inversion that Marx and Engels define alienation (*The German Ideology*, MEGA, Vol. 5, Moscow—Leningrad 1933, p. 48), they underline that "this inversion is real, not just postulated" (*Grundrisse*, ibid., p. 716), that it involves an entire historically necessary stage demanded by the creation of wealth at the expense of the majority (*Arkhiv Marxa i Engelsa*, Moscow 1933, Vol. II/VII, p. 34).

industrial level of the means of production and in the corresponding contours of human life, that in industrial civilization "the separation of the producer from the means of employment is the expression of an actual revolution of the mode of production itself"[1], that this changeover is embodied in the whole world of products, in everything around man, everything that he uses. And even when a socialist revolution has inverted its social implications, this contradiction persists for a time, fixed in its material, technical guise in the entire working and living environment of industrial civilization.

The stifling element is not an actual excess of technical means (as the romantics believe), but their limited, imperfect development, the bias of the artificial environment, where in the manifestations of their lives large sections of the working community play the part not of master, but of servants; far from enjoying opportunities for their own development, they are involved in reproducing their existing way of life and producing wealth for other spheres. Marx considered this civilization to be "the ultimate form of alienation" and simultaneously "the transit point", which in an inverted form enforces conditions for "abolishing all the restricted preconditions of production" and for "the total universal development of the productive forces of the individual".[2] Marx's criticism of the industrial civilization of capitalism conceived of alienation being overcome through a radical transformation of both the social and the corresponding technological conditions, producing a civilization in which every link in the environmental structure would embody an *element of human development* emanating the power of common endeavour.

When technology is weak, it confines and masters man; when, however, it is perfected and versatile, it gives him the entry to his own independent development. Automation, chemical processes, industrial biology, modern consumer techniques, communications and urbanistic facilities are all beginning to exclude human service to the material world. The scientific and technological revolution, by and large, can allow civilization to be transformed into *service to man* — through adaption of the production process, and by evolving environments suitable for the cultivation of the human being.[3]

---

[1] K. Marx, *Capital*, Vol. III/2, p. 700; similarly, *Theorien über der Mehrwert*, Vol. III, Stuttgart 1921, p. 596 f.

[2] K. Marx, *Grundrisse*, ibid., p. 414—415.

[3] J. D. Bernal has described the prospect offered by modern science as follows: "It will no longer be a question of adapting man to the world but the world to man" (*The Social Function of Science*, London 1939, p. 379).

/*The Culture of Work*/ 3.2.2

Under the classical factory system the work place was a necessary evil where human energies were expended. Giving work and its motivation a one-track bias, the system complicated all the appliances of industry until they surpassed the comprehension of the individual. The material effect was given priority over the anthropological; in place of adapting the means of production, the aim was to *adapt man*, even to the length of *ruthless selection*.

When the primary function of the worker in industry was reduced to the monotonous repetition of a few physical operations, technology and design could make do with the most elementary anthropological considerations. These were the days of Taylor's "one best way"[1] (and associated fields of psychotechnics) to find the most suitable movements, habits, organization and rhythm of work — in short, rationalized use of man as simple labour power. But the more advanced the technological and organizational structure within which this system operated, the more obvious its inherent limits set by the identification of man with the machine. Taylorian rationalization was therefore subjected to growing criticism, demanding greater attention to the human factors in industry, such as *human relations*[2] — although again confined to the purely productive aspects, to the same rationalization of simple labour power. Growing claims on the human conditions of the production process are evident — in contrast to their initial debasement in the age of industrialization.[3]

Insofar as socialism relies (and will continue to rely for some time yet) on the industrial system, the need for providing the most effective working environment will present itself with full urgency, involving the problems of rational operation and the working regime. But this is far from exhausting the factors of rational management in this field. From application of findings about the influence of lighting, noise, dust, smells, colours, etc., through planning the conditions for "human relations", to ways of compensating the evil effects of the machine system combined with all kinds of technical means for taking over arduous and stereotype operations, the socialist community is faced with the intricate

[1] F. W. Taylor, *The Principles of Scientific Management*, New York 1911.
[2] E. Mayo, *The Human Problems of an Industrial Civilization*, New York 1933.
[3] This rising pressure of human demands is making headway even against the resistance of the accepted order. Its beginnings were recorded by G. Friedmann in *La Crise du Progrès, esquisse d'histoire des idées* (1895—1935), Paris 1936.

task — if only for a transitional period — of creating a fitting working environment that would encourage the maximum cultivation of people's own powers, while reducing to a minimum the social burden imposed by the conversion of labour power into a cog in the mechanism of industry.[1]

At a higher level, technological advance makes both work and management highly intellectual and complicated; breaking the old set-up of the industrial machine-man system (and the rule of man's adaptation), it shifts the problem to the entirely different,[2] mediated linkage of man and the automatic system. Here *adaptation of technology and organization* comes to the fore — what is the optimal amount of information for man? What social and psychical circumstances will alter his ability to act and show initiative? Such questions indicate the extent to which "the human aspect" is emerging as the limiting factor throughout the modern industrial system. Considerations of hygiene, psychology, indeed of culture, can in these circumstances be genuinely decisive in the choice of techniques, or the size and composition of the work force, and set the course in operating and designing.[3] In the most advanced countries this trend is assuming practical forms, including institutions for *industrial sociology*[4] and *industrial psychology*,[5] subjects that have long since outgrown their original functions and are proving of real value, although, of course, they are still used for the smooth integration of the labour force in the regime of a firm and for damping down the conflicts in which the working-class movement tries it strength.

---

[1] While authors such as Adorno and Horkheimer have shown up some programmes for "humanizing work" as instruments for adapting the workers to bourgeois undertakings, one cannot deny the justification of such socialist writers as Hochfeld and Prudenski in calling for the elaboration of "humanization of work" projects for socialism, which would bridge over the period during which radical changes in the mode of work cannot be expected, and would ultimately serve as the instruments of such changes.

[2] Although the observation of human parameters in automated works, carried out by C. R. Walker, stemmed from an opposed concept, the difference between the machine and automated industries in their human aspects was evident at every turn (*Toward the Automatic Factory*, New Haven 1957).

[3] Many experts have argued that accidents, which have reached first place among the diseases of civilization, are in 80—90 per cent of cases caused by failure to master the human dimensions of production.

[4] In the USA and Great Britain, "human relations", in West Germany and Italy, "paternalism" and the like.

[5] Some of the most modern firms employ industrial psychologists to the extent of one for every few hundred employees (Western Electric, which was among the first to feel the need to tackle these questions, has one psychologist per 300 employees).

What we may call the culture of work comes rapidly to the fore in times of technological upheaval. Alongside the emergence of scientific disciplines concerned with applying psychology, labour sociology and physiology directly to design and construction and tackling their problems at the highest theoretical level (ergonomics), we see concentrated attention being devoted in the USSR and other socialist countries primarily to the most advanced approaches — psychological engineering, that offer socialism wide opportunities and are best fitted to the concern with the human dimensions of production required by the scientific and technological revolution.

In these circumstances the lag in industrial sociology and psychology and shortcomings in their application are a big handicap for a socialist country.[1] There is an urgently felt need for a network of departments of human work (sociology and industrial psychology) in large enterprises, branch managements, design organizations and technical schools, and in the system of basic research; such a network could bring a scientific approach to bear on questions of the working environment, channelling of skills and personal prospects, on personnel distribution and motivations in work, etc., and would ultimately imbue the entire system of modern production with the *human aspect*.

With the growth of the creative elements of work, there will in all probability be a shift towards individual care in cultivating people's abilities in their jobs. Even today psychological engineering and ergonomics are leading in some places to the replacement of the black, misshapen silhouettes of factories by harmoniously designed, psychologically conceived, aesthetic work places resembling laboratories, landscaped in greenery and equipped with all modern amenities. These are signposts to coming revolutions in the meaning of "employment" and in the role of "the work place" for man and society.

---

[1] In Czechoslovakia there has been a delayed start in this field. There are now about 200 labour psychologists. But the qualitative aspect of the problem is coming to the fore. If psychology is to be usefully employed in economic operation, the psychologists need to gain a broader view of production-economics in practice from the angle of future trends, while managing personnel will have to be capable of demanding psychological expertize and equally of applying its findings. The evident need is to concentrate the psychologists at the key centres of management and give management personnel thorough psychological preparation. Only the first steps in this direction have been taken so far.

/*Shaping the Environment*/

Since the start of industrialization, industrial agglomeration has exerted an inexorable centripetal pull to the cities, accompanied by vertical construction, the disintegration of traditional small-town units and the decline of farm settlements (see Table 3-5). Although the process of civilization has been linked from ancient times with the growth of urban settlements — those condensers of human relationships and of the productive forces built upon them — the history of modern civilization is *predominantly* that of the towns.[1]

Spontaneous economic pressures carried most weight here,[2] the town with its ring of suburbs allowed for the necessary aggregation of labour power divorced from the land and all means of production, and always at hand for use in industry. The classical industrial town arose as a murky stone agglomeration of machines for reproducing human labour power[3] — Manchester, Essen and Chicago of the old days laid bare the grim reality of the industrial city.

In the age of factories and the machine, the big cities undoubtedly manifested themselves as the only dynamic centres of opportunity and the only road to a higher level of civilization — both in consequence of the general division of labour, with the accompanying material equipment of the tertiary sphere (shops, services, transport) and in the opportunities — exclusive to the cities — for applying existing techniques and hygienic amenities in urban dwellings (electrification, gas, water supplies, sewerage, telephones, etc.)

In the industrially advanced countries, the towns absorbed the majority of the population; now, not only relative but also absolute decline in rural populations is increasingly frequent.[4] In the mid-sixties, the populations of towns and urban areas accounted for 85 per cent of the total population in Great Britain, 72 per cent in West Germany, 69 per cent in the U.S., 58 per cent in France, 53 per cent in the USSR[5],

[1] L. Mumford, *The City in History*, London 1961.
[2] This is noted by L. Wirth in *Urbanism as a Way of Life* (*Cities and Society*), Glencoe 1957, and J. Ziołkiewski, *Urbanizacja, miasto, osiedle*, Warsaw 1965.
[3] S. Chase, in his book *Men and Machines* (New York 1929), remarked, basing himself on A. Freeman, "Engines have ...created huge cities adjusted to the needs of themselves but totally unadjusted to the human beings..."
[4] In France, for example, the population of the countryside was 26.8 million in 1926, in 1962 17.2 million.
[5] The corresponding figure for Czechoslovakia today is 60 per cent. Within this high level of urbanization, however, the structure is diffuse — only 15 per cent live in

(while the world average was 30 per cent) and around the year 2000 it is generally expected that this figure will rise to 80—90 per cent.[1]

The urban sprawl is no longer confined to the immediate vicinity of the towns — feelers are reaching out to formerly untouched spots. The traditional town is "exploding" into a super-town, a conurbation. The march of urbanization is pressing with growing insistence on the boundaries beyond which the city acquires the nature of the megalopolis,[2] in which the vast uncontrollable massing of civilization's fruits brings man back to the elementary problem of the "inhabitability" of the artificial environment.[3] Escape from the cities, the mass spread of horizontal settlements of a recreational type — these are just the accompaniments of unfettered urbanization. This blind alley, this disturbance of the metabolism of man and nature, demonstrates that the traditional ideas of the industrial city as a localized concentration of people and industry has outlived its day and calls for radical revision;[4] what is needed is radical reconstruction with a view to re-styling and moulding the environment to human needs. This in its turn calls for a revolutionary change in man's objective status in civilization, combined with an entirely new technology for controlling the environment.[5]

The scientific and technological revolution therefore appears as a condition for a new departure in the process of urbanization, as a

towns of over 100,000 inhabitants, compared with 60 in U.S. and 30 for the USSR (see Table 3—4). The reason is the large number of small industrial towns and settlements (32 per cent of dwellers in communities of up to 5,000 inhabitants are connected with industry), and widespread commuting (50 per cent of gainfully employed people in communities of up to 5,000 inhabitants commute to work), and finally the general tendency towards levelling out and overlapping of town and countryside in Czechoslovakia.

[1] For instance, in *Land for the Future* (Baltimore 1960), M. Clawson and others have estimated that the share of the urban population in the U.S. will be 84 per cent in 2000.

[2] Jean Gottmann, *Megalopolis*, New York 1960.

[3] The long-term problem of "the inhabitability of towns" was first pointed out by K. Honzík in *Tvorba životního slohu*, Prague 1947, p. 93.

[4] Leaving aside the biassed "criticism of cities" that has accompanied the spread of urbanization since the days of Sir Ebenezer Howard, we can still trace the awareness of this urban crisis in Gropius's idea of decongestion, in Milyutin's proposals for zoned towns, in Neutra's "Rush City" projects, Abercrombie's polycentric towns and Giedion's concept of differentiated types of settlement.

[5] The fate of Western functionalism and Soviet constructivism demonstrates the futility of all ventures that fail to link social and technological innovations. O. Nový, *Konec velkoměsta* (The End of the City), Prague 1966; J. Hrůza, *Teorie měst* (Theory of Towns), Prague 1966.

dividing line in man's relation to all material reality — to the environment in which men and communities pass their lives and the ways in which people adapt nature, moulding it and making it fit for their habitation. The impact of the scientific and technological revolution on the process of urbanization can be expected to follow several courses:

a) It will relieve the concentration around industry (in view of the fall-off in the demand of the secondary sector for manpower); but it will also underline the importance of services as a focussing power and will ultimately evolve a strong attractive force in the shape of *scientific and cultural centres*. Indeed, in some parts of the United States today (Boston, Houston) we can see how industry is moving to centres of science.[1] There is little hope for the idea of promoting the development of small or medium towns if they are not treated as new focal points of civilization, with an interweaving of research, technological, educational and cultural facilities.

b) Advances in transportation and communications techniques have enormously increased the extent to which distance in urbanistic projects can be compensated by speed. They have given space a new quality, enabling it to be widely used as an optional dimension in man's environment. Growth of the transportation and communications systems is proving a potent factor in organizing concepts of urban development. In this connection we most frequently come across tendencies towards *structuring* towns, building planned systems of differentiated communities, residential quarters intermingled with recreation areas, projecting housing construction in natural settings and so on.

c) Modern technology introduces a new factor into urban development, heralding a complete change in the traditional materials and methods of construction,[2] through the use of new plastics, ceramic materials, aluminium, etc., and coordination of civil engineering works. New types of family houses produced by unorthodox mass production methods, terrace and patio houses on slopes, mobile dwellings, etc., can in some cases prove as sound a proposition as construction of many-storied buildings. Remembering that standardized dwelling in massive apartment blocks breeds demand for a second home (country cottage, etc.), the family house is not really so wasteful of land. Investigations have not confirmed that apartment houses as such foster a community

[1] Cf. I. Dubská, *Americký rok* (American Year), Prague 1966, p. 427.
[2] Cf. K. Janů, *Nové stavebnictví a architektura* (New Building and Architecture), Prague 1967, and E. Carter, R. Glass and others in *The World in 1984*, Vol. 2, Baltimore 1965.

spirit, or that family houses tend to disrupt social contacts; indeed, it seems that the crux does not lie in the type of dwelling, but in the nature of the environment.

Without trying to anticipate the results of more detailed examinations of these trends or forecasting the potentialities or time schedules of their application in practice, we cannot but see that some radical changes are already taking place in urban development; current theoretical projects[1] have in common the idea that as human development, human wants and the human aspect in general are underlined by the growing impact of science and technology, entirely new spatial dimensions and structures of settlement will be needed, including multifunctional area planning, covering regions, countries or, indeed, entire continents. Developments press for a balance among the economic, social, technological, cultural, recreational and other functions of the environment in the process of all-round cultivation of human power. The scientific and technological revolution will in all probability eliminate the traditional contrast between town and countryside by a harmonious blending of urban and rural features, of built-up and open areas, thereby giving shape to the vision of "the fusion of town and country".[2]

The key question remains whether in the coming decades man will encounter a differentiated material environment in which he will be able to enjoy the advantages of diverse types of dwelling that he can alternate and individualize. In this transition to independent, dynamic contriving, in other words, *creating a style of life* which alone can open the way to man's full self-realization in a technically advanced civilization, lie hitherto almost untapped sources of human power. Socialism is offered a unique opportunity to frame a far-sighted, comprehensive policy for shaping the environment,[3] whereby dwelling, working, transportation, services, culture and recreation would be integrated; the aim would be intensive *cultivation of entire regions* and changes in the structure of settlement — which in any event promises to be an indispensable condition of civilization.

These considerations will in the end have to apply to the priorities of

---

[1] Cf. Hillebrecht's idea of a city region, Pchelintsev's plans for urbanized areas or Doxiadis' *Ekumenopolis*.

[2] F. Engels, *Anti-Dühring*, New York, 1966, p. 323.

[3] This concept is advanced in the study, First Version of a Long-term Environment Forecast, prepared in 1966 by Z. Lakomý and others, which draws on broadly-based material provided by *Projekt R* (area planning) and *Studie Z* (analysis of investments and environment) made by the Research Institute for Construction and Architecture.

public investment in shaping the environment;[1] during the scientific and technological revolution investment in the cultivation of human potentialities will acquire growing importance.

/Application of Nature and Seeking a Home/ 3.2.4

Industry and urbanization divorced man from nature, imposing their mediation on all contacts between man and his environment. He was placed in an entirely new situation; his being in the world no longer derived from his natural attributes — evolved as a distinct historically moulded and modified, autonomous existence, in which Leonardo da Vinci already perceived the "second nature of man".

However, the more civilization confines man in artificial, but one-sided structures — in their totality uncontrolled and therefore remote from the conditions for human development — the more it evokes in him a new, specific need of civilized man: the *need for nature*, for contact with the original, natural surroundings that once played the double role of an accepted, welcoming home and the merciless, indifferent hand of fate. Growing power over the material things of nature, the ability to manipulate the whole structure of things he meets with, the prospect of changing his environment in terms of countries and continents, can be rightly viewed as the condition for genuine human self-realization and as a source of true human life.[2] However, such a power over nature must ultimately bring man (and society) back within his own limitations: in an industrial civilization it is, after all, merely an external, and in that sense quite limited, power based on the separation of man from

---

[1] Hitherto the means invested in Czechoslovakia in the environment have been limited by extensive industrialization. This has caused a lag in housing construction (about 60 per cent behind the USSR and Sweden), in the number of rooms per 100 inhabitants (about 20—30 per cent behind West Germany and France), in the sanitary equipment of dwellings (fifty per cent behind Britain and Sweden). While in Czechoslovakia some 15 per cent of investments is directed to housing and 10 per cent to public construction, in other advanced countries the figures are around 20 per cent for public facilities and 20 per cent for housing and its development, offering prospects for remarkably rapid modernization of their standards of accommodation, and their upward trend is a sign of the times (cf. Table 3—6).

[2] "...the restricted relation of men to nature determines their restricted relation to one another, and their restricted relation to one another determines men's restricted relation to nature, just because nature is as yet hardly modified historically" (K. Marx, F. Engels, *The German Ideology*, New York 1966, p. 20).

nature; the outcome is, therefore, nature reduced to a mere means or mechanism — a machine for human life. The artificially constructed environment again manifests itself as a power confining man, reducing him to a "denatured being" or machine.[1]

The natural ground having been lost, the certainties it afforded are also lacking and civilization inevitably appears as a harbinger of doom.[2] With the very first steps of industrial civilization — from the days of Novalis, Chateaubriand and Ruskin — this fact inspired a wave of romantic efforts to halt the invasion of nature by technology and to return from "the artificial world" to "the womb of nature". The industrial system was, indeed, still in a position to send people oppressed by the artificial environment of factories and towns to seek refuge in the evergreen, undefiled "tree of life"; they could seek compensation for industrial work in recreation and for city dwelling by going to the countryside.[3]

However, the present century has witnessed the acceleration and extension of man's intervention in the material, ecological, vegetational, biotic and climatic factors of his environment, while hand in hand with this process grows concern about "the man-made world".[4] The *technical world* seems to have come for good.[5] The artificial environment reaches out, encroaching step by step on all the refuges of nature. There is nowhere to run away.

The uncurbed technical advance intensifies the desperate need for nature, while eating away the soil that could satisfy the need. In the fruitless oscillation between industry and the cities at one pole, and recreation and nature at the other, modern man is driven backwards and forwards at breakneck speed along an endless road. Fifty years ago the average American made only a few visits in a life-time to the open country, a national park, forest or holiday resort; in 1964, he went almost every year; today, several times a year, and prognoses for the

---

[1] Francis Bacon inadvertently indicated this internal mechanism; Samuel Butler depicted it in *Erewhon*.

[2] E. Carpenter, *Civilization, Its Cause and Cure*, 1889.

[3] Here were the roots of the movement (Thoreau, Nansen and others) that sought new values of civilization in the enjoyment of unspoilt nature.

[4] Jacob Hommes, *Der technische Eros*, Freiburg 1955.

[5] Contemporary followers of the romantic critics of civilization have come to take this trend more or less for granted. Cf. A. Gehlen, *Die Seele in technischer Zeitalter. Sozialpsychologische Probleme in der industriellen Gesellschaft*, Hamburg 1957; H. Freyer, *Über das Dominantwerden technischer Kategorie in der Lebenswelt der industriellen Gesellschaft*, Mainz 1960.

year 2000 envisage a fantastic frequency of one visit in three weeks.[1] The frontal attack on the countryside, the swelling stream of recreation, is beginning to frustrate its own aims — overcrowded resorts are sprawling out, full of noise, polluted air, water and land. At the present rate, a few decades will see the devastation of the landscape.[2] The only salvation lies in a considered and consistent policy for conserving nature, starting with a halt to the dissemination of industry; it should include tall blocks combined with family houses, planned siting of leisure-time areas to suit all tastes, bungalow towns, camps, etc., delimiting nature reserves, national parks and "quiet areas". The only solution will be to plan the country, just as today a house or housing estate is designed and built.

Civilized man will not return to the arms of nature, but he can *use* protected nature as a boon of civilization; he can *apply* nature, turn it into an enormous laboratory for generating human power and so renew on a higher level the intimate contact without which he would be drowned in the technical flood sweeping over the earth.

When man outdoes nature, he loses his natural home and is forced to look for it in the world of his own creation. Once he has taken his leave of nature, he is left alone and he experiences an elementary urge for the beauties of forests, meadows and streams to enter into his everyday environment. As industry robs his activities of their function as genuine self-realization, it forces him to find other means of impressing his personal mould on his unique creations and incomparable deeds. To the extent that the city with its lack of intimacy[3] denies the opportunity to take refuge in the secure, cosy and familiar places of living, it makes the yearning for a home a modern obsession that people bear with them everywhere, inevitably transferring its implications to the whole world.[4]

In the civilization of coming decades all of us will find ourselves to some extent in the position of an astronaut for whom the artificial reconstruction and control of the elementary conditions of existence is a matter of life and death. A society that proved incapable of mastering

---

[1] *Resources in America's Future*, ed. H. H. Landsberg, L. L. Fischman, J. L. Fisher, Baltimore 1963.

[2] In a country as densely populated as Czechoslovakia, present trends promise the devastation of most natural areas in 20 years.

[3] Cf. *The Exploding Metropolis*, ed. Fortune, New York 1957, or P. H. Chombart de Lauwe, *Des Hommes et des Villes*, Paris 1965. A typical feature in this connection is the remoteness of modern towns from the child mentality.

[4] Cf. I. Dubský, Domov a bezdomovosť (Home and Homelessness) in: *Človek kto si?*, Bratislava 1965.

the production of a balanced artificial environment, of turning the global and often unbalanced onrush of technology to man's advantage, would undoubtedly be faced with the devastation of its natural conditions and a tragic disturbance of the biological and mental balance of its people.

/ The Necessity of Beauty /

3.2.5

The works, streets, houses and articles that we commonly meet in daily life bear unmistakable witness to the fact that the industrial revolution cast out of production and the life of the people *the aesthetic dimension* which the craftsman still had at his command. This accorded with the nature of civilization based on technical methods that had no need for people with special skills, but required, in the words of James Watt, merely "mechanical forces", a civilization whose bourgeois social order set no value on a varied assortment of human personalities, but needed a host of nameless, exchangeable units of labour — as demonstrated by Adam Smith and David Ricardo. Understandably, where people's activities and their way of life are deprived of the specific feature of self-realization, where their contact with the material environment has no room for the *free play* of human powers, in which Schiller perceived the essence of the aesthetic dimension,[1] the category of beauty loses its practical *raison d'etre*. From this stems the conviction that technology and art, springing in antique times from common roots, now lie irrevocably at opposite poles of this world; that the rational approach is at variance with emotional fruition and that, on the contrary, Brunetière's proclaimed "bankruptcy of science" paves the way for beauty to return to human life.

However, the freer the advance of science and technology, the more clearly they reveal the limits of this facile generalization. Beyond a divide set by the realization of the human dimensions in man's own handiwork, we see emerging from the hard planes and sheer, uncompromising contours of the human edifice, from the artificially evoked play of light and shade, from the strangely integrated harmony of colour and movement, unique technical beauty that enriches the senses with "*a fresh* kind of perception and pleasure".[2] Few would deny the thrilling

[1] F. Schiller, *Über die ästhetische Erziehung des Menschen*, letter 14, *Gesammelte Werke*, Berlin 1955.
[2] L. Mumford, *Technics and Civilization*, 1934, p. 334.

presence of aesthetic restraint in Le Corbusier's austerely integrated constructions, in modern urban units and sophisticated technical designs. And however incredible it may seem to the uninitiated, science today is absorbing the aesthetic element in growing measure: we can cite many reliable witnesses for the view that even modern "mathematics has a cultural and aesthetic appeal".[1]

Since the days of the Hawthorne studies, sociological and psychological investigations have provided plenty of evidence that the aesthetic appearance of work places and tools, the design of towns, apartments, vehicles, shops and services, attractive designing of consumer goods, gay packaging, good layout of books and newspapers — in short, the aesthetics of the whole range of articles composing man's artificial environment, have a far stronger influence on *human abilities and flexibility* than has ever been admitted hitherto. A well-composed product of human endeavour evidently stimulates the creative power and heightens the capacity of subjective sensibility. On the contrary, untended work places, shabby streets, comfortless dwellings, smoky railway stations, people and things of drab appearance stifle self-respect, make people demand less of themselves, and represent not inconsiderable obstacles to the progress of creative powers. In the age of the scientific and technological revolution, when everything depends on cultivating human abilities, beauty and feeling are "as indispensable" as reason and utility.[2] It is no accident that today aesthetic values are at least to some extent ceasing to be confined to luxury goods, that industrialists, who are far from forgetting to look to their profits, are requiring architects to produce artistic designs for factories and works, that the whole field of design is enlisting the aid of industrial aesthetics, that many countries, in the West and East, have laid down that a percentage of costs on industrial buildings has to be devoted to the aesthetic aspect, that contrary to all expectations, even in countries where artistic life has never been to the fore, the tendency towards a reinstatement of true aesthetic values is breaking through the wall of commercial "mass culture".[3]

[1] N. Wiener, *I Am a Mathematician; the Later Life of a Prodigy*, Cambridge 1964, p. 62. Wiener shocked the romantics by his contention that mathematics itself, with its free play of imagination, "is essentially one of the arts" (ibid., p. 65).

[2] The French prognoses, *Réflexions pour 1985* (ibid. p. 83), rightly link this circumstance with the current changes in civilization: "Today, at the threshold of the scientific and technological revolution, we are discovering that it is necessary to declare the right of every individual to live amidst beauty..."

[3] In the US, where until recently cultural matters have proverbially tended to take a back seat, sales of books of literary worth have doubled over the last ten years,

For architecture, technical aesthetics and all fields of cultural and artistic activity in a socialist context, these connotations of the scientific and technological revolution offer almost unlimited and hitherto unexploited opportunities — and imperative needs. In the transition — typified by job specialization, a one-track preoccupation with technical matters and the pressure of mass consumer culture, accompanied by a break-up of traditional artistic attitudes reflecting the drastic conflict between man and his creations that is being fought out on the fringes of modern civilization[1] — we may certainly expect a tendency to bias, amounting even to artistic insensitivity, which cannot, however, be countered by holding back science and technology, but solely by compensating the shortcomings with powerful work in the *artistic* sphere, with art that moves from within and evokes unrest and commitment rather than satisfaction — art that opens man to history and quickens the power to communicate the fundamental existential experiences of the human race.[2]

Only when man's activities start to assume the aspect of freely operating human powers, when cultivation of abilities will last a lifetime — only then will a situation exist in which receptivity to the higher artistic values will be encouraged[3] and they will be communicable to all. Only when the relationship to external nature assumes the aspect of man's self-realization through his work and through his fellow man — only then can we expect a merging of exact rational inventiveness with the sources of deep emotional and aesthetic experience.[4] Indeed, beyond a boundary set by existing barriers of civilization, the two spheres are in effect merely different dimensions of the same enriching of the human

there has been a sharp rise in the number of musical ensembles and interest in works of art has grown considerably.

[1] Many analyses of current civilization trends note in one form or another the relevance of the present-day artistic media and aesthetic concepts to the absurd limits reached by technology in its potential human implications. Cf. C. R. de Carlo in *Technology and Social Change*, ed. Ginzberg, New York 1964, p. 12; similarly, K. Chvatík, "Umění ve světě vědy a techniky" (Art in the World of Science and Technology), *Nová mysl* 2/1968.

[2] Cf. A Mokrejš, *Umění, skutečnost, poznání* (Art, Reality, Knowledge), Prague 1966.

[3] T. Veblen noted long ago in *The Instinct of Workmanship and the State of the Industrial Arts* (New York 1914, p. 30) that the "artistic instinct" was fading with the decline of the crafts and reviving in some fields of engineering and technical work.

[4] A. N. Whitehead regards the maturing of the human personality as a condition for both scientific creativeness and aesthetic sensitivity (*Science and the Modern World*, New York 1948, p. 199).

personality, the same development of man by man.[1] And *vice versa*. This unfolding of personality and individual talents and of the human aspects in all fields is the unique and indispensable role of the arts in the transformations through which civilization is passing.[2] Some significant correlations should be borne in mind for the future: none of the great scientists with whose names even the very beginnings of the scientific and technological revolution are linked has been known to lack culture and a love of the arts. This has deep-lying causes. Aesthetics is an essential dimension of all human creative powers and its theory is therefore a key to many problems of man's self-realization in the technological age.

/*Laying Hold of Space and Time*/ 3.2.6

The present course of civilization amounts in effect to a shrinking of space and dilation of time. The stream of scientific discoveries and technical innovations[3] now accelerating changes in the foundations of human life is overrunning a boundary of crucial importance for man and his existence. If the realities correspond to the generalization drawn from analyses of current happenings,[4] the time lag between the discovery of something new in science and its realization in practice has been reduced from 37 years (which at the start of the century was more than the average productive span of life) to 9—14 years (that is, one-quarter to one-third of the present average productive life span). This means that in a single lifetime one may experience three to four startling

[1] Marx conceived of the development of man and his powers in its fully human connotation as a mutual process of man's cultivation by science and the arts (cf. K. Marx, *Grundrisse*, ibid., p. 593). — Whereas "...the abstract hostility between sense and spirit is inevitable so long as the human sense for nature, or the human meaning of nature, and consequently the *natural* sense of *man*, has not been produced through man's own labor". In: *Marx's Concept of Man*, ed. E. Fromm, 1967, p. 148.

[2] Because "All true art has always invoked a humanity that did not yet exist" (E. Fischer, *The Necessity of Art*, London 1963, p. 219). The idea of the key place held by art in developing the individuality is discussed by Herbert Read in *Education Through Art*, London 1958.

[3] The volume of scientific findings is now doubled in less than ten years — compare the flow of inventions described in *Frontiers of Science* (1958) with the list in *Handbuch zur Geschichte der Naturwissenschaften und der Technik*, by L. Darmstaedter (1908).

[4] Cf. estimates by F. Lynn, made for the National Commission of Technology, Automation and Economic Progress (*Technology and the American Economy*, Washington 1966).

innovations induced by discoveries that few are in a position to foresee. The same accelerated rate of change is to be seen in the sphere of consumption; the increment in average real income which a working man could expect in a lifetime has now to be envisaged within ten years — that is, several times in the course of his life.[1]

The same interaction of higher *mobility* and *temporality* now spreading through industry and consumption can also be observed in relation to employment and occupations, skills and education, etc. The days are not long past when the general tenor of man's life was set at his birth by the level of civilization and culture. The feature of the present day, however — and we can expect it to be more pronounced in the future — is that a man's lot is not shaped by the world into which he is born, but by changes that the dynamics of civilization and culture — and man himself — will accomplish in the course of a lifetime. The future will evidently see a breaking of the bonds holding a man to one place, one occupation, one rhythm, one set of values for life — both the bonds originating in connection with the land and with absorption in the industrial agglomeration. The very beginnings of the scientific and technological revolution signalize strong pressure towards mobility of professions, occupations and dwellings — both for objective reasons (changes in technology) and subjective motivations (changes in skills).

Mobility in many dimensions is coming to be a feature of modern man and simultaneously a new anthropological characteristic. Bearing in mind the potential human implications of these movements — the path to the development and universality of man — we see them as entirely positive values, but people accustomed to the stable round of working to live and living to work are as yet rather unprepared for such changes and tend to feel that they are being debased and uprooted.

Advances in the techniques and speed of transportation have radically altered the meaning of *space*. The conquest of space by time has reached such lengths that for our terrestrial purposes distance is no longer a problem: any part of the globe can be reached in a matter of hours. The attack on the Moon and the planets is just a typical expression of this process by which man is staking his claim to space.[2]

[1] Calculated from figures in S. Lebergott, *Manpower in Economic Growth. The American Record Since 1800*. New York—San Francisco—Toronto—London, 1964.

[2] The systematic attention devoted since the first successes of the Soviet space programme to planning and elaborating space flights — including projects for interplanetary travel (cf. D. M. Cole, *Beyond Tomorrow, The Next 50 Years in Space*, Amhurst 1965), surpasses — at least in the USA — anything in other spheres of human undertaking.

Mobility is now making something of an Icarian symbol of free horizons (rapid movement in space, long journeys), but in its ungoverned aspect it is felt as an imposition,[1] a thief of free time.[2] We can expect some remarkable innovations, alongside sharp conflicts, in this field. With a nearly five-fold increase in the number of automobiles over the past thirty years bringing the total over the 200 million mark, we can look forward to entire countries being changed into motorized deserts by the end of the century.[3] Yet the majority of advanced European countries envisage that the next twenty years will raise the percentage of families owning automobiles from the present 10—15 per cent to the level in the USA today, i.e., almost as many cars as families.[4] But once the automobile is a universal amenity, it becomes unusable in urban areas; its speed drops almost to that of a pedestrian, while it fouls the air and assails the ears. Therefore various technical innovations are being considered, such as new means of propulsion, special fuel units, new methods of driving by connecting vehicles to electronic networks and by computer techniques, providing mass automatic control,[5] which would involve a completely novel concept of personal transportation. New public transport systems are also in course of preparation, relying mainly on high-speed elevated and underground railways, and hovercraft[6] for use on land and waterways. Forecasts up to the year 2000 envisage some 85 per cent of public transport taking to the air (see Table 3-8); intensive work is being put into the construction of vertical take-off planes and the development of rocket transport. Only a well-considered approach, combining modern high-speed public facilities with rational development in the private sphere, can avert a major traffic calamity.

However rapidly means of transportation may multiply, the urge towards *world travel* looks like outstripping them. People in the millions

[1] Total expenditures in transportation reaches in the USA the startling figure of 20 per cent of the gross national product (cf. G. S. Wheeler, "Problems in Transport in Cities of the United States" in Czechoslovak Economic Papers, Prague 1965/4, p. 9).

[2] Travel to and from work still occupies one hour and more a day on average in Western Europe; the figure for Czechoslovakia (where nearly a half of employees commute) is 40—50 minutes daily.

[3] Cf. *Traffic in Towns*, Buchanan Report, London 1963.

[4] In Czechoslovakia some 11 per cent of families own cars at present, but studies of motorism suggest a figure of one automobile to every second family by 1980. Most socialist countries anticipate a similar upswing.

[5] M. Glanville, "Roads and Traffic in 1984" in *The World in 1984*, vol. I, ed. N. Calder, London 1964.

[6] C. S. Cockerell, "The Prospects for Hover Transport" in *The World in 1984* (ibid.).

are on the move.[1] Over the last decade the number of people travelling abroad has trebled (see Table 3-9) and the trend is still upward.[2] In some countries 20—30 per cent of the population spend vacations abroad and present trends suggest that in 10—15 years it will be the general rule. Although at present rushed transportation, commercialism and prefabrication are robbing the tourist flood of many rewarding contacts with people and environments,[3] there is no doubt that authentic knowledge of many lands and continents will prove to be a most valuable approach in cultivating human potentialities.

Accelerating mobility is impinging on the world of human products, too: industrial plant, machinery and equipment grow obsolete in an amazingly short time — the cycle of modernization is contracting. Consumer goods outdate so rapidly that the habit of temporary repairs or immediate replacement is spreading. While these processes can place man above his products, they may also rob him of all respect for his own creations and lead to destructive attitudes. Indeed, the consumer system drives this "throw-away spirit" to the point of intentional waste.[4]

The steadily accelerating rate of obsolescence is rapidly encroaching on all fields of human life — the technological, economic, legal, educational, artistic and so on — undermining the traditional standards and customs; it is manifested as a debasing of all values, as "partaking for the moment without view to the past or future".[5] In reality it simply underscores the need for people to adopt a *flexible, original concept* for their own lives and that of society — and that is no easy matter, because in this case man's inner identity has to rely on values going deeper than the preoccupation with any immutable and superficial axioms. And who other than people who have experienced a great social revolution can be expected to show the disposition and undertaking for such a dynamic treatment of human life?

---

[1] "Vacation nomadism" is partly a reaction to the way in which people have hitherto been tied to their appointed station all the rest of the year. Cf. B. Filipcová, *Člověk, práce, volný čas* (Man, Work and Leisure), Prague 1967, p. 91.

[2] According to records of Union Internationale des Organismes Officiels de Tourisme, the figure of 25 million visits to other countries was topped in 1950 for the first time in the history of foreign travel; by 1958 the figure was 50 million; by 1964 there were 100 million visits and in 1966 close to 130 million travellers spent 13 billion dollars abroad, i.e., more than, for example, the earnings of the world oil trade.

[3] Cf. D. J. Boorstine, *The Image*, New York 1964.

[4] Vance Packard has patiently compiled a list of the monstrous wastages inspired by this "throw-away spirit" — cf. *The Waste Makers*, 1960.

[5] K. Jaspers in *Wo stehen wir Heute?*, Gütersloh 1960.

Technological civilization gives man an idea of the depth of space and the sharp taste of time, but it also lays their riches before him. Ever since cybernation has compressed incredible numbers of operations into a split second, and the space scientists have embarked on the practical investigation of Einstein's relations of space and time, it has been evident that man's mastery of time will be a real key to the secret of human existence in this world.

/ *Technology and Health* /   3.2.7

For the first time the original process of industrialization made the health of the working masses a private concern — a matter of indifference to the mode of production as such. But simultaneously the growth of civilization generalized the social nature of diseases (especially epidemics) to such a degree that health services had to be provided as a sector of the national economy. These two trends within the industrial system determined the conditions of man's life for a long time.

The injury to health caused by industrial exhalations (see Table 3-10), water pollution and soil erosion, sometimes outright devastation of the countryside, is well known. Workers were exposed to the evils of monotonous work, to noise, vibration, dust and noxious substances. The mode of life was deformed by speed-up accompanied by the loss of varied movement, by unbalanced diets of high carbohydrate content and deficient in proteins, vitamins, etc. Industrialization bore down on man with its uncontrolled urban ecology. These conditions were so immanently bound up with the very nature of extensive industrialization that no subjective effort, no amount of measures and regulations could cope with them adequately.[1] The cure has usually been found to be slower than the spread of the damage. There are grave indications that if expert regulation, based on the structure of economic interests, is not undertaken, the consequences of industrialization may well present such a danger to health that they will start to operate as a limiting factor of social advance.

The scientific and technological revolution can be expected to contribute some health-giving factors: the gradual shift to creative work, rising living standards, extension of leisure, control of most traditional

[1] Czechoslovakia has a highly developed system of free health services available to all; there is also legislation providing for protection of the environment, etc.

diseases by treatment and prevention, opportunities for the scientific management of many aspects of life — in their outcome, however, each of these factors may work in more than one way, and only some can be identified. With the importance that the "human factor" is assuming today, every question of *human health* is necessarily felt as a *social* problem; mounting expenditure on health care in the industrial countries is just a remote indication of this fact.

As the life span grows longer, the accepted rhythm of people's lives is disrupted. In the advanced countries the immediate future holds out the prospect[1] of "a third phase of life", "active old-age" lasting from 50—60 to 70—80 years of age — a phase with its distinct and as yet unidentified opportunities for work and social engagement (transfer to occupations requiring less physical effort and mental alertness, but where experience is of value). Mature scientific civilization can be expected to discard the outdated seniority principle and give the interplay of the generations in the social organism a more effective pattern.

The methods of countering the health risks of the technological environment are for the most part known to present-day science. Nevertheless, these material potentialities are usually held in check by the unfettered spread of civilization, in which the human aspects has as a rule appeared as a by-product of material endeavour and the operation of the industrial system; consequently health care, too, has usually come on the scene after the event and often too late. In face of the complexity of current revolutionary changes, the instability of such a state of affairs is only too clear. We know from experience that most dangerous aspects originate in the transition phases and the uneven advance of civilization. But we may be faced in the future with quite new, unknown factors of a physical, chemical, biological and psychological nature, or hitherto insignificant factors may come to the fore — and the most serious circumstance will be their long-term operation in small doses, their cumulative potential (e.g. new chemical substances in the environment and in foodstuffs, physical factors such as noise or radioactive materials). The artificial environment of modern civilization contains an increasing amount of mutagens that can upset the genetic code

---

[1] Cf. *Ciba Foundation Colloquia on Ageing*, London 1955—1959; Z. G. Frenkel, *Udlineniye zhizni i deyatelnaya starost*, Moscow 1949; J. Dumazedier, A. Ripert, "Troisième age et loisirs", *Revue internationale des sciences sociales* 3/1963, etc. Every ten years the span of human life is now extended by several years. Studies made by the Rand Corporation in the USA suggest that within the next hundred years the duration of life may grow by a half.

of the human body.[1] The growing consumption of new medicinal preparations is also potentially dangerous in that it may upset the mental balance, induce changes in the properties of bacteria through widespread use of antibiotics, etc. Nor are the advances in surgery and medicine without their problems, because by preserving the lives of defective individuals they may cause a temporary genetic handicap leading to deterioration in the quality of the population. Finally, it is hardly conceivable that a technologically advanced society can remain permanently indifferent to the population explosion,[2] which although it is induced by the successes of science and technology, squanders their fruits and presents a real threat of overpopulation.

Technological advances in industry are drastically reducing people's physical functions, prolonging the static loading of nervous and emotional tension; there are various alarming signs of physical deterioration due to lack of exercise. An imperative need in the future will be a rational regime of movement with excessive work loads compensated by sports and physical training as forms of active rest, which will be beneficial for mental as well as physical condition. Similarly, nutrition will have to be adjusted to changing conditions (a shift to high-nutrient proteins and optimal vitamin content, etc.).

The present state of our knowledge suggests that in man there will be only a limited capacity of the humoral adaptation mechanism and metabolism, so that the immediate menace presented by technology through chemical, physical and biological factors can in fact be countered only by technology. A serious problem — especially for *mental health* — will be the *indirect* consequences of technological changes, which are evinced through the medium of social factors.

In the transition phase of mechanization and partial automation, nervous tension is likely to be aggravated by heavy demands on the powers of concentration and by the weight of responsibility at the control desks;[3] at a later stage there will probably be difficulties caused by a widespread changeover to mental work. Transferring people to new

[1] J. Charvát, "Cesty civilizace" (Paths of Civilization) in *Kulturní tvorba* 34/1964.

[2] On the one hand, the intervention of medicine and hygiene has led to a population explosion in the "third world" by upsetting the natural equilibrium maintained by centuries of epidemics and hunger, while being incapable as yet of substituting an equilibrium of civilization. On the other hand, we have in recent years witnessed the pressure of the consumer system in an advanced country seeking to expand the market through a sharp rise in the number of children (an artificially inspired "baby boom"), and able to push up the level of population increments in the US to that of India.

[3] *Mental Health Problems of Automation*, WHO, Geneva 1959, p. 10.

jobs in response to a mass advance of automation can easily lead to conflict situations and secondary psychic traumatism. Violent upheavals in the mode of life and the increasing speed of living are liable to overstrain the individual's adaptability, with ill effects both physical and mental (hypertension, coronary thrombosis, stomach ulcers, etc.). The importance of scientific selection of personnel comes strongly to the fore (tests based on health and psychological criteria).

On the whole, however, modern technology is not irrevocably linked with mental health. The largest group of mental disorders recorded in technologically advanced countries — neuroses — still result mainly from emotional conflicts and personal relationships, where technology is usually in the background. Analyses indicate that neurosis can be induced as readily by failure and lack of technical facilities as by a superfluity. A notable part of mental illnesses in the technologically most advanced countries appears to be connected with discrepancies between the beginnings of the scientific and technological revolution and the social forms derived from the industrial system that have not been adapted to the new conditions (this applies especially to the traditional types of capitalist society).

As a species man is a highly adaptable creature. He is capable of coming to terms with the increasing variability of his environment and with the growing amount of information. Science (integration of concepts) and technology (cybernetic systems) are opening the door to new processes of life. The cerebral cortex still possesses incalculable and untapped capacities; they lie in components that are of later evolutionary age and therefore more adaptable than the humoral regulation mechanisms.

Findings in the fields of physiology, genetics, molecular biology and biochemistry appear to be bringing us to the verge of potential anthropological changes reaching at present beyond our ken, but probably destined to be one of the most vital parts of the whole scientific and technological revolution, for they can provide the key to man's purposive self-development and set in motion what have been hitherto the most immobile factors, that is, the human factors in our civilization. The prospects for artificial synthesis of proteins, transplantation of organs, regulation of embryological processes and intervention in the genetic code make the evolutionary capacities of human beings a practical proposition — and under certain conditions (still rather remote) may enable man to *control his own evolution*.[1]

[1] Cf., for example, P. B. Medawar, *The Future of Man*, London 1959 and conclusions by J. Lederberg on man's biological future in *Man and his Future*, London 1963.

Assuming that the scientific and technological revolution will be scientifically regulated, it can contribute to the uncompleted process of "humanizing man", of unfolding all his potential capacities (especially the rational) and his individual gifts. If this should not happen, there is a danger that the whole process will get out of hand and that its interference in life and man's natural functions will burden the world with the full weight of a misbegotten product of human endeavour.

/ *Participation in Civilization and Man's Self-Realization* /

In its day, the industrial revolution gave material substance to the inversion of subject and object that was inherent to capitalism as a relation of production. In place of the subjective activity of the craftsman through the medium of his tools — restricted as it was — it imposed the broad subjectivity of the machine system, through the medium of the working group. Under the industrial system materialized labour faces live labour as an omnipotent power.[1] In conveyer belt production, the entire process quite obviously relies on the operation of the machine system and not on the efforts of the workers. The more human labour is fragmented in the process of industrial mechanization into simple operations in the pores of the machine system, and the more it is divorced from any creative element, from management and decision-making, the more man's activity loses the quality of self-fulfilment, the peculiarly human element of subjectivity, its positive involvement in shaping civilization.

Moreover, the entire industrial system and the artificial evironment of modern civilization assumes the same aspect of a vast mechanism directing and manipulating man. The kaleidoscope of things that man meets with in everyday life conceals their true nature as man-made links in the chain gearing human beings to the spontaneous mechanism of industrial civilization.[2] Whatever the man of labour might feel about

[1] There is "active subsumption of living labour to materialised labour, not only by appropriating it, but also in the actual course of the productive process; the relation of capital as value that appropriates a value-forming activity is also imparted to fixed capital, existing in the guise of machinery, as the relation of the use value of capital to the use value of working capacity" (K. Marx, *Grundrisse*, ibid., p. 585).

[2] "It is not the worker who buys means of subsistence and means of production, but the means of subsistence that buy the worker in order to attach him to the means

the things that filled his personal life with cares and joys, he was never the one to set the course of this cycle of life. On the contrary, his life was the medium through which the extended reproduction of capital was accomplished. In his own activity the worker witnessed an alien subjectivity.

And the traditional bourgeois forms of society corresponded to the true position of man in industrial civilization: private property assumed exclusion of the workers from economic decision-making, while the formality of political participation and the implicit ineffectiveness of any popular involvement in public affairs are today beyond all doubt. The resultant feeling that one's life is a means to extrinsic ends has deep roots in reality. In effect people merely perform their given functions of working and living, without playing a part of their own within this civilization; they find no scope for active self-assertion in their daily lives. Indeed, this constraining of the human subjectivity, from which few are exempt, is the most formidable of all the barriers set up by industrial civilization. It represents the kernel, and still valid substance, of Marx's criticism — of more vital import than a mere protest against the material poverty of the workers.

Significantly, the implications of this criticism are not less, but more impelling as technology advances and wealth multiplies. Today "one of the greatest dangers would seem to be the insufficient participation of human beings in the world around them;"[1] this is the conclusion reached both by those who in one way or another base themselves on Marx, and by writers whose approach is quite different and who see the problem purely in terms of society without participation[2] on the one hand and the lonely man[3] on the other. In any event, these are the considerations that arouse the gravest fears for the future of our civilization.

In the present empirical reality, this structural boundary of industrial civilization, this constraining of man's "active self-assertion", is projected in the symptoms of social traumatization[4] of the technologically advanced world, in deprivation and delinquency,[5] the negative attitude

of production. Means of subsistence are a special form of material existence in which capital faces the worker." (*Arkhiv Marksa i Engelsa*, vol. II (VII), Moscow 1933, p. 60.)

[1] G. Friedmann, *Le Travail en Miettes, Spécialisation et Loisirs*, Paris 1959.
[2] M. C. Goodall, *Science and the Politician*, Cambridge 1965, p. 64.
[3] D. Riesman, N. Glazer, R. Denney, *The Lonely Crowd*, New York 1950.
[4] Cf. W. F. Whyte, *Money and Motivation, an Analysis of Incentives in Industry*, New York 1955.
[5] R. K. Merton, "Social Structure and Anomie", in: *Mass Society in Crisis. Social Problems and Social Pathology*, Rosenberg—Gerver—Howton, New York—London 1964.

203

of youth (gangs, etc.), which — it appears[1] — are not rooted in high or low living standards or the break-up of the family, but in this open wound — the lack of any true participation in industrial civilization. This lack is evinced in the physical and mental disorders of people who find themselves caught up day by day in the wheels of the civilization process like inanimate objects;[2] there can be little doubt that the always unsatisfied need for personal and collective creative effort inevitably evokes feelings of "being pitchforked into the world", "the futility and emptiness of existence" as reflected in the philosophy of existentialism.

Growing efforts to find a cure in various types of formal participation in capitalist profit or the cult of "personal prestige" are symptomatic, but fail to touch the true causes in their depth and totality. Therefore we have the ever-present background of synthetic compensation for "self-assertion" through "one-armed bandits", drastic entertainment, wild driving, drugs and the whole scale of escapist extravagances.

But increasingly a solution is being sought in more practical measures — primarily in the technological field — that actually aim beyond the bounds of the industrial system. Especially instructive are surveys of the rapid spread over the past two decades of various employee-participation committees in factories. Their results correspond to their half-hearted, reformist character.[3] It is found, however, that at a certain technological level the claims and opportunities for employee-participation in economic decision-making undergo a radical change. While in the days of intensive mechanization a few decades ago there was some justification in assuming the main axiom of the Taylor system to be valid — that the success of "scientific management" depended on excluding any participation by the workers[4] — doubts began to appear in the inter-war period,[5] and today in highly automated works, even of

---

[1] *Réflexions pour 1985*, ibid., p. 15.

[2] J. Bodamer, *Gesundheit und technische Welt*, Stuttgart 1955, p. 231. H. Sopp has demonstrated that as work becomes more creative and responsible, sickness declines (*Was der Mensch braucht. Erfüllung und Versagen im Beruf*, Düsseldorf 1958, p. 110).

[3] Some of the limitations are pointed out in a report by the National Institute of Industrial Psychology, *Joint Consultation in British Industry* (London 1952); M. Montuclard reacts similarly to French experiences in *Le dynamisme des Comités d'entreprise* (Paris 1963), and to West-German, P. V. Oertzen in *Analyse der Mitbestimmung — ein Diskussionsbeitrag* (Hannover 1965). The causes of the questionable results are examined by A. Matejka in *Praca i koleżenstwo*, Warsaw 1963.

[4] According to F. W. Taylor the task of a worker "is not to produce more by his own initiative but to execute punctually the orders given extending into the smallest details" (*Shop Management*, New York 1911).

[5] Cf. F. J. Roethlisberger, W. T. Dickinson, *Management and the Worker*, Cambr. 1964.

capitalist firms, it is possible to compute the ineffectiveness of management and decision-making when some participation by personnel is lacking, although the impression of "bilateral decision" may be illusory.[1] Naturally, such trends do not yet overstep the barrier of private ownership, but they undoubtedly suggest that the industrial managerial system has reached its limit and is on its way out.

In the technologically advanced countries today this structural impossibility of full self-realization within the industrial system, the lack of true creative participation in the process of civilization, is the main consideration attracting people to the idea of socialist revolution — as a process seeking a radical solution of this very question, and directed to overcoming the alienation and inversion of the subject-object relationship in modern civilization. Of course, insofar as socialism has been or is being built upon foundations taken over from the industrial system, it cannot develop its inner tendencies to the full; in that case the problem of "participation" is present, but with the significant circumstance that in this context there are prospects for handling it in its entirety.

Socialist revolution enabled millions of workers to intervene in the course of civilization in the *political sphere*. Indeed, the degree of mass participation was imposing: in 1924 the average worker in the USSR spent 109 hours a year on public political, or political and cultural activity.[2] However, when the elementary political tasks of revolution have been accomplished and the centre of change shifts to other areas, these opportunities for man's self-assertion naturally recede; by 1959 this type of social participation occupied only 17 hours of the average Soviet worker's annual time.[3] A similar trend in workers' time economy can be assumed in all socialist countries. Evidently this type of "participation" will in future be inadequate to fill the gap caused by the structure of the industrial system. Indeed, it is merely the first reflex of the nascent subjectivity within man and society; power and forms of ownership are not the sole issue here, for the crux lies deeper, in the genuine appropriation of the world by man, in his self-realization as man. If higher forms

---

[1] "Large plants can be operated at high productivity levels under decision-making conditions that are very different from the traditional management view" (S. Melman, *Decision-Making and Productivity*, New York 1958, p. 41).

[2] Cf. S. G. Strumilin, *Problemy sotsializma i komunizma v SSSR*, Moscow 1961.

[3] S. G. Strumilin, ibid. Surveys by Goncharenko and others give similar data. But the difference includes saving of time due to progress in communications and transport, etc.

of participation in the civilization process are not evolved in time, under socialism, too, the resultant vacuum will be a source of tension, affecting the personality of man and depressing motivation to the simplest levels.

Consequently, during the transition stage there is a level at which a strong social and anthropological value is assumed by sharing in *economic* decision-making, in the widest sense of the term. The most serious aspect of the directive management employed in the socialist countries when completing industrialization — a stage of typical industrial division of labour and rationalization[1] — is that it fails to take sufficient account of man's independent creative subjectivity, that it constrains it in the very sphere where it is already justified, and so in its outcome drives people once more into nihilism in face of civilization. The "economic reforms" taking place in the socialist countries, with their "new systems" of planning and management, will undoubtedly do much to promote mass participation in economic decision-making.

These circumstances underline the significance, especially for the socialist countries, of technological contributions towards eliminating purely operative work and shifting a growing proportion of the work force to the sphere of management, job-setting and to the growth of creative elements both in work and in the whole structure of life. Sociological and psychological analyses indicate that there is a direct relationship between the level of automation and the openings for individuals and groups to take part in decision-making and management.[2] Contrary to earlier ideas derived from the indubitable decline in creative intervention in production witnessed during the transition from craft work to industry, it would appear that at a higher level of the productive forces the structure of production once more opens up wide opportunities for *technical* initiative by workers, but this time on a scientific basis. In the most modern socialist enterprises we see a relative increase in inventions and

---

[1] D. A. Yermansky (*Teoriya i praktika ratsionalizatsii*, Moscow 1928) and the Soviet school NOT *(Nauchnaya organizatsiya Truda)* already pointed to the need to reverse the dehumanizing trends of rationalizing processes.

[2] At a sociology congress held in 1966 at Špindlerův Mlýn in Czechoslovakia, R. Supek reported on an investigation in 26 Yugoslav enterprises, which demonstrated that the higher the technological level, the more extensive and effective was the participation of employees in management and the stronger the sense of responsibility among all employees for the performance of the enterprise (cf. J. Filipec, *Industriální společnost v sociologické diskusi* (Industrial Society in Sociological Discussion), Prague 1967).

in the role of innovation proposals submitted by employees (who are predominantly highly skilled).[1]

The opportunities for self-assertion and participation in shaping the *social* conditions of human life — including the minor, local and quite individual aspects — are far from being exhausted. Such cultivation of human relations and welfare can mean a great deal, especially for people otherwise engaged in occupations in the lower range of skills.[2]

No small value may be attached to the advance of independent cultural activity on a mass scale. A typical sign of the times is the growing claim made by contemporary writing and art on the ability of readers, viewers and listeners to use their minds and emotions to complete what the author may merely hint at — in contrast to the ready-made, unquestioning and pure entertainment method of standard "consumer culture"; some new forms of art can be expected from this quarter, too.

Finally, socialism has opened up the first new opportunities in the world for the working people to participate in planned management of the future. But we are still at the beginning; there is often failure to appreciate the role of popular participation in projecting the future course, in choosing among alternatives for the advance of civilization — but, in fact, this participation represents fresh ground for the most varied approaches to man's creative self-assertion in modern civilization; the popularity of "futurological" writings is not fortuitous.

All this initiative and participation — despite the undoubted limitations of each field and form of expression — are miles ahead of any immediate intentions, calculated economies and the like; the human subjectivity of the scientific and technological revolution is asserting itself. Nevertheless, a radical solution will probably have to wait until the productive forces have undergone more radical changes in structure and dynamics — changes that will overstep the bounds of the restricted

---

[1] This tendency can be observed in the West, too. For example in the US there has been a renewed growth since the fifties in the numbers of technical proposals made by employees (cf. F. Machlup, *The Production and Distribution of Knowledge in the United States*, Princeton 1962). In the mid-fifties, their annual value was estimated at one billion dollars (R. H. Krauss, *Das betriebliche Vorschlagswesen als Mittel zur Rationalisierung und zur sozialen Betriebsgestaltung*, München 1956, p. 42). Relating these savings to the national income and employing comparable methods, we find that in the US technological initiative by employees reached a value of barely 0.5 per cent of the national income. In the USSR and Czechoslovakia the comparable figures for 1959—1960 were around 0.9 to 1.0 per cent of the national incomes.

[2] In practice the approach is often the opposite, which leads to people whose work already gives them ample opportunity for self-realization being overloaded.

(industrial) form of man's self-realization in his work — not by a return to the subjectivity of the individual within production (which is now impossible), but by excluding man from purely operative activity and expanding his subjectivity alongside and above it in the preparation and transformation of production, then subordinated to the power of "universal social labour".[1] In technological, organizational, scientific and artistic *creative activity* linked with man's development — where joint successes in transmuting the world rely upon the unique, subjective contribution of the human personality — active self-assertion and participation in the progress of civilization flow directly from the nature of the human way of life.

* * *

Civilization has not been brought to the present crossroads purely by the fantastic magnitude of the human achievement and all the potential ways of its external application. An equal share belongs to the essential nature of man today, with which the products of science and technology are indissolubly bound up. The dimensions that include man's development in the development of civilization present the scientific and technological revolution itself with many potential outcomes. What will be the consequences in the sphere of the fundamental problems of existence? In what direction will the shaping of man's "human nature" be impelled? What integration of values derived from previous development can be expected of the revolution in the deepest regions of human life? What new type of humanity will be given forth?

Usually the answer is embodied in the concept of a "totally" developed, all-round man; however, this concept cannot in itself represent something complete and closed; it is rather a project of human purport, merged with the movement of the world and with man's self-realization — a project through which man transcends external reality and his own self; in fact, man appears here in the role of both subject and object, and always in the aspect of a mobile, multidimensional process; he presents himself as a problem, and he indubitably is the key problem of the world today.

Clearly the scientific and technological revolution is bringing society right to the point at which its further progress will escape our theoretical grasp if a comprehensive *scientific view of man and his development* is not

[1] K. Marx, Capital, Vol. III (Kerr ed.), p. 124.

brought to bear. The greater the knowledge of nature and technology, the greater the need for knowledge of man.[1] But the present system of science is not prepared for this; its underlying purpose is still directed to mastering objective nature, in the spirit of Bacon or Descartes, and its evolution has for the most part followed the demands of industry and the progressive mechanization of the external world. To apprehend the vital questions of civilization today will undoubtedly require a more profound methodological basis, combining objective cognition with the autoreflexes of the subject — as found in Marxism; knowledge of man will have to be enormously expanded, *a system of sciences* of man constituted. Most of the questions involved will require special investigation from the anthropological point of view (with cooperation from sociology, economics, psychology, pedagogy, historiography, aesthetics, ethnography, biology, physiology, medicine, general technology, etc.), with philosophy approaching the subject as one demanding a certain ontological foundation. Indeed, for some years now the call for advancing the sciences of man has been heard from various quarters, especially from scholars concerned with theories of civilization and culture.[2] In such an undertaking — which may be expected to do much to prepare the ground for a new synthesis of sciences, as foreseen by Marx — socialist science may justifiably perceive its historical mission and great opportunity. Indeed, without such a scientific groundwork, socialist society might succumb to the worst possible eventuality — that of missing the opportunity to grasp the human dimension offered by the civilization of our day.

---

[1] In recent times the advance of the social sciences throughout the world has, compared with their traditional lag, begun to catch up with the rapid growth of the natural sciences.

[2] For instance, G. Friedmann's call for a "science of man" (*Où va le Travail humain?*, Paris 1950), L. Mumford's suggestions (*The Transformation of Man*, New York 1956), proposals for unifying sciences of man, from biology to aesthetics, made by Julian Huxley (in the symposium *Man and His Future*, London 1963), Adam Schaff's plan for widely-based anthropological research (speech at the sociological congress at Evian in 1966). The ideas on the tasks awaiting the science of man advanced by A. D. Aleksandrov at a meeting of the Soviet Academy of Sciences (*Stroyitelstvo Kommunizma i Obshchestvennye Nauki*, Moscow 1962) indicated an initiative towards bringing the sciences of man into a system.

NEW FEATURES OF SOCIAL DEVELOPMENT IN THE ERA OF THE SCIENTIFIC AND TECHNOLOGICAL REVOLUTION

4

The laws by which society develops are not predestined, they follow no set scheme. Flowing always from the matter of history, from the motion of society itself, they change with every turn in this essential substratum.[1] The profound intervention in the civilization base of human life signified by the scientific and technological revolution in its entirety — viewing it in its intrinsic correlation with the whole complex of social revolution of our day — cannot fail to impinge on the *elementary laws of history*. In many respects the course of civilization acquires a new logic and time scale.

The interconnections among the hitherto disparate forms in the life of man and society — in the chain of production technology, the economy, politics, ideology, etc. — have so far been posited primarily by the *limits* that each of these forms of human activity embodied in itself and in relation to the others. In earlier societies these forms were linked, mixed and fused out of all recognition. Only with the advent of the industrial age, with capitalism, was the economy disengaged from politics, politics from ideology, etc. As these components were launched on their relatively autonomous paths, scholars were at last able to discern their consistency and interrelationships. It became evident that a fairly developed, but still deficient level of the productive forces carries with it a specific class structuring of society; a restricted class structure underlies and calls for a political state; the specific development of the base, including its limitations, is reflected in the mediating status of an autonomous, distinct superstructure, and so forth.

In terms of this complicated mechanism of the historical process, our age is dominated by relationships and phenomena that can be derived

---

[1] The idea that Marx's theory is founded on a set pattern of historical development, therefore providing a universal key to every historical situation, derives from a grave misconception of the method of historical materialism, which Marx and Engels themselves refuted.

directly or indirectly from the logic of industrial civilization as shaped by capitalism; in this sense we can speak of the present developments as following certain *laws*. Yet simultaneously we find tendencies and phenomena that are suggestive of a far deeper type of movement, namely *a change in the laws* of civilization's advance. Assuming that:

a) the scientific and technological revolution reshapes and expands the productive forces (with new productive forces coming on the scene and assuming a leading role) and overcomes their deficient state,

b) the former frontiers of civilization's advance are not immobilized by social and class barriers (an eventuality to be reckoned with especially with the existence of capitalism),

we may envisage change in the matter of history ultimately generating essential and sweeping changes in the laws of historical development and in the ties linking the various forms of life within society. The dynamics of civilization will then grow more versatile, their features will be more clearly defined.

/Science and the Management of Affairs/ 4.1

The first sign of an impact by the scientific and technological revolution on the course of human affairs, and equally a condition of changes to come, is the new role assumed by science. There comes a stage when science, as a product of civilization on its forward march, emerges as a generator of advances in new directions. Obviously the moment when the way is opened for science to play a direct and full part in shaping social relationships and human life comes as soon as the frontiers of industrial maturity have been crossed. But what is the source of this special quality in current development?

/*The New Status of Science*/ 4.1.1

Today it is a commonplace to see the upsurge of science as the feature of our age. Fifty years ago there was nothing in the world to compare with the research centres of today, the network of laboratories, the new towns catering for scientists and universities. Science has penetrated the foundations of contemporary society,[1] infused the dynamics of historical

[1] R. B. Lindsay, *The Role of Science in Civilization*, New York 1963.

movement[1] so thoroughly that the whole pattern of change appears as a "research revolution"[2] and the coming age as one of "scientific civilization".[3] If we free the innumerable reflections on this subject from the fog of popular illusions that see science as a magic wand without identifying the social and human sources of its power, we discover that the crux lies in the *new status of science*. This type of human activity, which has hitherto served primarily as a factor of *social consciousness*, is now fully and self-evidently proving its worth as a *productive force*. Its value as a mode of man's activity, a specific form of existence in the modern world, is growing rapidly. This coincidence brings into play feedbacks in the historical process that the industrial mechanism failed to use or confined to a narrow sphere; the upward spiral of civilization and cultural progress has been opened out.

In its new role science takes off from a civilization base with *social* qualities shaped by previous development. Science itself represents an inherently social productive force in which the social aspect is far more pronounced than in all other productive forces that have ever been set in motion. While relying here and now on the integrated efforts of all who are contributing to present-day civilization, it is also a product of all bygone generations and the whole progress of society. It is manifested as "universal social knowledge" and society's "accumulated knowledge"[4]; for its full operation it requires a basis of all-inclusive social combination. The use of machines already showed the extent to which the production process was imbued with the social element — so permitting the application of science. But in the industrial use of science, the limits of its social quality were ever present; science was brought in now and then and in small doses. In referring to the machine and the industrial mechanism as "coagulated intellect"[5], Max Weber was really only repeating Marx's description of the machine and industry altogether as "the materialized power of human knowledge".[6] But Marx's concept went much deeper. For him the machine and the industrial system represented knowledge with specific limitations, that is always containing

---

[1] R. J. Forbes, "The History of Science and Technology" in *Rapports de XIe Congrès International des Sciences Historiques*, Stockholm 1960.

[2] L. Sylk, *The Research Revolution*, New York 1960.

[3] H. Schelsky, *Der Mensch in der wissenschaftlichen Zivilisation*, Köln, Opladen 1961.

[4] K. Marx, ibid. *Grundrisse*, pp. 594, 600, etc. And therefore only "associated labour is capable of employing the *general* products of human development such as mathematics, etc..." (*Arkhiv Marxa i Engelsa*, II/VII, Moscow 1933, p. 98).

[5] M. Weber, *Gesammelte politische Schriften*, Munich 1921, p. 151.

[6] K. Marx, ibid. *Grundrisse*, p. 594.

an element of what was *not known*, man's inability to reproduce the entire production process intellectually, and then technically, the impossibility of doing away with traditional, routine activity in which science had no say; in such a system every incarnation of the intellect implied stunting the intellectual growth of the majority.[1] With equal justification one can say with the first observers of industrialization that "ignorance is the mother of industry".[2] In this sense Marx saw the development of capital and the industrial system as an indication of "the extent to which general social knowledge has become an immediate force of production"[3] — and, conversely, of the extent to which it had *not* become.

With the changes now in process (and the accompanying association of production) science is, on the contrary, permeating the entire range of operations and merging with them; *all* productive forces are being converted in one way or another into applications of science, which is emerging as the most revolutionary and widespread — and ultimately in effect universal — productive force in society.[4] Therein lies the basis for the new status assumed by science in current civilization processes.

Science exercises this function in ways that are rather far removed from those of earlier productive forces — indeed, they do not fit in at all with the customary ideas about the role these forces should play. Science does not operate solely as a factor in the production of things and as an instrument for satisfying wants; it serves equally as a source generating new types of human endeavour, as an initiator and producer of new wants. That is to say, it is a productive force that can create new demands, conflicts and outlooks.

This unique cognitive function[5] endows science with a peculiar dynamic value in the interplay of civilization processes, making it the prime productive force of human life, an unquenchable source of human ad-

---

[1] K. Marx, *Notebooks on Technology*, quoted from *Bolshevik*, 1—2/1932, p. 21.
[2] A. Fergusson, *History of Civil Society*, Edinburgh 1767, p. 280.
[3] K. Marx, ibid. *Grundrisse*, p. 594, similarly p. 402 and elsewhere. Marx's reference to science as a productive force applied to the industrial system and capitalism, but only "to a certain degree".
[4] Marx's concept of science as a productive force was first used in characterizing the new course of events by J. D. Bernal (*Social Function of Science*, London 1939, p. 224) and later by S. Strumilin, "Rol nauki v razvitiyi proizvoditelnykh sil", *Voprosy filosofii* 3/1954, and G. Kosel, *Produktivkraft Wissenschaft*, Berlin 1957, and others.
[5] F. Šorm (*Věda v socialistické společnosti* (Science in Socialist Society), Prague 1967) shows that underestimation of this cognitive function of science is leading to a lack of understanding of the autonomous role assumed by basic research.

vance. For every want satisfied and every advance in knowledge, it breeds a multitude of new questions, a spate of human dissatisfaction.

Hand in hand with its newly-acquired status in civilization, science is undergoing a change in structure and dynamics. The features usually noted are the unprecedented force and intensity of discoveries, with one revolutionary advance following hard on another to transform the basic concepts of entire areas of knowledge;[1] changes in the most elementary theoretic fundaments of science are inducing more and more leaps[2] whose impact is felt in all fields. At first by turns and then all at once, scientific disciplines are on the move — from the most ancient (mathematics) to the youngest (biochemistry); and the chain of upheavals is reaching over the entire field.[3] New discoveries are now centred in the fringe sciences, at points of contact and in interdisciplinary areas of research.

With the sophisticated technical apparatus, the laboratories and research equipment now available, the work of the scientist is also far removed from the traditional image.[4]

Modern information and cybernation technologies represent an enormous force relieving scientists of many routine jobs, while calling for cooperation among big research teams on an uprecedented scale.[5]

Probably some deeper process underlies this trend. One has the impression that science today is crossing a divide. For centuries its successes were primarily derived from mastering the laws of mechanical systems or of systems that could somehow be converted to elementary abstract motion. A single absolute method was applicable to such reality. The appropriate scientific basis could be the Galilean approach and the Cartesian method, abstracting from changes on the part of the subject and

[1] For 200 years, Newton's principles were the basis of physics; but in the 60 years since Einstein's discoveries the picture of physical reality has undergone several transformations, and we are witnesses of what seems to be a permanent crisis in the physical sciences.

[2] T. S. Kuhn, *The Structure of Scientific* Revolutions, Chicago—London, 1962; B. M. Kedrov, Zakonomernosti rozvitiya nauki, *Organon* 2/1965.

[3] H. W. Bode, in a report *Basic Research and National Goals*, Washington 1965, p. 56.

[4] L. Brandt (*Die 2. industrielle Revolution*, Bonn 1956) has mentioned an estimate by German physicists to the effect that if Faraday's laboratory cost 100 Marks and Hertz's 1,000, the present price would be at least 5 million, and for a nuclear laboratory 500 million.

[5] D. J. de Solla Price (*Little Science, Big Science*, New York—London 1963) distinguishes between "big science" working with high-power technical equipment and "little science" conducted in the traditional manner by smaller groups with more modest means.

reducing the objective world, nature and society, in effect to a *machine*.[1]

Modern science derives its methodological approaches from the realm of self-movement, which is not confined to the bounds of mechanism (fundamental qualities of living matter, chemical synthesis, nuclear structure, social systems). As soon as it meets with areas in which the material dialectic of subject and object cannot be excluded or severely reduced, the Galilean-Cartesian reason is at a loss. Hence the signs of a deepening "crisis of science" and of the very foundations of rationality already referred to by Husserl.[2]

All enquiry into the objective world now involves focussing attention on the subject making the enquiry. Science is concerned with working out new means by which the transmutation of the world and man's self-creation can be rationally comprehended, methods that will be adequate to the new level attained by the practical dialectics of man and his handiwork in modern civilization. From the days of Clerk Maxwell to the birth of cybernetics, there has been growing demand for a multidimensional method in science that would take account of motion on the part of both object and subject,[3] for a cybernetic approach, systems analysis, etc. — demands also posed by the new types of research practice (team and multi-science cooperation, application of cybernation technologies etc.).

The discerning observer will not fail to notice that parallel with these changes, and as a symptom of them, a point has been reached where the searching eye of science is focussed not only upon the external world, but also upon the affairs of science itself. The contours of what has come to be known as "science of science"[4] have been taking shape for some

[1] Criticism of this basis was already contained in general terms in Marx's comments on "the abstract materialism of a natural science that excludes the historical process" and on a philosophy that excludes "man's dealings with nature" (*Capital*, Vol. I, p. 393, Dent ed.). He wrote of the prospect of a natural science of man just as the science of man would incorporate natural science (Economic and Philosophical Manuscripts, in *Marx's Concept of Man*, ed. E. Fromm, New York 1967, p. 137).

[2] E. Husserl, *Die Krisis der europäischen Wissenschaften und die transzendentale Phänomenologie*, Hague 1954.

[3] Cf. discussion by Heisenberg, Kolmogorov and many others. Though surprisingly little known, such a methodological approach was first outlined in Marx's theory including scientific cognition as such in the dialectic of subject and object, in the coincidence of changed circumstances and self-transformation, thereby replacing the traditional one-and-only absolute method by the method of methods, the method of matter in transformation.

[4] The term "science of science" seems to have been first used by the Polish authors M. Ossowska and St. Ossowsky (see "The Science of Science", *Organon* 1/1963); but

decades. This is helping to equip science with self-reflexions and the ability to demonstrate how its status in society is changing. In this respect one may say that the scientific and technological revolution is entering a new phase — it is acquiring *self-consciousness*.[1]

In its day, the industrial revolution tied scientific progress by and large to the degree of concentration and mechanization in production. These circumstances gave full validity to Engels' statement that impulses stemming from industry were the most important stimulus to science, much more effective than the dependence of technology on science.[2] Today it is still true — at least to a degree, if we take the average industrial countries — that the part played by science in the national economy is roughly in line with the industrial level. There comes a point, however, where the relation is inverted, and finally breaks free of all former patterns. Where once science followed in the wake of industry and technology, the tendency today is for it to control industry and lead technology.[3] Opinion polls have shown that the general public still tends to view science from the standpoint of the industrial revolution. Edison with his hundreds of discoveries and patents still figures as the model for the ideal scientist. But in the meantime the relation of science to practice has changed a lot. People like Watt, Fulton, Arkwright, Polsunov, whose inventions underlay the industrial revolution, were mostly men of affairs, engineers and craftsmen. Carnot derived his theoretical elaboration of the laws of thermodynamics from his experience with steam engines in practice. Now the tables have been turned — the foremost theoretical advances come direct from *basic research*. Einstein's theory heralded the harnessing of nuclear energy long before even laboratory types of atomic techniques were available; the science of cybernetics preceded the computers; macromolecular chemistry gave theoretical pictures of substances previously quite unknown. While at the start of his career Ford proclaimed the slogan that practical necessity is the mother of invention, his successors are now guided by the principle that invention is the mother of necessity. Science now pur-

it was signalized at the second international congress on the history of science held in London in the thirties — notably in contributions by British and Soviet delegates.

[1] J. D. Bernal, "After Twenty-Five Years", *Science of Science*, ed. M. Goldsmith, A. Mackay, London 1966, p. 286.

[2] See letter from Engels to H. Starkenburg, Jan. 25, 1894, in Karl Marx, *Selected Works*, Vol. 1, Moscow 1933, p. 391.

[3] J. D. Bernal, *Science in History*, London 1954, p. 512

sues its own, *independent* path as a revolutionary driving force of civilization. No modern concern can dispense with science, and within industry the lead is taken by branches based directly on science, for instance, electronics, chemicals, etc., where science finds its major response and application. A new pattern emerges — the more an industrial country advances, the more its economic (and subsequently social) progress is tied to the progress of science.

Science owes its new status primarily to its exceptional power of *generalization*. In contrast to other products, a scientific finding is not consumed by use, on the contrary it is improved on — and then "it costs nothing". Moreover, science possesses a peculiar *growth* potential. Every finding is both a result, and then a starting point for further research; the more we know, the more we can find out.[1] This intrinsically exponential quality distinguishes science sharply from all traditional activities of the industrial type.

According to various surveys and calculations, this trend in science is already clearly reflected in statistical data. The fantastic forecast of a drastic, tenfold expansion in scientific activity made by Prof. Bernal in 1939[2] — received with incredulity at the time — was soon outdone by reality. In most industrial countries the work force in science, research and development is doubled within eight to twelve years,[3] and in the USSR in seven years.[4] In this respect the annual growth rate of science is four times that of all other activities (see Table 4-1). Yet even this explosive advance proves inadequate.[5]

Expenditure on science and research now reaches enormous sums in some countries[6] (see Table 4-2), a hundred times above the level of 30—40 years ago. The world total is estimated at 60,000 million dollars

---

[1] "...science progresses in proportion to the mass of knowledge that is left to it by preceding generations, that is, under the most ordinary circumstances, in geometrical progression..." (*Umrisse zu einer Kritik der Nationalökonomie*, K. Marx-F. Engels, *Werke*, Band 1, Berlin 1961, p. 521).
[2] J. D. Bernal, *The Social Function of Science*, London 1939, p. 242.
[3] P. Auger, *Current Trends in Scientific Research*, Paris 1961, p. 15.
[4] G. M. Dobrov, *Nauka o nauke*, Kiev 1966, pp. 92, 99 ff.
[5] "Diverse requirements for the more highly trained engineers, mathematicians, and physical scientists are rapidly outstripping our capacity to produce them" (J. F. Kennedy in introduction to the report, Meeting Manpower Needs in Science and Technology, Washington 1962, p. V).
[6] C. Freeman, A. Young, *The Research and Development Effort in Western Europe, North America and the Soviet Union*, Paris 1965; "Role of Research in Growth'," *Chemical and Engineering News*, July 1955.

and is doubled every six to twelve years, in the USSR within a shorter time.[1]

By all appearances, this typical trend in the scientific and technological revolution will continue in coming decades. In the USA another doubling of investment in science is expected within ten years,[2] and in the number of scientific workers within eleven years.[3] In France and some other European countries doubling of outlays is envisaged every nine years, and so on.[4] It has been stated that half the scientific findings with which we operate in the most varied spheres have been obtained in the past 15 years and that the time scale is shrinking; of scientists who have made their mark in the history of mankind, 90 per cent are living today.

For the present there is no telling at what stage we should expect saturation effects induced either by big advances in the effectiveness of scientific work, or by social retarding factors.[5] In the meantime, any falling off is merely due to fluctuations or deformation of the growth curve, with a propensity in any case to absorb an incomparably higher share of human labour and means than envisaged by outlooks derived from the industrial system. There are factors whose significance for scientific advance is still hard to guess. The effectiveness of research may be enormously increased by modern information techniques and handing over some areas of science to computers; structural change within science is also a strong progressive factor. Enormous gains would

---

[1] V. G. Marakhov, J. S. Meleshchenko, "Sovremennaya nauchno-tekhnicheskaya revolyutsiya i yeyo sotsialinye posledstviya v usloviyakh sotsializma", *Voprosy filosofii* 3/1966.

[2] Annual research expenditure in the United States has topped the 20,000 million dollar mark and exceeds investments in the sectors of industry; in the manufacturing industries it amounts to two-thirds of all investment and in electronics to three times the total expenditure.

[3] *Long-Range Demand for Scientific and Technical Personnel*, Washington 1961.

[4] *Reviews of National Science Policy*, Paris 1966 (for France and other OECD countries).

[5] D. J. de Solla Price, who has computed long-term growth relations (*Science since Babylon*, New Haven 1961), expects a saturation point at the close of the century. He applied Lotka's law, according to which the effectiveness of science moves inversely to the number of scientific workers — a phenomenon that can, in fact, be observed in the USA since World War II (*Little Science, Big Science*, New York—London, 1963). G. M. Dobrov (*Nauka o nauke*, Kiev 1966), however, rightly points to the purely numerical interpretation of the data, which ignores the social causes and fails to answer the question of what really distinct level the role of science will achieve in the future.

ensue from releasing the vast scientific resources now tied down by armaments.[1] But in seeking the true limits of scientific advance, we find the key solely in man's abilities,[2] and once we have the opportunity to cultivate them consistently, there will be no more obstacles to the steady growth, and finally universal validity of science as human activity. At all events, in the phase now before us we shall have to discard our preconceived ideas about the status of science in society and the proportions it should assume.

/ *Conditions of Integration* / 4.1.2

As the industrial productive forces expanded, together with the capital market, they broke through the traditional local frontiers, or made them less and restrictive. The doors were opened to international contacts, and this in its turn provided the soil for using new productive forces of a more profound social nature; fragmentary history, restricted in place and time, was replaced by world history.[3]

The scientific and technological revolution advances this process to a new stage. Integration of economic, community and cultural life is enforced at high speed by science — the most social of all productive forces — until it embraces everything. As science permeates the life of society, any barrier, any monopoly, standing in its way is sooner or later felt as a burden. The effectiveness of science is in direct proportion to the breadth and depth of the base on which it relies — both nationally and internationally.[4]

Consequently the scientific and technological revolution demands an incomparably higher degree of integration than the industrial revolution.

---

[1] Sixty per cent of US scientific capacity is concentrated in the military field. Economists have been pointing out for decades that the country's scientific and technological undertakings are really by-products of advances in techniques of destruction (V. Perlo, "Sotsialnye posledstviya nauchno-tekhnicheskoy revolutsii", *Voprosy filosofii* 11/1959; N. Gauzner, "Kapitalizm i novaya tekhnika", *Kommunist* 10/1959, etc.).

[2] J. D. Bernal, ibid., *The Social Function of Science*, p. 312. In *Science in History* Bernal reiterates this view in a critical note to Price's forecast of saturation.

[3] Marx-Engels, *The German Ideology*, New York 1966, p. 27.

[4] S. Fabricant believes that the prime cause of the lead held by the USA over the West European countries in productivity stems from the breadth of the American production base ("Productivity and Economic Growth", in *Technology and Social Change*, ed. Ginzberg, New York—London 1964, p. 114).

Given certain preconditions (as far as the range of resources was concerned), industrialization could take place within the confines of the larger countries. On the contrary, the scientific and technological revolution is inconceivable without a wide international base.[1] It is obvious at first sight how on the soil of capitalism — especially in Western Europe — science and technology are enforcing intensive moves towards integration.[2] With its international character, socialism offers infinite prospects for cooperation in a different social context. By grasping all these opportunities, an adequate groundwork for the scientific and technological revolution could undoubtedly be laid.

There can be no question that a country like Czechoslovakia, with an economy that is not closed and with necessarily limited resources, has to play an active part in international division of labour and in the world of science and technology right at the approach to the scientific and technological revolution. Any local separation, any restrictions — on movements of people, information, literature and the like — are bound to take their toll in holding back economic growth. It is vitally important that all the opportunities offered, in the first place, by the world socialist system should be used. Although there are some encouraging examples of close cooperation among socialist countries,[3] there are wide areas waiting for integration. Should the socialist countries fail to reach a higher stage in sharing labour among their economies and coordinating science and technology, should they not outdo the capitalist world in overstepping the actual and the formal boundaries among themselves (primarily in the economic field, but then in all sectors), they will seriously hamper their transition to the scientific and technological revolution. If integration does not go forward quickly in the socialist world, even single countries

---

[1] "The possibilities which science does offer can only be realized by creating a new ordered and integrated political and economic system on a world scale" (ibid. *The Social Function of Science*, p. 386. A quarter of a century later Bernal returned to this idea — the question whether such integration, or at least coordination was possible in the divided world of today was "the great problem of our time" (ibid. *Science of Science*, p. 301).

[2] Alongside the long list of international societies in every branch of science, regional agencies (Euratom, ENEA, EIRO, ESRO, etc.) and institutions (CERN, Rome Computing Centre, etc.) are multiplying; cf. report by J. J. Salomon in *Ministers Talk About Science*, Paris 1965.

[3] In recent years nearly a hundred Czechoslovak research and development institutes have entered into active cooperation with their opposite numbers in the USSR, GDR, Poland, Hungary, etc. The Council of Mutual Economic Aid has undertaken coordination of scientific and technological development plans and is laying the basis for fuller integration. But this is only a beginning.

like Czechoslovakia will be unable to keep up with the most advanced countries that are able to rely on a broad international base. These considerations make it imperative to continue strengthening ties with the USSR and other socialist countries, without infringing the principles of national sovereignty.

Of course, there are bound to be obstacles on the path of integration, and these will not come solely from the general national disparities, but primarily as a result of the varying degrees of preparedness for the scientific and technological revolution. While some socialist countries are still at a stage of predominantly extensive industrialization, the more advanced — Czechoslovakia included — cannot go ahead without finding an approach to the scientific and technological revolution. Naturally this gives rise to substantial differences in outlook, in demands, and in the proportions and priorities of construction — nor are views unanimous on the model of a socialist society, and on the need for and limits of international integration itself.

Examination of models suggests that the world linkages corresponding to the immanent tendencies of the scientific and technological revolution will show an appreciably different quality to that we have known in the classical division of labour. The old division by sectors divorced the industrial metropolises from the agricultural and raw material outposts. The new distribution of activities is, on the contrary, of a more *technological* nature.[1] On the one hand this deepens the gulf between the developed and underdeveloped countries, on the other hand it offers opportunities for the industrially advanced countries to establish stronger ties apart from the old imperial constellations. Moreover, the separation of the mass production countries from the historical centres of culture and research is losing its meaning. Old ties are loosening, and the hub of much more intense integration processes is shifting right into the sphere of science and technology.

These transformations in the nature of international division of labour are nourishing the soil of *nationality* problems, reviving the spirit of nationalistic aspirations, so that entirely modern sentiments experienced at the brink of the new technological gulfs are being dressed up in ancient national costumes, which their very wearers once used to hold up to ridicule. On the one hand the quite unsentimental brain drain has reached such a pitch that the entire educational and scientific system

[1] M. Nikl, "Světové ekonomické vztahy a vědeckotechnická revoluce" (World Economic Relations and the Scientific and Technological Revolution), *Mezinárodní vztahy* 1/1968.

of Europe and, indeed, of the "third world", operates in some respects as an auxiliary supply for the US research machine. On the other hand, we have the parallel growth of US dependence on the intellectual potentials of many medium and small countries,[1] as a result of the far-reaching and growing role of basic research and new scientific concepts. The openings for applying science are not governed by the means devoted to "big science", and there is therefore still scope for the talents of many small and medium-sized cultural nations. Understandably, in these complicated and rapidly changing circumstances exceptional, indeed decisive, importance is assumed by a purposive scientific and technological programme, with creative activity wisely directed to the main lines of advance in the scientific and technological revolution and in science as such.

/ *Strategy of Science* /　　　　　　　　　　　4.1.3

With the new status of science in the structure of the productive forces, all countries — and wider groupings — are faced with the vital choice of the area or form in which to use the accelerating potential. This gave birth to the idea of a modern *strategy*, or *tactics* of science (alternatively, "scientific policy").

Theoretical analysis indicates — and many practical experiences in the world confirm — that even such circumstances as shortages of manpower, raw material resources, etc. need not debar a country such as Czechoslovakia from taking an active part in the scientific and technological revolution. One might even venture to say that the more developed a country, the less weighty are these traditional factors. Scientific and technological fertility is not governed by the size of the population, and with a measure of international integration it is quite possible to embark on the revolution with quite a modest raw material base — on the condition, of course, that a scientifically based dynamic course is chosen, which would allow the favourable elements in the country's growth to be used. Moreover, fresh opportunities would need to be discerned in good time and the internal management structure would have to be elastic enough to take advantage of them. The solution should be sought in:

[1] D. J. de Solla Price writes in this connection of "a Pareto-like distribution" of small countries in the spectrum of world research projects (ibid., p. 97).

a) maximum development of international cooperation, specialization and integration (drawing on all the potentialities of the socialist system), with special regard to the technology of mass production;

b) emphasis on *highly skilled* work with a big share of creative and intellectual elements — which is in line both with Czechoslovakia's traditions, and with the shift in the mainspring of growth to spheres of intellectual activity. Only in this way can the skills and technical aptitude which the Czechoslovak people possess in large measure find an outlet; the preoccupation with extensive industrialization, however, lets them lie fallow.[1]

The prime need for a country intending to embark on such a course is an adequate scientific base of good quality. An undoubted achievement of socialism in Czechoslovakia has been to establish an *integrated research base*, which is incomparably superior to the prewar facilities and in some sectors approaches world standards.[2] True, Czechoslovakia is a country whose circumstances make especially big claims on the extent, structure and quality of research, and from this angle her scientific base still has some grave weaknesses. As regards the work force in science, research and development (see Tables 4-3 and 4-4) Czechoslovakia — taking the ratio to all gainfully employed — is 15—20 per cent behind the most advanced countries, that is, the USA and USSR;[3] measured by the ratio to manpower in mining, manufacturing and construction, the gap is 35—50 per cent; but for both indicators Czechoslovakia is at or above the level of many industrial countries of Europe.[4] But when quality is compared, the picture is worse. The true range of research is better judged by the number of university people engaged[5] and here there is already an appreciable lag (see Tables 4-3 and 4-4).

[1] This concept holds out prospects of freeing surplus specialized capacities to help economically underdeveloped countries, and in the sphere where they will be most needed in the long view.

[2] If we take as the basis for comparison the discussion by S. Dedijer in "International Comparisons of Science", *New Scientist* 379/1964 and data by Ewell, Freeman and others.

[3] B. Levčík, J. Nekola, L. Tondl, "Kritéria rozvoje výzkumné a vývojové činnosti" (Criteria for the Development of Research and Development) *Politická ekonomie* 7/1966.

[4] So the lag in this respect is not a key factor, but the danger lies in the fact that growth of the research base in Czechoslovakia is slower in the sixties than it was in the fifties.

[5] The share of university-trained personnel in the research base in Czechoslovakia is not more than 21 per cent, while in the USSR the figure is 24 per cent, in Britain

Scientific and research personnel in 1962 (%)	Czecho-slovakia	USSR	USA	UK
— of gainfully employed	1.79	2.18	2.12	1.67
— of industrial workforce	3.85	7.15	7.15	3.57
University-trained personnel in science and research (%)				
— of gainfully employed	0.39	0.52	0.81	0.46
— of industrial workforce	0.81	1.72	2.74	1.00

A similar picture is presented by comparing the shares of national incomes devoted to science and research (see Table 4-5). Here Czechoslovakia (in 1961) was about half-way behind the USA, very little behind the USSR and Britain, and was on a level with the industrial countries of the European continent, or ahead of some.[1] Nonetheless, the weakness born of extensive growth emerges unmistakably from comparison by the most reliable indicator — the share of total investment in the economy devoted to science and research was in Czechoslovakia only 30—50 per cent of that in the most advanced countries.[2] (cf. Tab. 4-7). In such circumstances, of course, all research work is hampered; development especially tends in many ways to formality.

Research is generally a wasteful undertaking; some findings find no immediate application, others may suddenly change the world. There is no foreseeing the course and fruits of a research project. Consequently

---

28 per cent and in the USA 38 per cent. The biggest section of specialized personnel in Czechoslovak applied research are workers with only secondary education (see V. Richter, M. Doležel, *Vědeckovýzkumná a vývojová základna v ČSSR* (Research and Development Base in Czechoslovakia), Prague 1964.

[1] J. Nekola, J. Zelinka, "Trend čs. badatelského výzkumu z hlediska některých tendencí rozvoje vědy ve světě" (Trend of Czechoslovak Basic Research in the Light of Some Tendencies in World Scientific Development, *Věstník ČSAV* 1/1965.

[2] For a long time the share of investment in science stayed around 0.8 to 0.9 per cent of total investment and rose to 1.1 per cent in 1964 (V. Richter, M. Doležel, *Výzkumná a vývojová základna v ČSSR, organisace, řízení a plánování* (Research and Development Base in Czechoslovakia, Organization, Management and Planning), Prague 1966. The figure for the advanced countries is 2—3 per cent. Naturally this means that institutes are starved of equipment, conditions for research work are often seriously cramped (one-third of the standard area per scientist), some modern branches of the technical and natural sciences, and primarily the social sciences — economics, sociology, anthropology, etc. — lack a basis for development, and the universities, where 8,000 specialists are working, are inadequately engaged in research owing to the shortage of equipment and of auxiliary personnel.

science, and especially basic research, need much broader backing than can be provided by considerations of immediate practical advantage.[1] Some reflections on the future suggest that the ratio of scientific workers to industrial manpower should advance from the present 5 per cent to 15—20 per cent and over within 20 years.[2] The proportion of expenditure on science and research would, of course, rise accordingly.

These are purely the quantitative preconditions for an approach to the difficult question of framing a modern *strategy of science and research* in a small, advanced country[3] with means too modest to allow it to cover the whole field as presented today. The feature in recent decades has been the complexity and sophistication of the intellectual processes leading up to scientific findings, so that it can no longer be maintained that they have been made in response to "orders" placed by industry. On the contrary, more and more impulses stem from the needs of scientific cognition as such, from its systems linkages, methodological syntheses, inter-discipline confrontations, etc. And the source of revolutionary changes in the civilization base is shifting to the area of fundamental discoveries in basic research. The effectiveness of resources channelled to this area is generally regarded as being about four times that attainable in applied research. In short, a scientific view of the progress of science points in all respects to the prospect that *basic research* will take the *lead* and that its quality will increasingly set the tone for the entire field of a country's research effort. While in the 1953—1959 period, the share of basic research in the USA was 8.5 per cent, it is now approaching 12 per cent, and this falls far short of what could be achieved, indicating that the potentialities are still gravely underestimated.[4]

Circumstances are making the distinction between basic and applied

---

[1] The American report *Scientific Progress, the Universities and the Federal Government* (Washington 1960) formulates the following principles of modern policy: "...to increase our investment in science just as fast as we can, to a limit not yet in sight"... "any short-sighted calculation of return on investment is likely to be self-defeating".

[2] The prospect, both in the USSR and the USA, is that 10—14 per cent of the workforce will be engaged in science and research by 1970.

[3] L. Tondl, J. Nekola, "Nové rysy v úloze vědy" (New Features in the Role of Science), *Sociologický časopis* 2/1966.

[4] "At the present moment I feel that we are grossly underplaying the use of fundamental science" (J. D. Bernal, ibid., *Science of Science*, p. 306). The share of basic research is 12 per cent in the USA, 17 per cent in France, 19 per cent in Italy, 21 per cent in Belgium, 22 per cent in Norway, etc. (*The Overall Level and Structure of R and D Efforts in OECD Member Countries*, Paris 1967.) (See Table 4-8.)

research rather relative, but a remarkable feature is that the smaller countries usually show a higher share of basic research.[1] This suggests that Czechoslovakia should envisage raising the share of basic research[2] substantially and concentrating it in forward-looking areas of the scientific and technological revolution that are accessible to the economy: the choice should be made with due regard for the country's traditions, the capacities of schools and supply of talents. Such sources of initiative would provide a good basis for applied research, which cannot in Czechoslovakia advance independently on all fronts because that would involve unnecessary duplication of work in other countries and would dissipate the forces available. Its chief role should be to ensure *prompt and creative application* of scientific and technological findings from all parts of the world, while concentrating on sectors offering the best prospects for breaking new ground.[3]

Obstacles will certainly be presented by:

a) lack of *qualified staff* in enterprise and departmental research and development, where the proportion of university-trained personnel often falls short of 20 per cent;[4]

b) *information facilities* of entirely inadequate proportions, lacking proper technical equipment. They account for only 2.7 per cent of research capacity, although by the standards of advanced countries the figure should be doubled, not to mention the need for modern information techniques. It is vital for a small country to keep abreast with scientific developments throughout the world;

c) inadequate use of foreign *licences*, for which less than one per cent of expenditures on science and research is earmarked, compared with 5—40 per cent in Western Europe. In many fields licences could contribute to a rapid advance in the technical level of production.[5] A policy

---

[1] Cf. *Fundamental Research and the Politics of Government*, Paris 1966. Evidently the existence of certain "thresholds" (Freeman), or "critical masses" (Capisarow) in applying the findings of "big science" in various fields play a part here.

[2] The share of basic research in Czechoslovakia is today about 9 per cent, and there was a falling trend in the sixties.

[3] To this end it would be advisable to select priority branches and to decide in which sectors progress will not depend on independent development, but will rely on other means.

[4] Investigation by the Statistical Office has shown that university-trained staff refer to foreign sources far more than those with secondary professional education. Therefore low qualification in applied research operates as an isolating factor.

[5] Estimates for 1963 alone are that 35,000 licence agreements were concluded by non-socialist countries. The paper *Handelsblatt* stated in 1960 that contracts on licences

directed to this sphere would also enable more active steps to be taken to *offer* licences, provide advisory services, etc., which could yield good economic returns.[1]

The socialist countries cannot be indifferent to any scientific and technological progress in the world. It is vital for them to keep their eyes open to all new developments; they should be alert to take possession of the know-how of civilization wherever it comes from, to master and elaborate it to the benefit of socialist advance.

Given favourable circumstances, a well-directed scientific, cultural and economic policy could turn Czechoslovakia into an arsenal of technological advance in a number of branches — primarily of the socialist world. She could serve as a laboratory, pilot plant, prototype and rationalization centre, and as a storehouse of the social, cultural and humanistic values so vitally needed in the world today.

/*Atmosphere of Scientific and Technological Progress*/   4.1.4

Industry, in its traditional guise, has relied predominantly on operative activity. Science, being on the contrary a system of mainly *creative activity*, makes different claims on the social conditions and climate for its work.

The chief element in creating this atmosphere — at least at the present stage of development — is provided by economic motivation. In its separate discoveries science can offer fantastic advantages to this or that businessman, or more probably to a concern or monopoly. But in its overall advance, it is a civilization factor of an emphatically *society-wide* kind — which is all the more striking now when the sequence of discoveries is merging into a steady stream. The force of this factor can be appreciated to the full solely by society in its entirety.

were already the keystone of industrial enterprise. This view stemmed from the discovery that in most advanced industrial countries earnings from patents, licences and scientific findings were growing twice as rapidly as from the export of goods. Countries like West Germany and France spend four to five times more of their national incomes on buying licences than Czechoslovakia does.

[1] The United States — whose laboratories, of course, employ scientists from all parts of the non-socialist world — trebled net earnings on licences in a decade, from some 200 million dollars in 1950 to nearly 600 million in 1961.

Indeed, this fact is generally accepted today;[1] but few who acknowledge its truth are aware that they are dealing with one of the elements of Marx's theory, and indeed one of the pillars of socialism's position in the world today.[2]

A *social climate* conducive to scientific progress possesses, alongside the economic factors (and resting on them), its socio-political and psychological background, too. Science calls for quite a different type of management, working regime, different standards and rules in society's everyday life, than those suited to industry, because it involves a much higher degree of inner subjectivity and responsibility, a greater measure of initiative and self-realization. There has to be much greater "*reliance on man*", on his creative abilities and powers. In contrast to the hierarchy of the industrial system, science reaches a stage in its development where it demands fuller implementation of democratic principles.

There is a quite widespread view, ascribed to Max Weber, that modern science is inevitably subjected to the hierarchy of industry. True, such a process has taken place here and there, and can still be observed, but mainly at the fringes of science and usually to its detriment.[3] The discerning observer will be more likely to find in this confrontation the phenomenon of a transitory equilibrium that will give way

---

[1] "...most of the returns on investment in research may be social... The requirements of society for the rapid dissemination of new knowledge among all potential users in the interest of economic growth are thus to some extent in conflict with the interest of private enterprise" (C. Freeman, R. Poignant, I. Svennilson, in *Ministers Talk About Science*, Paris 1965, p. 104). *In Basic Research and National Goals* (Washington 1965, p. 136) E. Teller admits that "the economic and social benefits of basic research cannot be wholly recaptured by the private institutions that finance it, but only by society as a whole".

[2] True, writers specializing in the subject of science and society often refer in one way or another to the fact that the exceptional support for science on the part of the socialist government, which changed the USSR by the close of the thirties into a country where relative expenditure in this field was three times higher than the US, and nine times the British, played no small part in creating a favourable atmosphere for government promotion of science and technology in all industrially advanced countries. Max Lerner even writes of "the political mystique of science" in the USSR, the "belief that nothing is impossible for man once he has the weapons of science" (cf. *Education; An Instrument of National Goals*, New York 1962, p. 153).

[3] It was stated at a symposium of Soviet and Polish historians of science held in Lvov in 1966 that attempts to apply the traditional system of management by officials to science lead to a drop in effectiveness directly proportional to the number of staff raised to the fourth power. Three scientists enjoying freedom of choice and procedure can perform work equivalent to that of 81 researchers who merely obey instructions.

to a more long-term opposed trend. Modern science cannot tolerate the hierarchical principle that was adequate for industry. It dismantles the old industrial system, breaking up its elements one after another. Writers on the sociology of science have repeatedly pointed to an immanent correlation and aptness of science and democratic forms,[1] although the deeper significance and roots of this relationship have not been fully elucidated, because not only forms, but also the substance of the social system are involved. The climate for such scientific activity can be provided only by a completely open social system founded on multidimensional interaction — a structure of interacting development.

Industrially developed bourgeois society handled this problem by way of "autonomy of science", by cultivating a separate, specially paid and protected enclave living a life governed in greater or lesser degree by rules distinct from those applying in industry. Although this autonomy was merely an auxiliary means and was therefore frequently suspended in favour of higher class interests, it was not without a certain rationality. But the arrangement encounters obstacles as soon as science begins to permeate production and everyday life, requiring that the appropriate rules and standards be generally accepted.

Enquiries into the difficulties facing science today come up against the fact that "social barriers were often a greater obstacle to innovation than lack of knowledge";[2] in short, that the key issue appears to be to build an appropriate *"scientific infrastructure"* in all spheres of society; that the job will be to change the entire industrial system — "integration of science with general policy".

At this point we find that the relation of society to scientific cognition, the ability or inability to use scientific findings and technological innovations, is the touchstone by which to judge the progressiveness of a given social order.

In the long historical view, from the standpoint of the theoretical model, socialism and communism are inherently linked with science.[3]

---

[1] R. K. Merton, who has more than once called attention to these empirically observed correlations (*Science and Democratic Social Structure — Toward Codification of Theory and Research*, Glencoe 1949), speaks in this connection of some degree of "communism" of science — an attribution that carries far wider significance than accorded to it by the author himself.

[2] C. Freeman, R. Poignant, I. Svennilson, ibid., p. 131, 116, 168.

[3] Marx explained this inner linking of science and socialism, which is as inherent to science as it is to socialism (*Arkhiv Marxa i Engelsa*, Vol. II/VII, Moscow 1933, p. 344). "It is no accident that the revolutions in science and society should occur

Their vast reserves flow from an open social structure, from endeavours to establish relationships of mutual cooperation and development of all, which in fact extends the groundwork for science on this inclusive scale, too. Nevertheless, to use these opportunities is a different matter than to formulate them in words; experience has shown that it is a hard and thorny path.

Scientific and technological advance is coming to be seen in the socialist countries as the vital factor in their social endeavours. Various documents on the subject have been issued in Czechoslovakia.[1] Yet the economy has continued on the path of extensive industrialization, with scientific advance very much in the background. We may take as proved the fact that the retarding influences lie deeper in the substance or forms of social reality and that even generous government support for science and research in general is powerless to halt them. On the one hand, we are only gradually working our way towards a comprehensive understanding of all that is involved in the transition from industrialization to the scientific and technological revolution; on the other hand, under the system of management in force so far, what we have already grasped and elaborated has not been matched by adequate measures. Moreover, the economic preconditions carry with them some social factors that retard the growth of the atmosphere necessary for scientific and technological advance. Genuine application of science in today's system of civilization regulators can be accomplished only by educated people, with profound knowledge of the prospects offered by modernization and dynamically directed growth under present conditions. Management at all levels needs to be of incomparably higher quality — with education to match — than in the days of industrialization. The Czechoslovak economy is showing unmistakable signs of the extent to which lack of genuine, not merely formal, qualification can hold back technological progress and the modernization of the community.[2] Experience is a big help when the basic proportions are stable. But when

---

together, but it would be too simple a view to make either one the consequence of the other" (J. D. Bernal, *Science in History*, ibid., p. 492).

[1] Resolutions by the Communist Party Central Committee and the Government on the tasks of science in promoting development and improving the technological level of industry, dating from 1956; resolutions by these bodies on strengthening the role of science and technology in developing the country's productive forces.

[2] This can be seen in many spheres and at all management levels in Czechoslovakia today. Only 3.7 per cent of workers in research and development are scientifically trained. In 1962, only 25 per cent of directors and leading technicians in industrial

they change — and this is typical for the early stages of the scientific and technological revolution — modern education alone is effective. Science starts to oust routine and "commonsense" decision-making at points where it has never penetrated before. All over the world, in every possible institution, scientific advisory bodies are multiplying, almost all decisions draw on specialist expertise, there is a spreading network of consultants of scientific standing,[1] while scientists also play a direct part in the highest organs of state.[2]

The extent to which science is used depends very largely on the initiative of the scientists and technicians, highly-skilled workers, executives and other specialized personnel. So long as socialism is unable to make the conditions of work customary in scientific life the general rule, so long as available resources, the content of work and the educational level of the majority stand in the way, special conditions have to be provided in the sphere of science, with many divergences and an autonomous standing, not subject to the rules and modes of management current in industry. Such differences cannot be eliminated by levelling down to the existing standards of industry, but on the contrary by raising the conditions for all up to, and above, the existing level of conditions and rules now customary in scientific and creative work. The

enterprises had the appropriate university training (in 1966 the figure had risen to 31 per cent). The educational level of cooperative farm chairmen is still below the average for the population as a whole. A mere 29 per cent of department chiefs in government administration and 40 per cent of all leading officials have more than basic or lower vocational education, although 70 per cent are under 40, that is, they belong to generations for whom socialism afforded good educational opportunities. These figures (derived from data in the Czechoslovak Statistical Yearbook for 1966 and from the analysis of Census results in the book *Vývoj společnosti v ČSSR v čtslech*, Prague 1965) are out of all proportion to the general educational level in the country and give strong cause for doubt whether such a body of men is qualified to advance the scientific and technological revolution.

[1] Almost all industrially developed countries now have scientific advisory bodies at the highest levels (cf. S. Dedijer in *Science of Science*, ibid.). In the United States, alongside the National Academy and the Office for Science and Technology, there are 16 Senate Commissions and 20 Commissions of Congress, a special Presidential adviser for science, a Federal Council for Science, hundreds of brain trusts attached to central institutions. In the socialist countries, self-governing scientific bodies (Academies) are appointed by statute as government advisers and together with state commissions for technology they form a system framed to promote the participation of science in directing social advance.

[2] Members of Congress in America include 3 per cent who are scientists and technicians; for deputies to the Supreme Soviet in the USSR the figure is 25 per cent (quoted from *Science*, Sept. 30, 1960, p. 883).

future may be expected to bring an equalizing of living conditions and work regimes at a much higher level,[1] but in no case their *levelling* or depressing to the old level typical for industrial conditions today — that would conflict with true socialist progress and constrain the lives and initiative of intellectual workers.

In some socialist countries, the healthy equalizing of living standards among workers and intellectuals that occurred during socialist construction has degenerated from time to time into a general "averaging out", which is incompatible with remuneration according to work,[2] and with the significance of science in society. Even when this egalitarianism has been corrected, many specialists will lack the incentives existing under capitalism — social distinctions cannot be unduly sharpened. The greater then the need for socialist countries to contrive and safeguard a suitable regime for creative work,[3] leaving people as free as possible to do their special jobs;[4] the more important it is to raise the prestige of work in science and technology[5] and, most important, to give the socialist expert a wide field for freely creative self-assertion. Herein lies the moral stimulation that capitalism is unable to offer. It is a question of an atmosphere of *respect* for learning as the accumulated wealth of

---

[1] By examining the long-term statistics of differentiation in earnings and trying to extract from them the influence of science and technology, we may conclude that to a point the gap between pay for skilled and unskilled work widens, but as skill becomes widespread, it starts to close.

[2] Czechoslovakia holds pride of place for low pay differentials. For example, earnings of highly skilled workers are only about 20 per cent above the average workers' wages, and engineers and technicians draw 27 per cent above, while in the early sixties levelling was continuing. The total earned income of a university graduate working in research only catches up with the sum of wages earned by a worker in heavy industry when the former reaches the age of 46 to 47; a doctor reaches this point when he is 52—53 and a teacher never gets there. There are also strongly egalitarian tendencies in the working regime.

[3] N. Wiener pointed out long ago that long summer holidays for teachers and sabbatical years for scholars (with some freedom to order their working time) is no unwarranted privilege, but an absolute imperative; a society that ignores it has to pay in terms of a sharp drop in the effectiveness of creative work (cf. *I Am a Mathematician*, New York 1956).

[4] Many specialists in Czechoslovakia (mainly doctors, technicians, foremen, teachers and skilled workers) are obliged by lack of auxiliary personnel and a mistaken propensity towards egalitarianism to perform jobs that could be taken over by non-professional workers.

[5] Research by V. Brenner and M. Hrouda (*Věda a vysokoškolské vzdělání v prestiži povolání* — Science and University Education and the Prestige of Professions, Study Material 38/1967) has demonstrated various problems in this connection.

society, *confidence* in this "universal labour" as Marx termed it, *encouragement* for creative initiative. The expert is of service to socialist society when he points emphatically to the opportunities for advance and to the barriers, when he is fully informed about science, technology and cultural developments in other countries, when he breaks new ground with full confidence that what furthers socialism will find the recognition due to it. The expert who carries out instructions to the letter has no opinions of his own, avoids taking risks, or is timid, absorbed in his own worries and incapable of criticising superiors and subordinates when things need to be pushed ahead, is of no value to socialism. Today all types of society are facing a test of their ability to create the climate needed for free development and universal application of science.

/*Technology and Management.*   4.1.5
Cybernetic Model/

Industrial civilization knew two main types of management: *enterprise management*, which provided the real basis for all active, positive developments in this field,[1] and *administration*, with the prime function (insofar as it was not derivative of enterprise management, too) of negating movement, maintaining the status quo, the given industrial system. In between these two types lay a sphere of spontaneous motion, controlled by the general regulation process of capital.

Management within an enterprise — factory — consisted in directing the mechanical stream of things and their handling by men, with a purely utilitarian intent, precisely governed by the appropriate norms and with a maximum of objective rationality. The practice of administration has been to petrify this mechanism by confining people to set grooves, by treating them as things. In both cases the precondition and consequence of management was a large measure of non-subjectivity in the

[1] Max Weber understood "enterprise management" in the sense of an expert hierarchy, an incarnation of sober rationality, deprived of all value attributes. Consequently bureaucracy appears to him as a necessary outcome, and in fact an inherent element, of enterprise management (cf. *Wirtschaft und Gesellschaft*, Vol. I, Tübingen 1956, pp. 65 ff.). He elucidated the essential interrelation of bureaucratic administration with industrial enterprise management, but failed to grasp the overall integration of these management processes alongside the spontaneous movement of the capital market, that is, as a specific distribution of the components in the movement of industrial civilization. That is why they appear to him as imperative phenomena of management.

objects managed.[1] Changes within them were left aside, and only a limited circle of changing material circumstances was taken into consideration. This range of tasks could be handled by *directive decision* on things, and on people as things, according to the hierarchy of the industrial structure, with the backing of an equally directive decision on the part of the bureaucratic power machine.

These connections between industrialization and management have led people to identify the *deterministic model*, the rigid rationality of things, with the image of management as such.[2] They have brought the more acute observer, who tries to project the procedures of industrialization into the future, to the conviction that civilization is moving towards total bureaucracy, to "the utterly inescapable fettering of our entire existence".[3] He feels that the anonymous technicized apparatus of management is turning "totalitarian" and the rationality it embodies is seen as something in face of which "all counteraction seems impossible", if it is not placed outside the realm of reason altogether,[4] that, in short, the whole history of our life on earth threatens to be "no longer the history of people, but of an apparatus *(Apparate)*".[5]

However, such an outcome is relevant only in considering the typical industrial mode of management with its limitations. The situation changes the moment one or several factors are replaced by a *universal dynamism* in each of the many dimensions of the productive forces and in the endless maze of circumstances, as soon as the actual *subjectivity of the managed* emerges as a key element that cannot be left aside, that is, as soon as the mere rationality of things is replaced by the higher rationality of developing and mutable systems. And these are the

---

[1] The manifold ways of incorporating man in the system of enterprise management are recalled by W. H. Whyte in *The Organization Man*, New York, 1956.

[2] In any management effort people think precisely along the lines on which an engineer organizes an industrial plant (J. Burnham, *The Managerial Revolution*, New York 1941, p. 167).

[3] M. Weber, *Gesammelte Aufsätze zur Religionssoziologie*, Vol. I, Tübingen 1920, p. 1; similarly in *Wirtschaft und Gesellschaft*, ibid. p. 669 — there is constant growth of "the fettering of the whole material fate of the mass to the ever more precisely operating, ever more bureaucratic organization of private capital, and the idea that it can be abolished thereby becomes more and more utopian".

[4] H. Marcuse, *One-Dimensional Man*, Boston 1964, pp. XV and 9. "The web of domination has become the web of Reason itself, and this society is fatally entangled in it. And the transcending mode of thought seems to transcend Reason itself" (ibid., p. 169).

[5] Prof. Bertaus at a conference entitled "Machine — Denkmaschine — Staatsmaschine. Entwicklungstendenzen der modernen Industriegesellschaft", *Bergdorfer Protokolle*, Bd. 2, Hamburg—Berlin, p. 25.

features peculiar to science and creative cooperation among people. Thence, in the course of the scientific and technological revolution, they penetrate all aspects of life and manifest themselves at all levels as an insistent pressure towards a *new concept of management*.

The integrated systems common to all automated and highly technical processes cannot be managed by the old methods derived from determinist rationality.[1] New techniques and technology demand new types of organization and new people who will combine with them in a uniform system.[2]

The key to control of technical processes today seems to lie in *systems engineering*, which originated some ten to fifteen years ago, when serious breakdowns were being experienced in working with big automated units. The classical engineer, with his detailed knowledge of a given component of the system, its tangible mechanism, is out of his depth. The concern is more and more with managing aggregate and changing processes, the production system in its entirety, and this is the responsibility of the systems engineer.

The change applies with equal urgency to managers in departments with highly-developed technical equipment. The old idea that a manager's job was to organize the work of subordinated operatives becomes absurd when automation is progressively taking over all operations that can be programmed.[3] The modern manager is concerned with the working of complete systems equipped with internal linkages enabling them to regulate themselves and operate like "biological beings".[4] His role is no longer to introduce one or another regime, but to optimize and integrate the behaviour of systems.[5]

[1] W. Buckingham (*Automation. Its Impact on Business and People*, New York 1961) compares attempts to manage automated units by the old methods with the fate of the Brontosaurus, whose body grew more quickly than its brain, which led to its extinction.
[2] M. Král, "Vědeckotechnický pokrok a řízení společnosti" (Scientific and Technological Advance and Management of Society), *Věda a řízení společnosti*, Prague 1967.
[3] This process is, of course, just beginning. But modern technology clearly "tends to completeness" (cf. J. Ellul, *La Technique et l'enjeu du siècle*, Paris 1954).
[4] S. Beer, Cybernetics and Management London 1960.
[5] The old-type managers have been the victims of the new technological conditions of management for some time (*Automation and Technological Change. Hearings before the Subcommittee on Economic Stabilization to the Joint Committee on the Economic Report of the US Congress*, Washington 1965). According to M. Anshem, the manager who is not versed in systems procedures, cybernetics and modern mathematics will in a few years be a mere hanger-on of the experts he will have to call in (*Automation and Technological Change*, ed. J. T. Dunlop, Prentice Hall 1962).

In the industrial system it was possible to assume the validity of the *"necessitarian* model"[1], where the whole and all the parts operate in effect like an enormous machine, like Leibniz's predestined world, Laplace's mechanism, in which each past state determines each future state, where the managing directive can therefore intervene at every step with certainty as to the result, and dictate "the one best way" with complete authority.

But in modern production systems — and still more in the civilization processes of our day — we are confronted by a network of interlinked processes with *internal automatism*, and consequently with some measure of "will", with a system of automatic reaction, making it impossible to decide every parameter beforehand.[2] The working of these *cybernetic models* can be followed only by systems methods capable of operating with statistical laws, involving versatile, stochastic processes.[3] It is not by chance that the origin and spread of cybernetics has come just now. It is, in fact, today the sole possible basis for modern management and planning. Operational prediction, programming and the like are far removed from any attempts to regulate things directly from without. They rely on systems use of regulatory principles, on *indirect management*.

As pointed out by Norbert Wiener,[4] modern civilization is on all sides discarding the classical Leibniz picture of the world, where events are unequivocally determined beforehand according to the rules of the industrial mechanism. Society can no longer be run like a machine or system of machines operating according to the hard and fast principles of Laplace's laws. Any such attempt is bound to condemn management to impotency and inescapable self-deception: directives would operate in precisely the opposite direction to that intended.

---

[1] An interesting criticism of the "necessitarian model" has been made by V. Tlustý in an article "Obecné filosofické a sociologické problémy řízení" (Common Philosophical and Sociological Problems of Management) in M. Král et al. *Věda a řízení společnosti*, Prague 1967).

[2] F. H. George, *Automation, Cybernetics and Society*, London 1959. V. N. Mikhalevsky refers to the multisector models employed in modern planning as "self-enlarging systems, working under conditions of incomplete information, which embrace many elements of a qualitative nature that are not amenable to numerical description" (*Perspektivnye raschoty na osnove prostykh dinamicheskikh modeley*, Moscow 1964, p. 146.)

[3] For the relevance of these cybernetic linkages to nascent economic conditions see J. von Neumann, O. Morgenstern, *Theory of Games and Economic Behaviour*, Princeton 1953.

[4] N. Wiener, *I Am a Mathematician. The Later Life of a Prodigy*, Cambridge 1956, p. 328.

Modern production and social systems would be reduced to chaos if they did not employ systems of *self-operating processes* which are mediated through a variety of civilization instruments such as the market, commodity forms, money, democratic principles, legal norms, moral standards, etc. Civilization has in fact relied on the constitution of these self-operating regulators[1] from the outset. The system is now being completed, undergoing change and internal link-ups. At the level now reached by civilized society it is therefore impossible to direct anything without consciously employing (and adhering to) these regulators and rules — at least until such time as conditions are ripe for abolishing them. Management and planning can no longer consist in direct intervention in separate matters; they need to employ the far more effective method of controlling and applying the regulators, modelling "rules of the game" whose automatic operation then makes for the chosen goal — or rather shapes the goal and the subjectivity in the desired direction. In place of directive regulation of things, and people as things, we have scientific operation with regulating principles.

During the first stage, when revolution and industrialization were the order of the day, the socialist countries endeavoured to free themselves of the power of the capitalist element through generalizing the system of intra-enterprise management, that is, to organize society like one giant industrial concern[2] — but without capitalists. Moreover, they connected it with administration, with power in the hands of the working class, resorting here, too, to direct command, because the old economic and social rules were largely inapplicable and the new had to be worked out by degrees. The outcome was that the directive approach

---

[1] Engels in fact based his definition of civilization on the existence of these regulators: "Civilization is therefore... the stage of development of society at which the division of labour, the exchange between individuals arising from it, and the commodity production which combines them both, come to their full growth and revolutionize the whole of previous society" (*The Origin of the Family*, London 1941, pp. 198—199).

[2] In some of his writings, e.g. in the well-known article *On Authority* (Marx-Engels, *Werke*, Bd. 18, Berlin 1962, pp. 305—308), Engels used similar formulations in polemics with the anarchists, but with the knowledge that this was not an ideal for the new society, but a necessary stage on the road from the old society. The idea that to give general validity to the industrial enterprise type of management (by direct orders) would signify eliminating the rule of elemental powers over people and establishing the objectivired power of man ignores the fact that the industrial directive still embodies (even after class antagonism has been abolished) the conflict of managing and managed, creators and executors, which was placed there by the conditions from which this type of management originated.

became the general rule;[1] it ousted economic methods and abrogated many of the established rules of society (such as formal democratic legal standards, etc.). However, as industrialization drew to its close, this directive management inevitably reached a point beyond which it could lead only to absurdity. When the whole groundwork of life is on the move, there is really no hope of managing things by deciding about each individual change. The instruments of civilization used hitherto (such as market-money relations or democratic forms) cannot be superseded unless we use them, master them and thereby deprive them of their power as elemental forces. Automatic processes in modern civilization cannot be abolished. They can either be purposively applied, objectively modelled, and so indirectly (as with every automatic system) controlled, i.e., made to achieve planned ends — or, on the contrary, through constant subjective interference, directing, laying down the law, forcing or prohibiting, we in fact succumb to their power in the blind belief that we have "abolished spontaneity".

Everything depends on whether socialism succeeds in working out a system of *civilization regulators*, of means and rules for adjusting the economic, and also the social, political, psychological and cultural conditions for promoting man's creative activity and directing his interest to socialism, so that the approaches to the scientific and technological revolution may be opened up in a planned way. Modelling economic motivation, moulding the socialist style of life, stimulating democratic initiative, cultivating the collective reason — all these forms of indirect management also imply developing the actual *subject* in society, unfolding and reinforcing the subjectivity of sectors of management that meet the needs of transition to the scientific and technological revolution. Purposive subjectivity is not, after all, a ready-made quality that has just been waiting for a chance to assert itself in society; on the contrary, it is something that has to be cultivated and constantly renewed, and it comes to the fore only when the economic, social and cultural forms of socialist society have reached the peak of their development.[2]

Management of modern socialist society figures primarily as a problem of creative self-regulation. The new dimensions that people and groups introduce into the movement of society — and which have not been

---

[1] M. Weber deduced from this that industrial enterprise management and factory discipline are actually the prime principles on which socialism is founded and that consequently bureaucracy is its inevitable fate.

[2] Cf. R. Richta, *Ekonomika jako civilizační dimenze* (The Economy as a Civilizing Dimension), Study materials 42/1967.

prescribed beforehand — are part of its very essence, providing a new, specific quality, and they cannot be lightly ignored or frustrated. Regulation of the managed is no longer good enough; on the contrary, *all-inclusive* management now has to be conceived in a planned way. The job is to expand and articulate a system of civilization regulators capable of providing optimal conditions for accelerated growth, for the advance of human powers and for active participation by all management. If such indirect management is sometimes regarded as a lower and weaker type than the directive, this is an optical illusion dating from the days of industrialization. *Regulation of the regulators* is in fact a higher form of management, adapted to more versatile and powerful movements in society. Furthermore, it is the sole means by which to make the process of modern civilization amenable to planning and control. Since it allows the flow of information to be rationalized and then taken over by technical devices, with the greater part of management processes put into an algorithm,[1] it provides a sound basis for widespread application of modern computer technology, to which the directive system was deaf on principle. This technology in its turn again and again breaks through the circle of processes hitherto susceptible to management and transforms the nature of management as such.[2] This two-way countermotion will ultimately allow a reversal of the inherent propensity of the industrial system born of capitalism to erect a hierarchy and bureaucracy.[3]

Prejudices about management inherited from the industrial epoch go to the roots of man's position in civilization today. The trouble is that the traditional management model has no room for any change stemming from the self-assertion and self-transformation of individuals and groups on which so much depends.[4] Directive management culmi-

[1] P. Kapitsa refers to the prospect of building the machinery of state on the pattern of a cybernetic installation (*The Science of Science*, ibid., p. 139).

[2] Computer technology continually upsets the traditional ideas about management (M. Shanks, *The Innovators*, London 1967, p. 96).

[3] "The technological revolution that is now only just starting in offices leads to a breaking down of hierarchy similar to that already noticeable for some time at many points in production" (H. P. Bahrdt, *Industriebürokratie. Versuch einer Soziologie des industrialisierten Bürobetriebes und seiner Angestellten*, Stuttgart 1958, p. 101). Similar tendencies have been pointed out by K. Boulding in another connection (*The Organizational Revolution*, New York 1953), G. Osipov (*Tekhnika i obshchestvenny progress*, Moscow 1959). We leave aside here the question of how much scope is offered for this process by different social systems.

[4] Considerations about management systems under socialism are now centred on this point (see J. Bober, *Stroj, človek, spoločnost* — Machine, Man, Society — Bratislava

nates in an endeavour to turn civilization into a mechanism, thereby eliminating man, his initiative and creative activity from the world. In a quite elemental manner it once more confines society within the one-dimensional movement of industrialization from which it emerged itself. In contrast, management by planned regulation of regulators creates an elastic space for alternation, *individual and collective* enterprise and multidimensional growth, because it converts the managed links into autonomous subjective agents, which by their own growth set new dimensions in motion and so participate in management. This is a crucial point. Without such management socialism would be unable to work out its inner subjectivity and move resolutely along the road of scientific and technological revolution.

Modern man cannot free himself of the innumerable ties binding him to the vast apparatus of civilization, which today indubitably operates as a fateful power, the programmer of human life. Nevertheless, under certain conditions he can turn it step by step into the foundation and programmer of his own human initiative, and on this plane man's every compliance will signify his victory.

/ *Rationalizing the Flow of Information* /   4.1.6

Management is commonly viewed from its "power aspect", involving subordination, issuing orders, etc. The reason lies both in the fact that this aspect actually predominates in industrial management[1] (in enterprise management and public administration), and that when constant parameters could on the whole be expected, the other aspect of management — information — receded into the background. However, with the advance of science into production and everyday life, and with the acceleration of technological development, this hitherto neglected element is everywhere coming to the fore.

Since information is the medium of every innovation and an essential link in every application of science, the progress of information technology is one of the pivots of the scientific and technological revolution.

1963; and on a new basis P. Pelikán, *Člověk a informace* — Man and Information, Prague 1967).

[1] "Our whole concept of management is essentially naive and primitive, relying on an image of causality that is almost completely dominated by the principle of retribution. For the majority the management process signifies naked force; this throws a typical light on our civilization" (S. Beer, *Cybernetics and Management*, London 1960).

To the extent that technology in the past augmented man's physical abilities in the first place, the technology now revolutionizing our civilization base reinforces in addition, and primarily, the intellectual resources of society.[1]

The growth of officialdom and the administrative machine in recent decades gives a good idea of the amount of information required for the management of any sphere of modern civilization. This somewhat primitive, but until recently almost exclusive mode of obtaining, transmitting and storing information has obviously exhausted its possibilities. On the one hand, it is expensive, unwieldy and unreliable; it distorts information, delays or holds it back altogether, diverts and disperses its flow. On the other hand, it breeds a spate of senselessly repeated, superfluous information. Man is overwhelmed by this massive flow, but starved of what he needs.[2]

Modern civilization faces the urgent need to analyze and rationalize its information systems, to employ new and more rapid techniques for transmitting, elaborating and storing information — to evolve a new code and miniaturize recording. This presupposes finding answers to such questions as: what is and what is not information for a given institution; what are the appropriate methods for obtaining it; what are the optimal information patterns; what method of handling facts to choose; what principles should be adopted to ensure "clean" information? Only when the flow of information has been rationalized in this way can we expect cybernetic techniques to be harnessed to the full; mass cybernation will then yield quite startling results[3] and new implications.

There can be little doubt that cybernetic technology is capable of displacing a mass (in the long view, the bulk) of office work and the part of management in which decision-making can be programmed. A universal automatic system of handling information, which accepts, processes, abbreviates, codes and distributes, is already a theoretical proposition.

---

[1] M. Král, "Vědeckotechnická revoluce a řízení" (The Scientific and Technological Revolution and Management), *Sociologický časopis* 2/1966. A number of authors, like Crossman, Davis and others, see this as the essential aspect of the processes that we refer to in this book as the scientific and technological revolution (*Discussion of the Impact of Automation on the Occupational Distribution, Job Content and Working Conditions*, ed. University of California, January 1965).

[2] J. Zeman, *Poznání a společnost* (Knowledge and Society), Prague 1962.

[3] In the light of present developments we may expect that "we will be able to do more with information technology than we now can even imagine" (J. Diebold, The New World Coming, *Saturday Review*, July 27, 1966).

It can take over the work of entire offices and institutions.[1] Memory stores with capacities of hundreds of millions of "addresses" can provide an enterprise with an "immortal memory" where information will never be forgotten and is always on tap. In the long run it will be possible to arrange for a steady two-way flow of information — some kind of regular voting and consultation with public opinion, which would be a substitute for Rousseau's ideal of a meeting of all citizens in the Republic, and provide for democratic confrontation of every newly-introduced principle of regulation.[2]

Information technology is now highly important — 'and any lag is especially unfortunate — in the sphere of science itself. Despite a rapid extension of scientific information networks throughout the world, there are still innumerable discoveries of what has been discovered elsewhere. Various calculations estimate that in the USA and USSR alone (the countries with the best information systems) they amount to 10, 15 and 25 per cent of the total.[3] In many areas it is still easier to make a discovery anew from the start than to find out whether it has already been made. Some 20 to 50 per cent of an engineer's time is occupied by hunting for information.[4] Intensive work is therefore in progress on a complete technical conversion of the information system, on new types of computerized information centres, on projects for technical documentation, etc. A foundation for these plans exists in the type of scientific and technological information system that originated in the Soviet VINITI as the first in the world.[5] An ambitious scheme for the Western European countries was elaborated between 1957 and 1963.[6] President Kennedy took the initiative in 1963 in launching extensive projects for "bold new

[1] Cf. A. I. Berg, J. Chernyak, *Informatsia i upravleniye*, Moscow 1966.

[2] In a lecture to British radio-engineers, Dr. Zvorykin of RCA suggested that regular voting at short intervals could be arranged by means of the telephone, television and computer system. Commenting on this project, M. C. Goodall writes, "This could allow a very significant development of the democratic process" (*Science and the Politician*, Cambridge 1965, p. 65).

[3] For example, G. M. Dobrov in *Tekhnika i yeyo mesto v istorii obshchestva (materialy k soveshchaniyu)*, Moscow 1965, p. 48.

[4] V. I. Tereshchenko, *Organizatsiya i upravleniye (Opyt SShA)*, Moscow 1965.

[5] The VTEI system in Czechoslovakia is conceived on similar lines, but with a considerable technical lag (cf. J. Spirit, *Mechanizace a automatizace v soustavě* VTEI — Mechanization and Automation in the VTEI System — Prague 1965). Its efficiency is therefore still low, for instance a questionnaire in Czechoslovak steelworks showed that it satisfies a bare half of technical personnel.

[6] Including the "European centre" for scientific and technological information from the socialist countries.

methods" of scientific information in the United States,[1] capable of providing a steady flow of news about world science; they include: automatic central depots, specialized centres in big institutes, an international network supplying scientific information, a computer system providing scientists with information and to which they have direct access.[2]

In the USSR, in accordance with a decision of the Council of Ministers, work has been stepped up in recent years on a country-wide system of scientific and technological information. The socialist system — and especially Czechoslovakia — is feeling a growing need for an international linking of information systems that would make the most of the advantages offered by a social system where barriers to a full and even flow of information have been removed. Failing this, big opportunities peculiar to socialism would be neglected.

Strange as it may seem, the fates of social systems will be decided in large measure within the realm of man and information.

Seen as an entity, science is a young, emergent mode of human activity that still has to finish defining its inner principles — not to mention its full-scale application in society. But experience has already indicated the enormous benefits to be expected if its growth potential, anthropological qualities, rational motives and democratic principles should assume general validity — compared with the traditional narrow dynamism of industrialization and the inverted structure and hierarchical cleavages of the industrial system. This is vital for the future, because the basic rules of society and of management are always derived from the most progressive areas in which productive forces are created. If industrial mammoths have hitherto shaped civilization to their own likeness,[3] we may foresee the society of the future framing its life forms primarily on the model of creative scientific activity.

---

[1] "...strong science and technology is a national necessity and adequate communication is a prerequisite for strong science and technology" (*Science, Government and Information. A Report of the President's Science Advisory Committee*, Washington 1963, p. III).

[2] Experiments are being made with linking several hundred scientists directly to an information centre by means of a special typewriter and telephone.

[3] P. Drucker, *The New Society. The Anatomy of the Industrial Order*, New York 1950.

/Social Problems and the Ferment of Ideas in the Age of Science and Technology/

The scientific and technological revolution is essentially a part of the process of *constituting the subjective factor*, that is to say, the subjectivity of society, and then of man, who through its medium comes to master the processes by which the productive forces of human life are created, and this implies mastering the very well-spring of the changes underlying history. More precisely, in the course of this revolution, insofar as the necessary conditions have been generally established, these subjective factors discover that their own development offers radically new opportunities to intervene in the march of history.

Observing the course of industrial civilization in the West, we cannot fail to note how the progress of science, technology, education and culture calls with growing insistence for the most diverse new types of subjectivity (state intervention, assembling scientific bodies around centres of management, experiments in planning, setting up forecasting institutions, etc.). A detailed analysis would evidently reveal that in the context of modern capitalism these are retroactive phenomena — every step towards broadening the actual subjectivity of society and man involves further subordination of society and man to circumstances beyond their control — the outcome is, in fact, a pseudo-subjectivity. Nevertheless, the material so accumulated is remarkably explosive. We may assume that at a comparable level of the productive forces the pressure in this direction will be substantially stronger under socialist conditions, and will be able to find more adequate and effective media — indeed, empirical confirmation for this exists. In this case, the endeavour to expand the subjectivity of society and man that is typical of socialism cannot fail to make common cause with the nascent revolution in the structure and dynamics of the productive forces. At least in the long view, we would then be led to expect history to lose the aspect of a natural process,[1] which in the traditional industrial civilization has obscured the unchallenged course of events, interrupted only from time to time by a convergence of change in civilization.

That is the second radical change introduced by the scientific and technological revolution into the laws of the historical process — in the measure to which the world is changed, the practical activity of the mass

---

[1] "Thus past history proceeds in the manner of a natural process and is also essentially subject to the same laws of movement" (Letter from Engels to J. Bloch, London, September 21, 1890, in Marx-Engels, *Selected Works*, Vol. 1, Moscow 1933, p. 382).

ceases to be a mere *prop* of history. The *everyday* begins to lose its inexorable antinomy to the *historical* — insofar as it embodies elements of growing human abilities and hence of the gestation of new productive forces in society. What happens in this everyday individual life is simultaneously an autonomous factor of historical change. Such a process of civilization implies shaping history equally with one's own life.

/The Scientific and Technological Revolution and Social Stratification/   4.2.1

Every revolution in production — including the industrial revolution — has hitherto been the work of the class that was instrumental in promoting it and which replaced another class in this role, carrying out the whole process at the expense of the class that represented the majority. If the model we have constructed of the scientific and technological revolution corresponds to reality, we should assume that as a specific universal revolution in the productive forces its progress will be impracticable — at least on the whole front — without the *positive*, independent participation of the *majority*, and ultimately of *all* members of society. In one way or another, man can be forced from without to function as simple labour power, and the range of creative activities required to keep industry running is fairly restricted. But no one will be induced to engage in creative activity involving the development of his own powers if he is not committed freely, of his own will. And in the end no élite will be capable of opening up the sources of science, technology and culture adequately to meet the demands of a complete transformation of the productive forces of human life.

Consequently, the scientific and technological revolution is not, and can never be in its entirety, the concern of some exclusive group; it is beyond the power of any class confronting another class to bring it to a successful conclusion. On the contrary, in the material features of human labour and human life this revolution evidently embodies the fundamental aspiration and mission of the working class — that role which makes it the avant-garde of the communist movement, whereby it no longer figures only as a class, but as the true representative of society as a whole, as the motivator of a programme for "*abolishing all classes*". The working class is the first victorious class in history to have no vested interest in maintaining the conditions of its class or estate;

on the contrary, its concern is that they should be abolished and conditions for the full development of all men be established. The working class derives its position as the major social force of the century, in which the only real hopes of this civilization rest, from the fact that together with the objective conditions it changes itself and ultimately abolishes itself as a class — its own supremacy and all class supremacy[1] — and not only with regard to property, economic conditions, but also to the nature of work and life. The goal is the complete transformation of society, and this all-inclusive self-transformation is also the highest stage and an essential precondition for the self-liberation of the workers.

In this sense, carrying through the scientific and technological revolution is a condition and integral part of the mission that history has allotted to the working class. In its attitude to the development and application of science throughout the fabric of society we have a reflection of the extent to which this class is aware of this special task and how far it is actually concerned with it. The truly great and liberating element in the position of the working class — making it the avantgarde of the new society — does not derive from its momentary interests and pride of caste, which are often material for social demagogy, but from the ability to transform the world and society by harnessing the product of man's whole development that is embodied in science.[2]

Marx saw in this *union of the working class with science,* and in a full and thorough union alone, the promise of liberation for society and man. There is no question of subordination and compromise between them. (cf. Action Programme of the CPCz.) The more resolutely, dispassionately, uncompromisingly and ruthlessly science advances, the more it is in accord with the aspirations of the working class.[3] Socialism stands and falls with science just as surely as it stands and falls with workers' government.

Today, at the very outset of the scientific and technological revolution, when it is diffused among diverse social systems, the theoretical

---

[1] K. Marx, F. Engels, *The Communist Manifesto,* ibid., p. 28.

[2] "Only the proletarians of the present day, who are completely shut off from all self-activity, are in a position to achieve a complete and no longer restricted self-activity, which consists in the appropriation of a totality of productive forces and in the thus postulated development of a totality of capacities" (K. Marx, F. Engels, *The German Ideology,* New York 1966, p. 67).

[3] Cf. F. Engels, *Ludwig Feuerbach und der Ausgang der klassischen deutschen Philosophie, K. Marx, F. Engels Werke,* Band 21, Berlin 1962.

picture of the accompanying changes in the social structure may appear empirically unproved and dubious. Nonetheless, in one way or another it is taken into account in researches of the most varied trends, both from socialist positions,[1] and (in limited form) from other standpoints.[2] The trend of the scientific and technological revolution is manifested in the social stratification of the capitalist countries in a disparity — on the one hand, technological innovations undoubtedly reduce the relative importance, and sometimes the actual amount, of traditional worker labour, while on the other, they substantially expand the specialist category, to some extent that of clerical workers, employees in services, etc. From this stem ideas about the emergence of "a new middle class"[3], "levelling of the middle estate",[4] prediction of "deproletarization" induced by technological development,[5] theories about white-collar workers replacing manual workers,[6] prophesies that the government of affairs will be taken over exclusively by a growing force of professional technical personnel, and so on and so forth.[7]

However, these sociological efforts all agree in generalizing the purely transitory or secondary aspects of the present trend and abstracting from the second pole of the disparity, from the fact that the class framework of the processes remains unchanged. They identify the working class with manual workers and reduce the definition of a class to characterization of a social stratum. In terms of Marx's classification, the increase in specialist personnel induced by technological advance (with the exception of a small section comprising executives living mainly from profit — that is, a product of class differentiation within the intelli-

[1] "While the industrial revolution led to the origin of the working class, the socialist revolution, of which the scientific and technological revolution is an essential part, leads to abolishing the working class as a class" (K. Tessmann, *Probleme der technisch-wissenschaftlichen Revolution*, Berlin 1962, p. 136). Similarly, A. Mileikovsky, "Nauchno-tekhnichesky Progress i sorevnovanie dvukh sistem", *Pravda*, April 24, 1966).

[2] "The return of the worker to his home from which he was drawn by the first industrial revolution will constitute the second industrial revolution" (M. Pyke, *Automation: Its Purpose and Future*, London 1956). Pyke, however, does not distinguish between "the worker" and "the working class" and leaves aside the question of what social conditions allow of these changes.

[3] Cf. K. Mayer, *Transactions of the Third World Congress of Sociology*, vols. III—IV, Amsterdam 1956.

[4] E. Salin, *Industrielle Revolution*, Kyklos 1956.

[5] D. Bell in *Dun's Review and Modern Industry* 1/1962.

[6] H. Schelsky, *Die Sozialen Folgen der Automatisierung*, Düsseldorf—Köln, 1957, p. 18; also, *Auf der Suche nach Wirklichkeit*, Köln—Düsseldorf 1965.

[7] M. Young, *The Rise of Meritocracy*, London 1958.

gentsia) is simply a new phenomenon of the selfsame class polarization in society, because in these circumstances specialist employees, technical personnel, clerical workers and so on swell the ranks of the working class — even if they are not "blue-collared", and their status is not absolutely clearly defined, so that often they have illusions about it themselves.[1] On the other hand, the propensity to abolish worker jobs is to some extent countered by the mechanism of capitalist economy, which persistently reproduces and maintains the worker's function in society; every major intervention in the manpower structure is compensated by a shift of traditional labour to other spheres (see the compensation theory). In many cases divergences among strata are accentuated anew by deformations in technological development.[2] And so in the advanced industrial countries of the West we are witnesses of a growing disparity between occupational and class affiliations, between the changing structure of work and its fixed class frontiers.

A point of vital interest for a technologically advanced civilization is that socialism — insofar as it is founded on cooperation among all its people — radically alters the position of skilled workers, and of scientists, technologists and the intelligentsia in general. In times of class conflict, highly skilled workers are known to have figured largely in the role of a "working-class aristocracy", with their skills divorcing them from the general interests of their class. Under socialism, on the contrary, they appear in many respects as a true avant-garde, because their skills (insofar as they are not simply residual craft proficiencies) enhance their standing in the working group.

Marx already considered that technicians and specialists, insofar as they were employees, undoubtedly belonged to the "aggregate worker".[3] The intelligentsia owed its status as "an intermediate class" to the share in profits enjoyed by professional people, the ruling-class privileges, affinity with the bourgeoisie and its ideology, monopoly of education, etc. Under socialism, however, these economic and social considerations gradually drop away. When employment is on the same basis for all, remuneration is according to the amount of work done, there is free

---

[1] These employees are coming increasingly close to the workers, both in their economic position and in their living standards and social circumstances (cf. the results of an enquiry published in *World Marxist Review* 5/1960).

[2] This has been pointed out by F. Pollock in *Automation, Materialien zur Beurteilung ihrer ökonomischen und sozialen Folgen*, Frankfurt a. M. 1956, p. 105.

[3] Cf. K. Marx, *Capital*, Vol. I (Dent ed.), p. 448. K. Marx, *Theories of Surplus Value*, Moscow 1966, p. 398—399.

access to education and higher learning, power lies with the workers, there is a common orientation in matters of world outlook, and so on, the professional intelligentsia gradually comes to form an *inseparable part of the "aggregate worker"*,[1] a skilled and expanding group within the working class.[2] In such circumstances, to label people employed in scientific and technological work, and other intellectual workers, as an "intermediate" class, apart from the working class, implies lack of confidence in the victory of socialism; it means that the working class is not seen as a revolutionary class, but solely as the estate of manual labour. The outcome would inevitably be to loosen its bonds with the world of science, subordinating the broad historical mission to short-term, sectional interests. Such a view of the working class and its role could carry grave consequences for socialist countries at the threshold of the scientific and technological revolution. It would impel them into the sphere of extensive industrialization, where there has been little change in the aspect of the "aggregate worker" and society has no special need to link its affairs with science. It introduces into socialist life artificial antagonisms between the interests of the workers and of science, which in the future — when more and more of the working population will be moving to highly skilled technical and intellectual activities — could well undermine the social basis of the new society and erect an insuperable barrier to the scientific and technological revolution.

As the class structure under socialism changes (to the extent that unification takes place, or distinctions are overcome), the dominant feature in the social stratification starts to be differentiation primarily according to the content of work.[3] The long-term existence of two distinct strata working side by side — people performing exacting creative work and others occupied in simple operative jobs — will then have to be foreseen as a serious problem. Both types of work are equally necessary in the transitional phase, yet each is linked with rather divergent patterns of

---

[1] "The intelligentsia is gradually shedding its attributes as a distinct social stratum and is becoming an integral part of the working class and cooperative farming population" (*Resolutions of the Twelfth Congress of the Communist Party of Czechoslovakia*, Prague 1963, p. 24).

[2] Class attribution here loses much of its former antithetical significance (insofar as the social structure within the country is concerned) although, of course, this quality is an essential feature.

[3] P. Machonin et al., *Sociální struktura socialistické společnosti* (The Social Structure of Socialist Society), Prague 1966.

interests, motivations, wants, aspirations and style of living;[1] the distinctions they engender are no longer class distinctions.

So long as advances in science and technology are not rationally controlled in all their social and human implications, we shall be faced with a cleavage between the *professional* and *democratic aspects*. It may find expression in technocratic tendencies, which do not, however, stem from science and technology as such, but rather from conditions that heighten certain group and class interests to which science and technology are subordinated. The fact is that at the start of the scientific and technological revolution, the actual practice of management passes in many capitalist countries to a trained managerial élite, which under state monopoly acquires some degree of "independence"[2] at least in relation to the traditional capitalist groupings — although its status is still essentially one of servitude to capital.

There is nothing to be gained by shutting our eyes to the fact that an acute problem of our age will be to close the profound cleavage in industrial civilization which, as Einstein realized with such alarm, places the fate of the defenceless mass in the hands of an educated élite, who wield the power of science and technology.[3] Possibly this will be among the most complex undertakings facing socialism. With science and technology essential to the common good, circumstances place their advance primarily in the hands of the conscious, progressive agents of this movement — the professionals, scientists, technicians and organizers, and skilled workers. And even under socialism we may find tendencies to élitism, a monopoly of educational opportunities, exaggerated claims on higher living standards and the like; these groups may forget that the emancipation of the part is always bound up with the emancipation of all.

Government under socialism belongs to *all* working people, and not

---

[1] W. E. Moore points to the fact that both in economies where private ownership prevails, and in socialist countries, the magnitude of these distinctions varies inversely to the level of the civilization base (*Industrialization and Society*, ed. B. E. Hoselitz-W. E. Moore, Paris 1966, p. 354).

[2] Hence the interpretation in terms of a "managerial revolution" (Burnham). But technocratic theories always come to grief (even in their latest refined social versions) through failing to detect the overall change in man's position, so that they also miss the significance of human development in its entirety during the scientific and technological revolution.

[3] "We cannot hope to have a healthy American business body, an effective industrial organism, composed of distinctly separate units distinguished as the workers and the thinkers" (A. R. Heron, *Why Men Work*, Stanford 1948, p. 85).

to the professionals alone. Yet the working community cannot "govern" in a truly socialist manner without the aid of professionalism, of science. Ultimately the only solution will be to make professionals of us all[1] (while simultaneously abolishing by degrees the need to govern at all). Every step in this direction will facilitate further progress. And when the goal is set in these terms, the coincidence of the scientific and technological revolution with revolutionary social changes is essential.

In the transitional phase, however, when industrialization is being completed and the country is advancing towards the scientific and technological revolution, the opposite danger comes to the fore — the danger of *vulgar egalitarianism*, resistance to science, technology and education, a conservative pressure on the part of the less skilled, for whom the general objectives of revolution are overshadowed by their traditional attitudes and limited horizons, who debase, constrain and obstruct creative work and the development of human powers, and in their failure to grasp their own dependence on scientific, technological and cultural progress, spoil the soil for a rapid advance of civilization.[2]

Socialism will have to counter both these tendencies (which are not class antagonisms) by speeding up its approach to the scientific and technological revolution. Measures will need to include changes in work, extending education (breaking down any monopoly), offsetting the excessive authoritarianism in the management structure by reinforcing its rational aspects (less manipulation with people, job mobility in top posts, etc.), strict observance of the rules of socialist democracy, increasing participation in management of economic, social and cultural processes, humanizing conditions of life and opening up the available sources of human development for all.

Those workers who, because of the nature of their occupations and the restricted resources in society, are acutely aware of the need to transform human activity and develop their own creative powers, and who therefore improve their skills, transfer to more demanding jobs,

[1] A rather exaggerated formulation is "every member of society will become a scientist" (J. Davydov, *Trud i svoboda*, Moscow 1962, p. 113) — nevertheless, man's contact with science can be made at various levels and in more modest forms.

[2] Of course, these tendencies are to be found in the West, too. Note, for example, the frequent references in American scientific and educational projects to Whitehead's one-time prediction that a class which failed to appreciate the value of an educated intelligentsia would be doomed; and the continually felt need to attack the deep-rooted American propensity to anti-intellectualism, the disparaging attitude to "pen-pushers" and "eggheads" (cf. *Education for the Age of Science*, Washington 1959). But here the anti-intellectualism has an entirely different social context and trend for the future.

launch out as rationalizers, inventors, experts, organizers and pioneers of technological, social and cultural progress — socialist scientists, technicians, experts, cultural workers, for whom education and creative work is not a privilege to be guarded at the expense of others — working people who find the conditions for self-assertion solely in the revolutionary transformation of the productive forces of human life — in all these social groupings the scientific and technological revolution finds its potential *support*[1], they are the core of its pioneers and guarantors.

/Forms of Social Organization and Leadership in the Age of the Scientific and Technological Revolution/

4.2.2

Faced by the cleavage that industrial civilization has bestowed on us, one is led to the conclusion that even under socialism the working people will not be brought overnight into active participation in the scientific and technological revolution. The appropriate forms were lacking in previous social systems, and we cannot expect that the process will now be automatic and without problems, as indeed no stage of revolution has ever been. On the contrary, to bring into universal motion spheres that have seen no major changes for centuries will be possible only when all the subjective elements in society have been vitalized to the utmost. The first step is gradually to discard the old and evolve new forms of social organization that will not be merely mobile forms of given production relations, existing over people's heads or serving as instruments by which they are governed,[2] but in which the autonomous

[1] Cf. M. Svoboda, "Vědeckotechnická revoluce a změny ve stratifikaci" (The Scientific and Technological Revolution and Changes in Stratification), *Sociologický časopis* 2/1966.

[2] The forms of society's practical and theoretical development that we know today originated in their classical guise as mobile forms of the fundamental class division within industrial civilization. The relation into which men entered every day in the production of their life constituted itself as a self-moving substance-subject (capital) which governed all things under the sun in modern civilization, while human life, on the other hand, appeared rather as a link in this active organism, as an appendage. Thanks only to this material mystification could the classical economists such as Ricardo claim with some justification that private ownership in its active aspect (i. e., capital) was a subject ("ownership civilizes the world"), only because of this could sociologists follow Saint Simon in proclaiming order, the rule of principles over people, as the foundation of modern civilization. And Guizot could depict history as the product of civilization advancing like some kind of being, while Hegel was able to venture on the perilous

subjectivity of the human community and of every human being could always reconstitute itself and find support. So long as these forms have not been established and have not become the groundwork for social and human subjectivity, there is a need to bring together the *avant-garde forces* of society in an organization capable of employing the existing social forms to new ends, of converting them into instruments for unfolding people's creative activity — while also renewing and expanding their own principles and inner life all the time. Such an avant-garde organism emerges in the socialist countries in the shape of a party of a new type, the Communist Party, with a leading role to play.

The industrial system was not founded on any universal activity on the part of man; it had no need to develop and direct such activity. The original system of management in the socialist order was framed, in its turn, largely in the days of struggle for political power, for ending exploitation, promoting industrialization, etc. That is to say, it was built up within the very bounds of the conflicting spheres inherited from the old society. It was adapted for the job of handling elementary issues of the class struggle, it relied on the traditional means of power politics and administration — but they were in the hands of the people. In this narrow political guise, however, these forms are inadequate to deal with processes that no longer follow the laws of class struggle and cannot be handled by the exercise of power or by straightforward command.

If the avant-garde organization is to operate as the leading centre in society and the organizer of the scientific and technological revolution, with all its social implications — and herein lies the supreme and, by all appearances, the ultimate historical mission of the Communist Party — it will be equal to the task only if it oversteps the narrow bounds of rule by power and the corresponding means of administration, to evolve superior, more effective forms of *society-wide* ("socio-political") guidance.[1] In the process it will completely reshape its internal structure, which originated in the heat of class struggle and in the zone of earlier revolutionary goals.

The point here is to evolve a whole range of new, unorthodox approa-

---

but for this very reason symptomatic path of portraying the march of civilization as the forward movement of the "World Spirit". The abstract economic, political and ideological forms of life — in fact and in theory — were always, in this view, reflections of specific social relations prevailing in industrial civilization.

[1] Marx and Engels foresaw that the affairs of society would have to be managed in this wider sense, "the government of persons" being replaced by "the administration of things".

ches and forms, directed to adjusting technical, economic, sociological, psychological and anthropological conditions for people to engage in *universal creative activity*. Furthermore, existing approaches and forms will have to be rearranged and subordinated to the new.[1] In the spheres of the economy, technology, science, human abilities, etc., power pressures and administrative management assume the quality of external interventions emanating from the superstructure. They served their purpose in fighting the power of capital, large and small, but are incapable of arousing economic activity, stimulating rapid technological advance, and still less of generating scientific discoveries — in fact, they offer the best way of killing many such prospects.

Society has it in its power to encourage, organize and unify the growth of the abilities and talents peculiar to each individual by providing the appropriate conditions of civilization and the social background — and should the avant-garde party fail to fill this role, the former social forms would be unlikely to achieve any lasting success — but it will not get anywhere with injunctions and pressure. The more social progress relies on science and its advances, the greater the need for scientific control of the conditions enabling society, and science itself, to go forward; and the more possible and essential it becomes to relinquish any unnecessary and fruitless interference with the course of creative subjectivity, to give socialist man ample room to choose his independent path. The measure of success in guiding society is ultimately to be found solely in the degree and universality of creative communist activity that has been awakened.

The essential form of social activity in the scientific and technological revolution appears in the long view to be complex scientific management involving some kind of auto-regulation within society. When the frontiers of class objectives have been crossed, the entire leading role of the avant-garde party consists in bringing the class that is the potential agent of the most radical criticism of bourgeois industrial civilization into alliance with science, as the potentially most forceful means of shaping a new society and laying a new base for civilization. To fulfil this role, the avant-garde party will have to find an entire system of new forms for society and its own internal life.

An essential step is to establish a firm foundation in the *social sciences*,

---

[1] Lenin warned against trying to handle entirely new jobs by the old means — "directly as ordered by the proletarian state". He called this approach "a most dangerous" illusion that could solve nothing (V. I. Lenin, *Selected Works*, Moscow 1967, p. 642, and *Sochineniya*, Moscow 1950, Vol. 33, p. 147).

which should be coordinated and expanded as never before into a medium capable of comprehending and unfolding the material dialectic of intricate systems whose inner subjectivity will be elaborated to match the processes of modern civilization. While hitherto an approach based on the classical "three component parts" of Marxism[1] has in general been adequate — with the emphasis on "scientific socialism" which embodies the experience of class struggle — for the present, and still more the future, it will be impossible to proceed without a series of new sciences, or sectors arising on the sidelines of changes in the traditional media of society — that is to say, anthropology, social psychology, science of science, science of work, ergonomics, theory of civilization and culture, sociology of the environment, general technology, economics of human resources, future research and so on and so forth. In many cases the theoretical base for a clearly-formulated programme and reliable prognosis is still lacking, but in time these sciences are likely to reveal the vital opportunities for society's growth that flow from innate forces reposing in man and his interrelationships. Scientific communism will be capable of integrating these undertakings to provide a theoretic foundation for practical activity only when it emerges from the traditional boundaries of theory concerned with the strategy of class struggle and the ending of private ownership[2] to unfold Marxism in its full potential breadth as the *theory of man's social development*[3] — taking as its

---

[1] The socialist order of society originated by inverting the content of all social and ideological forms in which the most developed class formation moved. That it heralded its approach by a radical change in the consciousness of the working class, continued through the decisive stage of political revolution and culminated by transforming the political and economic set-up, followed from the structure of industrial civilization. This historical sequence was reflected in the logic that led Marx and Engels to *criticism* of all the classical forms of industrial society and its thinking, to settle accounts with "the former philosophical conscience" by criticism of politics and finally by criticism of political economy. There lies the source of the "three component parts of Marxism", which, however, provide only a negative expression of its actual substance — only in the shape of a confrontation with the former society, and so still in the forms of that society.

[2] Even in the days of the October Revolution some Marxists were able to express the inner logic of these stages in the practical criticism of all past civilization. L. Kritsman touched on the subject in an article "Ocherednye zadachi proletarskoy revolyutsii v Rossii" (*Narodnoye khazyaystvo* 5/1958) where he predicted that after the philosophical, political and economic revolution there would follow a stage of "technological revolution" involving the productive forces and once more advancing Marxism to new levels.

[3] The practical and theoretical forms hitherto current in society referred to human life in the abstract, seeing people simply as members of classes, units active in class conflicts.

basis the elimination of class antagonisms, and the existence of the scientific and technological revolution.

In the course of the said revolution, similar claims will be made on the social sciences as on the natural sciences, and they will have to be cultivated at an equivalent level. Most unaccustomed problems crop up at every turn as the revolutionary process spreads throughout society and its productive forces. With the complexity of the contemporary upheavals in civilization, rational knowledge can be acquired not only through a wide range of specialized research, but also through repeated departures beyond the horizons of the traditional disciplines to formulate broad synthetic concepts as to the nature of the current changes.[1]

Such problems can be resolved only when open, free and friendly discussion takes place. The more the scientific and technological revolution gathers momentum, the more rapidly many accepted ideas will turn into brakes on progress, the greater the intellectual capacity that will be needed to master the new dimensions and modes of movement. Thoroughly elaborated systems of instruments, rules and methods will be required to facilitate the more rapid and diversified passage through the social organism of progressive findings and ideas[2] that would give the avant-garde elements of social auto-regulation means of acceleration and would avoid the losses and delays caused by failure to appreciate new methods or by human fallibility.

/ *Dynamics of the Age and the Mode of Thinking* /   4.2.3

Preindustrial formations were static, their life moved in a circle and perfection persisted as their ideal. The industrial system endowed society with the dynamic of a single dimension of civilization that condemned the lovers of perfection to lasting frustration and brought on the scene that unending train of people who in striving after progress never achieve their goal.

---

[1] "Contemporary industrial civilization demonstrates that it has reached the stage at which "the free society" can no longer be adequately defined in the traditional terms of economic, political and intellectual liberties" (H. Marcuse, *One-Dimensional Man*, Boston 1966, p. 3).

[2] Evidently enquiry by the social sciences will have to employ a network taking in basic research, applied research and practical application, on the lines of the natural sciences.

With the scientific and technological revolution, the march of civilization finally assumed a *multiform universal aspect*. Revolutions that open up new dimensions of movement are coming to be everyday affairs[1] and this stems from the nature of the contemporary civilization process. Hitherto society has experienced movement governed by laws and proceeding within fixed relationships, because only one of its dimensions was subject to change. Now, however, we are approaching a point where we have to be prepared for the laws to change, implying that the elementary relationships will be cast aside and movement will proceed in all dimensions. There can be no doubt that such an era will make radically new demands in the realm of ideas, on mental alacrity, intellectual flexibility; people will need broad horizons, comprehensive information, they will have to be ever receptive to knowledge, to think soberly and critically. In short, all-round mobility in society and all-round development of man will be the need of the day.

In confrontation with the scientific and technological revolution all visions of a future free of conflict and struggle are doomed to disappointment. The idea that with socialism humanity will enter an epoch in which personal strain and individual effort will no longer be required, where society will care for all wants, is one of those illusions of industrial life that simply abstract from the two-edged manipulatory power of the industrial mechanism. And when it is found that the preoccupation with existential questions is nevertheless heightened, this should be seen as the inevitable opposite pole of passive unconcern. No cure can be found in referring back to commonsense, spontaneous faith or moral certainty, because it is in the dissolution of these traditional values under the impact of the contemporary dynamic that such tendencies are born.[2]

The hypothetical image of the scientific and technological revolution suggests that the civilization of the future will be marked by a rising

---

[1] "The age in which we live is one of deep and widespread ferment. We have been witnessing a revolution in politics, social order, science, economics, diplomacy and weapons.".. These words were not written by a Marxist or revolutionary — they are to be found in *Prospect for America*, The Rockefeller Panel Reports, New York 1961, p. XV.

[2] The frequent retreat to the age-old ideal of finite, closed perfection may, in these circumstances, have a double meaning. On the one hand it implies a search for an inner anthropological structure that gives man a mobile equilibrium in place of the one-sidedness and fragmentation of the industrial epoch, on the other, however, it embodies that romantic yearning for tranquillity which in our age is no more than wishful thinking.

stream of *conflicts*. To overcome the disproportions induced by the constant movement in the groundwork of life will become the permanent lot of every single one of us. Frictions may emerge among the most varied groups of people, primarily — probably in their most persistent form — engendered by differences in work content and the resultant disagreement in ideas on life apart from work. Such differences among social groups involve distinctions in the modes of self-realization, signifying divergent degrees and intensities of opportunity for man's own development. There may equally be a sharpening of misunderstandings among the generations, evoked by the widening gap set between modes of life in the course of two to three decades.[1]

The signs are that society will undergo a repeated and ever stronger polarization between *progressive* and *conservative* attitudes. This throws into relief the role of social conditions under which this divergence of forces and opening up paths for progressive trends will no longer be linked with an inexorable lifelong division of people by attributes of class, property and power, where, moreover, irreconcilable antagonisms no longer breed ruthless struggles. This calls for conditions allowing mobile, functional forms adequate to the actual dialectic of conflict. The drama of pioneering efforts by individuals and groups will, of course, involve risk, genuine collisions, with real victors and losers — although arbitrary power for the victors and humiliation for the defeated can and must disappear from the scene. And, indeed, the historic mission of socialism lies just there — in meeting such opening and closing of social splits that are not founded in conflicts among classes with a system of new, appropriate forms of motion, while employing for this purpose all suitable elements of former social forms — economic instruments, democratic social and political institutions, etc.

Indeed, such considerations speak for a bold concept of a classless, technologically mature society of the future, with a conflicting structure of a special type, whose form of existence will be dynamism and contra-

[1] Many of the conflicts among generations in the contemporary world are obviously caused by the growing mobility of the civilization base. As mastery of the world comes to rely less and less on the traditional approaches and experience, the less authority will parents enjoy in the eyes of their children as far as the ideals and techniques of life are concerned. The consequent scepticism experienced by the rising generation from childhood culminates with increasing regularity in a split (cf. H. Schelsky, *Die Skeptische Generation*. Düsseldorf—Köln 1963; similarly, E. Fischer, *Probleme der jungen Generation, Ohnmacht oder Verantwortung*, Wien 1963) — at least insofar as the mode of life, social forms, advance of education, etc. are not adjusted to the quickening stream of change.

diction.[1] The new quality that this structure introduces into life is not that it will resolve all social and human problems once for all, but that it will afford the means of resolving them through cooperative effort, and ultimately, in fuller measure, through mutual development of people.

In a technologically developed socialist society the clash of ideas cannot be expected to die down, but rather to intensify, assuming new roles for which it will be necessary to find new forms and rules differing from the modes of ideological battle inherent to class struggles and accompanying the campaigns of classes. Communication of ideas in this deeper sense signifies a transition to the method of *dialogue*, which follows rules distinct from those of political exposure employed in fighting a class opponent. There are no longer the informed and uninformed, because the cooperation and activity of all requires a state of universal information. The goal is not decided by tactics, but by the drive towards a factually satisfactory solution. The spread of knowledge is not divorced from self-knowledge, but demands it as a condition. The structure of dialogue knows no exclusive subject and object, and this allies it with theoretical activity, with science and research. Alongside economic and socio-political forms, and together with them, employing and giving institutional expression to such theoretical and ideological forms is of far-reaching significance for the processes of civilization today. In contrast to these opportunities offered by a social structure free of class conflicts there loom, however, like a big question mark, the explosive factors that are at work wherever the scientific and technological revolution makes its appearance in the context of the old class antagonisms. There can be no illusions about the violent tensions accompanying every forward step in science as long as it places modern military technology, the modern media of political power, the opportunities for manipulating people and so on at the service of monopolies and militarism. We must expect to see a whole range of new battlefields between the world systems, yet equally new prospects for maintaining peaceful coexistence.

As the scientific and technological revolution unfolds, people's intellectual life and the clash of ideologies in the world will be intensified,[2] with a considerable shift in emphasis to new areas.

---

[1] I. Dubská, J. Šindelář, "K ideologické problematice vědeckotechnické revoluce" (Ideological Issues in the Scientific and Technological Revolution), *Sociologický časopis* 2/1966.

[2] R. J. Momsen foresees a growth in ideological conflict in *Modern American Capitalism*, Boston 1963, p. IX.

a) The foremost issue will be to create and release the *motive forces* for the advance of civilization — which economic order, social structure and social forms will offer the broadest and most appropriate base for the new dynamics of the productive forces, for the scientific and technological revolution.[1]

b) Further, there will be problems concerning *civilization* — which type of society will be capable of correcting the bias of industrial development, of breaking through the paradox of means and ends embodied hitherto in all social institutions, of allowing man to play a real part in the advance of this civilization, giving him the opportunity to control and shape the conditions of his own life.[2]

c) Finally, there is the issue with the most profound humanist, anthropological or cultural connotation — under what conditions and to what extent will man's development and the cultivation of his powers be identified with the process of civilization, what social system will afford the best guarantee that this will be so and, all in all, in what measure will people be capable of unfolding their powers?[3]

We may expect the scientific and technological revolution to reveal where in practice the truth lies in this age-old dispute about man. The sudden popularity of philosophical anthropology would seem to suggest that the questions revolving around the subject of who is man and what is the human world have far outnumbered the answers hitherto provided.

As the ferment of ideas spreads and goes deeper, every integrated theoretical concept is offered the opportunity of proving its ability to give direction to modern civilization. And here the strength of Marxism can for the first time be manifested in its true light. However, if this is to be so, it will be essential to overcome the propensity to restrict Marxism within the bounds of objectives, media and ideas belonging to the single, initial stage of revolution, to cultivate its inner wealth in which

---

[1] Marx actually linked the justification of the existence of socialism with the handling of this issue. L. von Mises, on the contrary, advanced in this context his argument about the impracticability of socialism owing to the inadequacy of its stimuli.

[2] In opposition to Marx's idea that at a certain stage man can control the social conditions and the civilization base for his own development, Max Weber's argument operated with the process by which the hierarchical bureaucratic apparatus of the industrial system becomes autonomous — the process that keeps inverting means and ends and reveals the irrational basis of this rationality.

[3] Marx assumed that man possessed a universal capacity for development; there is a notable trend in modern anthropology, on the contrary (Gehlen and others), to revive the Platonic view that at most a few individuals are fit to cultivate their abilities.

the perspectives of the scientific and technological revolution merge with the humanistic intent of communism. Today there are already signs that where socialist theory is confined to traditional approaches derived from the conditions of industrialization alone, it is losing its appeal and power of orientation. Should it fail to master the new theoretical issues posed by the whole area of civilization today, should it fail to grasp the social and human implications, socialism would be powerless to meet the coming confrontations of ideas; the truths of yesterday would turn into empty phrases; in the context of the scientific and technological revolution, the most humanistic ideas of the past would inevitably lose their practical value.

/ *New Light on the Individual* /

Bourgeois revolution and industrialization broke up the traditional, manifold, individually-tinged, seminatural community groupings in which people were firmly bound in pre-industrial epochs. The original tangible community was converted into an abstract "society as such" and each of its members appeared as an autonomous abstract unit, "man in general".[1] Man was deprived of any attribution of his own whatsover and transfixed as a mere "member of a class", to which he belonged solely as "an average individual".[2] In the industrial system the individuality of man as labour power unmistakably recedes to the fringe of society, into the realm of privacy. The conveyor belt has no need for development of individuality, requiring simply a fragmented individual in the shape of a working unit, a robot. The individual is reduced to its external existence, to a set of definite social roles.[3] The anonymity of the

---

[1] "Man in general" seems, from afar, to be posited by nature, although in this abstract guise he is a product, achievement and also the boundary of class relations expanded into universality. So the antique lovers of the concrete, such as Aristophanes, were able to conceive of a being answering to the name of "man in general" solely as an impostor ("Plutos"). But the representatives of the bourgeois epoch knew full well that the abstract individual, "man as man", is primarily an independent owner, man as "owner of himself", as Fichte or Destutt de Tracy put it.

[2] K. Marx, F. Engels, *The German Ideology*, ibid., New York, p. 68. Today it is generally recognized among scholars that the industrial revolution instituted a "transformation of human attitudes" to the world (cf., for example, R. Aron's contribution to discussion in *World Technology and Human Destiny*, Ann Arbor 1963, p. 59).

[3] B. Baczko in the symposium *Socialist Humanism*, ed. E. Fromm, New York 1965, p. 177.

industrial machine, the mechanical causality, and interchangeability of things and people then dominate the way of life, wants, interests and relationships.

Within this zone of industrial civilization, movement of society flows from the actions of classes. As industrialization advanced, it increasingly confirmed and filled in de Tocqueville's picture of civilization[1] — the boundless anonymous mass of similar or identical people with the selfsame petty cares. The outlook was that this civilization would irretrievably destroy individuality,[2] confining it within the bounds of Ortega y Gasset's "mass society", turning people into ants à la Bergson or robots à la Saint Exupéry, disintegrating and cancelling all individuality, as predicted by Orwell and Huxley.

In the zone of industrial civilization, all movement in society is founded on the movement of classes. In fact, only the onslaught of classes and masses could threaten the stability of social conditions and the existence of classes in general. But victory of the nameless mass of working people could not signify rejection of individuality; on the contrary, it established a collective base (of universal cooperation) on which to unfold the wealth of the human personality — although the actual soil for this undertaking was still to be laid.

Individuality might appear to be "scurvy"[3] in the days when its development, or rather privileges and caprices, involved the exclusion of millions from their individual share in human progress. Nevertheless, the birth of this abstract individuality implied an enormous advance. There had appeared on the scene for the first time an individual who was not posited by nature, but fully mediated by society,[4] although the form was still abstract — that is to say, an autonomous individual, with his own base of movement, who has assumed a direct relationship to the world and human society in their entirety, and who can therefore open up the approach towards taking command of the conditions of his own

[1] A. de Tocqueville, *De la Démocratie en Amérique*, I—II, Paris 1864—1865.

[2] "Private space has been invaded and whittled down by technological reality. Mass production and mass distribution claim the *entire* individual... The result is not adjustment but *mimesis:* an immediate identification of the individual with *his* society and, through it, with the society as a whole". (H. Marcuse, One-Dimensional Man, p. 10).

[3] F. Engels, *Origin of the Family, Private Property and the State*, London 1941, p. 202.

[4] "...man is only individualized through the process of history. He originally appears as a *generic being, a tribal being, a herd animal*" (K. Marx, *Grundrisse,* ibid., ed. Hobsbawm, p. 96).

life that society has created and to universal self-realization on this basis. Only such an out-and-out socially-posited Faustian individuality, such a "self-alienated man", is in a position to appreciate his situation as signifying the total alienation of civilization, see its limits as his own limits and, on the contrary, comprehend and then overstep the boundaries by which man's universal appropriation of the world is confined. No longer can he accept the conditions of human life that have been shaped by the hand of man as being the work of natural or external fate; on the contrary, he feels them as "a crushing experience"[1] presenting both a threat of destruction and a Promethian summons.

Insofar as this reality engenders — alongside advances in science and technology — tangible opportunities that under favourable conditions could potentially allow each individual to develop his own powers, that could present everyone with the common opportunity to embody his purposes freely in his own life — thereby transcending the abstract confines of his own individuality and of human community — and insofar as this purposive self-creation of man simultaneously encounters fixed limits in society, man will inevitably be filled with a sense of frustration, and the conviction that his efforts to achieve individual self-realization are in vain.[2] The system of uniform mass consumption, by which even beyond the limits of necessity the abstract confines of individuality are reproduced with a remarkable persistence, in fact constitutes the unconscious and sterile frame within which the socially formed — and hence controllable (but by no means controlled) — conditions of man's mass development are accumulated. There therefore comes a stage in the mastery of nature when a fundamental choice is presented — which variant of this objectivized power of man will be realized? Purposive self-creation of the human personality, or man's self-destruction? For these alternatives are not posed from without; they constitute the absolute inner content of human liberty in a technologically advanced civilization; man will live with them[3] throughout the era of the scientific and technological revolution.

[1] F. Pappenheim, *The Alienation of Modern Man*, New York 1959, p. 115.
[2] "The social character of our time, being largely without goals, lacks this sense of meaning and purpose. This lack is experienced as futility, emptiness and longing. It forms a reservoir of restless energy which seeks attachment, presses for discharge. It is the explosive fuel for, among other things, mass movements" (A. Wheelis, *The Quest for Identity*, New York 1958, p. 87).
[3] Cf. R. Guardini, *Das Ende der Neuzeit*, Basel 1950, p. 95. The same note is struck by the somewhat mystical formulations of Heidegger's philosophy of technology (*Die Technik und die Kehre*, Pfullingen 1962).

Viewed from the opposite angle, however, people would be unable to free themselves of the rigid confines of their own relationships, even when the class barriers were overthrown, if productive resources were to remain restricted to the point of not allowing for the emergence of a society in which all individuals would share not merely as members of a class or as labour power, but directly through their manifold human *individuality*. This new relationship among people is conditioned, just as much as the relationship of man to his own self, by the new relationship of man to the world as "nature" created by man — and vice versa.[1]

Socialist revolution places a high value on self-sacrifice so long as society cannot advance without it. It subsumes individual needs and interests to those of society wherever resources are wanting and necessity rules. Consequently restriction of individuality may appear for a time — perhaps even beyond the frontiers that had something in common with the abstract individuality formerly imposed by elemental economic and social power (capital) — as a forerunner of a higher type of social development. But the goal and the lasting foundation can never be found in such subordination; a new social and production base is required, where the individual development of each will not conflict with the collective interest, but will, on the contrary, be the object of this interest, where general development will not demand that individual development be constrained, but will actually rely on it. Beyond the point when enriching the human personality no longer takes place at the expense of others, but becomes a part of the enrichment of all, society necessarily breaks the bounds within which self-sacrifice was required and free self-affirmation by the socialist individual was constrained. What is more, with every advance of technology and civilization, the course of history is then increasingly bound up with the social development of the individual; human abilities and powers rapidly gain in value. In a day a man can produce means for his own development and that of many others. We are witnesses in the modern world of how technology extends the sphere of creative work where social value merges with individual enjoyment. Beyond the limits necessary for reproducing labour power, it creates a realm of consumption (education, enquiry, culture, physical training, etc.) which in catering for the needs of individual development is not a matter of indifference or deprivation for other people, on the

[1] H. Marcuse rightly poses "control of nature" as a condition for the modern "domination of man by man" (ibid., *One-Dimensional Man*, p. 158). But the power that enables man to control man corresponds in another context to the stage when man's development by man is a feasible proposition.

contrary. Although the social barriers are still quite formidable, there are signs here that individuality is acquiring a new meaning in the process of civilization[1] and organization[2] — individuality that transcends its abstract existence through its development.

The supreme principle in industrial civilization continued to be as much that individuals were personally independent of each other, as that each of them was dependent on the tangible powers engendered by the interaction of these abstract individuals. Consequently, the liberal maxim to live and let live could suffice. However, there comes a quite advanced stage of technological civilization when, assuming that class antagonisms no longer exist (for in their ultimate form — that of capital — they are nothing less than a monopoly of social development), the price of progress in civilization ceases to be the denial of development to individuals, and vice versa. Practically and generally, every individual may through his own development as an end in itself serve as a means for the development of others.[3] Then, indeed, the free development of each is transformed into the condition for the free development of all, and vice versa.

The collectivity upon which the achievements of science and technology rely is a collectivity of interdependent individual development[4] —

[1] Cf. D. Riesman, *Individualism Reconsidered*, Glencoe 1955.

[2] P. Drucker (*Landmarks of Tomorrow*, New York 1959, p. 62) announces changes in the principles of modern organization stemming from the fact that conditions exist under which the success of organization as such depends not on subordination, but on the development of personality. There were already similar indications in K. Boulding's *The Organizational Revolution*, (New York 1953) — leaving aside his interpretation.

[3] This ends the conflict that accompanied the industrial revolution and confronted it with the dilemma — either general development at the expense of the individual as postulated by Ricardo and Hegel, or limitation of general development in favour of the individual according to Sismondi and Fichte. If it is true that few are so good that they will be willing to put the benefit of society first while suffering themselves, it is equally true that few are so bad that they will prefer injury to society while suffering injury themselves.

[4] Genuine collective cooperation in science, remarks J. D. Bernal, not only has no need (as distinct from traditional industry) for "loss of individuality", but excludes it (*The Social Function of Science*, ibid., p. 415). This quality of science as a productive force, its intrinsic connection with the individual development of all, reveals the profound significance for today of the ideas expressed by Marx and Engels in *The German Ideology*, MEGA, Abt. 1, Band 3, p. 334): "Private ownership is a form of intercourse necessary for a certain level of the productive forces, a form of intercourse that cannot be overthrown, that cannot be dispensed with for the production of immediate material life, so long as productive forces have not been formed for which private ownership will become a fetter."

a genuine community in the shape of a community of developing individuals. It was predominantly as a mass that the working people accomplished the objectives of political revolution. In face of the objectives of scientific and technological progress, each individual stands simultaneously to a much greater degree alone, and on his relation to himself, his self-development, depend his real contacts with all his fellows — to the same degree as in the reverse case. "Free individuality",[1] founded on the universal development of individuals in their joint udertaking, is not a work of nature, but of highly developed history; it is a potentiality stemming from the scientific and technological revolution, while being simultaneously a precondition of that revolution.[2]

These new connotations of individuality should compel us to review the position of the individual in the socialist community. Here there is certainly no future for the typical view of a whole that detracts from individual initiative in the name of collective customs, even when it is "collective" narrow-mindedness or backwardness. This is not the place to idealize the "average individual", because surpassing this average to the utmost is beginning to be the chief wealth of all.

True, modern science, technology and culture rely primarily on a collective base. But at the same time, when the first signs of the scientific and technological revolution are being manifested, the pioneer of a new life can be none other than an active, responsible individual, who decides independently, is not bound by convention, is enterprising, critical, with courage to make distinctions and call a spade a spade — prejudice is prejudice, even in the mass, and backwardness is backwardness, even when found in a leader. Such a man has a distinctive individuality and even shows a certain exclusiveness in practical life, because of his preoccupation with his special sphere of problems and activities. Where opportunities are open to all and the social value of individual development is heightened, the time has come to learn to respect such personal human development, to protect it against pressure making for average and egalitarian standards — to protect it as a social value without which the accelerating trends of our age would be lost.

Man cannot really take the production of his living conditions into his own hands until such time as he is capable not only of creating and reproducing them, but also of producing them as his own, that is, of pro-

---

[1] K. Marx, ibid. *Grundrisse*, p. 75.

[2] Consequently, the frequent contention of romantic critics that "asceticism... would be a signal of a new epoch" (A. Gehlen, *Sozialpsychologische Probleme der industriellen Gesellschaft*, Tübingen 1949, p. 12) holds out no prospect whatever.

ducing himself as a changing, developing being. The problem does not lie in the immediate mastery of things, but in the purposive creation — with the aid of his own handiwork — of human subjectivity. It will not be easy for people to find the path to realizing their own abilities, because civilization processes themselves are open to diverse interpretations; in the transitional zone they increase the pressure of external circumstances, of material and industrial systems; individuals are inevitably drawn into mass production, consumption, transport, amusement, etc., as abstract units, as particles carried along by the current. Only when a certain frontier has been passed can technological development and abundance beget the opportunity for individualization and generate it as an imperative of authentic orientation and man's participation in these civilization and cultural processes.

However surprising it may seem, in the long term perhaps the *most emphatic* impress made by the scientific and technological revolution on the laws governing the process of history in the soil of the new society will be a new position of the individual in the collective achievements of tomorrow.

/ *Constructing Perspectives* /   4.2.5

Some scholars see the broad and rapid stream of change, sweeping through our age, as an obstacle to reliable long-term forecasting of advance in civilization and culture.[1] There are philosophers and artists for whom this avalanche, which day by day outdates the progress achieved yesterday, spells the collapse of human values and a sign that man is unfitted to manage his life on this "wired-up globe".[2] Nevertheless, there has never yet on the face of the earth been so much tireless effort

[1] M. Massenet points out that the need to forecast the future is steadily growing, but also becoming increasingly difficult ("Introduction a une sociologie de la prévision", *Futuribles* 60/1963).

[2] In *1984*, Orwell reflects on the fact that the outlooks and utopias of the "first industrial revolution" were universally optimistic, while today they are mostly pessimistic. This rather exaggerated contention does, however, have a rational core in the divergent experiences that are extrapolated into the future. In the days of the industrial revolution they were the first experiences of machinery, today (as for Orwell) they are experiences of the industrial system in its totality, where the power of human achievement has grown enormously, but where the operation of the system has not yet changed.

to map the future,[1] to know it at a scientific level, at the level of Einsten's "poetry of the intense longing" for new human values.

This turn to the future is deeply rooted in the nature of contemporary civilization processes; it flows from the changes in its laws of motion and in the method of man's self-realization. Within the bounds of the industrial system, Saint Simon was able to proclaim the future as being merely the last link in a chain stretching from the past, for the past (past labour) dominated the present in this system,[2] and cast the future simply in the role of a derived function. But the tables are turned at the moment when the present life of man, as a process developing creative human powers, starts to assume a universal role as an independent factor introducing new dimensions into the future, dimensions that are not imposed by external necessity and do not prolong the past course of history — when the future and purposive begin to operate as genuine components of human and social interests and endeavours in the present. Then the present starts to dominate the past, and the future emerges as an independent value open to freedom of choice.[3] At that moment, free human endeavour can cross the frontier set by the mere use of chance within the necessity of historical development, and begin gradually to endow the future — which is a dimension of man's self-realization in the present[4] — with the potentialities created by human development itself.

[1] In almost all industrially developed countries, long-term plans or forecasts have been worked out. The Soviet long-term plans were formulated in the Programme of the Communist Party of the Soviet Union. Development in the USA has been projected in several directions up to the year 2000 (*Resources in America's Future. Patterns, Requirements and Availabilities 1960—2000*, ed. Landsberg, Fischman, Fisher, Baltimore 1963); similarly, in the work of the National Commission for Year 2000, headed by D. Bell. An original method is applied in French prognoses up to 1985 (*Réflexions pour 1985*, ed. P. Massé, Documentation française 1964). British forecasts cover the period up to 1984 (*Britain 1984. Unilevers Forecast. An Experiment in the Economic History of the Future*, ed. R. Brech, London 1963), the West-German to 1975 (*Deutschland 1975. Analysen, Prognosen, Perspektiven*, ed. U. Lohmar, Bielefeld 1965), etc.

[2] K. Marx, F. Engels, *The Communist Manifesto*, ibid., pp. 35—36.

[3] "In the triarchy of past-present-future, the future now gains a quite different status-value than the past" (O. K. Flechtheim, "Utopie, Gegenutopie und Futurologie" in *Eine Welt oder Keine?*, Frankfurt a. M. 1964, p. 44).

[4] This concept has nothing whatever in common with giving the future priority over the present (e.g. L. Armand, M. Drancourt, *Plaidoyer pour l'avenir*), which simply implies sacrificing the present to the future. Nonetheless, under certain conditions in the zone of civilization processes hitherto, such elements (and just such elements) may be an expression of man's self-realization; in general, however, the said concept, on the contrary, solves the dilemma of present and future.

Yet to the extent that the historical process ceases to bear the stamp of an inexorable course of civilization, direct predictability of the future is, from another angle, less readily attainable; the possibility of treating the future as the last link in a natural process rooted in the past now disappears. More and more elements charged with new dimensions and prospects enter into its progress,[1] revealing a multiplicity of *variants* for the future. We are confronted here in theoretical form with an entirely new type of social movement. Therefore its import cannot be comprehended by the empirically limited approaches and their corresponding closed models that served their purpose and were, or still are, adequate for analyzing industrial civilization and capitalism. Seemingly, the scientific and technological revolution should be included among the new social processes whose logic may be — and from the other angle also has to be — discerned at some stage in their development; not waiting in the classical manner till the system is closed, because the very knowledge of them is a major factor in their progress and the mature classical system (closed model) is definitely not their appropriate form — in fact, movement does not proceed within predetermined dimensions, but at every stage opens up new dimensions.

The rhythm of civilization is always determined by the decisive subjects of its development. Time was when the natural reproduction of the primitive community set the tone, and to this day the natural yearly cycle of subsistence in these enclosed units provides the dominant time scale over a great part of the world. In the classical industrial civilization, the period of *capital turnover* in the process of expanded reproduction is known to have been the starting point for all surmises about the future and for speculations, usually calculated some years ahead. Similarly, the five- or seven-year planning terms of socialism — although not often based on an awareness of the connection — corresponded to the overall turnover period of *social labour*, of the assets concerned. Once *science* and its application start to determine growth, these outlooks based on the determinant subjectivity of stable economic relations are inevitably found wanting, although almost all practical perspectives continue to be drawn from them.[2] Today, however, the cycle

---

[1] B. de Jouvenel, *The Art of Conjecture*, New York 1967, p. 278.

[2] The majority of economic prognoses have hitherto employed extrapolation of economic series. American prognoses, for example, describe their method as indicating "the way in which things will be heading if most major trends continue" (*Resources in America's Future*, Baltimore 1963, p. 6).

of scientific discovery and education[1] is starting to decide the calendar of our civilization. Therefore, investigation of the future is today concentrated on forecasting scientific and technological advance, and from the opposite angle, wherever science and technology enter as key factors into the groundwork of the productive process and society's development, planned shaping of the future appears as an imperative.[2] Scientific development plans are now embracing the leading existential problems of social development and human life.[3] With increasing frequency they form the hub of society-wide programmes[4] — both in matter and method.[5] Within and beyond them, however, other agencies are coming forward to shape the future, and they match the new, emergent subjectivity of man and the community, that is, they are introduced into the process by the development of man and his powers. And here appears the need to record expectations and make plans or programmes[6]

---

[1] The cycle of innovation based on scientific findings (the path from findings to realization) is now estimated at an average of twenty years; this tallies with the duration of technological reconstruction of the production base and the time required to prepare research personnel. And this is the period on which most current plans and prognoses of future development are founded.

[2] "Technology, under all circumstances, leads to planning; in its higher manifestations it may put the problems of planning beyond the reach of the industrial firm" (J. K. Galbraith, *The New Industrial State*, Boston 1967, p. 20).

[3] Hence the noticeable growth in the self-consciousness of science. As I. I. Rabi notes in a contribution entitled *Der Wissenschaftler und das öffentliche Leben*, there can be no scientist today who "shows no concern about where things are leading" (*Unsere Welt 1985*, R. J. Jungk, H. J. Mundt, München—Wien—Basel 1965, p. 25). This distinguishes our times from all previous civilization: "All previous modes of production have been directed solely to achieving the nearest, most immediate use-effect of labour. The more remote consequences that made their appearance later... were completely ignored" (F. Engels, *The Part Played by Labour in the Transition from Ape to Man*, MEGA, Sonderausgabe, Moscow—Leningrad 1935, p. 704).

[4] In the thirties, Soviet experiments in planning science evoked widespread discussion on the relation between science and planning (cf. S. Dedijer, "The Science of Science. A Programme and a Plea". *Minerva* 4/1966, p. 277).

[5] The Rand Corporation long-term forecasts are usually based on anticipated movement in the sphere of science, ascertained by the "Delphi" technique (*Report on a Long Range Forecasting Study*, Santa Monica 1964).

[6] In a methodological analysis made for OECD (cf. E. Jantsch, *Technological Forecasting in Perspective*, Paris 1966) a distinction is made between an economic programme, economic plan and economic expectation. The first two are normative, while expectation simply tells us what will probably happen under certain assumptions. A national programme is a normative study of the overall long-range prospect for the national economy, while an economic *plan* is defined as a programme of action adopted as a law directing the economic policies of governments.

to steer the totality of society's growth, the deeper spheres of the civilization process, the conditions for man's self-creation.[1] All this is making for an enormous spread of long-range planning, boosting its prestige and prolonging the time scales. In all probability the span of scientifically-based outlooks will be stabilized around the term of active human life and will merge with the shaping of the outlooks purposively set by man for himself. The gulfs still dividing the long-term extrapolation of economic series, forecasts for science and the images of man's future self-realization are a sensitive indicator of the spontaneous rhythm by which civilization has hitherto progressed.

The socialist order, where the endeavour to plan the future undoubtedly originated, can, when its development has reached the necessary level, offer especially good opportunities for advancing to more sophisticated methods of *constructing perspectives;* matching the conditions provided by the scientific and technological revolution, such methods could evolve in line with the growing, practical power of new subjectivity in social and human development. Today lack of long-range outlooks is already felt as a brake on development; because in the upshot the prospects for science, technology and education are subordinated to the pressures of momentary economic worries and there is no chance of really consciously shaping human life. Moreover, people who take no part in outlining perspectives, or who are merely presented by the planners from time to time with ready-made projects which they have little chance of changing, cannot accept the plan and its drafting as their own work; more likely, the whole matter becomes just one of the conditions of life to which they have to accommodate themselves.[2] A far more satisfactory approach would seem to be to change the construction of perspectives at the right moment into a long-range, lasting concern of the *entire community*, with broad participation by scientists,

[1] This has evoked the remarkable emphasis on an overall theoretic concept of future development, on socioanthropological images, models of man, his life and future — both in futurological writings, and in official projects for the future. The significance of detecting "networks of the future" is stressed with a philosophical bias by R. Jungk (cf. *Wege ins neue Jahrtausend*, ed. R. J. Jungk, H. S. Mundt, München 1964); the above-mentioned OECD analysis underlines the fact that overall images, hypotheses, blue-prints, are essential for serious attempts at planning and prediction. Strong pressure in this respect emanates from the planning organs of the socialist countries.

[2] A number of authors (e.g. D. Riesman, N. Glazer, R. Denney, *The Lonely Crowd*, New York 1950) go so far as to stress the need for utopian thinking as the source of a realistic approach to outlining perspectives, which would offset the positivist and passive attitude to human life typical of modern civilization.

technologists, and specialists engaged in mapping the future, including the new social and technological features in the socialist mode of life.

For such long-range projecting to become a permanent social process, it would be necessary:

a) to acquaint the public with the general problems foreseen for a longish period (twenty to thirty years) in the most open manner — including the chief goals, problems, limits, and the alternative solutions offered by the given level of science, technology, the social structure, work, etc.;

b) to invite scientists, technologists, other specialists, economists and working groups to put forward their own suggestions on how to advance the civilization base of human life, how best to gear the country to the scientific and technological revolution in the world, to the process of shaping a socialist mode of life, etc.;

c) to initiate long-term open discussion, in which the public could assess the alternatives, giving all citizens the opportunity to voice their proposals for the future, to express their opinions on how to mould the profile of human life, how to advance the powers of man;

d) to choose and adopt on this basis the most mature and progressive alternatives at the appropriate decision levels.

Such far-sighted construction of perspectives would greatly enhance the authority of science, technology, education, and also of socialism and its progressive elements. Moreover, it could do much to make planning the future more perceptive, qualified and attractive, arousing attitudes of confidence and criticism towards such work. People would be made equal to their historic undertakings. It would be a step forward towards imbuing men with individual purpose, and equipping socialist life with a more adequate armoury of ideas. Socialist participation in advancing civilization would be notably extended, planning made more democratic (especially in connection with choice of variants) and an unhealthy piling up of responsibilities for the course of social development would be avoided. By linking up with the new system of management now being introduced, the construction of perspectives would encourage a socialist spirit of enterprise. For the young people — at least in the future — the benefits would be outstanding, because never having experienced the fervour of class struggle in their own country, their attitude to socialism can spring only from the exhilaration to be found in science, technology, culture, creative work, man's development and human contacts. Since young people today are quite naturally aspiring to take part in genuine, informal construction of their own future and their style of living, such a sharpening of society's collective reason might well help them to find their place in the world of today and tomorrow.

Naturally, such far-ranging discussion of perspectives would produce all kinds of variants and opinions, including sharp arguments about the road that socialist society should follow. But far from damaging the communist idea, such a democratic advance could only strengthen it, because the traditional expedients of parliamentary democracy are obviously outdated and the objective advanced by the founders of Marxism has no serious rivals in the world today — indeed, with the outlooks of the scientific and technological revolution in mind, it appears as an imperative.

This method of constructing perspectives might well succeed in bringing the essential matter of socialist society to the fore. When confronted with new civilization processes, any type of society is impelled to find ways of bringing all the creative powers of its working community into play. There is little reason to doubt that with the growing pace of technological and social change, the claims on planning and shaping the future will far exceed those customary in the industrial epoch; in all probability there will be pressure towards a stable system allowing everyone to take a hand in clearing the roads to the future.

/ *The Scientific and Technological Revolution in Modern History* /

4.2.6

The advanced economies of the modern world draw for the most part on the fruits of *industrial civilization*, with its typical limitations and contradictions. True, some previously unknown elements are apparent to a greater or lesser degree; but while belonging at bottom to the new type of civilization process, the scientific and technological revolution, they are interwoven in the chain of processes still directed towards concluding or carrying further the undertakings of the industrial revolution; they are obscured or compensated by many opposing trends. Moreover, alongside all this are areas that are only just embarking on industrialization.

If the hypothesis advanced in this work as to the nature of the scientific and technological revolution corresponds to the facts, the only adequate approach to this phenomenon is that of *world history*. That is the forum in which science — as an international force par excellence — penetrates to the centre of the productive forces and into the foundations of human life, and only here can the whole process be traced, although, of course it is far from impinging on all areas at once or to the same degree.

As a rule we find that signs of the revolution or its various currents can be detected at different stages in the history of different countries. Analysis of economic data has led many investigators to the opinion that in the USA the start is to be met with in the inter-war years, linked with signs of intensive growth; data on the social structure, however, suggest a rather later date. In the case of the advanced European countries, technological and economic indicators suggest locating it not earlier than the fifties or sixties. In the USSR, while some preparatory elements — especially in the sphere of science — appear in the fifties,[1] overall economic growth is still primarily of the industrialization type. This would imply dating the onset of the scientific and technological revolution throughout the world within a broad segment of the half-century, from the twenties to the sixties.

We can arrive at a far more rational conclusion if we follow the process according to the model proposed, that is, by the inner logic of the said revolution,[2] remembering that it passes through various preparatory phases, periods when its elements are matched by the industrialization trends, periods when it starts to gain the upper hand and finally when its victory is complete.

Among the first steps towards the scientific and technological revolution we must count the great *revolution in science*, signalized by the rapid succession of findings in basic research that since the turn of the century has been building up an unprecedented potential in the fields of nuclear physics, macromolecular chemistry, cybernetics, biology, sociology, etc.[3] The series goes on and is nowhere near its end; with growing

---

[1] *Puti razvitiya tekhniki v SSSR*, Moscow 1967.

[2] We have to bear in mind that mere analogies are not enough. The industrial revolution had only two basic components — the evolution of machinery and turning people into proletarians. The logic of the scientific and technological revolution is far more complex.

[3] An attempt to present the specific features of this stage has been made by M. Teich in "K některým otázkám historického vývoje vědeckotechnické revoluce" (Some Questions Concerning the Historical Trend of the Scientific and Technological Revolution), *Sborník pro dějiny přírodních věd a techniky* 10/1965. Bernal originally saw the beginnings in Einstein's discoveries; later he has tended to place more stress on the successes in the science of electricity. Kapitsa refers to the work of Rutherford and others in this connection.

clarity, however, we can see that the trend is towards a radical change cn science altogether, not only in its external operation, but equally — and hand in hand with this — in its internal constitution, in a new concept of the object-subject dialectic, in the approach to reality and to science itself.[1]

This phase, however, reaches far back into the first decades of the century. At first new scientific findings existed alongside the traditional industrial base. Later they entered production one after another, taking hold of some processes and segments, but not yet by means of any qualitative change in production technology; the advance was rather through some elements of organization, in some cases in the guise of accelerated growth of qualified personnel outside the immediate production sphere — still using the traditional technological principles, mechanization and a considerable force of unskilled labour.[2]

However, the first steps in the scientific and technological revolution will not be on firm ground until the key role of science in the structure of the productive forces is reflected in the *technological* apparatus of production, in the civilization base, until the scientific revolution joins with the technological and starts to be a substitute for growth in the mass of simple labour, so that innovations in technology, raw materials and power, combined with radical changes in organization and education, turn the trend of economic growth permanently towards the intensive model. Only then will it be possible to regard technological innovation as a lasting process that opens up the inner logic of the scientific and technological revolution, embodying prospects for its own continuation. In this phase the revolution starts to be a social process,[3]

---

[1] S. Shibata was one of the first to reply to the question — does the scientific and technological revolution signify a "revolution in science" or a "revolution through science"? (*Historischer Materialismus und Sozialforschung*, Berlin 1966, p. 27). It signifies both, because if there were no revolution in science, there would be no penetration by science into the foundations of life, and vice versa.

[2] This was the case, for example, in many industrial sectors in the United States of the twenties, with rationalization advancing rapidly on the basis of large-scale, conveyor-belt production. That is also why economic growth models record an accelerated rise in output per man-hour in that period, with a certain decline in capital-output ratios and intensive factors acquiring greater importance. Although up to the fifties these changes were not universal and stable, and were subject to regressions, we can safely speak of the first signs of the scientific and technological revolution as having been evident in the United States between the wars. This first milestone is mentioned by J. D. Bernal in *Science in History*, I, p. XVI.

[3] Comprehension of this linkage between the technological and social revolutions was a big step forward in Tessmann's concept (see *Probleme der technischen-wissen-*

but at first its influence is felt only in growth of the economy, without any decisive impact on the mass of existing labour, that is, without changing the industrial social structure as such, but tending rather to erect elements of a new structure alongside and above it. Within these limits the initial phases can proceed irrespective of the social order — a favourable climate for innovation, whatever the underlying motives, is enough.[1]

The period from the fifties up to the present day can be regarded with full justification as representing the above phase and can be identified as the onset of the scientific and technological revolution in the world.

However, it would be absurd to expect this process to be straightforward, without hold-ups and diversions. It is not a matter of a few years, but a vast historical upheaval[2] in terms of decades, in a sense of centuries, a process that can only be compared with the three major milestones in human history, leading from barbarism to civilization, then to cultivation of the soil and ultimately to the industrial system[3] — and even this comparison is inapt when we consider the substance of the emergent changes.

Probably in the leading countries the next two to three decades will see the scientific and technological revolution gradually assuming the

---

schaftlichen Revolution, Berlin 1962; *Teoretische Probleme der wissenschaftlich-technischen Revolution*, Rostock 1964). We find a similar idea in Kolman's contribution at Royaumout in 1961 ("Tekhnicheskaya revolutsiya i obshchestvenny progress" in *Kakoe budushcheye ozhidayet chelovechestvo*, Praga 1964) and elsewhere.

[1] This has been the situation in the USA since the war, and in Europe for the most part since the late fifties and early sixties. J. D. Bernal (ibid.) dates the scientific and technological revolution from this point.

[2] If we take any kind of advance in science and technology to be identical with the scientific and technological revolution, it might appear that everywhere — in Czechoslovakia, too — the process is in full stream and that it is enough to wait for the results. But our analysis leaves no doubt that Czechoslovakia, in common with a number of other industrial countries, is now at the stage of seeking for her approaches to the scientific and technological revolution and that the advance to it will not be a matter of a few years, but of an entire phase, the length of which cannot be seriously stated without more thorough investigation. All one can do, indeed, is to warn against the superficial attitude that sees the scientific and technological revolution — this objective historical process — in terms of a campaign that can be carried out according to a predetermined schedule. On the other hand, it would be an equally fatal error if the country failed to concentrate here and now on a resolute search for the paths leading to its most rapid and intensive entry into the stream of scientific and technological revolution in the world.

[3] We employ here a comparison made by Bernal, Mumford, Toynbee and other historians of science, technology and civilization.

role of the dominant dynamic force. It would thereby enter on a new stage — as long as the social conditions were favourable — while where this was not the case it would come into sharp conflict with the social barriers. Around the turn of the century modern automation technology may be expected to take over the majority of production processes and to displace an appreciable amount of operative human labour from production proper. The general run of operations will be performed by cybernetic devices. Nuclear technology will yield practically unlimited resources of power for industry. And developments of such magnitude will undoubtedly signify a radical change in the civilization base of human life. Only when they have reached this stage will changes in the structure and dynamics of the productive forces make their full impact on industrial labour and in this connection pose the urgent question of a social order offering a suitable *social structure*.[1] This linking of changes in the technological base of civilization and in the growth models with changes in the social structure and the social conditions of human life is now posed as an immediate issue, and we may expect to see it at as the profound motif running right through the concluding phase of the twentieth century. It signifies the approach to the decisive stage of the scientific and technological revolution which will show whether the sequence of causes and effects will join up in a consistent historical process of a new type.

If we are to avoid indulging in speculation, we are hardly in a position today to estimate the time limits required by this vital stage of the scientific and technological revolution. But it is almost a foregone conclusion that in its course, and close on its heels, a further stratum and a further stage will make their appearance and that they will be associated with accelerating effects of these changes on the development of *man* and his powers, with inversion of most accepted proportions, forms and ideas of life today. The more we advance on to the actual ground of the scientific and technological revolution, the more diverse will be the ends to which its processes lead, and the more unknown variants it will reveal.

No satisfactory answer has yet been given to the question of what influence these stages in the transformation of civilization may have

---

[1] Soviet scholars S. V. Shukhardin, A. I. Kuzin and others link this phase with a "new production revolution". We could also cite the beginnings of biochemistry. But the actual basis of the new concept was, in fact, indicated by Marx. (Cf. *Sovremennaya nauchno-tekhnicheskaya revolutsiya. Istoricheskoye issledovaniye*, Moscow 1967).

on the periodization of modern history. One thing alone is clear — the scientific and technological revolution is emerging as an elementary fact in the civilization process of the twentieth century.

* * *

We have said that the development of science, technology and modern productive forces has posed a whole range of social problems and that without science and technology the human problems of our day would not exist. It only remains to add that their human solution would also be wanting.

Harnessing science and technology within a unified social context, promoting the effective interest of all in raising the productivity of social labour, planned use of modern technology, providing conditions for creating and asserting all human abilities — these are the potential means, and indeed the sole guarantee, of victory for the new social principles within civilization as we know it today. With them socialism and communism stand or fall — it is essential that everyone should realize that without a scientific and technological revolution the new society must perish — irrespective of any wishes, determination or the best intentions.

Granted that today the nature of the productive forces is the feature by which socialism and capitalism are comparatively least distinguishable, it looks as if the antithesis between the two worlds will reach its climax and in the course of the scientific and technological revolution in one way or another find its solution there. For this is the process whereby practical expression is given to the society-wide unification that allows scientific progress and man's development to operate as specifically new civilization forces of social revolution. And viewed from the opposite angle, only when the productive forces of human life have reached this level will opportunities exist for new relationships among people and a new concept of human life.

We are standing today on the soil of the historically formed industrial civilization, but we are beginning to cross its frontiers and go forward into the unknown civilization of the future. At this intricate crossroads, the movement aspiring to transform the world to the benefit of man is obliged to rely on the delicate compass of science and the power of creative thought.

EPILOGUE

/*Practical Aspects. Some Ideas for Consideration*/

The study undertaken by the authors of this book has been concerned with theoretical concepts; we have moved in the realm of basic research. The scientific and technological revolution, including its social and human implications, is so radical a movement that at the present stage and with the knowledge at our disposal we cannot lay down detailed measures to be applied in practice and certainly not prescribe any ready-made recipes; any such steps will have to be independently conceived and handled by responsible authorities. Nevertheless, we would like here to call attention to some general aspects, without giving them any absolute significance. They have a bearing on the approach that will be made to the whole question. We are not concerned with the actual course to be taken, but with suggesting the main lines on which the ground may be prepared.

A) A country that has traversed the stage of industrialization and socialist reconstruction finds itself face to face with the beginnings of the scientific and technological revolution — as an organic component and vital condition of further profound social transformations. The scientific and technological revolution is by its nature a universal, continuous transformation of all the productive forces in society and human life, involving their entire structure; consequently, it is a profoundly revolutionary social process with far-reaching implications for the position of man in producing his own life and for all social relationships; it impinges on the structure and nature of work, the levels of skills, extent and type of education, the configuration of life and wants, the breadth and intensity of human contacts, the nature of the environment, the relation between man and nature, the laws and forms of historical development, the position of the individual in society, the type of management and modes of thinking.

While the scientific and technological revolution carries forward the fruits of the industrial revolution (industrialization), it differs in its substance and its implications and in many respects produces completely opposed effects. The need therefore arises:

a) to adopt in the whole range of undertakings (whether programmes or economic prognoses, practical decisions or theoretical schemes), the methodological principle that it is now impossible to formulate any concepts concerning the development of society without reference to the new conditions and demands engendered by the scientific and technological revolution;

b) to arrange for conducting integrated interdisciplinary investigation of the scientific and technological revolution, its social and human implications, at the level of basic research (involving philosophy, economics, sociology, "science of science", psychology, pedagogy, aesthetics, law and history, theory of architecture, hygiene, political science, anthropology, ergonomics, cybernetics, the natural sciences, technology, medicine), to be followed by applied research. It will be necessary in this connection to see how far new branches are prepared and fill any gaps in the system of the sciences of man;

c) to acquaint the public with the true facts and the outlooks offered by the scientific and technological revolution, so that they may be prepared for the scale of future changes in the basis of civilization, in the style of human life and for unaccustomed lines of advance — and particularly, that they should grasp the vital necessity of such happenings from the standpoint of socialism and communism and be able to play a really effective part.

B) In an advanced socialist country such as Czechoslovakia, the main barrier in approaching the scientific and technological revolution is placed by some elements of immaturity in the economic structure, in the impulses and means linking the ordinary man with the advances of science and technology and with progress in the productivity of social labour in the mass. In these circumstances, socialism cannot conclusively manifest its essential nature or achieve effective scientific and technological development (and ultimately human development, too). Consequently, full implementation of fundamental measures underlying a new system of economic management is the main step in a decisive turn to intensive growth of the productive forces and the precondition for an approach to the scientific and technological revolution. In this connection it is of crucial importance for the stimulation of scientific and technological advance that incentives to fostering a spirit of socialist enterprise be freely operated and the categories of value adjusted in practice as an essential groundwork for guiding the objective and subjective elements in the processes of civilization.

C) The vital question for coming decades will be the extent to which science — as the leading agent in the dynamic civilization of our day — will permeate and be operative in the life of society. This requires:

a) rapid development of research capacities at a level adequate to the present trends in the world and geared to the long-range perspectives of economic growth. This implies eliminating some unhealthy symptoms of purely formal growth (inadequately qualified personnel in applied research and development) and envisaging science and research growing into a significant sector of the national economy (about 15 per cent of the industrial work force by 1980), on a scale bearing no comparison with the era of industrialization;

b) elaboration of a strategy for science in a small, advanced country, relying on an increased share of basic research in the distribution of scientific and technological resources, concentrating applied research in selected fields, drawing on work in other countries (cooperation within the socialist group and purchase of licences), expanding information services to provide comprehensive surveys of the state of science in the world;

c) organization of the media and channels by which scientific findings may flow into all sectors of the community: employing to this end primarily economic means; further, through scientific advisory bodies attached to all top institutions, and insistence on expertise or competitive selection preparatory to every fundamental decision by leading authorities on fundamental projects; finally, through building up an atmosphere of scientific progress based on confidence, recognition for creative effort, free and friendly discussion on disputable problems, etc.

D) The scientific and technological revolution is an intricate social process in which advance of science and technology is intimately connected with various social and human preconditions and implications. An effective approach can be made only if all new trends in science and technology (drawing on various lines of work hitherto undertaken to complete industrialization, aggregate production, etc.) are judiciously combined with the prospects offered by integration within the socialist system and with the special circumstances of the country concerned. An important point is to make the maximum use of favourable factors, such as the tradition of a labour force with expert knowledge and skills, and to compensate some drawbacks such as restricted raw-material resources. With this in mind, it is essential to project the course of the scientific and technological revolution, embracing the whole body of innovations in technology, raw materials, power, and in skills and organization, into long-range technico-economic concepts, always linked with considerations of the social and human implications of the respective intents (impact on structure of work, skills, development of human powers, working and living environments, etc.). This should not be a system of allocating directive assignments, but a social and technological programme, outlining the substance of the process and the measures available (a programme of comprehensive mechanization and automation, application of chemical processes, computer techniques, biological processes, handling of the power problem, modernization of machinebuilding, reform of agricultural techniques, treatment of urbanization problems, etc.), which should be followed up by the state plan and would provide scope for initiative by economic interests.

A vital factor in the success of this dynamic orientation of growth in Czechoslovakia will be the ability to integrate and to achieve division of labour within the socialist system, to engage in close international cooperation in science and technology along the lines envisaged for the course of the scientific and technological revolution.

E) The scientific and technological revolution inverts the elementary technological, economic, social and anthropological conditions of civilization's progress. In contrast to industrialization, we find that gradually, in more and more areas, science and its technical application, and through this medium man and the development of his creative powers, are providing the crucial dimension of growth of the productive forces. In these circumstances there is no use in automatically applying the growth patterns and the proportions of reproduction inherited from the age of industrialization. Effective growth is less and less dependent on multiplying labour inputs and industrial plants. The gap between the growth rate of groups I and II is gradually narrowing. The new basic growth pattern (intensive growth) now implies science being ahead of technology, and technology ahead of industry. We can no longer insist that the growth of production proper must be the most rapid — that is, insofar as its effect can be equalled or outdone by more effective generation of productive powers in the pre-production stages (science and research), and also in care for people and the development of human powers (the "quaternary sector"). Division into a "productive" (production proper) and "nonproductive" area loses its value for delimiting proportions in the national economy (investments, etc.) and has to be subordinated to a higher division deduced from the new logic of generating productive powers, in whatever sector the process may take place. In view of the multidimensional dynamics of the productive powers today, a progressive orientation (optimalization) of intentions can only be ensured if it stems from a well-planned and functioning economic system of interests, geared to absolute growth in the productivity of all social labour, and if it is combined with a scientific system of time economy drawing on modern economic growth theories, including the economics of human resources, mathematic modelling, an efficient computer network, etc. Elaboration of such a system makes it possible to determine at any given time the area (be it production, science, education, services, care for people, etc.) which, under the given conditions, affords the maximum preparation of the productive powers of human life.

F) The time will soon be ripe for a major intervention in the structure of the nation's work, employing the latest know-how, automation equipment, transportation techniques, chemical processes, computer techniques, modernization of machine parks, etc. and better utilization of human powers. Wherever it is technically possible and economically advantageous, it will be necessary to make considerable manpower cuts in industry and other sectors. The primary concern will be to free unskilled labour — from jobs such as materials handling, intra-plant transportation, auxiliary and completory operations, clerical record-keeping, work in out-of-date plants, etc. — and direct it to progressive branches, thereby improving the utilization of capital assets, saturating services and distribution and by degrees achieving a much better utilization of human powers in work involving mental capacities. In the long term we should expect new trends in job redistribution — some reduction of the share of manpower in industry (in Czechoslovakia, by 1980, below 35—33 per cent), a further outflow of labour from production as such (agriculture by 1980 down to 10 per cent) and strengthening of the tertiary sector. After a transition stage, this shift will move increasingly (if proper use is made of human powers) to science and research, technological preparation, highly skilled occupations and to public welfare (education, health services, etc.). The only possible basis for radical social and technological progress in the socialist context at the present stage is skilled, creative work.

G) Of equal urgency from the standpoint of generating productive powers are considered measures to cure the infrastructure of its chronic backwardness. This implies: judicious input of resources designed in the long term to bring about a substantial reduction in the time expended on acquiring means of subsistence and to cut down on wastage engendered by shortcomings in the working and living environments, that is, developing and modernizing transportation, services, distribution, etc. The aim will be to lighten the burden of subsistence cares and to extend (about threefold) disposable time, i.e., provide far wider scope for human abilities (education, active rest, technological and cultural activities, social participation, travel and so on). Under the conditions of the scientific and technological revolution in the socialist countries, such measures promise to contribute far more to growth of the civilization base than some costly investments in other sectors.

H) A start should be made now in preparing the ground for the rising claims on knowledge and skills to be anticipated during the next decades; special provision should be made for modern dynamic specialization on a broad universal base. Within the span of twenty years we should envisage the need for 60 to 70 per cent of workers to be equipped with modern skills. In this case, training methods at present directed in the main to trade skills will have to be adapted to provide the broad technological background required by modern types of production — and by increasing mobility among occupations. The share of trained technicians will rise to a level of 25 per cent of the work force and of university-educated engineers to 6—6.5 per cent. With this outlook, secondary education for all will be essential (polytechnical education with a balanced share of the humanities) and a plan for its introduction should be worked out. Rising demands on academic qualification require that a substantial proportion (after 1980 about one-third) of young people should receive university training. In the next few years we should also establish a system affording diverse opportunities for people to learn throughout their lives (adult education), and prepare for further expansion by providing the technical and institutional groundwork. To build up a modern educational system necessarily implies giving due emphasis to the new type of rationality in science and progressing from education to self-education. It would be an impossible undertaking without a broadly-based plan for introducing technology into instruction — both didactic technology and modern communication media (radio, television, the videotape-recorder, computers, etc.). Education theorists have a big job before them in mastering the multifarious implications of these innovations.

I) The scientific and technological revolution brings into play a new, independent growth factor — human development on a broad front. Far more is expected of individual activity, the fullness of man's inner

life, the ability to surpass oneself and to cultivate one's own capacities —
and growth of the individual acquires a wider social significance.
Hitherto individual socialist endeavour has tended to be put at a disadvantage, the horizons of "reproduction life" have been hard and fast —
in short, individual initiative has been curbed by a mass of directives.
We now face the necessity to supplement economic instruments with
socio-political and anthropological instruments that will shape the contours of human life, evoke new wants, model the structure of man's
motivation, while enlarging, not interfering with, freedom of choice, in
fact relying on a system of opportunities and potentialities in human
development. Otherwise, instead of progressively providing scope for
new wants (due to be felt with full force when present consumption has
been something like trebled), the approaching transition phase of "mass
consumption" will revolve in a closed circle. An urgent task in this field,
in which scientific and technological advance can make an especially
hopeful contribution, is to bring into operation a variety of ways by
which the individual can share in directing all controllable processes of
contemporary civilization and to do away with some of the restricting,
dehumanizing effects of the traditional industrial system.

J) If the artificial environment created by industrial civilization is
not to get out of control and hold back the advance of human powers,
it is imperative that we make considered use of the means afforded by
the scientific and technological revolution to regulate conditions of life
and work. A valuable contribution would be to work out a project for
a balanced environment, with the maximum resources devoted to generating human powers. Such a programme would have to include measures
in the sphere of work culture, the environment, air and water purity,
nature preservation, healthy modes of life, mental health, etc. It should
be backed up by a system of scientific standards set by the appropriate
branches of knowledge (rational nutrition, consumption, exercise, etc.).
A broadly-conceived concept of environment creation would have to be
elaborated, with a view to integrating the processes of dwelling, working,
recreation, transportation, culture, consumption, contact with nature,
and a rational, aesthetic and emotional life. Moreover, the speed-up in
the cycle of changes within the civilization base of work and daily life
underlines the need for a flexible approach in framing new concepts of
individual and social life.

K) The transition to the scientific and technological revolution, with
its manifold dynamic relations, will rule out any possibility of directing
the progress of society by the methods of administration that were

adequate in the days of industrialization. Everything depends on whether we can enlist the aid of science in finding suitable regulators (system of objective instruments and rules inducing self-operating processes) in the economic, socio-political, legal, moral, psychic, anthropological and other spheres of life. Such regulators would enable the objective and subjective conditions of activity to be modelled with the aid of cybernetic linkages affording ample scope for alternation, and for individual and collective initiative; they would raise the planned management of social development to a higher level, and would lay the basis for quantifying social processes and making effective use of cybernetic techniques in management. We shall have to train a body of experts for work with these methods (systems engineering, modern management of economic and social processes). Rationalization of the information flow in all fields calls for attention. We must bear in mind that if the apparatus of management is not equipped with substantially higher training it will be unable to keep pace with the dynamics of the scientific and technological revolution. Experience shows that unskilled management drives society along the old paths of extensive industrialization.

L) The growing role of subjective agencies in the context of the scientific and technological revolution will call for diverse forms of management:

a) it is necessary to take into account all the implications of changes in the social structure that allow socialism to approach the scientific and technological revolution with an effective deployment of forces (specialists, technologists and scientists become a component part of the working class, the significance of the skilled sections of the workers grows);

b) the Communist Party's leadership will increasingly rely on science and on ways of promoting scientific advance. In this connection it will be of the utmost importance to elaborate and stabilize means, rules and forms whereby new scientific concepts and progressive projects can be realized without the lengthy period of gestation customary with traditional methods and without the delays and waste occasioned by mistrust of or failure to understand unorthodox departures;

c) in the context of the scientific and technological revolution, the Communist Party, as the leading force, will find it necessary to look beyond the horizon of patterns solely directed to tackling issues arising from class struggle (and the structure of political power as such); it will have to evolve a diversity of new approaches and more effective means, taking in technology, the economy, social, psychological and anthropological factors, by which to adjust conditions for socialist endeavour.

M) The scientific and technological revolution introduces a radical change in the demands made on intellectual life, sound critical thinking, mental alertness and general knowledge. With all the problems of civilization and alternative roads opening up in the socialist world, the prospect is that, rather than dying down, intellectual life and conflicts of ideas will intensify, striking out into new fields where it will be necessary to find media and rules other than those accompanying class struggle within a country. Questions to be tackled will include the disparities and changes in modern civilization, the inversion in the relationship of man and his handiwork, of subject and object, the break-down in traditional modes of life and thought. It is, therefore, imperative to compile a survey of the leading civilization problems with an indication of the Marxist approach to handling them, which would be founded on a thorough analysis and serious comparative study of the operation of the scientific and technological revolution within the two world systems. Failing this, Marxist theory would inevitably lose its effectiveness. A grave shortcoming in our theoretic armoury has been a tendency to underestimate the impact of changes in the structure and dynamics of the productive forces on the character of social processes and on the position of man in modern civilization.

On an international scale, new tensions and conflicts of the technological age will probably cause a gradual shift in emphasis towards new elements in the motive forces within the different social systems — such matters as the application of science in all spheres of human life, promoting the development of human powers on a broad front, overcoming the conflicts and limitations of industrial civilization, mastering the social and human implications of the scientific and technological revolution.

N) In view of the fact that the changes in the status of science and the new implications of developing human powers lend increasing significance to long-term considerations and that in the transition phase the problem of people's involvement in the advance of civilization is felt with growing urgency, it will evidently be useful to adjust forecasts to the present cycle of scientific knowledge (20 years) and then to the effective span of human life (40 years); such undertakings should be accompanied by widespread initiative on the part of scientists, technologists, all specialists and working people, who would freely discuss all possibilities and alternative courses and how to shape the socialist style of life.

We are convinced that practical steps in this direction will be found to be merely the starting point for far more radical undertakings.

STATISTICAL TABLES

TABLE 1-1

THE PROGRESS OF COMPUTER TECHNIQUE
(Number of installed computers)

	1963	1964	1965	1970 forecast	Per one million inhabitants in 1965
USA	15,867	22,495	30,205	55,000	154
USSR[1]	.	.	3,500	10,000	15
Japan	870	1,081	1,837	.	19
FRG	993	1,657	2,291	.	41
Great Britain	626	1,100	1,600	.	30
France	791	1,043	1,500	.	31
Italy	592	882	1,100	.	22
Netherlands	149	275	380	.	31
Sweden	147	257	360	.	48
Switzerland	160	260	380	.	62
Belgium	142	232	350	.	37
CSSR	.	.	48	200	4
World total	23,000	32,000	45,000	90,000	13

[1] Estimate

Sources: Ukazatelé hospodářského vývoje v zahraničí (Indicators of Economic Development Abroad), UTEIN, Prague 1966; D. Rakouš, Samočinné počítače ve světě (Computers in the World), Hospodářské noviny 20/1966. Přehled o stavu a tendencích ve využívání výpočtové techniky v zahraničí (Survey on the Situation and Tendencies in Utilization of Computer Technique Abroad), UTEIN 1965, and further information of the Centre for Scientific, Technical and Economic Information, Prague

TABLE 1-2

PRODUCTION OF PLASTICS
(thousand tons)

	1937	1950	1955	1960	1965	Forecast 1970	Per capita production in 1964
USA	60	908	1,762	2,849	5,163	7,800	26.8
FRG	.	99	430	964	1,968	.	33.4
Japan	.	22	158	570	1,700	.	14.7
Great Britain	30	158	322	570	933	.	17.8
USSR	10	75	177	332	821	2,200	3.2
Italy	5	23	96	297	898	.	17.4
France	10	33	102	347	697	1,470	14.2
GDR	.	40	80	136	219	.	12.9
CSSR	.	9	20	64	124	190	8.8
World total	300	1,700	3,125	6,400	14,300	26,000	3.9

Sources: Ukazatelé hospodářského vývoje v zahraničí (Indicators of Economic Development Abroad) 1965, UTEIN, Prague 1966; Výroba plastických hmot v některých státech v posledních letech a její pravděpodobný vývoj do r. 1970 (Production of Plastic Materials in Selected Countries in Recent Years and Probable Development up to 1970), UTEIN, Prague 1966; Statistical Yearbook, UNO, 1965; Statistische Grundzahlen der EWG 1966

TABLE 1-3
GROWTH OF ELECTRICITY PRODUCTION IN SELECTED COUNTRIES
(in billions kwh per year)

	1920	1937	1950	1965	Projections 1970	Projections 1980	Projections 2000	1965 kwh per capita
USSR[1]	1	36	91	507	840	2,400	12,500	2,199
USA	57	146	389	1,158	1,590	3,000	10,000	5,946
Great Britain	9	24	57	196	241	390	—	3,607
France	6	20	33	101	151	290	—	2,068
Italy	5	15	25	79	120	260	1,000	1,536
FRG	—	49	—	45	169	250	450	1,325	3,025
GDR[1]	—	49	—	16	54	—	140	560	3 145
CSSR[1]	1	4	9	34	49	95	—	2,415
Canada	—	30	55	144	—	—	—	7,303
Sweden[1]	—	8	18	49	—	—	—	6,348
Switzerland	—	7	10	24	—	—	—	4,110
Japan	—	31	45	192	300	600	1,600	1,960
World total	—	411	872	3,340	—	—	—	1,002

[1] Gross

Sources: Statistická ročenka (Statistical Yearbook) ČSSR 1966. — Strana Sovetov za 50 let (50 Years of USSR), Moscow 1967. Beschinsky et al.: Problemy perspektivnogo electrobalansa SSSR, Moscow 1966. — Federal Power Commission: Annual Report 1965, Washington 1966; National Power Survey 1964. — United Nations: Statistical Yearbook Nuclear Power, Washington 1967. — Ukazatelé hospodářského vývoje v zahraničí (Indicators of Economic Development Abroad), UTEIN, Prague 1966. — Premier Programme Indicatif pour la Communauté Européenne de l'Energie Atomique, Bruxelles 1966.

TABLE 1-4 (A—B)

DEVELOPMENT OF NUCLEAR POWER
A. *Nuclear Programmes*

	First nuclear plant commissioned	by 1.1.1968 MW(e)	1970 MW(e)	1975 MW(e)	1980 MW(e)	1990 MW(e)	2000 MW(e)
USSR	1954	1,200	2,200	—	—	—	—
France	1956	1,174	2,000	8,000	20,000	68,000	170,000
Great Britain	1956	4,748	7,100	15,000	45,000	110,000	185,000
USA	1956	2,830	11,200	60,000	150,000	—	850,000
FRG	1960	557	1,000	7,500	18,000	53,000	110,000
Canada	1962	245	782	2,800	7,000	14,500 (1985)	—
Italy	1962	631	631	3,650	12,000	24,000	91,000
Belgium	1962	11	11	2,000	4,000	—	—
Sweden	1963	10[1]	610	1,000	4,000	—	—
Japan	1963	179	830	5,000	—	35,000 (1985)	165,000
GDR	1966	70	140	940	—	30,000	50,000
Switzerland	1966	7	663	—	—	—	—
Bulgaria	—	—	—	800	—	—	—
Hungary	—	—	—	800	—	—	—
India	—	—	580	2,600	10,000	—	—
Spain	—	—	610	2,250	4,850	—	—
Nuclear power program of Euratom[2]	1956	2,373	4,000	22,000	60,000	135,000	370,000
World total	1954	11,662	30,000	115,000	300,000	700,000	—

[1] With district-heating equipment of 70 MW(th) capacity
[2] France, FRG, Italy, Belgium, Netherlands, Luxembourg

Sources: Programmes of specific countries and reports in scientific and technical journals

TABLE 1-4

B. *Expected Growth of Share of Nuclear Power in Total Electric Power Generation*

	Nuclear power generation		Share of nuclear generation in total power output per year				
	Total by December 31, 1967	in 1967	1967 (%)	Projections			
	bill. kwh	bill. kwh		1970 (%)	1975 (%)	1980 (%)	2000 (%)
USSR	29 (est.)	6.8 (est.)	1.1	—	—	—	—
France	7.6	3.2	2.8	7	23	50	over 90
Great Britain	91.8	25.1	11.0	14	18	33	—
USA	32.0	8.5	0.6	3	17	28	over 60
FRG	1.9	1.2	0.6	7	40	66	86
Canada	0.8	0.2	0.1	—	—	—	—
Italy	13.2	3.1	3.2	4	15	25	—
Belgium	0.2	0.1	0.4	—	—	—	—
Sweden	0.1	0.03	0.001	—	—	—	—
Japan	1.3	0.9	0.4	—	6	27 (1985)	47
GDR	—	—	—	—	—	—	over 50
Switzerland	—	—	—	10	30	—	—
Euratom[1] Member states (together)	17.6	5.7	1.4	5	15	over 25	70
World total	over 140	over 40	1.1	—	—	—	over 50

[1] France, FRG, Italy, Netherlands, Belgium, Luxembourg

Sources: Nucleonics Week 8/1968; programmes of specific countries
Worked out by S. Medonos, State Commission for Technology, Prague

TABLE 1-5
CHANGES IN THE SHARE OF MAN, ANIMALS AND TECHNOLOGY IN EXPENDED ENERGY
(in percentages based on U.S. data)

	1850	1900	1930	1950	2000 (estimate)
Man	15	10	4	3	0.5
Animals	79	52	12	1	—
Technology	6	38	84	96	99.5

Sources: W. F. Ogburn, N. F. Nimkoff, Sociology, New York 1950; G. Osipov, Technika a společenský pokrok (Technology and Social Progress), Bratislava 1960; F. Baade, Weltenergiewirtschaft, Hamburg 1956; Der Weltlauf zum Jähre 2000, Oldenburg, Hamburg 1961

TABLE 1-6 (A—D)
DEVELOPMENT OF FUEL AND ENERGY BALANCE
A. ČSSR

Year	Total consumption of fuel and energy million metric tons per year	Solid	Liquid	Gaseous	Electricity produced in hydro-electric plants	Nuclear energy
1929	24.5	97.1	1.75		1.15	—
1937	21.1	95.7	3.0		1.3	—
1950	31.9	95.8	2.1		2.1	—
1955	42.5	93.3	4.05		2.65	—
1960	63.8	88.5	6.2	2.6	2.7	—
1965	72.6	84.6	12.3	1.5	1.6	—
1970 (forecast)	84.5	78.2	18.4	2.1	1.3	—
1980 (forecast)	120	66	26	6	1	1

Sources: Homola, F.-Rataj, M.: Razvitiye elektrifikaciyi v Chekhoslovatskoy sotsialisticheskoy respublike, Moskva—Leningrad 1961; Flemming, B.-Lidický, F.-Procházka, K.: Analysis of Structural Changes in the Czechoslovak Energy Balance. Paper No. 155 presented to the World Energy Conference in Tokyo, October 16—20, 1966

B. USSR

TABLE 1-6 (continued)

Year	Total consumption of fuel and energy — million metric tons hard coal equivalent per year[1]	Share of (percentages)						
		Wood	Coal	Peat	Shale	Crude oil	Natural gas	Hydro and nuclear electricity
1908	93	63.1	23.3	1.0	—	12.6	—	0.0
1927/28	115	52.9	29.2	2.9	—	14.6	0.3	0.1
1940	239	14.2	58.8	5.7	0.3	18.6	1.9	0.5
1950	313	8.9	65.6	4.8	0.4	17.3	2.3	0.7
1958	673	10.7	54.5	3.1	0.7	25.0	5.0	1.0
1965	1065	5.1	41.5	2.6	0.7	32.2	16.7	1.2
1970[2]	1320[3]		36.8	2.5	0.7	38.0	22.0	
1980[4]	2640[4]		31.3			37.3	31.4	

[1] hard coal equivalent — 7000 kcal/kg
[2] estimate on the basis of data presented to the 23rd Congress of the CPSU
[3] wood, hydroelectric and nuclear power excluded
[4] estimate on the basis of data published at the 20th Congress of the CPSU (only coal, crude oil and natural gas)

Sources: Feld, S. D.: Yediniy energeticheskiy balans narodnogo khozyaystva (problemy optimizatsii), Moskva 1964; Směrnice XXIII sjezdu KSSS pro pětiletku 1966—1970 (Guidelines of the 23rd Congress of the CPSU for the 5-year Plan 1966—1970). In: "XXIII. sjezd KSSS" (23rd Congress of the CPSU), Prague 1966, pp. 427—474; Melentiev, L. A.-Styrikovich, M. A.-Shteyngauz, Ye. O.: Toplivno-energeticheskiy balans SSSR (Osnovniye voprosy ekonomiki i planirovaniya), Moscow—Leningrad 1962

TABLE 1-6 (continued)

C. USA

Year	Total consumption of fuel and energy — mill. metric tons hard coal equivalent per year	\multicolumn{7}{l}{Share of (percentages)}
		wood	coal	crude oil	natural gas	liquid gas	Hydro electric energy	nuclear energy
1850	85	90.7	9.3	—	—	—	—	—
1880	100	57.0	41.1	1.9	—	—	—	—
1890	255	35.9	57.9	2.2	3.7	—	0.3	—
1910	600	10.7	76.8	6.1	3.3	—	3.1	—
1920	775	7.5	72.5	12.3	3.8	0.2	3.7	—
1940	910	5.4	49.7	29.6	10.6	1.1	3.6	—
1945	1180	3.9	48.8	29.4	11.8	1.5	4.6	—
1955	1475	2.6	28.7	40.0	22.1	2.9	3.7	0
1960[1]	1650		23.3	44.5	28.3		3.9	
1970[2,3]	2200		20	43	32.4		3.6	1
1980[2,3]	3000		18	37	35		3	7
2000[2,3]	6000		17	28	23		2	30

[1] From 1960 only coal, crude oil, natural gas, hydroelectricity and nuclear energy
[2] Forecast
[3] Estimate

Sources: Schurr, Netschert and coll.: Energetika v ekonomike SShA (Energy in the Economy of the USA) 1950—1975, Moscow 1963; Landsberg, Fischman, Fisher: Resources in America's Future, Baltimore 1963; Felix, F.: Nuclear Energy to Dominate Power Plant Construction, Electr. World 165 (1966), No. 18

TABLE 1-6 (continued)

D. *World*

Year	Total consumption of fuel and energy — mill. metric tons of hard coal equivalent per year	Share of (percentages)					
		agri-cultural waste[1]	wood	coal	crude oil	natural gas	electricity (hydro and nuclear)
1860	554	16.7	57.11	25.30	0.02	0.87	—
1880	806	16.7	39.60	42.03	0.78	0.89	—
1890	1020	16.7	30.33	50.56	1.57	0.84	0.002
1910	1830	16.7	15.02	63.48	3.74	1.02	0.07
1920	2115	16.7	11.76	63.12	6.80	1.44	0.18
1940	3165	16.7	5.57	59.33	14.18	3.73	0.49
1945	2835	16.7	5.62	51.11	19.12	6.77	0.68
1950[2]	2607			61.6	26.9	10.0	1.5
1955[2]	3291			54.8	31.2	12.2	1.8
1960[2]	4298			51.0	32.5	14.5	2.0
1964[2]	5093			44.0	36.6	17.3	2.1

[1] Estimate
[2] From 1950 only coal, crude oil, natural gas, hydroelectric and nuclear energy

Sources: Putnam, P. C.: Energy in the Future, Princeton—Toronto—London—New York 1956, pp. 439—444; World Energy Supplies 1929—1950 to 1961—1964, UNO, New York 1952—1966
Worked out by S. Medonos, State Commission for Technology, Prague

TABLE 1-7 (A—B)

CHANGES IN THE STRUCTURE OF PRODUCTION

A. *Growth of Industrial Production, Production of Automatic Equipment, Chemical Products and Electric Energy*

	Industrial production	Production of automatic equipment	Production of chemical products	Production of electric energy
Annual growth rate in 1955—1962 (per cent)				
USA	2.9	7.0	6.1	6.0
Great Britain	2.0	17.4	4.6	7.9
FRG[1]	6.7	31.5	11.4	9.5
Relation of annual growth rates of selected industries to the rate of growth in industrial production				
USA	1	2.4	2.1	2.1
Great Britain	1	8.7	2.3	4.0
FRG[1]	1	4.7	1.7	1.4

[1] Average for the years 1955—1961

Sources: Ukazatele hospodářského vývoje v zahraničí (Indicators of Economic Development Abroad) 1955, Prague 1966; UTEIN Prague, SIVO 402, 1964; data of UVTEI, Prague

TABLE 1-7 (continued)
B. *Development of Industrial Production and Production of Electricity in Selected Industrial Countries*[1]
(1950 = 100)

	CSSR	USSR	GDR	FRG	France	Great Britain	USA
Production of electricity 1965 (index)	368	556	276	388	307	339	280
Industrial production 1965 (index)	365	456	381	332	251	160	192
Growth of electricity output related to the growth of industrial production	1.01	1.22	0.73	1.17	1.22	2.12	1.56

[1] In view of differences in defining the index of industrial production, the data of socialist and capitalist countries are not entirely comparable

Sources: Statistická ročenka (Statistical Yearbok) ČSSR, pp. 225, 561, 563 and 1959, p. 508; Adlivankina, R. Ya.-Gladtsinov, B. N.-Kachevsky, V. I.: Energetika SShA, Moscow 1965, p. 247; Ukazatele hospodářského vývoje v zahraničí (Indicators of Economic Development Abroad) 1965, I, Prague 1966, p. 185
Ukazatele hospodářského vývoje v zahraničí (Indicators of Economic Development Abroad) 1967
Worked out by S. Medonos, State Commission for Technology, Prague

TABLE 1-8

PROCESS OF MECHANIZATION OF AGRICULTURE: NUMBER OF TRACTORS
(in thousands)

	Before the Second World War	1950	1962	Tractors per 100 ha of arable land 1962
USSR	531	595	1329	1
USA	1400	3685	4670	3
FRG	30	140	999	12
Great Britain	50	325	427[1]	6
France	36	142	804	4
Italy	36	57	305	2
Austria	2	15	148	9

[1] About 1000 tractors in tractor stations excluded

Source: Ukazatele hospodářského vývoje v zahraničí (Indicators of Economic Development Abroad) 1965, UTEIN, Prague 1966

TABLE 1-9 (A—B)

CHANGES IN THE CAPITAL-OUTPUT RATIO
(Constant Prices)

A. *Development of Capital-Output Ratio (at Constant Prices)*

	USA				Great Britain
Year	Manu-facturing	Mining		Year	National economy
1880	0.54	1.16	Period of industrialization	1875	3.51
1890	0.73	1.36		1895	3.72
1900	0.80	—		—	—
1909	0.97	1.80		1909	3.80
1919	1.02	2.30		1914	3.40
1929	0.89	2.14		1928	3.53
1937	0.74	1.57[1]		1938	2.68
1948	0.61	1.34	Initial phase of the scienti-	—	—
1953	0.59	1.26	fic and technological revolution	1953	2.55

[1] 1940

Sources: S. Kuznets, Capital in the American Economy, Princeton 1961; Creamer, Dobrovolsky, Borenstein, Capital in Manufacturing and Mining, New York 1960; C. Clark, The Conditions of Economic Progress, London 1957

TABLE 1-9

B. *Development of Fixed Assets — Net Material Product-Ratio (at Constant Prices)*

USSR			CSSR[2]	
1928	1.45	Period of industrialization		
1940	2.08			
1950	2.37		1949—1953	2.42
1955	2.56		1954—1959	2.16
1960	2.79		1960—1964	2.58
			1965—1966	2.87

[2] up to 1960 at constant prices for 1955, subsequently at constant prices for 1960. Average ratio for the period concerned

Sources: B. N. Mikhalevsky, Perspektivniye raschoty na osnove prostych dinamicheskikh modeley, Moscow 1964; Statistická ročenka (Statistical Yearbook) 1965, Prague; Statistické přehledy (Statistical Surveys), Prague 1966
Worked out by M. Toms and M. Hájek, Institute of Economics, Czechoslovak Academy of Sciences, Prague

TABLE 1-10
SOURCES OF ECONOMIC GROWTH (A—C)

A. *Factors of Economic Growth in the USA 1839—1957 (per cent)*

Period	Average annual growth rate (NNP)	Contribution of extensive factors (capital, labour)	Contribution of intensive factors (technological progress)	Share of intensive factors in growth	
1839—1849	5.2	5.4	—0.2	— 3.8	
1849—1859	6.2	6.1	0.1	1.6	
1859—1869	2.3	3.7	—1.4	— 60.9	
1869—1879	6.2	4.2	2.0	32.3	period of industrialization
1879—1889	6.3	5.1	1.2	19.0	
1889—1899	4.5	2.9	1.5	33.3	
1899—1909	4.2	3.1	1.1	25.6	
1909—1919	3.8	2.3	1.5	39.5	
1919—1929	3.1	1.6	1.4	45.2	
1929—1937	0.2	—0.9	1.1	550.0	
1937—1948	4.4	2.2	2.2	50.0	beginning of scientific and technological revolution
1948—1953	4.7	2.2	2.4	51.1	
1953—1957	2.2	0.7	1.5	68.2	

TABLE 1-10 (continued)
DISAGGREGATION OF INTENSIVE GROWTH FACTORS FOR 1929—1960 (PER CENT)[1]

	1929—1947	1947—1960
1. Rate of growth of net national product	100.0	100.0
2. Extensive factors	34.5	28.6
3. Intensive factors	65.5	71.4
a) capital improvement	37.9	37.1
b) improvement of quality of labour	34.4	28.5
c) impact of organization of management	—6.8	5.8

[1] Preliminary attempt based on estimates

Sources: Trends in the American Economy in the Nineteenth Century, Princeton 1961; J. W. Kendrick, Productivity Trends in the United States, Princeton 1961; R. R. Nelson, Aggregate Production Functions and Medium-Range Growth Projections, The American Economic Review, September 1964

TABLE 1-10 (continued)

B. *Factors of Economic Growth in Selected Countries 1949—1959*
(annual increments, percentages)

Country	Gross Domestic Product	Contribution of Extensive Factors	Contribution of Intensive Factors	Share of Intensive Factors in Rate of Growth
(1)	(2)	(3)	(4)	(5) = (4):(2)
FRG	7.4	3.9	4.5	67.81
Italy	5.9	1.8	4.1	69.49
Netherlands	4.8	2.2	2.6	54.17
France	4.5	1.1	3.4	75.56
Norway	3.4	1.6	1.8	52.94
Sweden	3.4	0.9	2.5	73.53
Belgium	3.0	1.0	2.0	66.67
Great Britain	2.4	1.3	1.1	45.83
Japan	7.9	4.9	3.0	37.97

Sources: Some Factors in Economic Growth in Europe during the 1950s, UN, Geneva 1964, p. 36; O. Aukrust: Factors of Economic Development — A Review of Recent Research, Productivity Measurement Review, February 1965

TABLE 1-10 (continued)

C. *Factors of Economic Growth in the USSR, 1951—1970*

	1951—1963		1959—1963		1964—1970[1]	
	Annual increment (%)	Share of factors (%)	Annual increment (%)	Share of factors (%)	Annual increment (%)	Share of factors (%)
1. National income[2]	7.00	100.00	4.41	100.00	5.28	100.00
2. Extensive factors	4.77	68.19	4.17	94.42	4.29	81.18
3. Intensive factors	2.23	31.81	0.25	5.58	0.99	18.82

[1] Plan
[2] Net material product

Source: B. N. Mikhalevsky, Makroekonomicheskaya proizvodstvennaya funktsiya kak model ekonomicheskogo rosta, Ekonomika i matematicheskiye metody No. 2/1967
Worked out by M. Toms and M. Hájek, Institute of Economics, Czechoslovak Academy of Sciences, Prague

TABLE 1-11

OUTPUT PER UNIT OF LABOUR INPUT
Average annual increments per man-hour in the USA
(Gross domestic product per man-hour; per cent)

	Total economy	Manufacturing industry	Agriculture	
1889—1899	2.3	1.5	1.3	industrial revolution,
1900—1909	1.8	1.3	1.1	initial stage of
1910—1919	1.7	1.1	0.5	imperialism
1920—1929	2.4	5.4	1.2	
1930—1939	2.0	2.6	1.8	
1940—1949	3.0	1.7	3.3	
1950—1959	3.2	2.8	6.1	initial stage of the scientific and technological revolution
1960—1964	3.2	3.0	5.6	

Sources: Historical Statistics of the US, Colonial Times to 1957; Historical Statistics of the US 1789—1945; Economic Report of the President, 1965

TABLE 1-12

SOURCES OF ECONOMIC GROWTH IN CSSR

A. *Share of Influence of Extensive and Intensive Factors of Economic Growth (Percentage)*

Period	Increments during period of		
	National income	Total[1] sources of social labour	Productivity of total sources of social labour
1949—1953	56.3	29.5	20.7
1954—1955	14.2	9.8	4.0
1956—1960	40.5	32.5	6.1
1961—1965	10.2	29.9	—15.2
1966	10.8	4.5	6.0

[1] Average annual sources of social labour = average annual value of capital assets plus labour input, expressed with the help of wage and income relations for years whose price levels were used as constant comparable prices (1955—1960). For details see V. Nachtigal, Extenzita a efektivita hospodářského vývoje ČSSR (Extensiveness and Efficiency of Economic Growth of the ČSSR), in: Politická ekonomie No. 4, 1966

(continued)

TABLE 1-12 (continued)

Average annual growth rate of			Share of	
National income	Total sources of social labour	Productivity[1] of total sources of social labour	Extensive factors (sources of social labour)	Intensive factors (productivity of sources of social labour)
9.3	6.0	3.7	57.8	42.2
6.9	4.8	2.0	70.6	29.4
7.0	5.8	1.2	82.6	17.4
2.0	5.4	—3.3	270.7	—170.7
10.8	4.5	6.0	43.0	57.0

Sources: Statistické ročenky (Statistical Yearbooks) ČSSR. Worked out by V. Nachtigal, Institute of Economics, Czechoslovak Academy of Sciences, Prague

TABLE 1-12 (continued)

B. *Sources of Economic Growth of the Non-Agricultural Sector[1] in Czechoslovakia in the period 1949—1966 (percentage)*

Year	Growth rate of national income	Contribution of extensive factors	Contribution of intensive factors	Share of intensive factors in the growth rate
1949	7.81	3.29	4.52	57.90
1950	9.82	4.36	5.46	55.64
1951	14.24	4.67	9.57	67.18
1952	13.49	3.72	9.77	72.45
1953	5.93	3.16	2.77	46.71
1954	6.37	4.56	1.81	28.37
1955	10.09	3.52	6.57	65.15
1956	6.75	3.80	2.95	43.67
1957	8.29	4.61	3.68	44.38
1958	8.90	3.95	4.95	55.67
1959	8.49	5.25	3.24	38.20
1960	8.47	5.68	2.79	32.91
1961	8.30	5.67	2.63	31.63
1962	4.09	4.92	—0.83	—20.24
1963	4.17	3.53	—7.70	—184.62
1964	1.37	4.32	—2.95	—215.03
1965	5.78	3.84	1.94	33.56
1966	10.05	4.64	5.41	53.80

[1] Total economy without agriculture and forestry. The results were obtained by a different method than in part A, namely by the use of the substitution production function. Shares of factors of the national income were chosen as parameters. For method of application consult M. Hájek, M. Toms, Determinanty ekonomického růstu a integrální produktivita (Determinants of Economic Growth and Integral Productivity) Politická ekonomie, No. 10. 1966

Sources: Statistické ročenky (Statistical Yearbooks) ČSSR. Worked out by M. Hájek and M. Toms, Institute of Economics, Czechoslovak Academy of Sciences, Prague

TABLE 1-12 (continued)
C. *Disaggregation of the Sources of Economic Growth in the CSSR; 1951—1964*[1]

	Growth Rate	Structure
Growth rate of national income	5.90	100.0
1. Growth of extensive factors	4.79	81.19
a) contribution of capital	4.71	79.83
b) contribution of employment	0.08	1.36
2. Growth rate of intensive factors	1.11	18.81
a) contribution of technological progress	0.33	5.59
b) contribution of growing quality of labour	1.82	30.84
c) influence of the system of organization and management	—1.04	—17.62

[1] Preliminary attempt based on estimates.
The results were obtained by the application of a modified form of the Cobb-Douglas function. For details of procedure and the solving of methodological problems consult M. Hájek, M. Toms, Determinanty ekonomického růstu a integrální produktivita (The Determinants of Economic Growth and Integral Productivity), *Politická ekonomie*, No. 10, 1966

Sources: Statistické ročenky (Statistical Yearbooks) ČSSR. Worked out by M. Hájek and M. Toms, Institute of Economics, Czechoslovak Academy of Sciences, Prague

TABLE 1-13
CHANGES OF RENTABILITY (PRODUCTIVITY) OF SOCIAL LABOUR[1] IN THE PRODUCTION OF CSSR, 1955—1966

A. *Annual Increments of Labour Productivity (net output divided by average annual number of workers) in per cent*

	1955	1956	1957	1958	1959	1960
Total output	8.7	4.2	6.7	8.4	7.7	8.7
Manufacturing and mining industry	8.4	5.9	4.3	8.1	5.9	3.8
Agriculture	9.4	—0.5	4.3	5.5	—6.5	15.4
Construction	15.4	7.3	2.4	1.8	10.1	8.3

	1961	1962	1963	1964	1965	1966
Total output	6.1	0.5	—2.0	0.3	2.6	9.0
Manufacturing and mining industry	6.4	2.8	—2.8	0.4	3.7	5.9
Agriculture	3.3	—15.0	17.9	—2.8	—13.5	19.3
Construction	0.5	—4.9	—13.3	11.6	10.4	12.1

B. *Annual Increments of Capital Productivity (net output divided by average annual value of equipment) in per cent*

	1955	1956	1957	1958	1959	1960
Total output	4.9	—0.1	1.3	1.7	—0.8	0.5
Manufacturing and mining industry	5.0	2.7	2.0	2.5	1.0	1.4
Agriculture	5.7	—8.1	—5.6	—4.6	—20.8	—3.5
Construction	9.1	7.8	—3.9	—4.8	2.9	—4.8

	1961	1962	1963	1964	1965	1966
Total output	—0.8	—5.7	—7.9	—4.3	—1.1	5.8
Manufacturing and mining industry	1.6	—2.5	—9.3	—3.7	1.0	3.6
Agriculture	—9.5	—22.1	11.6	—9.1	—18.7	14.6
Construction	—8.2	—14.5	—19.9	9.0	8.9	10.0

(continued)

TABLE 1-13 (continued)

C. *Annual Increments of Productivity of All Sources of Social Labour*[1]
(net output divided by average annual sources of social labour) in per cent

	1955	1956	1957	1958	1959	1960
Total output	5.5	0.5	1.9	2.1	0.3	1.2
Manufacturing and mining industry	5.4	3.2	2.2	3.2	1.6	1.7
Agriculture	6.3	—6.6	—5.1	—5.1	—17.8	—2.2
Construction	11.2	8.7	—0.5	—0.9	5.3	0.0

	1961	1962	1963	1964	1965	1966
Total output	0.3	—4.8	—7.1	—3.8	—0.6	6.0
Manufacturing and mining industry	2.2	— 1.9	—8.6	—3.3	1.3	3.9
Agriculture	—6.9	—19.6	12.1	—8.4	—17.9	14.4
Construction	—4.9	—10.5	—17.3	10.0	9.0	10.6

[1] Average annual sources of social labour = average annual value of equipment and labour input, expressed with the help of wage and income relations of years, whose price levels were used as constant comparable prices (1955, 1960)
For details see V. Nachtigal, Extenzita a efektivita a efektivita hospodářského vývoje ČSSR (Extensiveness and Efficiency of Economic Growth of the ČSSR), *Politická ekonomie*, No. 4, 1966

Sources: Statistická ročenka (Statistical Yearbooks) ČSSR
Worked out by V. Nachtigal, Institute of Economics, Czechoslovak Academy of Sciences, Prague

TABLE 1-14
DEVELOPMENT OF INVESTMENT IN INDUSTRY AND IN RESEARCH AND DEVELOPMENT IN CZECHOSLOVAKIA
(Index base year 1955, at constant prices)

	1955	1956	1957	1958	1959	1960
Total investment	100	114	124	141	169	189
In industry	100	117	128	159	193	216
Construction investment	100	129	142	174	213	231
Technological equipment	100	107	117	148	178	204
In research and development	100	174	160	147	169	209

← Period of industrialization ──

	1961	1962	1963	1964	1965	1966
Total investment	203	198	176	197	212	233
In industry	233	244	222	241	255	283
Construction investment	253	261	228	235	242	256
Technological equipment	216	232	216	246	267	290
In research and development	205	224	222	279	330	379

── Period of industrialization →

Sources: Statistické ročenky (Statistical Yearbooks) ČSSR, 1963, 1965, 1966 and 1967. Worked out by V. Nachtigal, Institute of Economics, Czechoslovak Academy of Sciences, Prague

TABLE 1-15
PATENT APPLICATIONS AND PATENTS GRANTED IN THE WORLD

Average number (in thousands) of patents granted per year	Switzerland	Sweden	Federal German Republic	United Kingdom	Czechoslovakia	United States of America	Union of Soviet Socialist Republics	Netherlands
1946—1949	6.4	2.8		14.2	0.8	25.5	4.8	1.8
1950—1954	7.7	4.3	24.7	16.9	1.2	41.3	4.9	2.4
1955—1959	7.9	4.3	19.2	20.5	2.0	44.3	6.7	3.2
1960—1964	8.5	5.3	18.8	28.4	3.9	49.0	9.5	3.5
Per 100,000 inhabitants during:								
1964								
a) Patent applications filed	283	204	115	98	56	46	46	127
b) Patents granted	200	101	35	60	27	25	6	32
c) National patent applications filed	87	58	68	44	44	35	45	18
d) National patents granted	65	25	22		23	20	6	5
1965								
a) Patent applications filed	313	221	117	101	55	48	44	140
b) Patents granted	324	103	29	62	28	32	5	19
c) National patent applications filed	98	62	67	44	45	37	45	20
d) National patents granted	94	22	17		25	25	5	3
1966								
a) Patent applications filed	318	231	117	85	59	45	46	149
b) Patents granted	378	103	39	68	30	35	7	18
c) National patent applications filed	94	62	64	26	45	34	45	21
d) National patents granted	104	22	23		26	28	7	3

Sources: La propriété industrielle, Stat. ročenky (Statistical Yearbooks) ČSSR. Worked out by A. Verner, Czechoslovak Patent Office

TABLE 1-16

STATUS OF SCIENCE AND EDUCATION IN OCCUPATIONAL STRUCTURE

Country	ČSSR	Poland	United Kingdom	USA	FRG	Japan
Number of investigated occupations	30	29	30	90	38	30
Rank in order of prestige						
Physician	1	2	1	2	2	5
University professor	2	1	—	7	1	2
Scientist	3	—	—	8	—	—
Engineer-technician	4	4	—	23	7	—
Teacher	6	3	10	36	9	11
Judge, lawyer	14	6	3	12	—	3
Architect	10	—	—	15	—	7

Source: V. Brenner, M. Hrouda: Věda a vysokoškolské vzdělání v prestiži povolání (Science and University Education in Occupational Prestige), Sociologický časopis 6/1967 and 1/1968

A. DIAGRAM OF A CLOSED WORK CYCLE[1]

TABLE 2-1

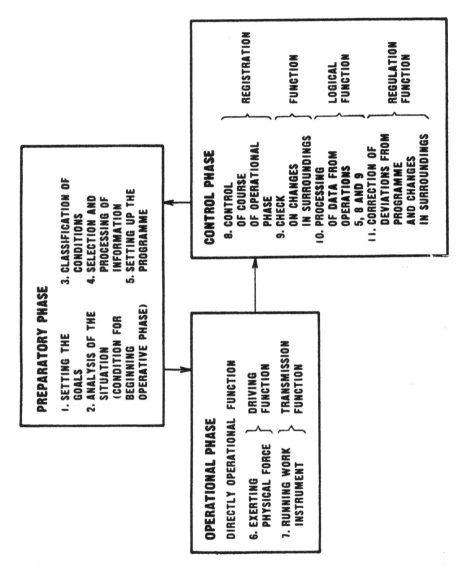

[1] For details see F. Kutta, Podstata a postavení automatizace v technickém rozvoji (The Substance and Position of Automation in Technical Progress), in: Politická ekonomie, No. 10, 1960, pp. 853—867

B. THE MODEL OF THE WORK CYCLE IN THE PERIOD OF MECHANIZATION

TABLE 2-1

FUNCTION OF THE MACHINE

DRIVING MECHANISM	DRIVING FUNCTION
TRANSMISSION MECHANISM	TRANSMISSION FUNCTION
WORKING MECHANISM	INSTRUMENT OF WORK
FUNCTION:	TRANSMISSION DIRECTLY ACTIVE

FUNCTION OF MAN

EFFECTIVE ORGANS OF THE HUMAN BODY	REGULATING FUNCTION
SENSORY ORGANS OF HUMAN BODY	FUNCTION OF REGISTRATION
NERVOUS SYSTEM	LOGICAL FUNCTION

WORK OBJECT

Prepared by F. Kutta, Institute of Economics, Czechoslovak Academy of Sciences

316

TABLE 2-1

C. THE MODEL OF THE WORK CYCLE IN THE PERIOD OF AUTOMATION

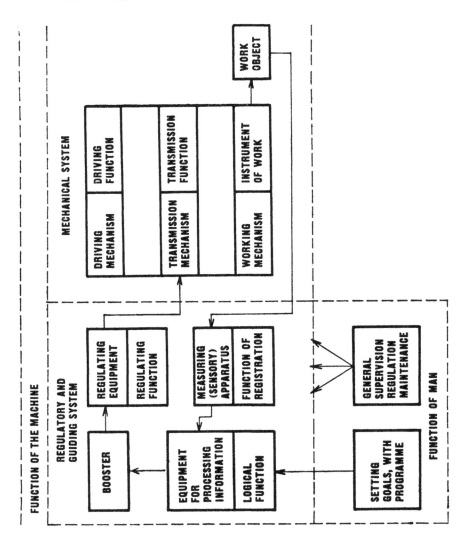

Source: F. Kutta, Vliv technického rozvoje na změny v pracovních funkcích člověka (Influence of Technological Development on Changes in the Work Functions of Human Beings), Filosofický časopis, 6/1964

TABLE 2-2

CLASSIFICATION OF TECHNICAL PROGRESS FROM THE
POINT OF VIEW OF WORK (A—C)

A. Degrees of technical development (according to J. Auerhan)

1. Hand tool
2. Tool driven by other than human energy
3. Universal tool
4. Semi-automatic machine (or apparatus)
5. Mechanized production line (semi-automatic machine or apparatus with mechanized feed of material and removal of finished products)
6. Automatic machine (or automatic production line or apparatus)
7. Automatic equipment (machine, transfer line or apparatus) equipped with automatic measurement of progress, conditions and results of the process (among these also belong the automatic signalization of breakdowns, automatic protection devices, switching off the machine in case of a threat of imminent breakdown, etc.)
8. Automatic machinery equipped with automatic regulation (this includes of course the automatic changing or re-adjustment of machine-tool tools)
9. Automatic machinery equipped with automatic evidence of the characteristic indicators of the production process (for example devices which automatically record the consumption of material and energy, the quantity produced, idle time etc.)
10. Automatic machinery, which automatically adapts itself to the changing conditions of its operation, automatically searches and selects the optimum means for fulfilling its assigned task (so-called automatic optimalizing systems; automatic adaptive systems; automatically self-adapting systems; automatic machines capable of "learning", etc.; the applications known today include certain controlling ing exchanges)
11. Automatic equipment which on the basis of the results of an evaluation of its own activity and of information about the development of the demand, about the requirements of the customers, etc., automatically according to the obtained complex data determines the optimum quantity, assortment and quality of production, chooses a technology of production and selects the material, i.e., performs not only technical but also economic tasks; equipment of this kind is for the time being almost non-existent in the actual production process.

TABLE 2-2

B. *Classification of the function of man in the production process*

1. *The active phase*
   a) sources of power;
   b) handling of the tool, or other forms of acting on the working tool;
   c) supplying material and semi-finished products, removal of the finished products and waste material;
2. *The controlling phase*
   a) maintenance of the necessary sequences of the operations;
   b) measuring the progress, the conditions and the results of the production process;
   c) control, i.e., maintenance of the production process within the limits set by the results of the measurement;
   d) optimalization and adjustment of the production process to changing conditions;
3. *The preparatory phase*
   a) inspection of the machine, its setting up, repair, maintenance;
   b) selection of material, tools, determination of the working methods and of the production technology and the organization of production;
   c) stipulation of the goals of production (the quantity, quality and assortment of the products, the economic criteria of production);
   d) improvement of production, i.e., research and development (of the product, the production machinery, the technology and organization of production);
4. *The inspection phase*
   a) the evidence of the overall characteristic indicators of the production process, i.e., comparison of the actual results with the set targets, analysis of the causes of the deviations, etc.;
   b) conclusions for determining the goals for production (3c), for the selection of the material, tools, the technology and organization of production (3b), for research and development (3d).

C. *Correlation between the function of man and the level of technological progress*

Function of man in the production process		Degree of technological progress										
		1	2	3	4	5	6	7	8	9	10	11
1. Active phase	a)		=	=	=	=	=	=	=	=	=	=
	b)			=	=	=	=	=	=	=	=	=
	c)				—	=	=	=	=	=	=	=
2. Controlling phase	a)				—	—	=	=	=	=	=	=
	b)							=	=	=	=	=
	c)								=	=	=	=
	d)										=	=
3. Preparatory phase	a)										—	—
	b)											=
	c)											=
	d)											
4. Inspection phase	a)									=	=	=
	b)											=
	c)											—

Note: The level No. 11 is listed here as a theoretical case, which represents the logical climax of the present-day tendencies in the development of automation. No doubt a number of intermediate levels which are omitted here will appear in the future between this level and level No. 10

blank space: function performed by man
      = function performed by machine
      — function performed partly by machine

Source: J. Auerhan: Technika, kvalifikace, vzdělání (Technology, Skill, Education), Prague, 1965

TABLE 2-3

CHANGES IN THE OCCUPATIONAL STRUCTURE

A. *Annual Increments of Occupations in the USA, 1950—1960 in per cent*

Office machine operators	+ 8.5
Cashiers	+ 7.4
Laboratory workers	+ 6.0
Engineers	+ 5.1
Secretaries	+ 3.8
Foremen	+ 3.5
Waiters	+ 2.6
Mechanics and repairmen	+ 2.5
Natural scientists	+ 2.5
Drivers	+ 2.5
Toolmakers	+ 1.8
Salesmen	+ 1.2
Physicians	+ 0.8
Metal workers	0.0
Labourers	— 0.1
Furnacemen and smelters	— 1.6
Self-employed managers	— 1.7
Stokers	— 2.7
Farm labourers	— 3.2
Farmers	— 3.3

(continued)

TABLE 2-3 (continued)

B. *Annual Increments of Occupations in the USSR, 1939—1959 in per cent*

Drivers	+ 7.5
Telegraph workers	+ 6.9
Scientists	+ 6.6
Engineers	+ 6.3
Jobsetters and repairmen	+ 5.9
Foremen	+ 5.3
Laboratory workers	+ 5.3
Combine workers	+ 5.2
Physicians	+ 5.1
Tractor drivers	+ 4.2
Turners	+ 4.1
Miners	+ 3.3
Teachers	+ 3.1
Railway conductors	+ 3.1
Agronomic specialists	+ 2.5
Sales workers	+ 2.5
Cashiers	+ 2.0
Charwomen	+ 0.5
Bakers	0.0
Farm workers	— 0.3
Cobblers	— 2.0
Diggers	— 2.2

Sources: Computed on the basis of data from Rutzick, S. Swerdloff, The Occupational Structure of US Employment 1940—1960, Monthly Labour Review, 11, 1962 and Report of the State Statistical Office of the Soviet Government, Voprosy ekonomiky, No. 1, 1961

TABLE 2-4

LONG-TERM DEVELOPMENT OF THE ECONOMICALLY ACTIVE POPULATION BY SECTORS OF THE NATIONAL ECONOMY In %)

Country	Year	Industry[1]	Agriculture[2]	Services[3]
USSR	1913	9	75	16
	1928	8	80	12
	1937	24	56	20
	1950	27	48	25
	1958	31	42	27
	1964	35	33	32
USA	1820	12	72	16
	1850	17	65	18
	1900	27	38	35
	1920	33	28	39
	1940	35	19	46
	1950	37	13	50
	1964	34	7	59
	1972—estimate	31	5	64
	2000—estimate	—	2.5	—
Great Britain	1811	39	34	27
	1841	44	23	33
	1871	49	15	36
	1901	47	9	44
	1921	49	7	44
	1951	49	5	46
	1963	47	4	49
	1970—estimate	47	3	50

TABLE 2-4 (continued)

Country	Year	Industry[1]	Agriculture[2]	Services[3]
France	1866	26	51	23
	1906	30	43	27
	1921	31	41	28
	1936	31	36	33
	1954	37	28	35
	1963	39	21	40
	1985— estimate	40	11	49
Germany	1882	37	43	20
	1907	40	35	25
	1925	42	31	27
	1939	42	26	32
German Democratic Republic	1952	45	23	32
	1963	48	16	36
Federal Republic of Germany	1954	46	21	33
	1964	48	11	41
Czechoslovakia	1921	43	32	25
	1930	44	27	29
	1955	39	34	27
	1964	46	22	32
	1970— estimate	47	18	35

[1] Industry includes mining and quarrying, manufacturing industries and construction.
[2] Agriculture includes agriculture, forestry, hunting and fishing
[3] Services include commerce, transport and communications, storage and warehousing, financial institutions, government administration and services

Sources: The National Plan, London 1965; Nation's Manpower Revolution (Senate Hearings), 1963; Réflexions pour 1985, Levallois—Perret 1964; C. Clark, The Conditions of Economic Progress, London 1951

TABLE 2-5
TYPICAL DEVELOPMENT OF THE LABOUR FORCE BY BRANCHES OF THE NATIONAL ECONOMY

Branches of the national economy	Percentage distribution of the economically active population		
	beginning of industrialization	process of industrialization	beginning of scientific and technological revolution
Agriculture	70—60	45—25	20—3
Mining and quarrying	2—3	3—5	4—2
Manufacturing	10—12	25—35	30—25
Construction	2—3	5—7	8—10
Transport and communications	2—3	4—6	8—6
Commerce	7—8	9—10	11—16
Services	8—12	10—14	20—35

Sources: T. Frejka, Vývoj odvětvové struktury společenské pracovní síly, Institute of Economics, CAS, 1966

TABLE 2-6

EMPLOYMENT OF WORKERS BY INDUSTRIES IN MANUFACTURING, 1958—1966
(increase +, decrease —, in per cent)

Industry	Belgium[1]	Denmark	France[1]	Austria	Sweden[2]	Switzerland	USA	ČSSR
Food	+ 9	+24	} + 3	} + 6	+11	+23	} — 5	} + 4
Beverages	— 5	+21			— 7	+38		
Tobacco	— 3	0	.	—24	—11	—10	—15	
Textiles	— 2	+ 1	— 9	—12	—20	— 3	+ 2	+ 3
Clothing	+ 8	+ 9	— 6[3]	+11	—11	+16	+19[3]	+13[3]
Wood-working	} + 6	+21	} — 4	} + 1	+10	+24	} + 9	} +13
Furniture		+84			+19	+20		
Paper and paper products	+22	+18	+11	— 5	+ 1	+12	+15	+ 7
Printing, publish.	+19	+28	+13	+48	+ 5	+29	+16	+12
Leather, leather products	—10	— 4	— 2[4]	—14	— 9	+16	— 2	+27[4]
Rubber products	— 1	—11		+24	+23	+12	+52	+38
Chemicals	+18	+16				+28	+16	+37
Products of petroleum and coal	—12	+15	} +13	} +25	} +15		—22	+36
Non-metal mineral products	+ 9	+35	+ 5	+ 8	+18	+29	+12	+13
Basic metal ind.	+ 5	+ 2	0	+10	+17	} +28	} +27	+31
Metal products		+38			+27			
Machinery (non-elec.)		+44			+22		+39	} +28
Electrical machinery	+25	+36	} + 6	} +11	+20	} +25	+54	
Transport equipment		0			+16		+21	
Miscell. manufact.	+40	+46	.	.	+ 5	+15[5]	+10	+26[6]
Mining & quarrying	—50	.	—25	—27	—33	.	—16	0[7]

326

TABLE 2-6 (continued)

NOTES
1. Including salaried staffs
2. Not exactly comparable, new prices linked to former prices
3. Excluding footwear
4. Including footwear
5. Watchmaking, jewellery, musical instruments
6. Including production of electric energy
7. Fuel mining and quarrying

Belgium, Austria — Statistics of compulsory social insurance; France, Sweden, USA — Statistics of establishment

Sources: Year Book of Labour Statistics 1967, ILO Geneva, Statistická ročenka ČSSR (Statistical Yearbook of the CSSR), Prague 1967
Worked out by J. Coufalíková, Institute of Economics, CAS

TABLE 2-7
PERCENTAGE DISTRIBUTION OF WAGE-EARNERS AND SALARIED EMPLOYEES BY BRANCHES OF THE NATIONAL ECONOMY

USSR	1940	1950	1960	1965
All wage-earners and salaried employees (excluding armed forces)	100	100	100	100
Workers in the material sphere of production	82	80	78	75
including: industry and construction	23	27	32	35
agriculture and forestry	54	48	39	32
Workers in other branches of the national economy	18	20	22	25
including: commerce	5	5	6	6
education, health, science and research	6	8	11	14

Czechoslovakia	1950	1960	1966
All wage-earners and salaried employees	100	100	100
Workers in the material sphere of production	78.0	75.1	71.0
including: agriculture and forestry	38.6	25.9	20.6
industry	30.0	37.3	38.6
construction	6.3	8.3	8.1
transport and communications	3.1	3.6	3.7
Workers in other branches of the national economy	22.0	24.9	29.0
including: commerce	8.6	8.2	8.7
education	2.9	4.7	5.9
science and research	0.4	1.7	2.3
health and social security	1.9	2.9	3.4

TABLE 2-7 (continued)

USA	1947	1957	1962	1966
All wage-earners and salaried employees	100	100	100	100
Workers in the material sphere of production	59.2	53.1	48.3	45.9
including: agriculture	15.8	10.5	8.6	5.9
industry	31.6	30.5	28.8	29.1
construction	3.8	4.9	4.4	4.8
transport and communications	8.0	7.2	6.5	6.1
Workers in other branches of the national economy	40.8	46.9	51.7	54.1
including: commerce	17.2	18.4	19.1	19.5
financial institutions, insurance and real estate	3.4	4.2	4.6	4.5
different services	9.7	11.4	12.8	14.1
government administration	10.5	12.9	15.2	16.0

Sources: F. Kutta, B. Levčík, Vliv vědeckotechnické revoluce na změny v obsahu práce a struktury pracovní síly, Sociologický časopis 2/1966; Manpower Report of the President and a Report on Manpower Requirements, Resources, Utilization and Training, Washington 1965; Narodnoye khozaystvo SSSR v 1965 godu; Statistická ročenka ČSSR 1967; Statistical Abstract of the US 1967
Worked out by J. Coufalíková, Institute of Economics, CAS

TABLE 2-8

A. *Changes in labour skills in the national economy of the United Kingdom (per cent distribution)*

Skills	1951	1961	1970 (estimate)
Managerial	10.1	15.0	15.6
Clerical	18.0	19.7	17.3
Qualified professional and technical manpower	3.2	4.0	7.8
Craftsmen	37.0	30.7	35.8
Operatives	19.6	14.6	14.3
Unskilled	12.1	16.0	9.2
Total	100.0	100.0	100.0

Sources: UTEIN, Sivo 650

Percentage distribution by occupational groups of the labour force in the USA

	1947	1955	1966
White-collar workers	34.9	39.0	45.0
including: professional, technical and related workers	6.6	9.2	12.6
administrative, executive and managerial workers	10.0	10.2	10.0
clerical workers	12.4	13.3	16.0
sales workers	5.9	6.3	6.4
Blue-collar workers	40.7	39.2	36.7
including: skilled wage-earners	13.4	13.2	13.0
semiskilled wage-earners	21.2	20.2	18.7
unskilled wage-earners	6.1	5.8	5.0
service workers	10.4	11.3	13.1
agricultural workers	14.0	10.5	5.2
Total	100.0	100.0	100.0

Sources: F. Kutta, B. Levčík, Vliv vědeckotechnické revoluce na změny v obsahu práce a struktury pracovní síly, Sociologický časopis 2/1966; Statistical Abstract of the US 1967

TABLE 2-8 (continued)
B. *Percentage distribution by skill of wage-earners in the industry of the USSR*

	Process of industrialization		Beginning of the scientific and technological revolution
	1925	1950	1961
Skilled	18.5	49.6	64.6
semiskilled	41.3	47.9	34.2
unskilled	40.2	2.5	1.2

Sources: A. A. Zvorykin, Nauka, proizvodstvo, trud, Moskva 1965; V. E. Komarov, Stroitelstvo kommunizma i professionalnaya struktura rabotnikov proizvodstva, Moskva 1965

Percentage distribution by skill of wage-earners in the U.S. economy (excluding agriculture and services)

	Closing phase of industrialization				Beginning of scientific and technological revolution	
	1920	1930	1940	1950	1964
Skilled wage-earners and foremen	32.3	32.3	30.1	34.4	36.0
semiskilled	38.8	40.0	46.2	49.6	50.1
unskilled	28.9	27.7	23.7	16.0	13.9

Sources: Economic Report of the President, 1965; Historical Statistics of the U.S. Colonial Times to 1957, Washington 1960

TABLE 2-9

PATTERN OF SKILL STRUCTURE OF THE LABOUR FORCE AT DIFFERENT LEVELS OF TECHNOLOGICAL DEVELOPMENT (IN PER CENT)

Level of skill	Level of technological development							
	mechanization			automation				
	3[1]	4	5	6	7	8	9	10	11
Unskilled	15	7	—	—	—	—	—	—	—
Semiskilled	20	65	57	38	11	3	—	—	—
Skilled	60	20	33	45	60	55	40	21	—
With high school education	4	6.5	8	12.5	21	30	40	50	60
With university or college education	1	1.5	2	4	7	10	17	25	34
With postgraduate education	—	—	—	0.5	1	2	3	4	6

[1] Levels 1 and 2 of technological development are related to manual work

Level 3 — universal machine
„ 4 — semiautomatic machine
„ 5 — mechanized transfer-line
„ 6 — automatic machine
„ 7 — automatic equipment
„ 8 — automatic equipment automatically controlled
„ 9 — automatic equipment automatically recording characteristic indicators of production process
„ 10 — automatic equipment automatically optimizing
„ 11 — fully automatic production equipment

Sources: J. Auerhan, Technika, kvalifikace, vzdělání (Technology, Skill, Education), Prague 1965

TABLE 2-10
A. *Number of students enrolled in universities and colleges for every 100,000 inhabitants*

Country	1930—1934	1935—1939	1940—1944	1945—1949	1950—1955	1955—1959	1960—1964
Bulgaria	.	174[1]	408[2]	580[3]	509	590	886[4]
Czechoslovakia	201	182[5]	.	450	450	563	877
France	201	172	237	319	348	409	785[4]
Japan	260	263	410	539	549	687	863[6]
Yugoslavia	109	106[7]	.	349	355	472	832[4]
Canada	318	319	311	594	493	537	934[8]
Hungary	164	138	.	249	350	269	409[4]
GDR	.	.	.	.	227	390	407[4]
FRG	.	.	.	.	325	418	587[10]
Norway	177	195	154	256	184	192	327[4]
Poland	.	.	.	380	538	571	688[4]
Austria	331	214	158	416	281	366	627[4]
Rumania	.	.	.	304[3]	414	417	548[4]
USSR	.	.	.	.	789	1024	1389[4]
Sweden	166	183	188	215	265	384	654[4]
Switzerland	238	261	320	377	329	345	467[4]
USA	884[11]	1046[12]	947[13]	1608[14]	1617[15]	1738[16]	2264[17]

[1] 1939
[2] 1944
[3] average for 1948, 1949
[4] average for 1960, 1963, 1964
[5] average for 1935—1936
[6] average for 1960, 1962, 1963
[7] average for 1935—1938
[8] average for 1960, 1962, 1963
[9] including West Berlin
[10] average for 1960, 1961, 1962, 1963
[11] average for 1931, 1933
[12] average for 1935, 1937, 1939
[13] average for 1941, 1943
[14] average for 1945, 1947, 1949
[15] average for 1951, 1953, 1954
[16] average for 1955, 1957, 1958, 1959
[17] average for 1960, 1961, 1963, 1964

Sources: World Survey of Education, IV. Higher Education, UNESCO 1966
Statistical Yearbook 1965, UNESCO, Paris 1966
Demographic Yearbook 1965, New York 1966
Statistika školství a kultury, Prague 1964

TABLE 2-10

B. *Share of students enrolled in the first year of study at universities and colleges in the given age group (in %)*

	OECD data			Report of the Robbins committee (all forms of study)	
	1950	1963	1970	1958/59	1968/69
USA	24.0	34.0	38.2	35	46
Canada	9.0	16.9	23.1	24	—
New Zealand	—	—	—	15	24
Great Britain	3.4	—	—	12.4	17
France	4.6	12.2	13.9	9	15
Sweden	4.0	9.1	11.7	11	18
Italy	4.8	10.0	12.5	—	—
Belgium	3.3	7.4	8.9	—	—
Denmark	3.3	5.1	8.9	—	—
FRG	—	7.3	7.8	6	—
Czechoslovakia	—	9.7[1]	9.9	—	14

[1] Average for the years 1963—1965

Sources: Ressources en personnel scientifique et technique dans les pays de l'OCDE Paris; Higher Education, Report (Robbins), London 1963

TABLE 2-11
LEVEL OF EDUCATION
(in %)

	Proportion of persons with university or college education in the economically active population	Proportion of persons with secondary education in the economically active population
	1961	1961
Czechoslovakia	2.60	13.50[1, 2]
USSR	4.05[3]	18.32[3, 2]
USA	8.89[3]	36.39[3]
Great Britain	4.43	16.44
Canada	4.27	22.64
Federal Republic of Germany	3.82[4]	—
Japan	3.48[3]	25.95[3]
France	2.58	—
Norway	2.58[3]	10.84[2, 3]
Sweden	2.06[3]	20.62[3]

[1] With incomplete secondary education 23.82
[2] Excluding general education
[3] Year 1960
[4] Microcensus of the FRG

Sources: Statistical yearbooks of the CSSR and USSR; Deployment and Utilization of Highly Qualified Personnel, Paris 1966

TABLE 3-1

PERSONAL CONSUMPTION INDICES
(at constant prices: 1950 = 100)

	1953	1955	1957	1959	1961	1963
USA	109	118	124	133	139	151
Sweden	105	113	118	125	134	145
Federal Republic of Germany	131	151	175	193	236	257
Norway	109	116	122	127	143	152
Denmark	101	108	110	122	138	148
Great Britain	102	111	114	122	130	138
France	116	128	143	148	165	187
Belgium	100	110	115	117	126	137
Netherlands	104	118	128	134	151	170
Italy	100	106	114	123	141	166
Austria	114	134	149	163	182	201

Sources: B. Stíbalová, Výdaje na lidského činitele ve vybraných západoevropských zemích a USA (Výzkumné práce VUNP č. 110/1967); worked out from "Yearbook of National Accounts Statistics", 1957, 1960 and 1963 (UNO)

TABLE 3-2

PERCENTAGE DISTRIBUTION OF PERSONAL CONSUMPTION EXPENDITURE

A. *Sweden, Austria and Czechoslovakia in comparable data*[1]

	Sweden 1955	Sweden 1963	Austria 1955	Austria 1963	Czechoslovakia 1955	Czechoslovakia 1963
food	28.7	25.1	38.7	} = 40.4	46.2	41.2
beverages	7.7	6.0	7.5		7.3	7.0
tobacco	3.2	3.4	3.1	3.3	3.4	3.1
clothing	12.7	12.8	14.9	14.0	13.3	13.8
rent and water charges	9.4	9.8	4.6	3.9	2.6	2.4
fuel and light	5.1	5.8	4.6	5.0	3.1	3.1
furniture and household equipment	5.9	7.5	6.0	7.7	5.4	6.8
household operations	2.6	2.2	3.0	2.8	2.9	4.1
personal care and health	3.3	4.0	2.8	3.4	0.9	1.3
transport and communication	11.7	14.6	7.7	10.2	6.2	7.5
recreation and entertainment	8.2	7.2	5.2	7.5	5.5	5.9
different services	1.5	1.6	1.9	1.8	3.2	3.8
expenditures consisting chiefly of goods	60.1	57.7	74.8	70.4	78.7	75.0
expenditures consisting chiefly of services	39.9	42.3	25.2	29.6	21.3	25.0

[1] Higher percentages in the consumption of goods (including food) and lower percentages in the consumption of services in Czechoslovakia are partly due to the fact that many services in Czechoslovakia are given either free of charge or at subsidized prices.

Sources: B. Stíbalová, Z. Urbánek, Rozbor výdajů na soukromou spotřebu ve vybraných evropských zemích a ČSSR, VUNP

TABLE 3-2 (continued)

B. *France*

	1950	1960	1970 (estimate)	1985 (estimate)
food and beverages	41.5	36.8	28.9	21.7
clothing	12.2	12.2	12.1	10.0
housing	15.5	16.4	17.7	19.2
health and personal care	8.1	9.9	12.9	15.2
transport and communications	6.0	7.8	10.2	12.9
including:				
purchase of cars	1.0	2.1	3.1	—
mass transportation	3.0	2.5	2.2	—
culture and recreation	7.3	8.0	9.1	11.4
including:				
education, theatres and books	4.6	4.9	5.5	—
broadcasting, television and photography	0.5	1.1	1.9	—
hotels and restaurants	9.4	8.9	9.1	9.6

Sources: Réflexions pour 1985, Levallois-Perret 1964

TABLE 3-2 (continued)

C. *Great Britain*

	1900	1938	1960	1984 (estimate)
food	32.9	30.1	29.3	30.0[1]
beverages and tobacco	13.1	10.9	12.9	10.5
clothing	9.3	10.3	9.8	9.0
housing	20.0	22.0	20.3	21.2
mass transportation and communications	3.6	4.4	4.3	3.3
domestic help	3.7	2.8	0.5	0.4
purchase of cars	0.1	1.1	3.5	3.5
books and newspapers	0.9	1.4	1.5	1.6
equipment for recreation and sport	—	1.0	1.3	1.5
entertainment	1.2	1.5	1.5	0.8
foreign travel	—	0.8	1.7	3.0

Sources: Britain 1964. An Experiment in the Economic History of the Future

D. USA

	1930	1940	1950	1960	2000 (estimate)
food	25.3	23.3	24.3	21.3	15.0
beverages and tobacco	2.0	7.6	6.3	5.3	3.2
clothing	13.0	11.7	11.4	9.7	7.2
housing	25.4	23.2	22.7	23.7	26.5
local transportation and communications	2.3	2.2	2.0	1.9	1.9
purchase of cars	2.3	3.1	5.5	4.8	5.0
health care	4.5	4.4	4.4	5.6	7.5
travelling	1.6	0.8	1.1	1.4	2.5
education	2.7	2.3	2.1	2.8	4.3
entertainment	2.3	2.5	1.8	1.7	1.7
culture and sport	2.0	2.2	2.6	2.9	3.6

Sources: Landsberg, Fischman, Fisher, Resources in America's Future

TABLE 3-3

A. *Hours of work per week in the USA*

Year	In agriculture	In non-agricultural industries	Weighted average	Decrease of work hours per decade (in per cent)	
1850	72.0	65.7	69.8	—	
1860	71.0	63.3	68.0	2.5	industrialization
1870	70.0	60.0	65.4	2.9	
1880	69.0	58.8	64.0	2.1	
1890	68.0	57.1	61.9	3.3	
1900	67.0	55.9	60.2	2.7	
1910	65.0	50.3	55.1	8.1	enactment of 48 hour
1920	60.0	45.5	49.7	9.5	work-week in the USA
1930	55.0	43.2	45.9	7.5	
1940	54.6	41.1	44.0	4.0	
1950	47.2	38.8	40.0	9.1	initial stage of the scientific and technological revolution
1960	44.0	36.5	37.5	6.3	

Sources: America's Needs and Resources (Dewhurst), 1955; M. Kaplan, Leisure in America: a Social Inquiry, New York—London 1960

339

TABLE 3-3

B. *Work Hours per Week in the Manufacturing and other Industries (Hours)*[1]

Country	1950	1955	1960	1964	1980 (forecast)
Sweden[3]	41.2	40.5	38.5	38.0	.
USA[3]	40.7	40.9	40.0	39.7	38.4[6]
Canada[2]	42.3	41.0	40.4	41.0	.
USSR[3]	.	48.0	41.5	41.3[5]	35.0
Austria[3]	.	45.5	43.5	42.7	.
Federal Republic of Germany	.	48.8	45.6	43.6	.
Switzerland	47.5	47.7	46.1	45.4	.

[1] Criteria differ from Table A (all paid leave included)
[2] Manufacturing industry
[3] Industry
[4] Manufacturing, construction, commerce and services
[5] 1963
[6] American forecasts do not assume a substantial decrease in hours worked, except for agriculture where the level of other industries is supposed to be achieved

Sources: Ukazatelé hospodářského vývoje v zahraničí, Prague 1966; Year Book of Labour Statistics 1965, Geneva 1966; Programme of the CPSU; 22nd Congress of the CPSU, Nová mysl 10/1961

TABLE 3-3

C. *Composition of Time-Budget According to American Source (in per cent)*

	1900	1950	2000 (forecast)
Time per year for total population	100	100	100
Sleep	39.7	38.7	38.9
Work	12.9	9.9	7.1
School	1.7	2.4	3.1
Household	9.2	5.1	3.2
Time for children	4.5	4.2	3.8
Personal care	5.5	5.6	5.6
Total	73.5	65.9	61.7
Residual	26.5	34.1	38.4
Leisure time during day	10.8	14.2	12.9
Weekend	7.5	13.5	16.7
Vacation	2.5	2.6	6.3
Retirement	0.9	1.8	1.9
Other	4.8	2.0	0.5

Sources: M. A. Holman, "A National Time-Budget for the Year 2000", Sociology and Social Research, 1/1961 October

TABLE 3-4

POPULATION DISTRIBUTION BY SIZE GROUP OF LOCALITIES
(in per cent)

Size group of locality	ČSSR %	FRG %	France %	Italy %	Austria %	Belgium %	GDR %
under 2,000	42.8	21.9	32.7	7.9	34.5	17.7	28.9
2,000— 5,000	16.3	12.0	12.1	17.4	17.1	19.6	12.8
5,000—10,000	8.7	9.2	8.4	16.6	6.3	16.2	9.7
10,000 and more	32.5	56.9	46.8	59.1	42.1	46.5	48.6

Source: Investice a životní prostředí (Investments and Environment of Life), mimeographed report of VÚVA (Research Institute of Construction and Architecture), Prague

TABLE 3-5

URBANIZATION IN THE USA

Year	Urban population[3] (millions)	Urban population increase as percentage of total increase	Percentage of urban population	
1850	3.54	—	7	
1860	6.22	33	20	
1870	9.90	44	25	
1880	14.13	42	28	
1890	22.11	62	35	
1900	30.16	63	40	period of
1910	41.40	70	45	industrialization
1920	54.16	91	51	
1930	68.96	89	56	
1940	74.42	61	56	
1950	88.93	74	59	
1950[1]	96.47	—	64	
1960	125.00	101	69	initial stage of the scientific and technological revolution
1980 (forecast)	193.00	104[2]	79	
2000 (forecast)	279.00	100[2]	84	

[1] Change of classification
[2] American forecasts do not take change of trends into account
[3] Localities with a population of 2500 and more having a legal urban status

Sources: M. Clawson et al., Land for the Future, Baltimore 1960; Landsberg, Fischman, Fisher, Resources in America's Future, Baltimore 1963

TABLE 3-6
ESTIMATION OF COSTS REQUIRED FOR EQUIPMENT IMPROVING WORKING CONDITIONS IN THE CSSR

Share of building investments in industry for	1965 %	1975 %	1985 %
electrical and illumination installations	2.5	3.5	4.0
air-conditioning	6.0	8.0	9.0
social facilities	3.9	4.5	5.0
dust removal	1.2	1.6	1.4
desulphurizing	—	6.0	4.0
building of sewage treatment plants	1.25	1.50	1.50
TOTAL	14.85	25.10	24.90

Sources: Investice a životní prostředí (Investments and Living Environment), study, VÚVA, Prague

TABLE 3-7
VISITS TO PRINCIPAL RECREATION AREAS IN THE USA
(Per thousand population in year indicated)

	National parks and recreation areas	National forests	State parks	Total
1920	9	—	—	—
1930	26	65	—	—
1940	·82	122	—	—
1950	144	180	753	1,077
1960	229	516	1,439	2,184
1980 (forecast)	520	1,760	3,460	5,740
2000 (forecast)	1,180	6,070	8,370	15,620

Sources: Landsberg, Fischman, Fisher, Resources in America's Future, Baltimore 1963

TABLE 3-8
CHANGES IN (DOMESTIC) PASSENGER TRANSPORT
in per cent

USA	1916	1940	1950	1960	Forecast 1980	Forecast 2000
Railway	98	63	42	23	9	7
Bus	—	31	41	27	14	7
Inland waterways	2	3	2	3	2	1
Air travel	—	1	15	47	75	85

Sources: J. F. Dewhurst et al., America's Needs and Resources, 1955; Landsberg, Fischman, Fisher, Resources in America's Future, Baltimore 1963

TABLE 3-9
EXPANSION OF TOURISM
(Frequency of visits in 1963 expressed by index: the best prewar year = 100)

Country	Growth of number of visitors
Belgium	322[1]
Greece	438
Great Britain	535
Italy	461
Yugoslavia	642
Netherlands	522[1]
Austria	472
Switzerland	339
Spain	4,536
Czechoslovakia	176

[1] Overnight stays

Source: B. Markos, "Die Psychologischen Motive der touristischen Expansion und ihrer geographischen und quantitativen Entwicklung", Revue de Tourisme, Bern, XX/2 1965

TABLE 3-10
CONCENTRATION OF SULPHUR DIOXIDE IN INDUSTRIAL AREAS

Year	Town	Year average
1955—1964	New York	0.4 mg. in a cube of metre
1955—1964	Los Angeles	0.2 ,,
1964	London	0.4 ,,
1963	Duisburg	0.3 ,,
1960—1962	Most (Bohemia)	0.3 ,,
1964	Chomutov	0.5 ,,

According to the legal norms the maximum tolerable concentration in Czechoslovakia is 0.15 mg/m^3, in California 0.59 mg/m^3.

Sources: Arch. of Env. Health; Investigation of the hygienic and epidemiological stations; V. Smil, Vesmír 5/1966

TABLE 4-1
NUMBERS OF WORKERS EMPLOYED IN RESEARCH AND DEVELOPMENT NETWORK

	1928	1940	1950	1955	1960	1964	1970 (forecast)
USSR							
thousands of persons	82	361	714	992	1,763	2,497	about 4,00
average annual growth	—	—	—	+6.9	+12.2	+9.1	+9.0
ČSSR							
thousands of persons	—	2[1]	24	71[1]	92	127	161
average annual growth	—	—	—	+24.0	+5.4	+6.9	+4.7

[1] Estimates

Sources: Narodnoye khozyaystvo SSSR v 1960 g., 1964 g.; Richter-Doležel, Vědecko-výzkumná a vývojová základna v ČSSR; šetření VVZ 1962

345

TABLE 4-2

A. *Expenditures for research and development (A—B)*

USA	1920	1930	1940	1950	1955	1960	1963	1965
Total expenditures for research and development in millions of dollars	180	400	1100	3400	6390	13,890[1]	18,200[2]	22,000
Annual percentage growth	—	—	—	—	+13.5	+16.9	+9.3	+10.0
of which expenditures for basic research in millions of dollars	—	—	—	—	547	1,256	1,815	2,450
Annual % growth	—	—	—	—	+13.0	+18.2	+13.2	+16.2
Share of basic research in the total expenditures for research and development	—	—	—	—	8.6	9.1	10.0	11.2[3]

[1] Of which about 60% is military, space and atomic research
[2] New series replacing former series
[3] The research in social sciences is covered only partly so that the real share of basic research is estimated at 12%

Sources: Statistical Abstract of the U.S., 1959 and 1965; R. A. Ewell, "Role of Research in the Growth", Chemical and Engineering News, July 1955; Předpoklady vědy a techniky, ÚVTEI, Prague

TABLE 4-2

B. *Expenditures for reseach and development in Czechoslovakia by sources of funds between 1960 and 1966 (millions of crowns)*[1]

	1960	1961	1962	1963	1964	1965	1966[2]
Total noninvestment expenditures	3260	3780	4320	4710	5300	5860	6290
of which from state budget	2010	2200	2520	2760	3110	3440	3750
from funds of enterprises	1250	1580	1800	1950	2190	2420	2540
Total investment expenditures[3]	420	500	530	480	610	600	500
Total expenditures	3680	4280	4850	5190	5910	6460	6790
Share of total expenditures in the national income (in %)	2.3	2.5	2.8	3.0	3.5	3.7	3.5
Share of total noninvestment expenditures in the national income (in %)	2.0	2.2	2.5	2.7	3.1	3.4	3.3

[1] All data are rounded off
[2] The plan
[3] Investment expenditures from state budget only

Sources: J. Nekola - J. Zelinka, "On the Scope and Structure of R+D Activity in Czechoslovakia", Minerva, Spring 1968

TABLE 4-3

WORKERS EMPLOYED IN RESEARCH AND DEVELOPMENT

Year 1962	ČSSR thousand pers.	%	Great Britain thousand pers.	%	USSR thousand pers.	%	U.S.A. thousand pers.	%
Total number of workers employed in research and development	112	100	405	100	2213	100	1450	100
of which:								
A. Experts with university education	24	21	113	28	529	24	550	38
of which:								
1. Natural and technical sciences	19	17	90	22	450	20	400	28
of which:								
a) natural scientists[1]	4	4	45	11	90	4	130	9
b) engineers	15	13	45	11	360	16	270	19
2. Social and medical sciences	5	4	23	6	79	4	150	10
B. Others[2]	88	79	292	72	1684	76	800	62

[1] Mathematicians, physicists, natural scientists and agricultural scientists (theoretical disciplines)

[2] Experts with secondary education, craftsmen, clerical workers and unskilled workers

Sources: B. Levčík, J. Nekola, L. Tondl, Criteria of the Development of Research and Scientific Activity, in: Czechoslovak Economic Papers No. 8

TABLE 4-4
DEMOGRAPHIC ASPECTS OF WORKERS EMPLOYED IN RESEARCH AND DEVELOPMENT

Year 1962	ČSSR	Great Britain	USSR	USA
For every 10,000 inhabitants from 15 to 59 years of age there are[1]:				
a) workers employed in research and development	137	132	162	139
b) workers employed in research and development with university education	29	37	39	53
c) workers employed in research and developement with university education in technical or natural sciences	23	29	33	39
For every 10,000 economically active persons[2] there are:				
a) workers employed in research and development	179	167	218	212
b) workers employed in research and development with university education	39	47	52	81
c) workers employed in research and development with university education in technical and natural sciences	30	37	44	59
For every 10,000 wage-earners and sallaried employees in industry[3] and construction there are:				
a) workers employed in research and development	385	357	715	715
b) workers employed in research and development with university education	81	100	172	272
c) workers employed in research and development with university education in technical and natural sciences	64	79	147	200

[1] Inhabitants from 15 to 59 years of age
[2] Economically active persons excluding armed forces and unemployed (USA and Great Britain)
[3] Industry includes mining and quarrying, manufacturing and electricity, gas and water production

Sources: B. Levčík, J. Nekola, L. Tondl, Criteria of the Development of Research and Scientific Activity, Czechoslovak Economic Papers No. 8

TABLE 4-5

SHARE OF RESEARCH AND DEVELOPMENT EXPENDITURES IN THE NATIONAL INCOME

(Share of research and development expenditures in the national income calculated in conformity with the methodology used in socialist contries — in %)

Country	1960	1961	1962	1963	1964
USA	4.5	4.8	5.0	5.0	5.2
Great Britain	—	3.2	—	—	3.5
Federal Republic of Germany	2.3	2.4	2.7	3.0	3.3
France	1.8	2.0	2.6	3.0	3.3
Sweden	2.6	2.6	2.6	—	—
Netherlands	2.4	—	3.0	3.2	3.1
USSR	2.2	2.4	2.6	2.8	2.9
ČSSR	2.0	2.2	2.5	2.7	3.1

Note: National income is calculated in conformity with the methodology of Marxist economics. Research and development expenditures in Czechoslovakia and USSR refer to non-investment expenditures only. Data for other countries include in different degree the expenditures for machinery and instruments.

Sources: J. Nekola - J. Zelinka, "Trend čs. badatelského výzkumu z hlediska některých tendencí rozvoje vědy ve světě", Věstník ČSAV 1/1965; statistical yearbooks in quoted countries

TABLE 4-6 (A—B)

A. *Percentage distribution of expenditures for research and development by activities*

Year 1963	Basic research	Applied research	Development
USA	12.4	22.1	65.5
Great Britain[1]	12.5	26.1	61.4
France	17.3	33.9	48.8
Italy	18.6	39.9	41.5
Belgium	20.9	41.2	37.9
Norway	22.2	34.6	43.2
Austria	22.6	31.9	45.5

[1] = year 1964—1965

B.

Year 1963	Share of the state expenditures for R + D in the total R + D expenditures (in %)	Share of the military, space and atomic research in the total R + D expenditures (in %)
USA	64	63
Great Britain[1]	54	40
France	64	45
Italy	33	21
Belgium	24	4
Norway	54	14
Austria	40	12
Sweden[2]	48	34
Canada	55	26

[1] Year 1964—1965
[2] Year 1964

Sources: International Statistical Yearbook for Research and Development. A Study of Resources Devoted to R and D Member Countries, 1963—1964, Vol. I.: "The Overall Level and Structure of R and D Efforts of OECD Member Countries", OECD Observer, October 1967, No. 30

TABLE 4-7

CURRENT RESEARCH AND DEVELOPMENT EXPENDITURES IN CZECHOSLOVAKIA BY SECTOR AND SOURCE IN 1960 AND 1966

	1960				1966			
	from state budget		total		from state budget		total	
	millions Czech. crowns	percentage	millions Czech. crowns	percentage	millions Czech. crowns	percentage	millions Czech. crowns	percentage
Academy of Sciences	310	15.4	310	9.5	580	15.5	580	9.2
Universities	30	1.5	30	0.9	110	2.9	110	1.8
Industry	970	48.2	2,160	66.3	1,910	51.0	4,210	66,9
Building construction	130	6.5	180	5.5	100	2.7	250	4.0
Transportation and telecommunications	50	2.5	50	1.5	70	1.8	100	1.6
Agriculture	290	14.4	290	8.9	590	15.7	590	9.4
Health care	130	6.5	130	4.0	200	5.3	240	3.8
Other	100	5.0	110	3.4	190	5.1	210	3.3
TOTAL	2,010	100	3,260	100	3,750	100	6,290	100

Source: J. Nekola and J. Zelinka, Research and Development in Czechoslovakia — MINERVA Spring 1968

TABLE 4-8
MANPOWER GROWTH IN THE "RESEARCH AND DEVELOPMENT BASE" IN CZECHOSLOVAKIA 1960—1970

A. *Manpower in "Research and Development Base" in Czechoslovakia by Sector and Level of Educational Qualification for 1965*

	University graduates Number	University graduates percentage	University graduates with advanced scientific degrees Number	University graduates with advanced scientific degrees percentage	Total number of workers
Academy of Sciences	4,410	38.6	2,120	18.6	11,420
Universities	930	54.8	385	22.7	1,700
Industry	15,920	19.0	995	1.2	83,710
Building construction	1,180	26.3	48	1.1	4,500
Transportation and telecommunications	710	29.4	29	1.2	2,400
Agriculture	2,860	20.8	416	3.0	13,710
Health care	1,370	24.5	485	8.7	5,600
Other	1,830	35.3	343	6.6	5,180
Total "research and development base"	29,210	22.8	4,821	3.8	128,220

Source: J. Nekola and J. Zelinka, Research and Development in Czechoslovakia — MINERVA Spring 1968

TABLE 4-8 (continued)

B. *Manpower in "Research and Development Base" in Czechoslovakia by Sector and Level of Educational Qualification for 1970*

	University graduates		University graduates with advanced scientific degrees		Total number of workers
	Number	Percentage	Number	Percentage	
Academy of Sciences	5,580	40.5	3,599	28.2	13,750
Universities	1,380	31.7	551	12.6	4,360
Industry	25,720	24.7	2,910	2.8	104,160
Building construction	2,020	33.4	227	3.8	6,050
Transportation and telecommunications	1,180	40.4	100	3.4	2,920
Agriculture	3,780	25.8	1,161	7.9	14,730
Health care	1,560	27.0	887	15.3	5,790
Other	2,780	32.0	1,111	12.7	8,700
Total "research and development base"	44,000	27.4	10,546	6.6	160,460

Source: J. Nekola and J. Zelinka, Research and Development in Czechoslovakia — MINERVA Spring 1968

BIBLIOGRAPHY

Abercrombie P., Town and Country Planning, London 1966
Adorno T., On Popular Music, in: Studies in Philosophy and Social Science, 1941
Aleksandrov A. D., Stroyitelstvo kommunizma i obshchestvenniye nauki, Moscow 1962
Allen, Hart, Miller, Ogborn, Nimkoff, Technology and Social Change, New York 1957
Anderson N., Dimensions of Work. The Sociology of a Work Culture, New York 1964
Andrieux A., Lignon J., L'ouvrier d'aujourd'hui, Paris 1960
Aron, R., Le développement de la société industrielle et la stratification sociale, Paris 1958
Aron R., Dixhuit leçons sur la société industrielle, Paris 1962
Arzumanjan A., Sovremenny kapitalizm, Moscow 1959
Ashby R. W., Design for a Brain, London 1952
Auerhan J., Automatizace a její ekonomický význam, Prague 1959
Auerhan J., Technika, kvalifikace, vzdělání, Prague 1965
Auerhan, Balda, Dráb, Říha, Základní problémy automatizace, Prague 1963
Auerhan, Bažant, Kolmer, Nekola, Nováček, Svoboda, Studie o rozvoji vědy a výzkumu do roku 1980, Prague 1962
Auger P., Current Trends in Scientific Research, Paris 1961
Auger, Barrère, Hirsch, Piganiol, Ponte, Thibault, Aspects économiques et sociaux du progrès technique et de la recherche scientifique, 1964 Paris
Baade F., Der Weltlauf zum Jahre 2000, Oldenburg—Hamburg 1960
Babbage Ch., On the Economy of Machinery and Manufactures, London 1932
Baczko B., Marx and the Idea of Universality of Man, in: Socialist Humanism, ed. E. Fromm, 1965 New York
Bahrdt H. P., Industriebürokratie, Stuttgart 1958
Balke S., Vernunft in dieser Zeit, Düsseldorf—Wien 1962
Barák et al., Studie o některých problémech rozvoje vzdělanosti a potřebě odborníků v národním hospodářství, Praha 1966
Baran P. A., The Political Economy of Growth, New York 1957
Bareš G., Zrození atomového věku, Prague 1958
Barjonet A., Conséquences humaines de la révolution technique, in: Cahiers Internationaux 87/1957
Bartoš E., Vplyv technického pokroku na vývoj spoločenskej pracovnej sily, Bratislava 1965
Beer S., Cybernetics and Management, London 1959
Belkin et al. Tekhnichesky progress i noviye professiyi, Moscow 1962
Benham F., Economic Aid to Underdeveloped Countries, London 1961
Bernal J. D., Science in History, London 1954
Bernal J. D., Social Function of Science, London 1939

Bernal J. D., World without War, London 1958
Bezouška J., Vyskočil J., Šetření o využití času v Československu, in: Demografie 3/1962, 4/1963
Bittorf W., Automation. Die zweite industrielle Revolution, Darmstadt 1956
Bober J., Stroj, človek, spoločnosť, Bratislava 1963
Bodamer J., Gesundheit und technische Welt, Stuttgart 1955
Borstine D. J., The Image, New York 1964
Boulding K. E., The Meaning of the 20th Century — the Great Transition, New York 1965
Boulding K. E., The Organizational Revolution, New York 1953
Bowman M. J., Schultz, Denison and the Contribution of "Eds" to National Income Growth, in: Journal of Political Economy 5/1964
Brabec F., Některé aspekty zabezpečení technického rozvoje v budoucím dvacetiletí, in: Techn. práce 12/1961
Brady R. A., Organization, Automation and Society. The Scientific Revolution in Industry, Berkeley 1961
Brandt L., Die zweite industrielle Revolution, Bonn 1956
Breyev B. D., Technichesky progress i struktura rabochikh kadrov, Moscow 1963
Brenner V., Hrouda M., Věda a vysokoškolské vzdělání v prestiži povolání, in Sociologický časopis 1, 2/1966
Bright J. R., Automation and Management, Boston 1958
Bright J. R., Opportunity and Threat in Technological Change, in: Harvard Business Review 6/1963
Brown A. I., Introduction to World Economy, London 1959
Brunner J. S., On Knowing. Essays for the Left Hand, Cambridge 1962
Brunner J. S., The Process of Education, New York 1963
Brus W., Modely socialistického hospodářství, Prague 1964
Buckingham W. S., Automation and Society, 1959
Buckingham W. S., Automation. Its Impact on Business and People, New York 1961
Buckingham W. S., New Views on Automation, New York 1960
Burnham J., The Managerial Revolution, New York 1941
Bushnell D. D., R. de Mille, J. Purl, The Application of Computer Technology to the Improvement of Instruction and Learning, in: Technology and the American-Economy — Appendix, Washington 1966
Cairncross A., Introduction to Economics, London 1944
Carpenter E., Civilisation: Its Cause and Cure, London 1908
Chase S., Men and Machines, New York 1929
Chvatík K., Umění ve světě vědy a techniky, in: Nová mysl 2/1968
Clark C., The Conditions of Economic Progress, London 1951
Cleater P. E., The Robot Era, London 1955
Cole D. M., Beyond Tomorrow. The Next 50 Years in Space, Amhurst 1965
Conant J. B., The American High School Today, 1960
Correa H., The Economics of Human Resources, Haag 1962
Creamer D., S. P. Dobrovolsky, J. Borenstein, Capital in Manufacturing and Mining, Its Formation and Financing, Princeton 1961
Crossman E. R. F. W., European Experience with the Changing Nature of Jobs Due to Automation, ed. Univ. of California 1964
Cvekl J., Vědeckotechnická revoluce a kultivace lidských sil, in: Sociologický časopis 2/1966

Cvylyov R. I., Sotsialno-ekonomicheskiye posledstviya technicheskovo progressa v SShA, Moscow 1960
Černý S., Socialistická rozšířená reprodukce pracovní síly, Prague 1961
Červinka A. et al., Práce a volný čas, Prague 1966
Čihák M., Vědeckotechnická revoluce a její důsledky v soudobém kapitalismu, Prague 1966
Davidovich V. G., Planirovka gorodov i rayonov, Moscow 1964
Davydov J., Trud i svoboda, Moscow 1962
Dedijer S., International Comparisons of Science, in: New Scientist 379/1964
Dedijer S., The Science of Science: A Programme and a Plea, in: Minerva 4/1966
Denison E., The Sources of Economic Growth in the US and the Alternatives before Us, New York 1962
Dewhurst et al., America's Needs and Resources, New York 1955
Dickinson T. A., The Real Revolution, in: Machinist Monthly Journal, Nov. 1949
Diebold J., Automation. The Advent of the Automatic Factory, Princeton 1952
Diebold J., Automation — Its Impact on Human Relations, New York 1955
Diebold J., Automation — Perceiving the Magnitude of the Problem, in: Advanced Management Journal, April 1964
Diebold J., The New World Coming, in: Saturday Review, July 27, 1966
Disman M., Volný čas a kulturní život, Prague 1966
Dobb M., Capitalism Yesterday and Today, New York 1962
Dobrov G. M., Nauka o nauke, Kieff 1966
Dobrov G. M., Perspektivy rozvoje vědy, in: Věda a život 8/1965
Dobrov G. M., Tekhnika i yeyo mesto v istorii obchestva (materialy k soveshchaniyu), Moscow 1965
Domar E. D., Essays in the Theory of Economic Growth, New York 1957
Domar E. D., On the Total Productivity and All That, in: Journal of Political Economy, December 1962
Drucker P. F., America's Next Twenty Years, New York 1955
Drucker P. F., Landmarks of Tomorrow, New York 1959
Drucker P. F., The New Society, New York 1950
Dubček A., Úloha technického pokroku ve vyspělé socialistické společnosti, Prague 1960
Dubská I., Americký rok, Prague 1966
Dubská I., Objevování Ameriky, Prague 1963
Dubská I., Šindelář J., K ideologické problematice vědeckotechnické revoluce, in: Sociologický časopis 2/1966
Dubský I., Domov a bezdomovosť, in: Človek, kto si? Bratislava 1965
Dumazedier J., Vers une civilisation du loisir?, Paris 1962
Dumazedier J., Ripert A., Troisième age et loisirs, in: Revue internale des sciences sociales 3/1963
Dvorkin I. N., Nauchno-tekhnichesky perevorot i burzhuaznaya politicheskaya ekonomiya, Moscow 1964
Ellul J., La Technique et l'enjeu du siècle, Paris 1954
Engels F., L. Feuerbach und der Ausgang der klassischen deutschen Philosophie, Marx - Engels Werke, Band 21, Berlin 1962
Engels F., The Origin of the Family, Private Property and the State, London 1941
Ewell R. A., Role of Research in Growth, in: Chemical and Engineering News, July 1955
Feldman G. A., Soobrazheniye o strukture i dinamike narodnogo khozaystva SShA s 1850 po 1925 gg. i SSSR s 1926/27 po 1940/41 gg., in: Planovoye khozyaystvo 7/1927

Feldman G. A., K teorii tempov rosta narodnogo dokhoda, in: Planovoye khozyaystvo 11—12, 1928
Feldman G. A., O limitakh industrializatsii, in: Planovoye khozyaystvo 2/1929
Filipcová B., Člověk, práce, volný čas, Prague 1967
Filipec J., Člověk v křivém zrcadle, Prague 1963
Filipec J., Člověk a industriální společnost, Prague 1966
Filipec J., Industriální společnost v sociologické diskusi, Prague 1967
Filipyov J. A., Tvorchestvo i kibernetika, Moscow 1964
Fischer E., The Necessity of Art, London 1963
Fischer E., Probleme der jungen Generation, Wien 1963
Flechtheim O. K., Utopie, Gegenutopie und Futurologie, in: Eine Welt oder keine?, Frankfurt a. M. 1964
Forbes R. J., The History of Science and Technology, in: Rapports de XIe Congrès International des Sciences Historiques, Stockholm 1960
Forbes R. J., Man the Maker. A History of Technology and Engineering, New York 1950
Ford H., My Life and My Work, 1928
Fourastié J., Le grand espoir du XXe siècle, Paris 1950
Fourastié J., La grande métamorphose du XXe siècle, Paris 1962
Fourastié J., Les 40 000 houres, Paris 1965
Fourastié J., Idées majeures. Pour un humanisme de la société scientifique, Paris 1966
Fourastié et al., Migrations professionelles, Paris 1957
Francois W., Automation. Industrialization Comes of Age, New York 1967
Freeman C., Young A., The Research and Development Effort in Western Europe, North America and the Soviet Union, Paris 1965
Frejka T., Rozbor odvětvové struktury pracovní síly, Praha 1965
Frenkel Z. G., Udlineniye zhizni i deyatelnaya starost, Moscow 1949
Freyer H., Über das Dominantwerden technischer Kategorien in der Lebenswelt der industriellen Gesellschaft, Mainz 1960
Friedmann G., La Crise du Progrès, Paris 1936
Friedmann G., Problèmes humains du machinisme industriel, Paris 1946
Friedmann G., Où va le travail humain?, Paris 1950
Friedmann G., Industrial Society, Glencoe 1955
Friedmann G., Sept études sur l'homme et la technique, Paris 1967
Friedmann G., Le travail en miettes. Spécialisation et loisir, Paris 1966
Friedmann G., Naville P., Traité de Sociologie du Travail, Paris 1961
Friedrichs G., Soziale Folgen der Umstrukturierung, in: Strukturwandel der Wirtschaft im Gefolge der Computer, Frankfurter Gespräch der List Gessellschaft (Sonderdruck)
Fromm E., Let Man Prevail, New York 1960
Fromm E., The Sane Society, New York 1958
Gaganova V., Ne radi korysti, Moscow 1959
Galbraith J. K., The Affluent Society, Boston 1958
Galbraith J. K., The New Industrial State, Boston 1967
Garaudy R., Perspectives de l'homme, Paris 1959
Gauzner N., Kapitalizm i novaya tekhnika, in: Kommunist 10/1959
Gauzner N., Ekonomicheskoye sorevnovaniye dvuch sistem i nauchno-tekhnichesky progress, in: Mirovaya ekonomika i mezhdunarodniye otnocheniya 11/1961
Gehlen A., Die Seele im technischen Zeitalter, Hamburg 1957

Gehlen A., Sozialpsychologische Probleme der industriellen Gesellschaft, Tübingen 1949
George F. H., Automation, Cybernetics and Society, London 1959
Gillmann, J. M., The Falling Rate of Profit: Marx's Law and Its Significance to 20th Century Capitalism, London 1957
Goetz-Girey R., Aspects économiques et sociaux du progrès technique et de la recherche scientifique, Paris 1964
Goldmann J., Kouba K., Economic Growth in Czechoslovakia, Prague 1969
Goldmann J., Flek J., Model hospodářského růstu za socialismu a kritérium efektivnosti soustavy plánovitého řízení, in: Plánované hospodářství 3/1966
Gonseth F., De l'humanisation de la technique, in: Dialectica 1956
Goodall M. C., Science and the Politician, Cambridge 1965
Gottl-Ottlilienfeld F., Vom Sinn der Rationalisierung, Jena 1929
Gottmann J., Mégalopolis, New York 1961
Gutton A., L'Urbanisme au service de l'homme. Conversations sur l'architecture VI, Paris 1962
Guardini R., Das Ende der Neuzeit, Basel 1950
Habermas J., Die Dialektik der Rationalisierung, in: Merkur 8/1954
Hájek M., Toms M., Determinanty ekonomického růstu a integrální produktivita, in: Politická ekonomie 10/1966
Hájek M., Toms M., Dva modely růstu, Prague 1965
Hanna P. R., An Instrument of National Goals, New York 1962
Harbison F., Myers Ch. A., Education, Manpower and Economic Growth, New York, Toronto, London 1964
Harrington H., The Accidental Century, New York 1965
Harrod R. F., Towards a Dynamic Economics, London 1956
Havelka J., Vědeckotechnická revoluce a změny ve struktuře práce, v kvalifikaci pracujících a v úrovni vzdělání, in: Sociologický časopis 2/1966
Havelka J., Vývoj a ekonomické postavení nevýrobní sféry, Prague 1966
Havlínová M., Hledání podstaty osobnosti, 1965
Heidegger M., Die Frage nach der Technik, in: Vorträge und Aufsätze, Pfullingen 1954
Heidegger M., Die Technik un die Kehre, Pfullingen 1962
Hely A. S. M., New Trends in Adult Education, Paris 1962
Hermach J., Filosofie a řízení, Prague 1965
Hermach J., Nástin řešení problému rozvoje socialistického člověka a jeho potřeb, in: Sociologický časopis 2/1966
Herlitius E., Historischer Materialismus und technische Revolution, in: Wissenschaftliche Zeitschrift der TV Dresden 4/1966
Heron A. R., Why Man Work, Stanford 1948
Herzberg, Mausner, Peterson, Capwell, Job Attitudes, Pittsburgh 1957
Hetman F., L'Europe de l'abondance, Paris 1967
Heyden C., Die marxistisch-leninistische Philosophie und die technische Revolution, in: Deutsche Zeitschrift für Philosophie, Sonderheft 1965
Hill S. E., Harbison F., Manpower and Innovation in American Industry, Princeton 1959
Hodek A., Technická revoluce a společenský pokrok, in: Nová mysl 5/1961
Hoch A. A., Roboti na postupu, Prague 1956
Hommes J., Der technische Eros, Freiburg 1955
Honzík K., Tvorba životního slohu, Prague 1947
Honzík K., Z tvorby životního slohu, Prague 1966

Horkheimer M., Adorno Th., Dialektik der Aufklärung, Amsterdam 1947
Hrouda M., Vysokoškolské vzdělání a vědeckotechnická revoluce, Prague 1964
Hrůza J., Theorie měst, Prague 1966
Huizinga J., Homo Ludens, Boston 1950
Husserl E., Die Krisis der europäischen Wissenschaften und die transzendentale Phänomenologie, Haag 1954
Huxley A., Brave New World, New York 1932
Huxley J., The Future of Man, in: Bulletin of the Atomic Scientists, Dec. 10, 1959
Hyman S., Society and Management, London 1964
Ivanov P. N., Tekhnichesky perevorot i rabochij klass v glavnykh kapitalisticheskykh stranakh, Moscow 1965
Jaffe A. J., Steward Ch. D., Manpower Resources and Utilization, New York 1951
Janů K., Nové stavebnictví a architektura, Prague 1967
Jantsch E., Technological Forecasting in Perspective, Paris 1966
Jaspers K., Die Atombombe und die Zukunft des Menschen, München 1958
Jouvenel B. de, The Art of Conjecture, New York 1967
Jungk R., Die Zukunft hat schon begonnen, Stuttgart 1954
Kahler E., The Tower and the Abyss, New York 1957
Kahn H., Wiener A. J., The Year 2000, New York, London 1967
Kaydalov D. P., Zakon peremeny truda, Moscow 1962
Kalecki M., Zarys teorii wzrostu gospodarki socjalistycznej, Warszawa 1963
Kamayev V. D., Lenskaya S. A., Rol avtomatizatsii v stroyitelstve kommunizma v SSSR, Moscow 1963
Kamiač A., Kvalifikácia a analýza nákladov na vzdelanie a reprodukciu kvalifikovanej pracovnej sily, Bratislava 1967
Kantorovich L. V., Ekonomichesky raschot nayluchshego ispolzovaniya resursov, Moscow 1959
Kaplan M., Leisure in America, New York, London 1960
Kapp E., Grundlinien einer Philosophie der Technik, Brunswick 1877
Kedrov B. M., Zakonomernosti razvitiya nauki in: Organon 2/1965
Keldysh M. V., Sovietskaya nauka i stroyitelstvo kommunizma, in: Pravda, June 13, 1961
Kendrick J., Productivity Trends in the US, Princeton 1961
Kerr C., Labor and Management in Industrial Society, New York 1964
Keynes J. M., Essays in Persuasion..., London 1931
Keynes J. M., General Theory of Employment, Interest and Money, London 1936
Kheynman S. A., O zakonomernostyach stroyitelstva materialnotekhnicheskoy bazy kommunizma, in: Zakonomernosti stroyitelstva kom. ekonomiky i yikh ispolzovaniye v nar. khozyaystve SSSR na sovremennom etape, Moscow 1963
Killingsworth C. C., Automation, Jobs and Manpower, in: The Nation's Manpower Revolution, part 5, Washington 1963—1964
Klages H., Technischer Humanismus, Stuttgart 1964
Klaus G., Kybernetik und Gesellschaft, Berlin 1964
Klein O., Vědeckotechnická revoluce a životní sloh, in: Sociologický časopis 2/1966
Klír, Valach, Kybernetické modelování, Prague 1965
Koeck W., Existenzfragen der Industriegesellschaft, Düsseldorf 1962
Kohout J., et al., Sociologie a psychologie v hospodářské praxi, Prague 1966
Kolman A., Tekhnicheskaya revolutsia i obshchestvenniy progress, in: Kakoye budushcheye ozhidayet chelovechestvo, Prague 1964
Kolman A., Výhledy do budoucna, Prague 1962

Kolmogorov A. N., Automaty a lidé, Prague 1962
Kosel C., Produktivkraft Wissenschaft, Berlin 1957
Kosta J., Odborní a řídící pracovníci v západoněmecké ekonomice, Prague 1966
Kosta J., Strukturální změny společenské pracovní síly ve světle mezinárodního srovnání, in: Politická ekonomie 1/1967
Kotásek J., Pařízek V., Vědeckotechnická revoluce a vzdělávací systém, in: Sociologický časopis 2/1966
Kotásek J., Škoda K., Teorie vzdělávání dospělých, Prague 1966
Kouba K., Tempo růstu výroby výrobních prostředků a spotřebních předmětů, in: Politická ekonomie 7/1964
Král M., Vědeckotechnická revoluce a řízení, in: Sociologický časopis 2/1966
Král M. et al., Věda a řízení společnosti, Prague 1967
Krauss R. H., Das betriebliche Vorschlagswesen als Mittel zur Rationalisierung und zur sozialen Betriebsgestaltung, München 1956
Kritzman L., Ocherednie zadachi proletarskoy revolutsii v Rosii, in: Narodnoye khozyaystvo 5/1958
Kržižanovskij G. M., Marx o revolučním pokroku techniky za socialismu, in: Výbor (Anthology), Prague 1960
Kudryashov A. P., Sovremennaya nauchno-tekhnicheskaya revolutsiya i yeyo osobennosti, Moscow 1965
Kuhn T. S., The Structure of Scientific Revolutions, Chicago 1962
Kurakov I. G., Rol nauki v sozdanii materialnotekhnicheskoy bazy kommunizma, in: Voprosy filosofii 6/1961
Kurakov I. G., Nauka i tekhnika v period razvernutogo stroyitelstva kommunizma, Moscow 1963
Kutta F., Budování materiálně technické základny komunizmu, Prague 1962
Kutta F., Podstata a postavení automatizace v technickém rozvoji, in: Politická ekonomie 10/1960
Kutta F., Technika práce a člověk, Prague 1966
Kutta F., Úloha automatizace v technickém rozvoji a její ekonomické a sociální důsledky, Prague 1959
Kutta F., Levčík B., Vliv vědeckotechnické revoluce na změny v obsahu práce a struktury pracovní síly, in: Sociologický časopis 2/1966
Kutta, Rufert et al., Metodika mikrorozborů a projekce vlivu nové techniky na pracovní síly, Prague 1965
Kuznetsov A. D., Razvitiye proizvodstvennoy i neproizvodstvennoy sfer v SSSR, Moscow 1964
Kuznetsov I., Tekhnichesky progress i sozdaniye materialnotekhnicheskoy bazy kommunizma, Moscow 1964
Kuznets S., Capital in the American Economy, Princeton 1961
Kuznets S., Proportions of Capital Formation to National Product, in: The American Economic Review, May 1952
Kuznets S., Six Lectures on Economic Growth, Glencoe 1959
Kvasha J. B., Klasifikatsiya mashin uchota oborudovaniya, Moscow 1934
Kwant R. C., Philosophy of Labor, Pittsburgh 1960
Kýn, Pelikán, Kybernetika v ekonomii, Prague 1965
Labini P. S., Oligopolis e progresso tecnico, Turin 1961
Lakomý Z., Životní prostředí a jeho tvorba, in: Životní prostředí a kultura práce, Prague 1966

Landa L. N., Algorifmy i programmirovannoye obucheniye, Moscow 1965
Lange O., On the Economic Theory of Socialism, in: The Review of Economic Studies 1966—1967
Lange O., Czlowiek i technika w produkcji, Warszawa 1965
Lange O., Teoria reprodukcji i akumulacji, Warszawa 1965
Lansdell N., The Atom and the Energy Revolution, Harmendsworth 1958
Largentière V., Le capitalisme contemporain et la croissance, in: Économie et Politique 107—108, 109/1963
Larrabee E., Meyersohn R., Mass Leisure, Glencoe 1958
Lauwe P. H. Chombart de, Des Hommes et des Villes, Paris 1965
Lebergott S., Manpower in Economic Growth, New York 1964
Lefèbvre H., Critique de la vie quetidienne, Paris 1958, 1962
Lengellé M., La Révolution Tertiaire, Paris 1966
Lengrad P., Adult Education, in: Fundamental and Adult Education, 3/1958
Lenin V. I., Imperialism, the Highest Stage of Capitalism, Selected Works, Vol. 1, Moscow 1963
Lerner M., America as a Civilization, New York 1957
Lerner M., Education: An Instrument of National Goals, New York 1962
Levčík, Flek, Kružík, Ekonomické soutěžení mezi kapitalismem a socialismem, Prague 1961
Levčík, Nekola, Tondl, Kritéria rozvoje výzkumné a vývojové činnosti, in: Politická ekonomie 7/1966
Ley H., Dämon Technik?, Berlin 1961
Lilley S., Automation and Social Progress, London 1957
Lilley S., Men, Machines and History, London 1965
Lindsay R. B., The Role of Science in Civilization, New York 1963
Lisichkin C. S., Plan i rynok, Moscow 1966
Litt T., Technisches Denken und menschliche Bildung, Heidelberg 1960
Longo G., Longo L., Il miracolo economico e l'analisi marxista Roma 1962
Losiyevsky V. I., Avtomatizatsiya proizvodstvennykh protsessov, II, Moscow 1958
Machát F., Dějiny vědeckého řízení v kapitalistickém průmyslu, Prague 1966
Magnane G., Sociologie du sport, Paris 1964
Machlup F., The Production and Distribution of Knowledge in the United States, Princeton 1962
Machonin P. et al., Sociální struktura socialistické společnosti, Prague 1966
Maier H., Bildung als ökonomische Potenz, Berlin 1967
Maier H., Schilar H., Bildung als Ziel und Faktor des ökonomischen Wachstums in der sozialistischen Produktionsweise, Berlin 1967
Málek I., Biologie v budoucnosti, Prague 1961
Mantoux P., La Révolution industrielle au XVIIIe siècle, Paris 1906
Marakhov V. G., Meleshchenko J. S., Sovremennaya nauchno-tekhnicheskaya revolutsiya i yeyo sotsialniye posledstviya v usloviyakh sotsializma, in: Voprosy filosofii 3/1966
Marcuse H., Industrialisierung und Kapitalismus, in: M. Weber und die Soziologie heute, Tübingen 1965
Marcuse H., Kultur und Gesellschaft, Band I, Frankfurt a. M. 1967
Marcuse H., One-Dimensional Man, Boston 1964
Marcuse H., Reason and Revolution, New York 1941
Marková K., Vztah vědeckotechnické a kulturní revoluce, 1966

Marx K., The Economic and Philosophic Manuscripts of 1844, N. Y. 1967
Marx K., Aus den Exzerptheften, MEGA, Vol. I/3
Marx K., Capital, London 1933
Marx K., Grundrisse der Kritik der Politischen Ökonomie, Berlin 1953
Marx K., Theories of Surplus Value, Moscow 1966
Marx, Engels, Arkhiv Marxa i Engelsa, Moscow 1933
Marx, Engels, Manifesto of the Communist Party, London 1935
Marx, Engels, The German Ideology, New York 1966
Massé P., Le Plan ou l'Anti-hassard, Editions Gallimard 1965
Massenet M., Introduction à une sociologie de la prévision, in: Futuribles 60/1963
Matejka A., Praca i koleźenstwo, Warszawa 1963
Matoušek O., Růžička J., Psychologie práce, Prague 1965
May R., Man's Search for Himself, New York 1953
Mayer K., Transactions of the Third World Congress of Sociology, vols. III—IV, Amsterdam 1956
Mayo E., The Human Problems of an Industrial Civilization, N.Y. 1933
Mayzel I., Kommunizm i prevrashcheniye nauki v neposredstvennuyu proizvoditelnuyu silu, Moscow 1963
Medawar P. B., The Future of Man, London 1959
Medonos S., Přínos jaderné energie pro čs. energetiku, in: Nová mysl 8/1963
Medynsky J. N., Entsyklopediya vneshkolnogo obrazovaniya, Moscow 1923
Meleshchenko J. S., Chelovek, obshchestvo i tekhnika, Leningrad 1964
Meleshchenko J. S., Tekhnichesky progress i yego zakonomernosti, Leningrad 1967
Melman S., Decision-Making and Productivity, New York 1958
Merton R. K., Science and Democratic Social Structure, in: Social Theory and Social Structure — Toward Codification of Theory and Research, Glencoe 1949
Michael D. N., Cybernation: The Silent Conqueror, Santa Barbara 1962
Mikhalevsky B. N., Perspektivniye raschoty na osnove prostykh dinamicheskykh modeley, Moscow 1964
Mileykovsky A., Nauchnotekhnichesky progress i sorevnovaniye dvukh sistem, in: Pravda, April 24, 1966
Millionshchikov M. D., Osnovniye napravleniya tekhnicheskogo progressa v zvyazi s dostizheniyami nauky, in: Vestnik AN SSSR 2/1966
Mills C. W., The Sociological Imagination, New York 1959
Mills C. W., White Collar. The American Middle Classes, New York 1951
Milonov J., Revolutsiya v tekhnike, Moscow 1922
Mises L. von, The Anti-Capitalist Mentality, Princeton 1956
Mises L. von, Die Gemeinwirtschaft, Jena 1932
Momson R. J., Modern American Capitalism, Boston 1963
Mokrejš A., Umění, skutečnost, poznání, Prague 1966
Montuclard M., Le dynamisme des comités d'entreprise, Paris 1963
Moore W. E., Man, Time and Society, New York 1963
Morgenstern O., Neumann J. von, Theory of Games and Economic Behaviour, Princeton 1953
Mumford L., The Conditions of Man, New York 1944
Mumford L., Technics and Civilization, London 1946
Mumford L., The Transformation of Man, New York 1956
Mumford L., The City in History, London 1961
Myasnikov I. J., Avtomatizatsiya i kommunizm, Moscow 1964

Myrdal G., International Economy, New York 1956
Musgrave P. W., The Sociology of Education, London 1965
Nachtigal V., Extenzita a efektivita hospodářského rozvoje ČSSR, in: Politická ekonomie 4/1966
Naville P. et al., L'automation et le travail humain, Paris 1961
Naville P., Vers l'automatisme social?, Paris 1963
Nekola J., Zelinka J., On the Scope and Structure of R and D Activity in Czechoslovakia, Minerva, Spring 1968
Nemchinov V., Ekonomiko-matematicheskiye metody i modely, Moscow 1962
Neumann J. von, Morgenstern O., Theory of Games and Economic Behaviour, Princeton 1953
Neumann J. von, The Computer and the Brain, New Haven 1958
Nikl M., Světové ekonomické vztahy a vědeckotechnická revoluce, in: Mezinárodní vztahy 1/1968
Notkin A. I., Tempo a proporce socialistické reprodukce, Prague 1964
Nový O., Konec velkoměsta, Prague 1964
Oertzen P. V., Analyse der Mitbestimmung — ein Diskussionsbeitrag, Hannover 1965
Omarov A. M., Tekhnika i chelovek, Moscow 1965
Oppenheimer J. R., Atomkraft und menschliche Freiheit, Hamburg 1957
Ortega y Gasset J., Meditación de la técnica, Buenos Aires 1939
Osipov G., Tekhnika i obshchestvenny progress, Moscow 1959
Osipov G., Avtomatizatsiya v SSSR, Moscow 1961
Osipov, Kovalenko, Petrov, Sovietsky rabochiy i avtomatizatsiya, Moscow 1960
Owoc K., Automatizacja i jej skutky spoleczne w kapitalizmie, Warszawa 1964
Ossowska M., Ossowski St., The Science of Science, in: Organon 1/1963
Packard V., The Waste Makers, 1960
Papalekas J. Ch., Wandlungen im Baugesetz der industriellen Gesellschaft, in: Zeitschrift für die gesammte Staatswissenschaft, 1959
Pappenheim F., The Alienation of Modern Man, New York 1959
Pauwels L., Bergier J., Aufbruch ins dritte Jahrtausend, Bern 1962
Pavlík O., Automatizácia a škola, Bratislava 1963
Pavlík O., Škola vo svetle súčasnej vedeckej a technickej revolúcie, in: Pedagogika 2/1967
Pelikán P., Člověk a informace, Prague 1967
Perlo V., Militarism and Industry, New York 1963
Perle V., Sotsialniye posledstviya nauchno-tekhnicheskoy revolutsii, in: Voprosy filosofii 11/1959
Petrochenko P. P., Organizatsiya i normirovaniye truda na promyshlennykh predpriyatiakh, Moscow 1962
Philp H., Education in the Metropolis, 1967
Pirker T., Büro und Maschine, Basel 1962
Polák M., K "vojenskému" charakteru současné vědeckotechnické revoluce, in: Sborník Vojenské akademie A. Zápotockého 6/1964
Pollock F., Automation, Frankfurt 1964
Popitz, Bahrdt, Jürres, Kesting, Technik und Industriearbeit, Tübingen 1957
Prager T., Wirtschaftswunder oder keines?, Wien 1963
Prudensky G. A., Vremya i trud, Moscow 1964
Purš J., Průmyslová revoluce v českých zemích, Prague 1960
Pyke M., Automation, Its Purpose and Future, London 1956

Read H., Education through Art, London 1958
Reis T., Aspects économiques des applications industrielles de l'énergie nucléaire, Paris 1958
Reuss E. G., Management im Zeitalter des Elektronenrechners, Basel 1965
Riesman D., Individualism Reconsidered, Glencoe 1955
Riesman, D., Abundance for What and other Essays, New York 1964
Riesman, Glazer, Denney, The Lonely Crowd, New York 1950
Richta R., Člověk a technika v revoluci našich dnů, Prague 1963
Richta R., Podstata a souvislosti vědeckotechnické revoluce, in: Sociologický časopis 2/1966
Richta R., Komunismus a proměny života, Prague 1963
Richter V., Doležel M., Výzkumná a vývojová základna v ČSSR, organizace, řízení a plánování, Prague 1966
Robinson J., Essay in the Theory of Economic Growth, London 1962
Rodwin L., The Future Metropolis, New York 1961
Roethlisberger F. J., W. J. Dickson, Management and the Worker, Cambridge 1964
Rostow W. W., The Stages of Economic Growth, Cambridge 1960
Russel B., The Impact of Science on Society, New York 1946
Řezníček J. et al., Vědecká organizace řídící práce, Prague 1965
Říha L., Ekonomická efektivnost vědeckotechnického pokroku, Prague 1965
Saarinen E., The City, New York 1949
Sachse E., Automatisierung und Arbeitskraft, Berlin 1959
Sachse E., Technische Revolution + Qualifikation, Berlin 1965
Sachse E., Was bringt die Automatisierung den Arbeitern in den kapitalistischen Ländern, Berlin 1957
Salin E., Industrielle Revolution, (Kyklos) 1956
Santayana G., The Sense of Beauty, New York 1961
Sartre J. P., Critique de la raison dialectique, Paris 1960
Schaff A., Filozofia czlowieka, Warszawa 1965
Schaff A., Marxizm a jednotka ludska, Warszawa 1965
Schelsky H., Auf der Suche nach Wirklichkeit, Köln—Düsseldorf 1965
Schelsky H., Der Mensch in der wissenschaftlichen Zivilisation, Köln—Opladen 1961
Schelsky H., Die Skeptische Generation, Düsseldorf—Köln 1963
Schelsky H., Die soziales Folgen der Automatisierung, Düsseldorf—Köln 1957
Schelsky H., Schule und Erziehung in der industriellen Gesellschaft, Würzburg 1959
Schenk G., Die Grundlagen des 21. Jahrhunderts, Berlin 1963
Schmid C., Mensch und Technik, Bonn 1956
Schultz T. W., Investment in Human Capital, in: The American Economic Review, 1/1961
Schultz T. W., Investment in Man, in: The Social Science Review, June 1959
Schumpeter J. A., Capitalism, Socialism and Democracy, New York 1950
Schurr, Netschert, Eliasberg, Lerner, Landsberg, Energy in the American Economy 1850—1975, Baltimore 1960
Selucký R., Ekonomie a život, Prague 1962
Servan-Schreiber J.-J., Le défi Américain, Paris 1967
Shukhardin S. V., Osnovy istorii tekhniki, Moscow 1961
Shanks M., The Innovators, London 1967
Skinner B. F., Pask G., Teaching Machines and Programed Learning (a source book), Washington 1961

Snow C. P., The Two Cultures and a Second Look: An Expanded Version of the Two Cultures and the Scientific Revolution, New York 1964
Solla Price J. D. de, Science since Babylon, London 1962
Solla Price J. D., Little Science, Big Science, New York, London 1963
Solow R. M., Technological Change and the Aggregate Production Function, in: The Review of Economics and Statistics 3/1957
Sominsky V. S., Ekonomika novykh proizvodstv, Moscow 1965
Sopp H., Was der Mensch braucht. Erfüllung und Versagen in Beruf, Düsseldorf 1958
Souček, Tauchmann, Vergner, Příprava dlouhodobé prognózy ekonomického rozvoje v ČSSR, in: Plánované hospodářství 9/1965
Sova, Teichman, Dohnalová, Problémy dlouhodobého vývoje životní úrovně, Prague 1961
Spengler O., Der Mensch und die Technik, München 1931
Steinbuch K., Automat und Mensch, Berlin—Heidelberg—New York 1965
Stranzky R., Kybernetik ökonomischer Reproduktion, Berlin, 1966
Strumilin S. G., Ekonomicheskiye problemy avtomatizatsii proizvodstva, Moscow 1957
Strumilin S. G., Effektivnost obrazovaniya v SSSR, in: Ekonomicheskaya gazeta, 14/1962
Strumilin S. G., Problemy ekonomiki truda, Moscow 1964
Strumilin S. G., Problemy sotsializma i kommunizma v SSSR, Moscow 1961
Strumilin S. G., Rol nauki v razvitii proizvoditelnykh sil, in: Voprosy filosofii 3/1954
Strzelewicz W., Industrialisierung und Demokratisierung, Hannover
Svoboda M., Vědeckotechnická revoluce a změny ve stratifikaci, in: Sociologický časopis 2/1966
Sweezy P. M., The Theory of Capitalist Development, London 1946
Sychrová H., Dlouhodobé změny vzdělávacích systémů a problémy naší vzdělávací soustavy, Study material 2/1967 (cyclostyled)
Sylk L., The Research Revolution, New York 1960
Šik O., Ekonomika, zájmy, politika, Prague 1962
Šik O., K problematice socialistických zbožních vztahů, Prague 1964
Šik O., Příspěvek k analýze našeho hospodářství, in: Politická ekonomie 1/1966
Šindelář J., Technika a humanismus v současném západoněmeckém myšlení, 1965
Šorm F., Věda v socialistické společnosti, Prague 1967
Štraub A., Vývoj spotřeby a přechod do stadia intensivního růstu, in: Politická ekonomie 5/1967
Taylor F. W., Shop Management, New York 1921
Taylor F. W., The Principles of Scientific Management, New York 1911
Teich M., K některým otázkám historického vývoje vědeckotechnické revoluce, in: Sborník pro dějiny přírodních věd a techniky 10/1965
Teller E., Basic Research and National Goals, Washington 1965
Tereshchenko V. I., Organizatsiya i upravleniye (Opyt SShA) Moscow 1965
Tessmann K., Probleme der technisch-wissenschaftlichen Revolution, Berlin 1962
Tessmann K., Theoretische Probleme der wissenschaftlich-technischen Revolution, Rostock 1964
Tessmann K., Technische Revolution und Sozialismus, in: Einheit 2, 4/1965
Thompson G., The Foreseeable Future, Cambridge 1955
Tinbergen J., The Design of Development, Baltimore 1958
Tlustý Z., Agregátní model dlouhodobého rozvoje ekonomiky ČSSR, Prague 1965

Tocqueville A. de, De la Démocratie en Amérique, I.—II., Paris 1864—1865
Togliatti P., I destino dell'uomo, Rinascita, March 30, 1963
Tollingerová D., Knězů V., Kulič V., Programové učení, Prague 1966
Toms M., Hájek M., Determinanty ekonomického růstu a integrální produktivita, in: Politická ekonomie 10/1966
Toms M., Hájek M., Příspěvek k vymezení extenzívního a intenzívního růstu, in: Politická ekonomie 4/1966
Tondl L., O vývoji a perspektivách vědy ve světle současné technické revoluce, Prague 1960
Tondl L., O povaze současné vědy, in: XX. století, Prague 1962
Tondl I., Nekola J., Nové rysy v úloze vědy, in: Sociologický časopis 2/1966
Tondl, Nekola, Voborník, Věda o vědě, in: Zprávy ČSAV 10/1964
Touraine A., L'Évolution du travail ouvrier aux Usines Renault, Paris 1955
Toti G., Il tempo libere, Roma 1963
Toynbee A. J., Civilization on Trial, New York 1948
Trapeznikov V. A., Avtomatika i chelovechestvo, in: Ekonomicheskaya gazeta 29. 6. 1960
Turing A. M., Computing Machinery and Intelligence, in: Mind 236/1950
Vaizey J., The Residual Factor and Economic Growth, Paris 1964
Valenta F., Efektivnost socialistického průmyslu, Prague 1964
Varga J. S., Kapitalizm dvadsatogo veka, Moscow 1961
Veblen T., The Instinct of Workmanship and the Industrial Art, New York 1914
Veblen T., The Place of Science in the Modern Civilization, 1920
Veblen T., Vested Interests and the State of the Industrial Arts, New York 1919
Vergner Z., Souček M., Teoretické otázky ekonomického růstu ČSSR, Prague 1967
Vincent A., Grossin W., L'enjeu de l'automation, Paris 1958
Vopička E. et al., Ekonomické a sociální podmínky a důsledky automatizace v kapitalismu a socialismu, Prague 1958
Vytlačil J., Šetření a využití času v Československu, in: Demografie 3/1962, 4/1963
Walker C. R., Modern Technology and Civilization; New York, Toronto, London 1962
Walker C. R., Towards the Automatic Factory, New Haven 1957
Walker C. R., Guest R. H., The Man on the Assembly Line, Cambridge 1952
Walter H., Automation und technischer Fortschritt, Köln 1962
Weber M., Wirtschaft und Gesellschaft, Tübingen 1922
Weber M., Wissenschaft als Beruf, in: Gesammelte Aufsätze zur Wissenschaftslehre, Tübingen 1951
Weber M., Fragen der Rationalisierung, Zürich
Wheeler G. S., Kapitalismus a automatizace, Prague 1961
Wheeler G. S., Problems in Transport in Cities of the United States, in: Czechoslovak Economic Papers, Prague 4/1965
Wheeler G. S., Technological Revolution, in: Political Affairs, May 1965
Wheelis A., The Quest for Identity, New York 1958
Whitehead A. N., Science and the Modern World, New York 1948
Whyte W. F., Money and Motivation, an Analysis of Incentives in Industry, New York 1955
Whyte W. H., The Organization Man, New York 1956
Wiener N., Cybernetics, Cambridge 1948
Wiener N., The Human Use of Human Beings. Cybernetics and Society, New York 1954

Wiener N., I Am a Mathematician, Cambridge 1964
Wiener N., God and Golem, Cambridge 1964
Wilenski H. L., Industrial Society and Social Welfare, New York 1958
Williams B., Science and Technology in Growth, Paris 1965
Wirth L., Urbanism as a Way of Life, Glencoe 1957
Woodburg C., The Future of Cities, Chicago 1956
Worthy J. C., Organizational Structure and Employee Morale, in: American Sociological Review, April 1950
Wright F. L., The Living Cities, New York 1958
Yelmeyev V. J., Nauka i proizvoditelniye sily obshchestva, Moscow 1959
Yermansky O. A., Teoriya i praktika ratsionalizatsii, Moscow 1928
Young M., The Rise of Meritocracy, London 1958
Zeman J., Poznání a informace, Prague 1962
Zeman J., Poznání a společnost, Prague 1962
Zhezhelenko, Ovchinnikov, Sharipov, Technika, trud i chelovek, Moscow 1963
Zvorikin A. A., Avtomatizatsiya proizvodstva i yeyo ekonomicheskaya effektivnost, Moscow 1958
Zvorikin A. A., Nauka, proizvodstvo, trud, Moscow 1965
Ziolkiewski J., Urbanizacja, miasto, osiedle, Warszawa 1965

Action Programme of the CPC, Prague 1968
Die Arbeiter und die Fliessbandarbeit, Moscow 1929
The Automatic Factory, What Does It Mean? (Report of the Conference held at Margate, June 1955), London 1955
Automation (ed. C. C. Killingworth), Philadelphia 1962
Automation and Technological Change. Report of the Subcommittee on Economic Stabilization to the Joint Committee on the Economic Report of the United States Congress, Washington 1956
Automation and Technological Change, ed. J. T. Dunlop, Prentice Hall 1962
Automation and Major Technological Change: Impact on Union Size, Structure and Function, Washington 1958
Automation. Great Britain, Department of Scientific and Industrial Research, London 1956
Automation, Jobs and Manpower, in: Manpower Revolution, 1963—1964
Automation — Risiko der Chance, Oberhausen 1965
Automation und technischer Fortschritt in Deutschland und in den USA, Frankfurt 1963
Basic Research and National Goals (Report to the Committee on Science and Astronautics, US House of Representatives, by the National Academy of Sciences), Washington 1965
Boy idet za cheloveka (I. Kon et al.), Leningrad 1965
Britain 1984 (R. Brech), London 1963
Ciba Foundation Colloquia on Ageing, London 1955—1959
Comparisons of the United States and Soviet Economics. Hearings before the Joint Economic Committee of the United States, Washington 1960
Le Concept d'information dans la science contemporaine, Paris 1965
Conférence mondiale sur l'éducation des adultes, Paris 1960
Le contre-plan (J. Ensemble), Paris 1965

The Crossroad Papers. A Look into the American Future, New York 1965
Culture of the Millions (ed. N. Jacobs), New York 1959
Chelovek i epokha (ed. P. N. Fedoseyev), Moscow 1964
Daedalus (Journal of the American Academy of Arts and Sciences), Toward the Year 2000: Work in Progress, 1967
Deutschland 1975. Analysen, Prognosen, Perspektiven, ed. V. Lohmar, Bielefeld 1965
Digest of Educational Statistics, Washington 1965
Discussion of the Impact of Automation on the Occupational Distribution, Job Content and Working Conditions, ed. Univ. of California January 1965
Dvacet let rozvoje ČSSR, Prague 1965
Economic Change, New York 1953
Economic Growth and Manpower, London 1963
Economic Report of the President, Washington 1963
Education for the Age of Science (Statement by the President's Science Advisory Committee), Washington 1959
Efektívnosť nár. hospodárstva, základných fondov, investícií a technického rozvoja (ed. H. Kočtúch), Bratislava 1965
Ekonomicheskiye problemy sovremennogo imperializma (S. I. Vygodsky), Moscow 1963
Europe's Future Consumption, Amsterdam 1964
The Exploding Metropolis, ed. Fortune, New York 1957
Factory Management and Maintenance, New York 1957
Fundamental Research and the Policies of Government, Paris 1966
The Growth of World Industry 1938—1961. International Analyses and Tables, New York 1965
The Guaranteed Income, ed. R. Theobald, New York 1966
Harvard University Program on Technology and Society (Annual Report I, II and III of the Executive Director) E. G. Mesthene, Cambridge 1965, 1966, 1967
Has Capitalism Changed? An International Symposium (ed. Tsuru), Tokyo 1961
Hearings before the Subcommittee on Employment and Manpower of the Committee on Labor and Public Welfare, US Senate-88th Congress, Washington 1963
Higher Education Report (Lord Robbins), London 1963
Historischer Materialismus und Sozialforschung, Berlin 1966
Hlavní směry zdokonalování plánovitého řízení národního hospodářství (SKOŘ), 1965
Industrialization and Society, ed. B. F. Hoselitz, W. E. Moore, Paris UNESCO 1963
Joint Consultation in British Industry, London 1952
Les implications sociales du progrès technique, Paris 1959
Investice a životní prostředí (Červenka, Kasalický, Stach, Matoušek), Prague 1966
Investment in Human Beings, in: Journal of Political Economy 5 (2), 1962
Jobs, Men and Machines: Problems of Automation (ed. Ch. Markham), New York, London 1964
Kapitalismus našeho věku (Urban et al.), Prague 1966
Kibernetika na sluzhbu kommunizmu (ed. I. Berg), Moscow 1961
KPSS v rezolutsiakh i resheniakh syezdov, konferentsiy i plenumov TsK, Moscow 1955
Kultúra práce, Bratislava 1962
20 let rozvoje ČSSR, Prague 1965
Long-Range Demand for Scientific and Technological Personnel, Washington 1961
Long-Range Projections for Economic Growth, Washington 1959
Long Term Economic Growth 1860—1965, US Department of Commerce, Bureau of the Census, Washington 1966

Man and His Future. A Ciba Foundation Volume, ed. G. Wolstenholme, London 1963
Management of Human Resources, New York, San Francisco, Toronto—London 1964
Manpower Report of the President, March 1965, Washington
Marxistická antropologie (ed. K. Mácha), Prague 1966
Die Marxistisch-leninistische Philosophie und die technische Revolution, in: Deutsche Zeitschrift für Philosophie, Sonderheft 1965
Maschine — Denkmaschine — Staatsmaschine. Entwicklungstendenzen der modernen Industriegesellschaft, Hamburg, Berlin 1963
Mass Communications and Popular Conceptions of Education: A Cross-Cultural Study, G. Gerbner, Urbana 1964
Mass Society in Crisis (Rosenberg, Gerver, Howton) New York, London 1964
Materialy XX. syezda KPSS, Moscow 1956
Materialy XXII. syezda KPSS, Moscow 1961
Materialy yunskogo Plenuma TsK KPSS, Moscow 1959
Materiály z konference o životosprávě, uspořádané věd. radou min. zdravotnictví, Prague 1965
Meeting Manpower Needs in Science and Technology (A Report of the President's Advisory Committee), Washington 1962
Mensch und Automation. Selbstentfremdung. Selbstverwirklichung, herausgegeben von W. Bitter, Stuttgart 1966
Mental Health Problems of Automation, WHO, Geneva 1959
Metodologicheskie voprosy izucheniya urovnya zhizni trudyashchikhsya, Moscow 1962
Ministers Talk about Science, OECD, Paris 1965
Modelle für eine neue Welt (ed. R. Jungk, H. J. Mundt) München—Wien—Basel, a series
Modern Technology and Civilization (ed. Ch. R. Walker), New York—Toronto—London 1962
Nation's Manpower Revolution, Senate Hearings, 1963
Nauka i tekhnika v period razvernutogo stroyitelstva kommunizma, Moscow 1963
The New Europe and Its Economic Future (ed. Twentieth Century Fund), 1964
New Views on Automation (Paper Submitted to the Subcommittee on Automation and Energy Resources. Congress of the US), Washington 1960
Noviye yavleniya v ekonomike sovremennogo imperializma, Moscow 1963
O hlavních směrech vědeckotechnického pokroku na rozvoji výrobních sil a uspokojování potřeb společnosti v dlouhodobém výhledu (SKT), 1965
O plánování ve vědě, Prague 1960
The Overall Level and Structure of R and D Efforts in OECD Member Countries, Paris 1967
Policy Conference on Economic Growth and Investment in Education, OECD, Paris 1962
Politická ekonomie socialismu (ed. K. Kouba), Prague 1964
Problemy sovremenney nauchno-tekhnicheskoy revolutsii (conference reports), in: Voprosy istorii estestvoznaniya i tekhniki, 19/1965
Programme of the Communist Party of the Soviet Union, Moscow 1961
Projections of Educational Statistics to 1974—1975, Washington 1965
Prospect for America. The Rockefeller Panel Reports, New York 1961
Puti razvitiya tekhniki v SSSR, Moscow 1967
Réflexions pour 1985 (ed. P. Massé), Levallois—Perret 1964
The Rate and Direction of Inventive Activity: Economic and Social Factors (ed. R. R. Nelson), Princeton 1962

Report of the Thirteenth Congress of the Communist Party of Czechoslovakia, Prague 1966
Report on a Long-Range Forecasting Study, Santa Monica 1964
Resolutions of the Twelfth Congress of the Communist Party of Czechoslovakia, Prague 1963
Resources in America's Future. Patterns, Requirements and Availabilities 1960/2000 (ed. Landsberg, Fischmann, Fisher), Baltimore 1963
Ressources en personnel scientifique et technique dans les pays de l'OCDE, Paris 1961
Science, Government, and Information. A Report on the President's Science Advisory Committee, Washington 1963
Revolution der Roboter. Untersuchungen über Probleme der Automatisierung, München 1956
The Science of Science (ed. M. Goldsmith, A. Mackay), London—Toronto 1966
Scientific and Technical Manpower Resources, Washington 1964
Scientific Progress, the Universities and the Federal Government, Washington 1960
Survey on the structure of the working class, in: World Marxist Review 1960
Sessiya po nauchnym problemam avtomatizatsii proizvodstva, Moscow 1957
Sociální struktura socialistické společnosti (P. Machonin et al.), Prague 1966
Sotsialno-ekonomicheskiye problemy tekhnicheskogo progressa (Materialy nauchnoy sessii otdeleniya ekonomicheskikh, filosofskikh i pravovykh nauk Akademii nauk SSSR), Moscow 1961
The Sociology of Science (ed. B. Barber, W. Hirsch), New York—London 1967
Some Factors in Economic Growth in Europe during the 1950's, Geneva 1964
Sovremennaya nauchno-tekhnicheskaya revolutsiya. Istoricheskoye issledovaniye, ed. Shukhardin, Moscow 1967
Sozialismus, Wissenschaft, Produktivkraft (ed. G. Heyden), Berlin 1962
Společenská produktivita práce v ČSSR, Prague 1966
Spravochniye materialy po trudu i zarabotnoy plate, Moscow 1960
Studi Gramsciani, Atti di Convegno tenuto a Roma nei giorni 11.—13. 6. 1958, Roma 1958
Technika i yeyo meto v istorii obchestva (materiyaly k soveshchaniyu), Moscow 1965
Tekhnichesky progress i voprosy truda pri perekhode k kommunizmu (ed. A. N. Grzhegorzhevsky), Moscow 1962
Technischer Fortschritt und gemeinsammer Markt (Europäische Konferenz, E. G. K. S. und EURATOM), Brussels, Dec. 1960
Technology and the American Economy. Report of the National Commission on Technology, Automation and Economic Progress, Washington 1966
Technology and Social Change (ed. Ginzberg), New York 1964
Teoria wzrostu ekonomicznego a wspolczesny kapitalizm, ed. J. Zawadski, A. Lukaszewicz, Warszawa 1962
Theoretische Probleme der wissenschaftlich-technischen Revolution (ed. Parthey, Tessmann, Vogel), Universität Rostock
Theorie der Lage der Arbeiter, Berlin 1955
Towards a Unified Theory of Management (ed. H. Koontz), New York 1964
Traffic in Towns (Buchanan Report), London 1963
The Triple Revolution. Complete Text of the Ad Hoc Committee's Controversial Manifesto, New York 1964
Udlineniye zhizni i deyatelnaya starost, Moscow 1949
Ukazatelé hospodářského vývoje v zahraničí 1965 (UTEIN), Prague 1966

Unsere Welt 1985, ed. R. Jungk, H. Mundt, München 1967
Usnesení ÚV KSČ a vlády o úkolech vědy při zabezpečování rozvoje a zvyšování technické úrovně čs. průmyslu, 1956
Usnesení ÚV KSČ a vlády o zvýšení úlohy vědy a techniky v rozvoji výrobních sil v ČSSR, in: Hospodářské noviny 44/1962
Usnesení ÚV KSČ o hlavních směrech zdokonalování plánovitého řízení národního hospodářství a o práci strany, in: Rudé právo January 30, 1965
ÚV KSSS o urychlení technického pokroku, Prague 1959
Věda a řízení společnosti (M. Král et al.), Prague 1967
Veda, technika a spoločnosť, Bratislava 1965
Vestnik Moskovskogo Universiteta 6/1964
Vnerabocheye vremya trudyashchikhsya, Novosibirsk 1961
Wege ins neue Jahrtausend, ed. R. Jung, H. Mundt, München 1964
Eine Welt oder keine?, Frankfurt a. M. 1964
The World in 1984, ed. N. Calder, Baltimore 1965
World Technology and Human Destiny; ed. R. Aron, Ann Arbor 1963
Za další technický pokrok (SVRT), Prague 1960
Za další všestranný rozvoj naší socialistické společnosti, XIII. sjezd KSČ; Prague 1966
Zásady urychlené realizace nové soustavy řízení (SKOŘ), 1966
Zásady a metody perspektivní přestavby našich měst (VÚVA), Brno 1963
Zur Ökonomik und Technik der Atomzeit (ed. H. W. Zimmermann), Tübingen 1957